CHAPTER 102 … WHILE WISHING TO NOT GO WRONG AGAIN, AT LEAST… (PART ONE)

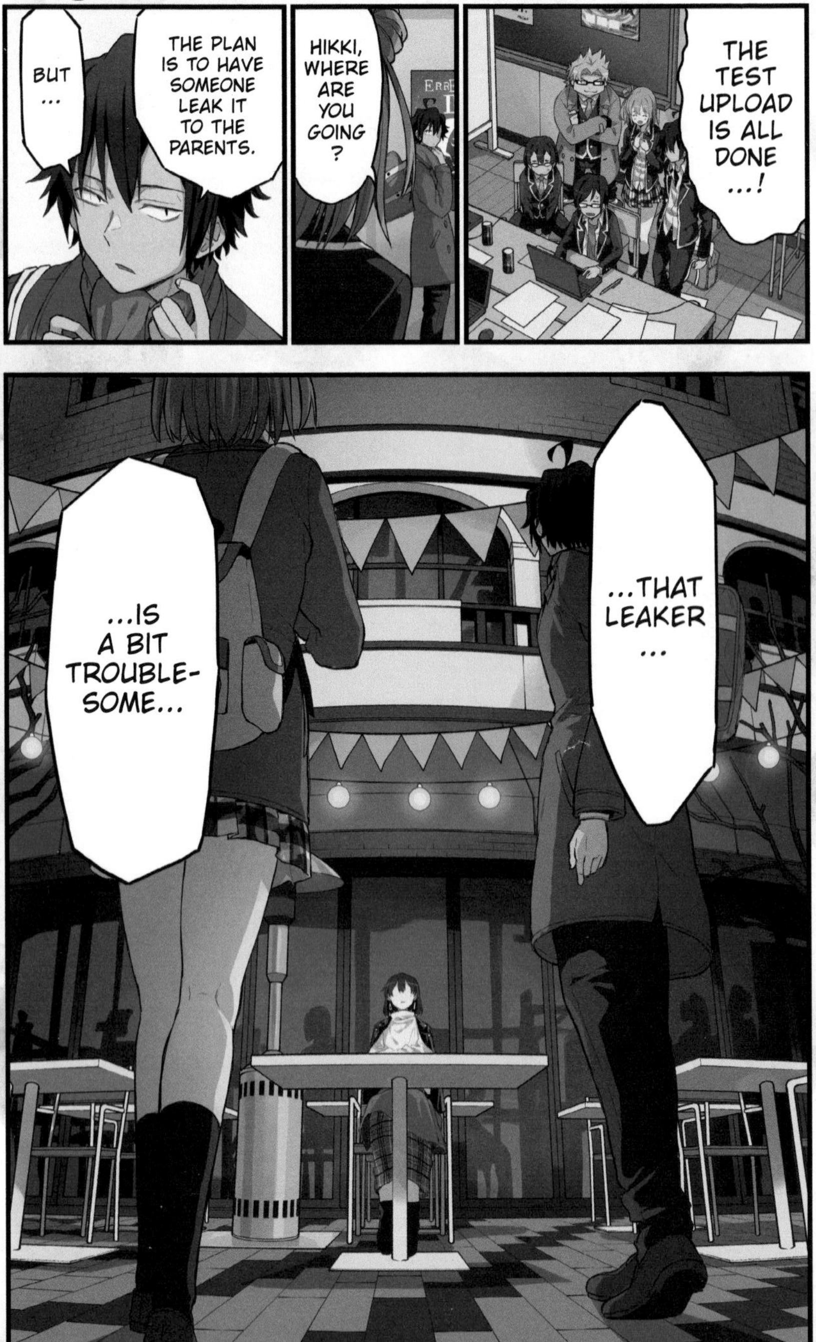
THE TEST UPLOAD IS ALL DONE …!
HIKKI, WHERE ARE YOU GOING?
THE PLAN IS TO HAVE SOMEONE LEAK IT TO THE PARENTS.
BUT …
…THAT LEAKER …
…IS A BIT TROUBLE-SOME…

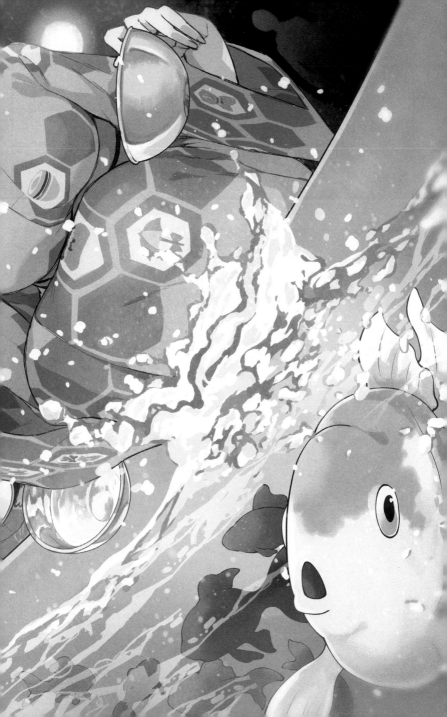

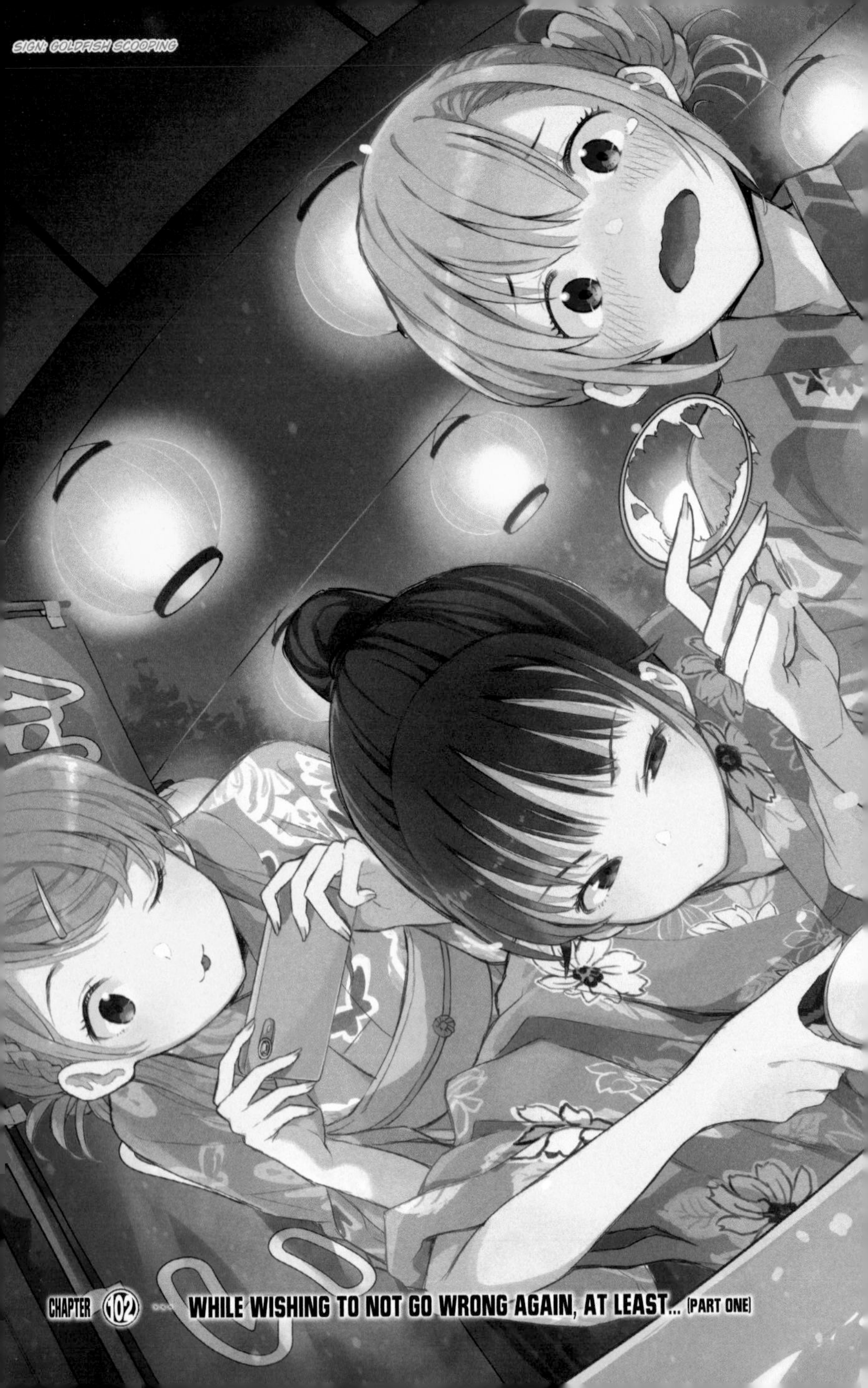
SIGN: GOLDFISH SCOOPING
CHAPTER 102 WHILE WISHING TO NOT GO WRONG AGAIN, AT LEAST... (PART ONE)

MY YOUTH R♥MANTIC C☺MEDY is WRØNG, AS I EXPECTED @comic

19

▌Original Story
Wataru Watari

▌Art
Naomichi Io

▌Character Design
Ponkan⑧

MY YOUTH ROMANTIC COMEDY IS WRONG, AS I EXPECTED @COMIC

CHARACTERS + STORY SO FAR

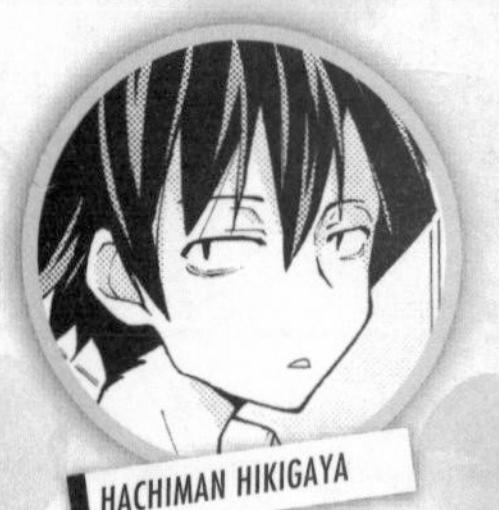

HACHIMAN HIKIGAYA

LONER AND A TWISTED HUMAN BEING. FORCED TO JOIN THE SERVICE CLUB. ASPIRES TO BE A HOUSEHUSBAND.

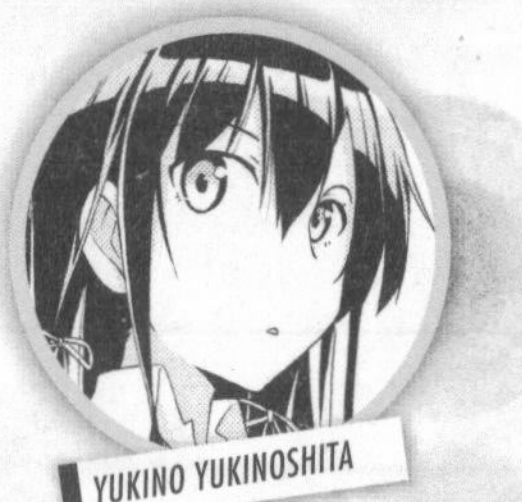

YUKINO YUKINOSHITA

PERFECT SUPERWOMAN WITH TOP GRADES AND FLAWLESS LOOKS, BUT HER PERSONALITY AND BOOBS ARE A LETDOWN. PRESIDENT OF THE SERVICE CLUB.

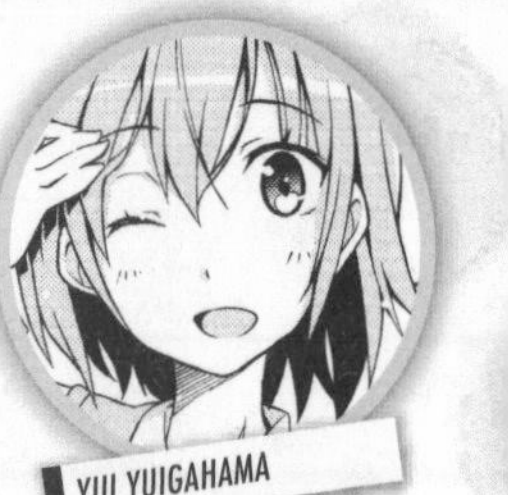

YUI YUIGAHAMA

LIGHT-BROWN HAIR, MINISKIRT, LARGE-BOOBED SLUTTY TYPE. BUT SHE'S ACTUALLY A VIRGIN!? MEMBER OF THE SERVICE CLUB.

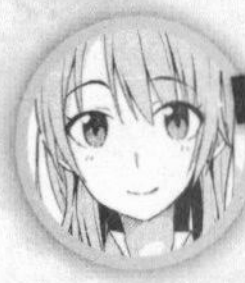

IROHA ISSHIKI

SOCCER CLUB ASSISTANT. FIRST-YEAR.

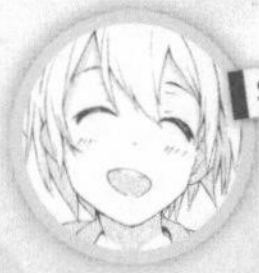

SAIKA TOTSUKA

THE SINGLE FLOWER BLOOMING IN THIS STORY. BUT...HAS A "PACKAGE."

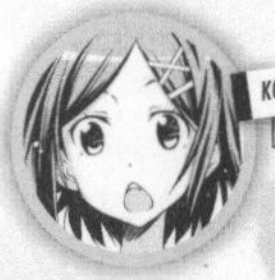

KOMACHI HIKIGAYA

HACHIMAN'S LITTLE SISTER. IN MIDDLE SCHOOL. EVERYTHING SHE DOES IS CALCULATED!?

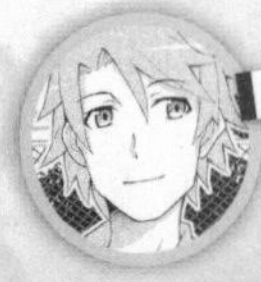

HAYATO HAYAMA

TOP RANKED IN THE SCHOOL CASTE. HANDSOME MEMBER OF THE SOCCER TEAM.

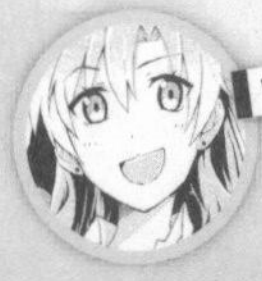

YUMIKO MIURA

THE HIGH EMPRESS NONE CAN OPPOSE.

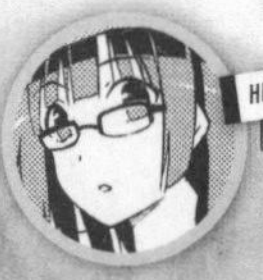

HINA EBINA

A MEMBER OF MIURA'S CLIQUE BUT A RAGING FUJOSHI ON THE INSIDE.

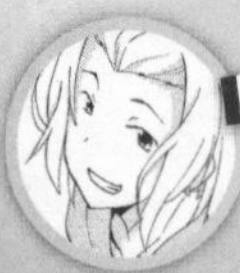

KAKERU TOBE

ALWAYS OVEREXCITED. MEMBER OF HAYAMA'S CLIQUE.

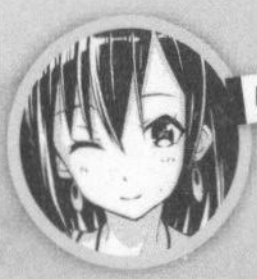

HARUNO YUKINOSHITA

YUKINO'S SISTER. UNIVERSITY UNDERGRADUATE. IS QUITE INTERESTED IN HACHIMAN.

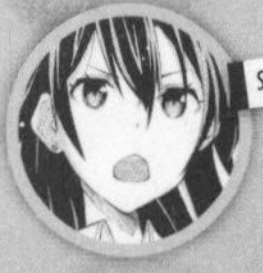

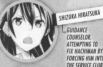

SHIZUKA HIRATSUKA

GUIDANCE COUNSELOR. ATTEMPTING TO FIX HACHIMAN BY FORCING HIM INTO THE SERVICE CLUB.

THE STORY SO FAR

YUKINO AND IROHA HAVE BEEN PLANNING A PROM. IN ORDER TO MAKE IT HAPPEN, HACHIMAN COMES UP WITH AN OPPOSITION DUMMY PROM. HE GETS YUI, ZAIMOKUZA, AND THE U.G. CLUB TO HELP HIM WITH HIS PLAN, AND THEY MAKE A WEBSITE AND ROPE IN KAIHIN HIGH. THE PLAN MOVES ALONG SMOOTHLY, AND ALL THAT'S LEFT IS TO GET THE PARENTS' APPROVAL. HACHIMAN KNOWS SOMEONE WHO COULD LEAK THE DUMMY PROJECT TO THE PARENTS, BUT THAT PERSON IS...

CONTENTS

MY **YOUTH**
R♥MANTIC C☺MEDY
is **WRØNG,** AS I EXPECTED
@ *comic*

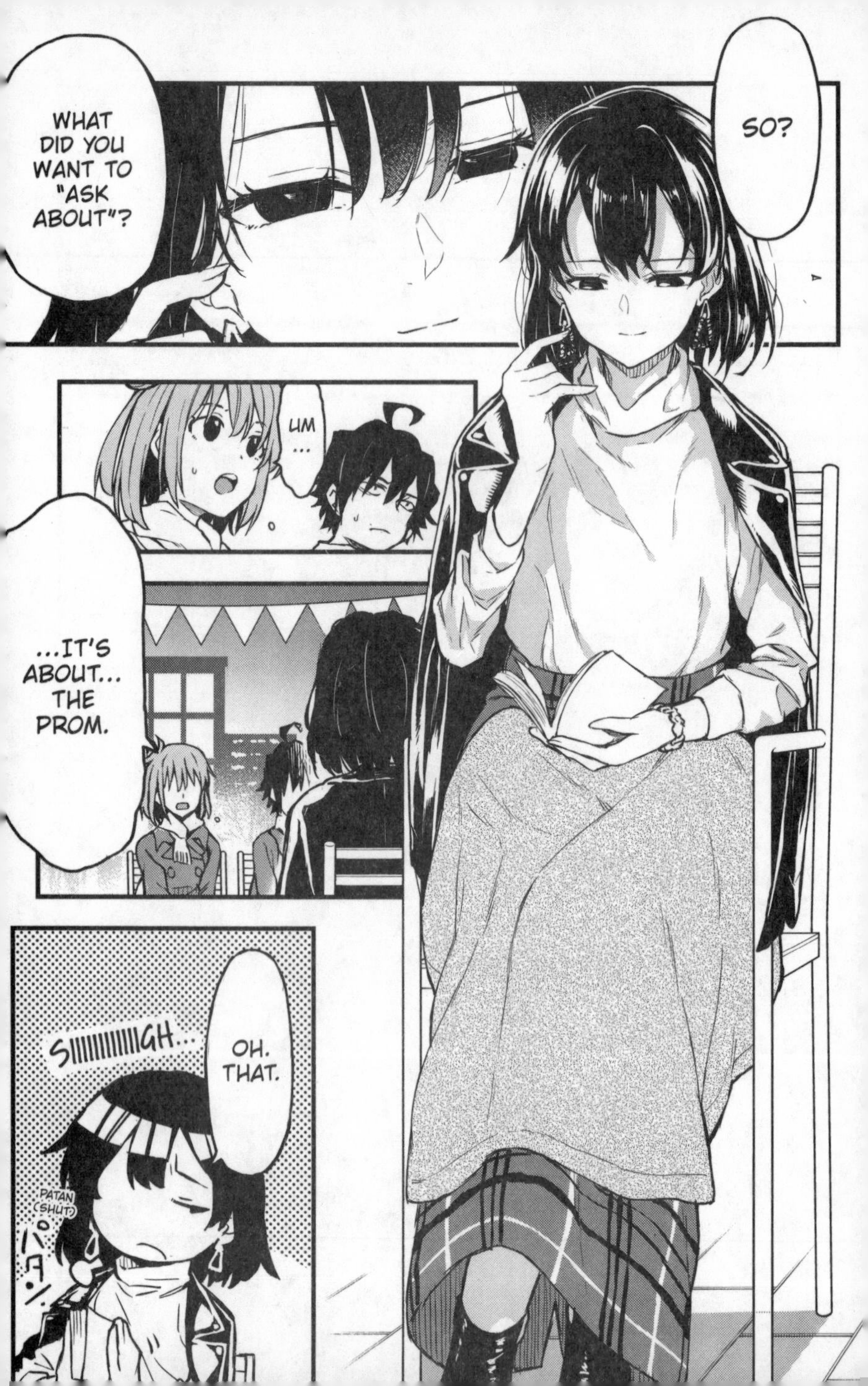
SO?
WHAT DID YOU WANT TO "ASK ABOUT"?
UM...
...IT'S ABOUT... THE PROM.
OH. THAT.
SIIIIIIIIIIIIIIIIGH...
PATAN (SHUT)

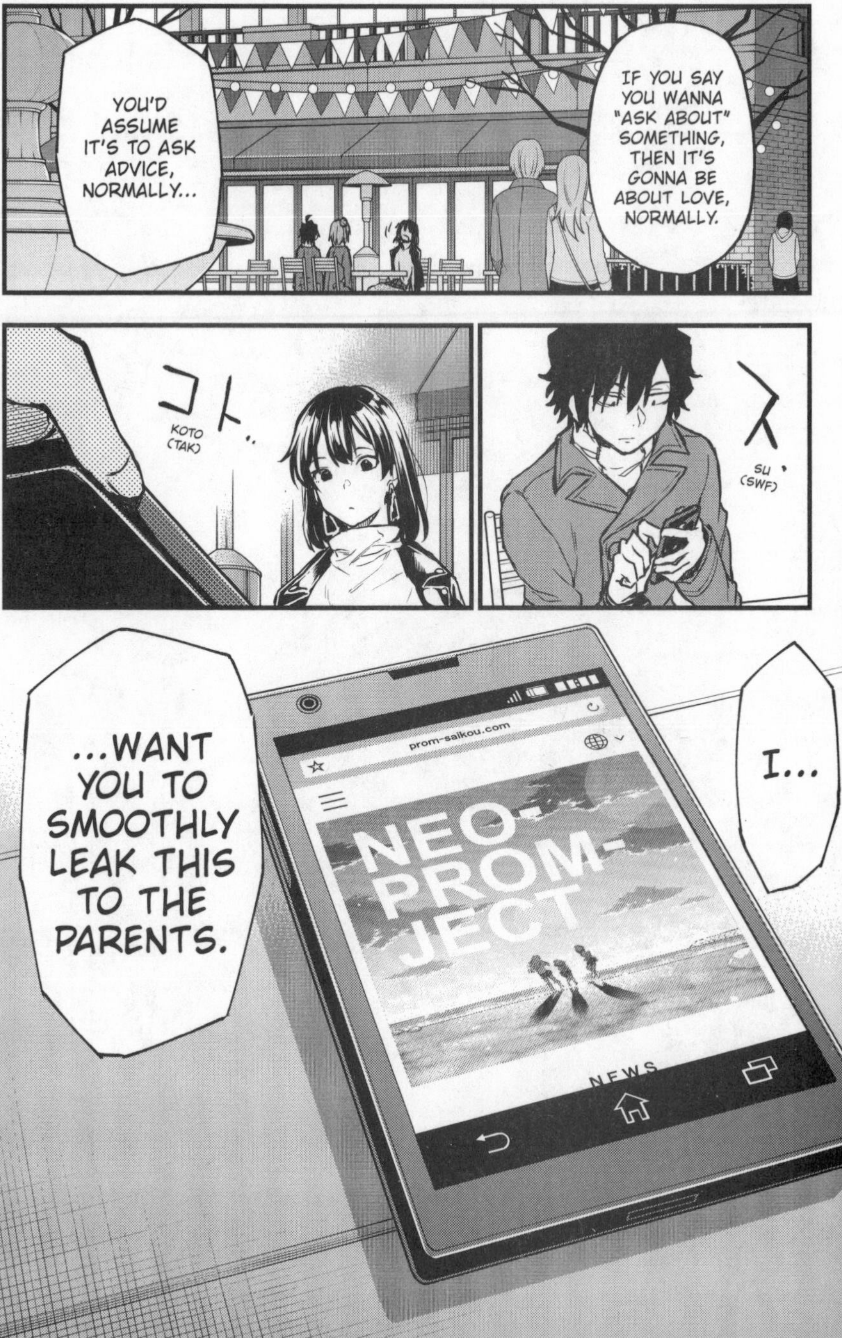
IF YOU SAY YOU WANNA "ASK ABOUT" SOMETHING, THEN IT'S GONNA BE ABOUT LOVE, NORMALLY.
YOU'D ASSUME IT'S TO ASK ADVICE, NORMALLY...
ス
SU (SWF)
コト
KOTO (TAK)
I...
...WANT YOU TO SMOOTHLY LEAK THIS TO THE PARENTS.
prom-saikou.com
NEO-PROM-JECT
NEWS

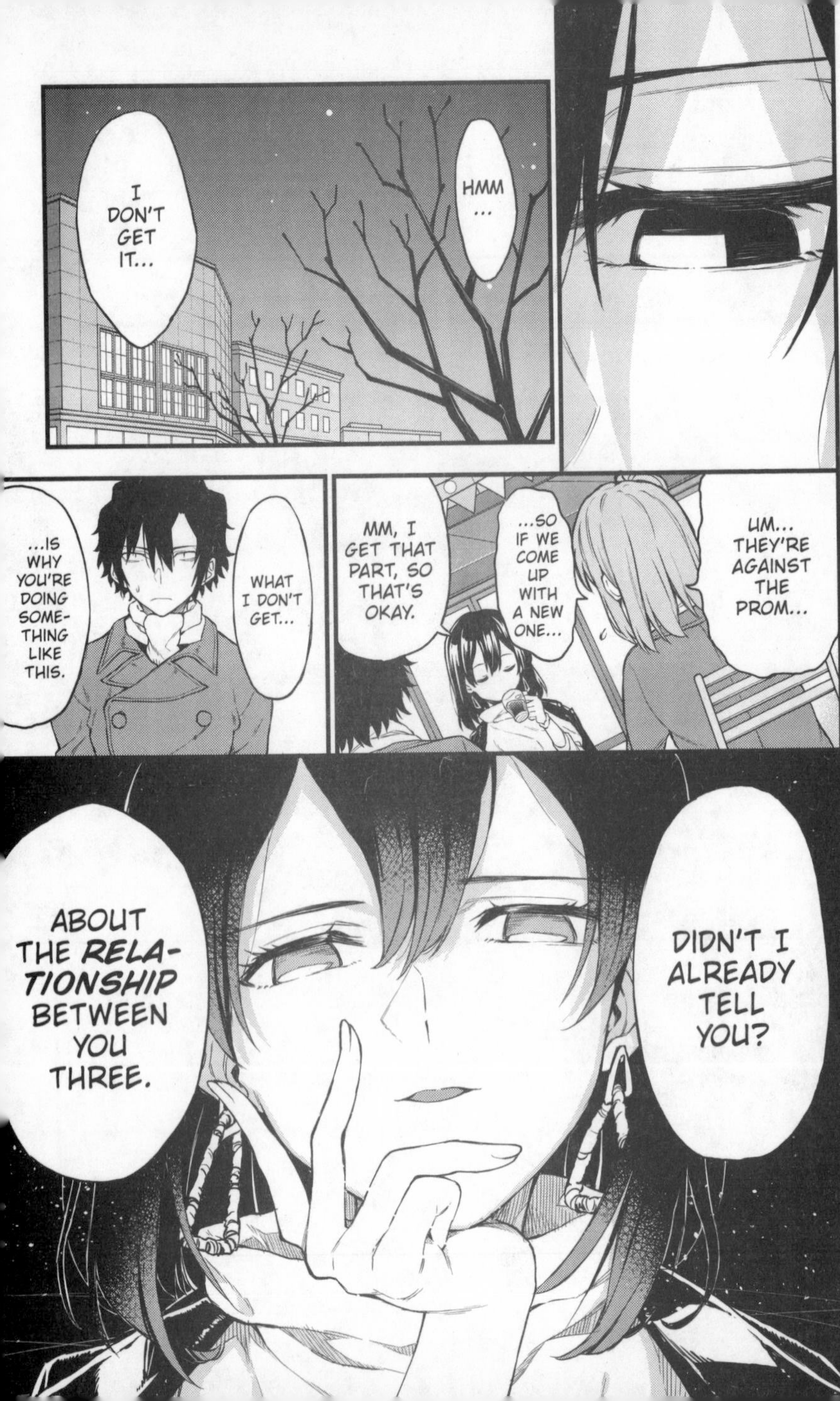
HMM...
I DON'T GET IT...
UM... THEY'RE AGAINST THE PROM...
...SO IF WE COME UP WITH A NEW ONE...
MM, I GET THAT PART, SO THAT'S OKAY.
WHAT I DON'T GET...
...IS WHY YOU'RE DOING SOMETHING LIKE THIS.
DIDN'T I ALREADY TELL YOU?
ABOUT THE *RELATIONSHIP* BETWEEN YOU THREE.

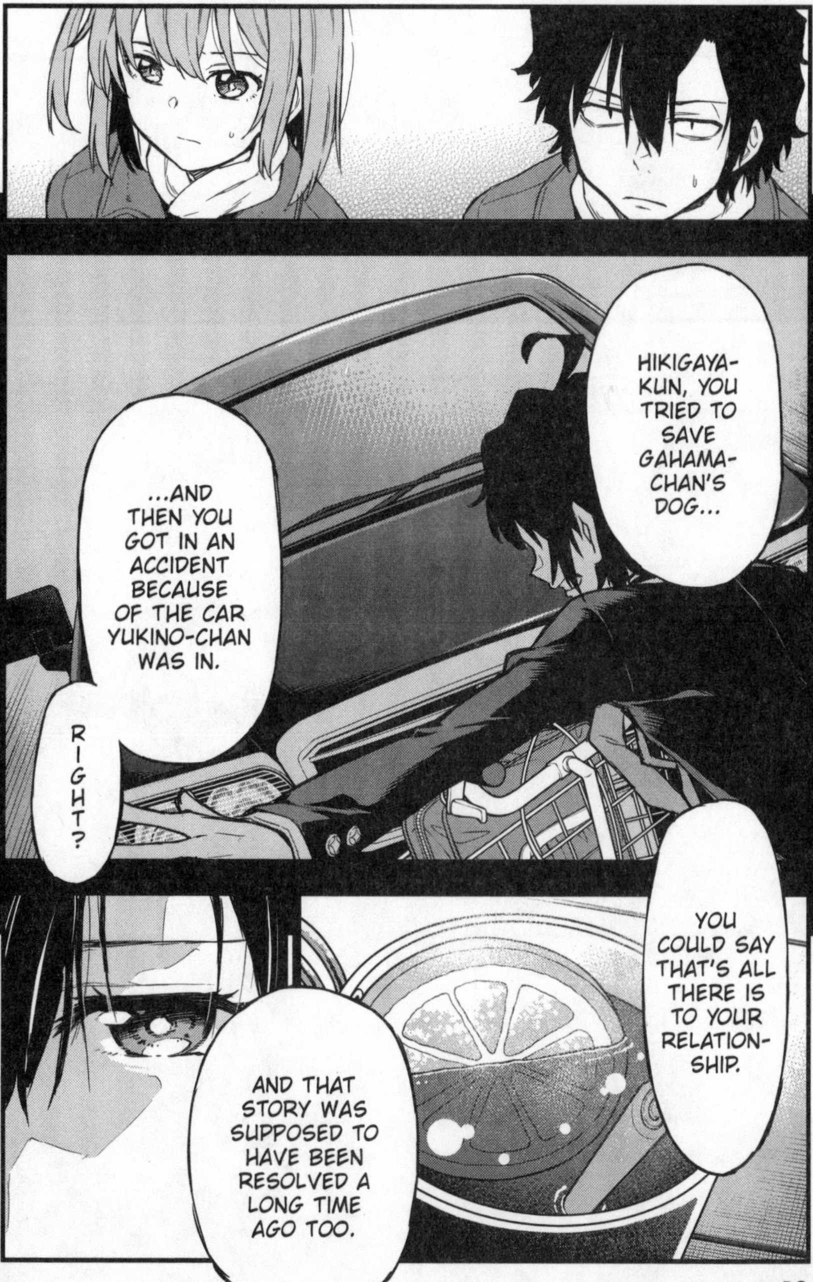
HIKIGAYA-KUN, YOU TRIED TO SAVE GAHAMA-CHAN'S DOG...
...AND THEN YOU GOT IN AN ACCIDENT BECAUSE OF THE CAR YUKINO-CHAN WAS IN.
RIGHT?
YOU COULD SAY THAT'S ALL THERE IS TO YOUR RELATIONSHIP.
AND THAT STORY WAS SUPPOSED TO HAVE BEEN RESOLVED A LONG TIME AGO TOO.

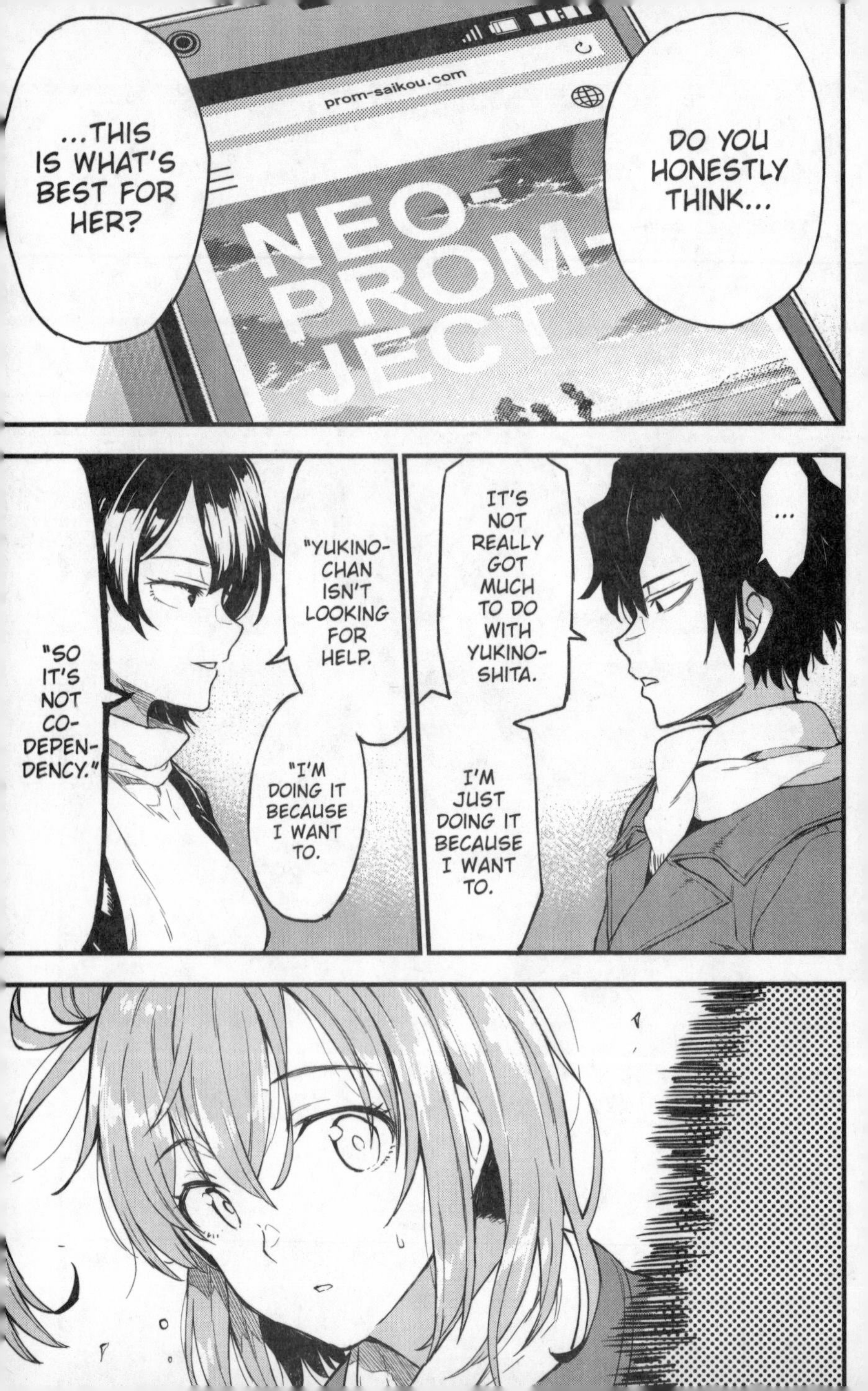
DO YOU HONESTLY THINK...
prom-saikou.com
NEO-PROM-PROJECT
...THIS IS WHAT'S BEST FOR HER?
...
IT'S NOT REALLY GOT MUCH TO DO WITH YUKINOSHITA.
I'M JUST DOING IT BECAUSE I WANT TO.
"YUKINO-CHAN ISN'T LOOKING FOR HELP.
"I'M DOING IT BECAUSE I WANT TO.
"SO IT'S NOT CO-DEPENDENCY."

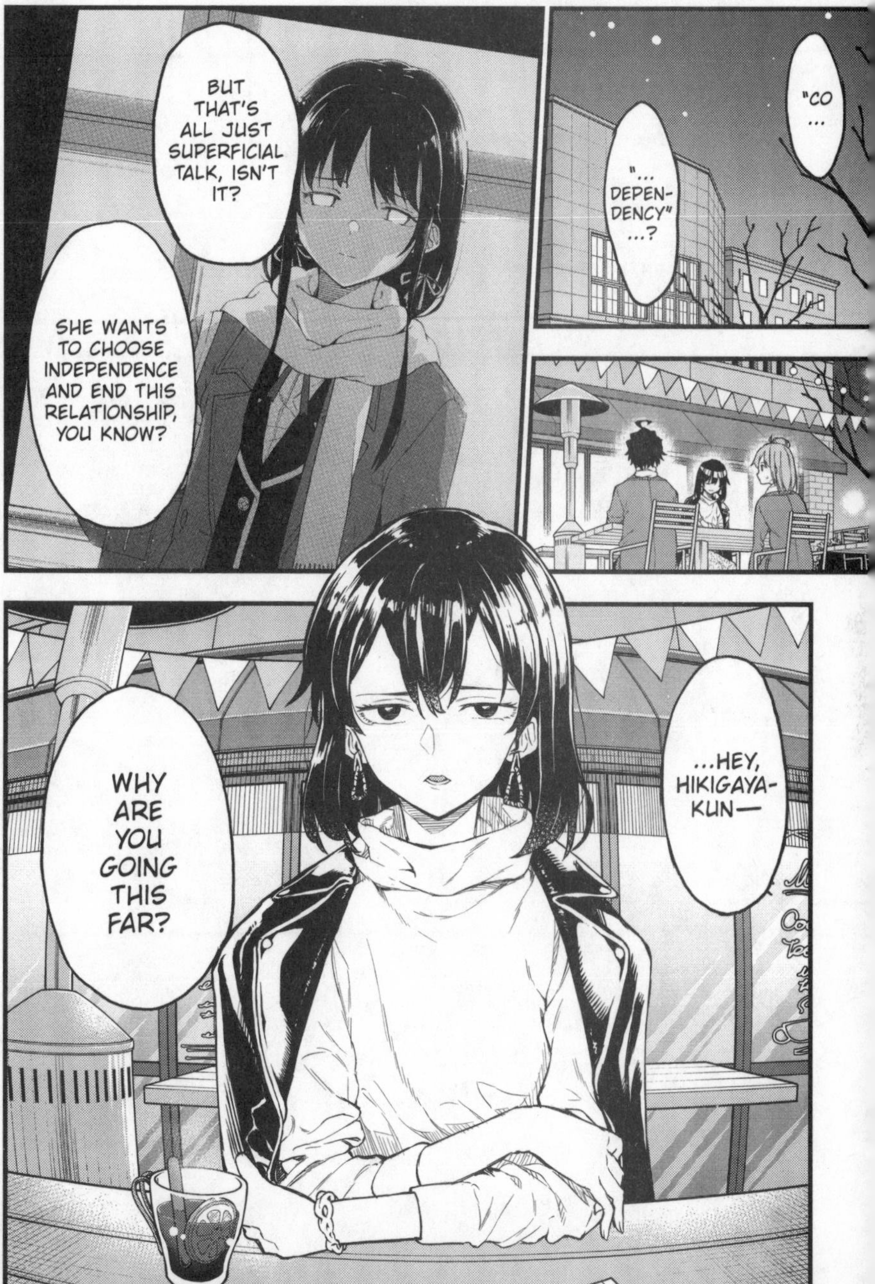
"CO...
"...DEPENDENCY"...?
BUT THAT'S ALL JUST SUPERFICIAL TALK, ISN'T IT?
SHE WANTS TO CHOOSE INDEPENDENCE AND END THIS RELATIONSHIP, YOU KNOW?
...HEY, HIKIGAYA-KUN—
WHY ARE YOU GOING THIS FAR?

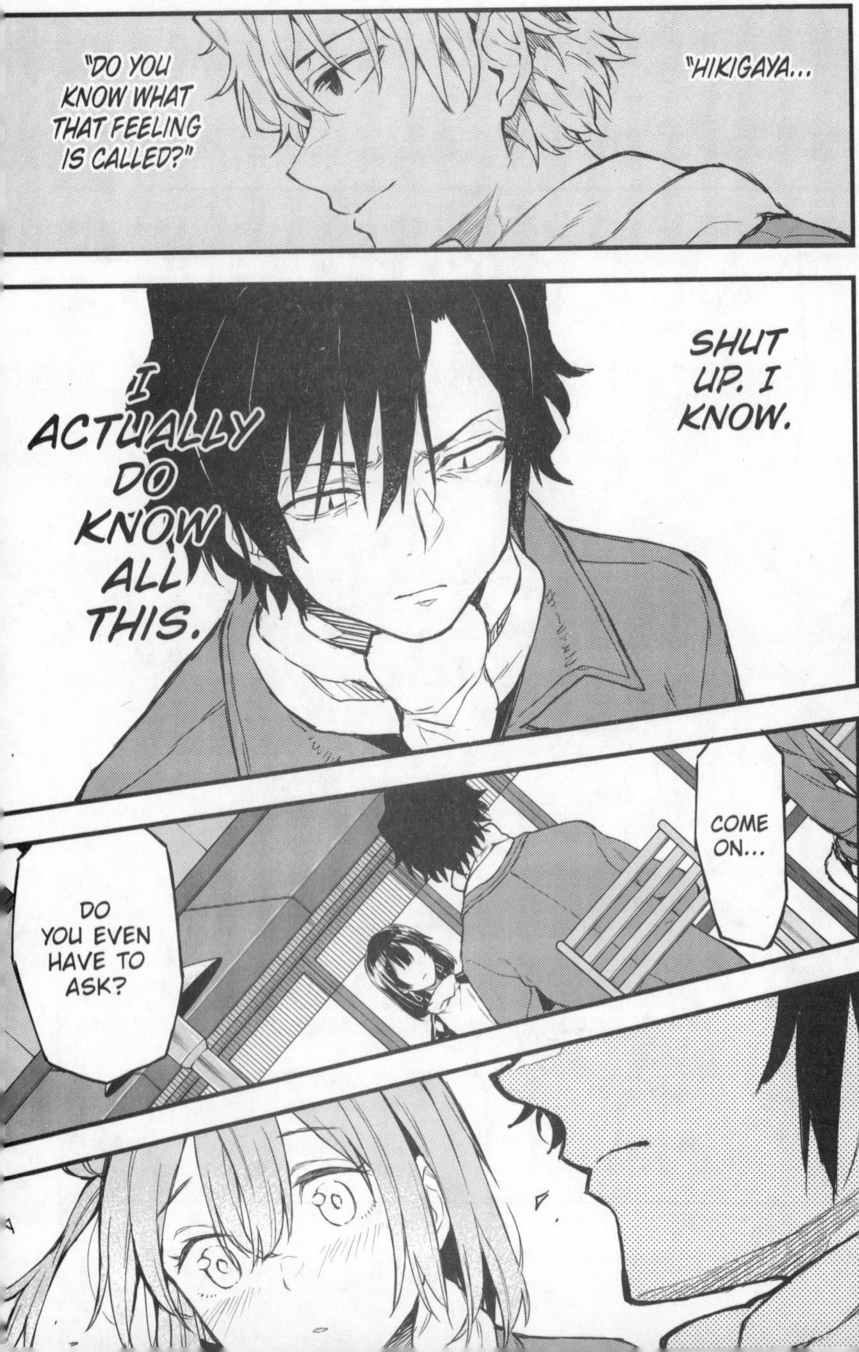
"HIKIGAYA...
"DO YOU KNOW WHAT THAT FEELING IS CALLED?"
SHUT UP. I KNOW.
I ACTUALLY DO KNOW ALL THIS.
COME ON...
DO YOU EVEN HAVE TO ASK?

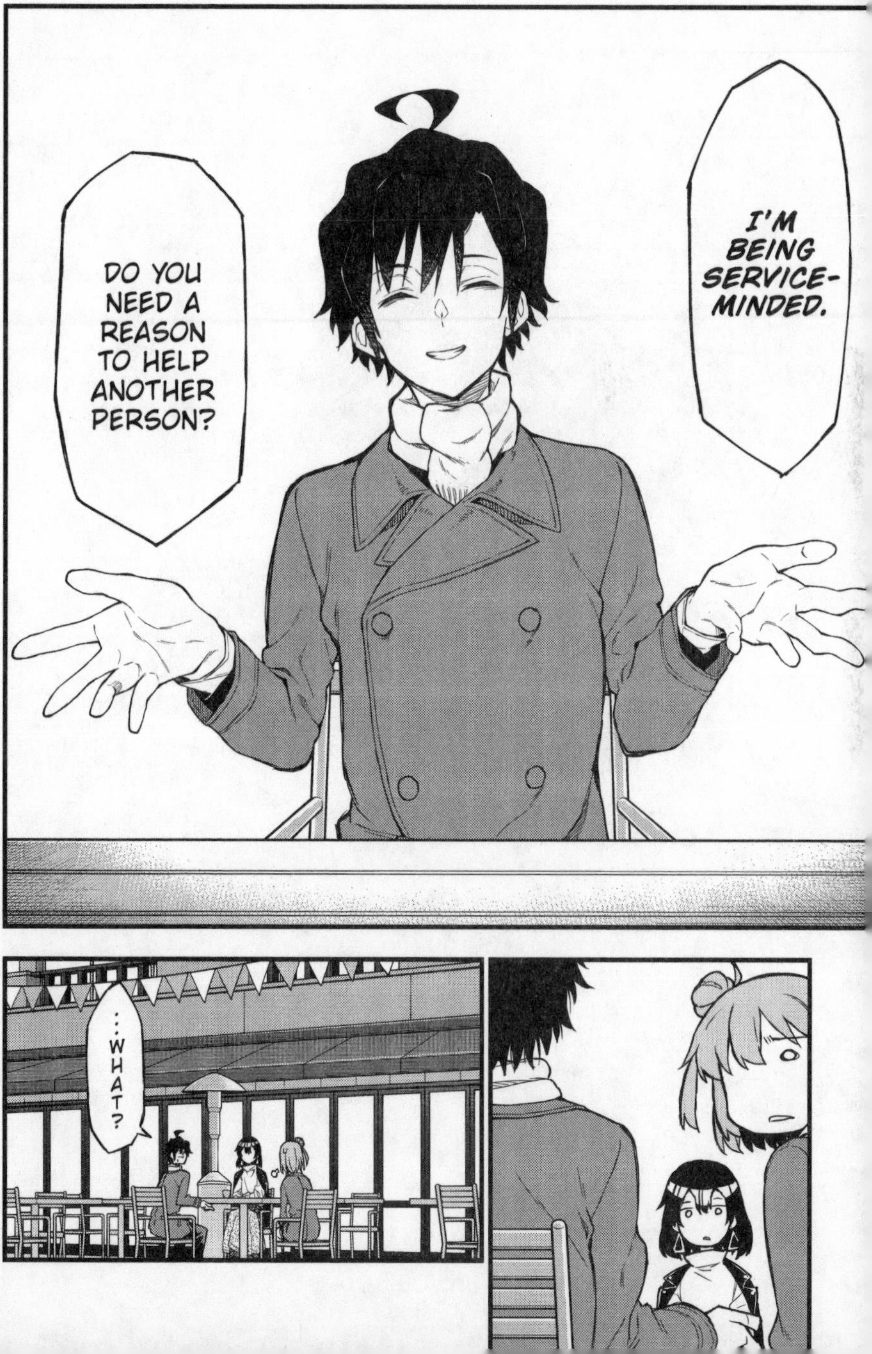
I'M BEING SERVICE-MINDED.
DO YOU NEED A REASON TO HELP ANOTHER PERSON?
...WHAT?

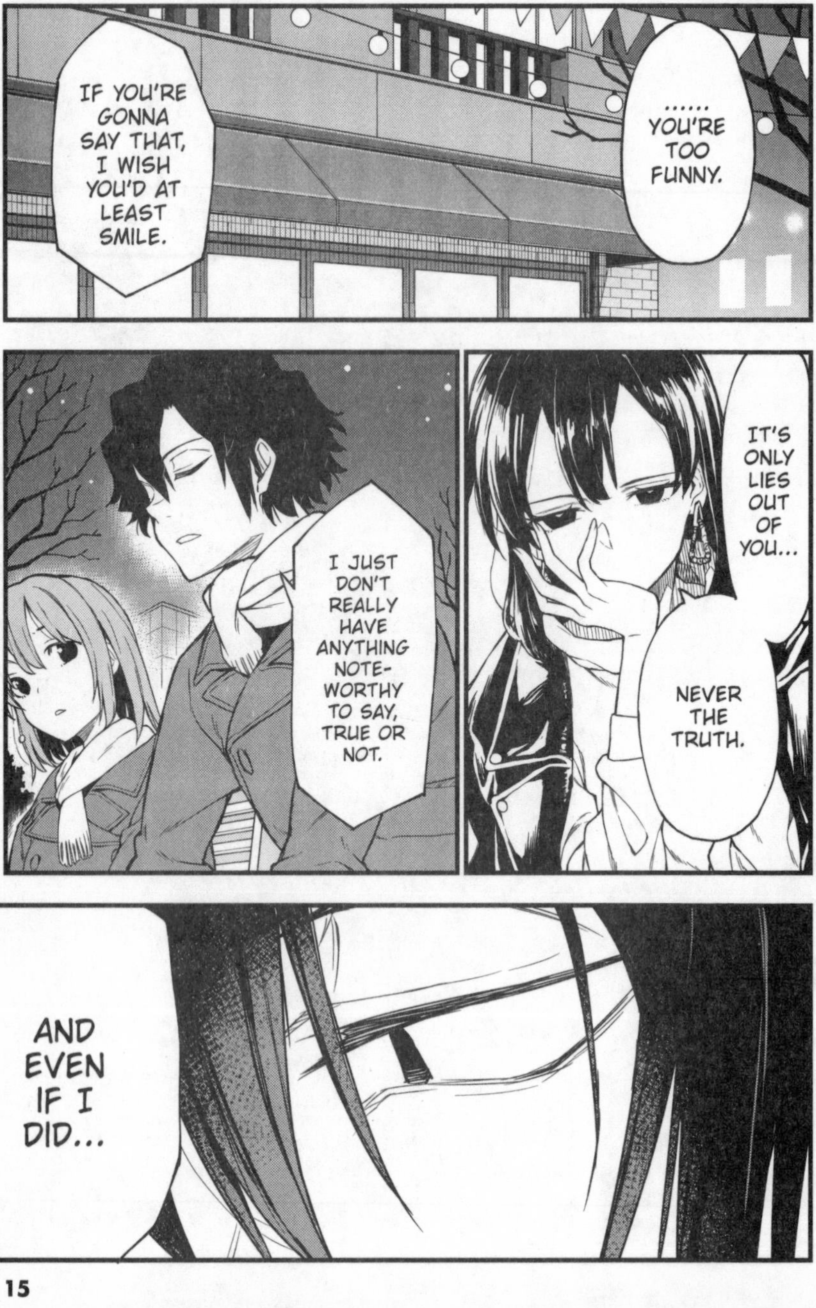
...... YOU'RE TOO FUNNY.
IF YOU'RE GONNA SAY THAT, I WISH YOU'D AT LEAST SMILE.
IT'S ONLY LIES OUT OF YOU...
NEVER THE TRUTH.
I JUST DON'T REALLY HAVE ANYTHING NOTE-WORTHY TO SAY, TRUE OR NOT.
AND EVEN IF I DID...

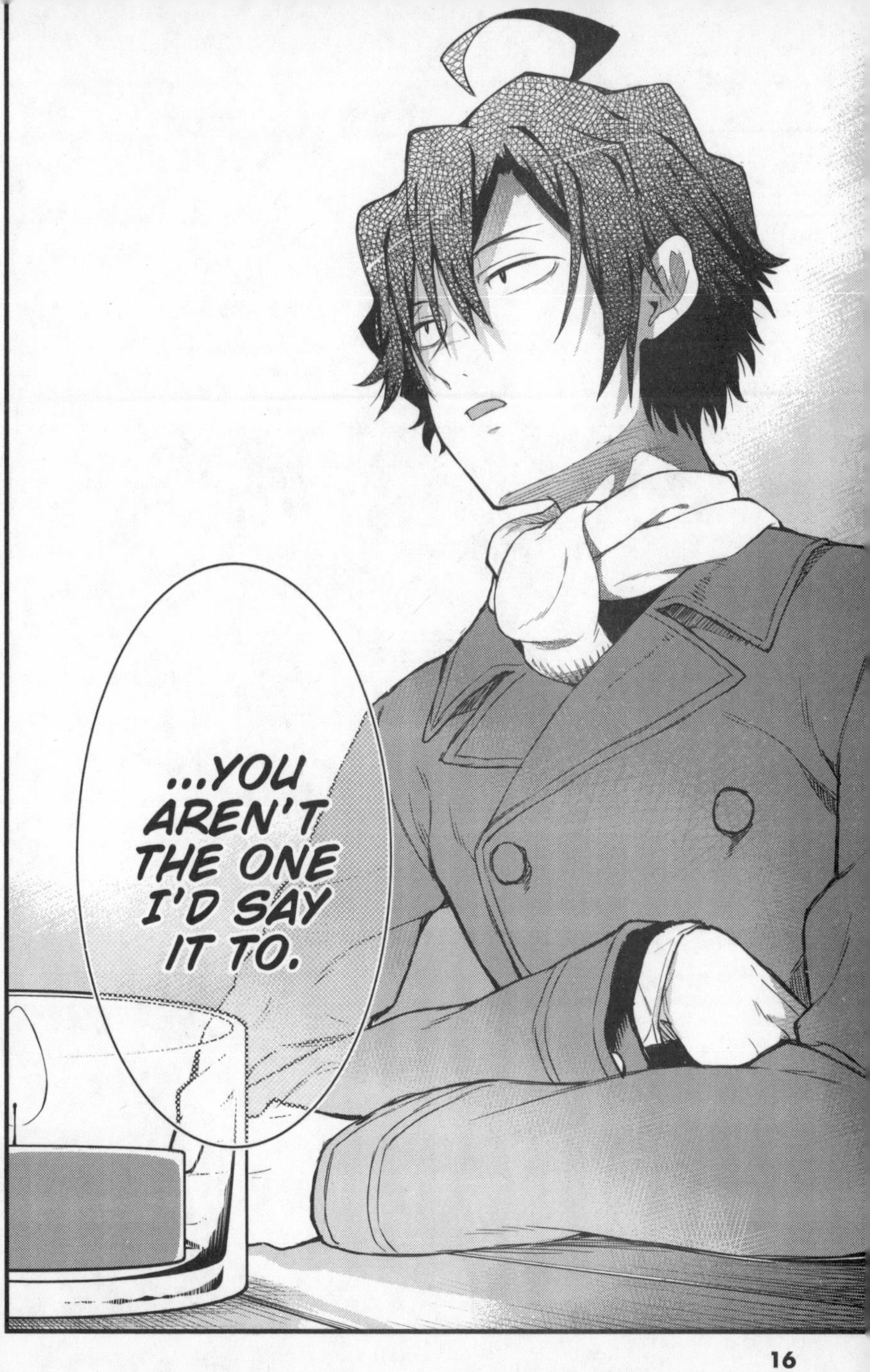
...YOU AREN'T THE ONE I'D SAY IT TO.

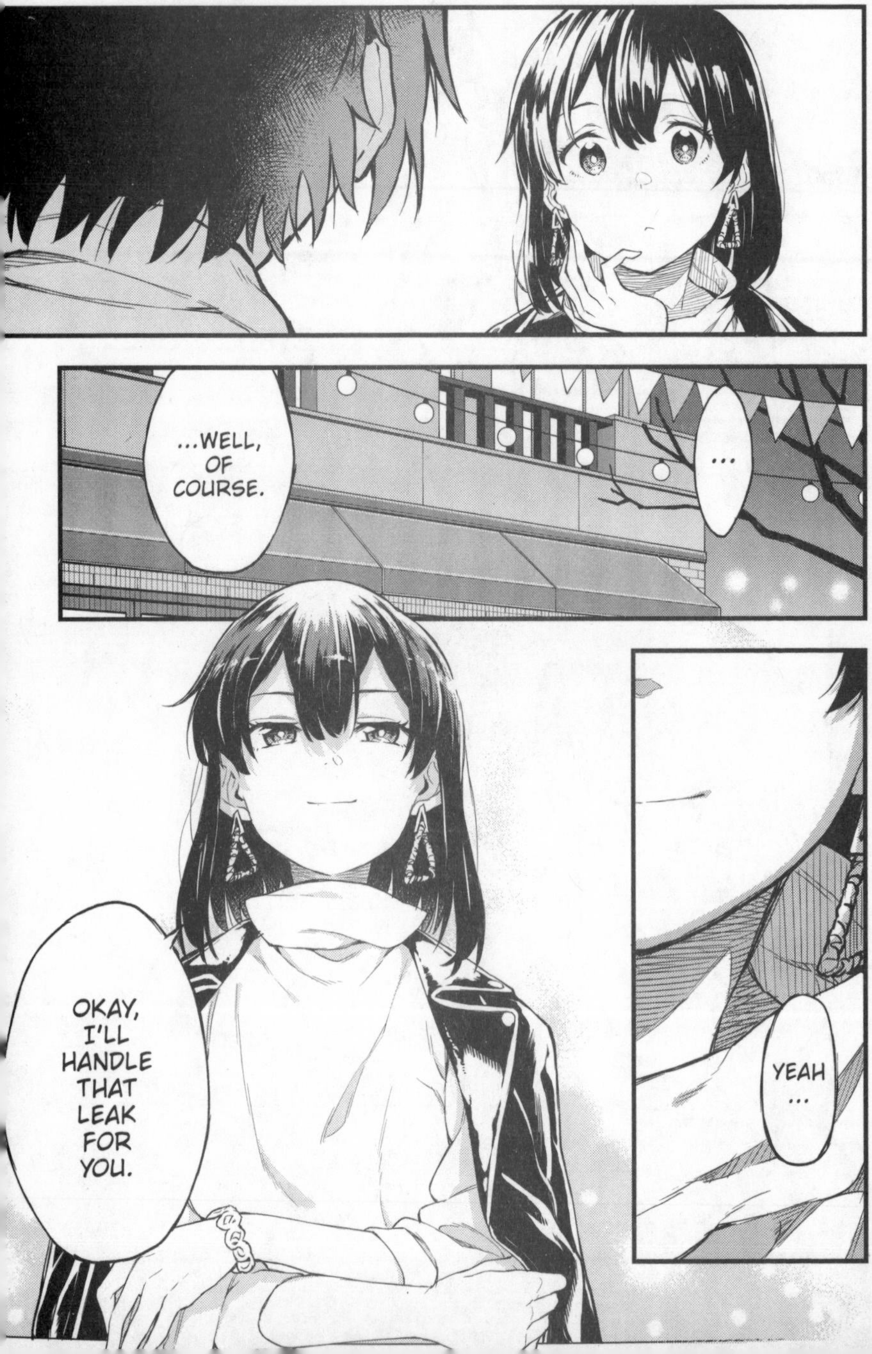
...
...WELL, OF COURSE.
YEAH ...
OKAY, I'LL HANDLE THAT LEAK FOR YOU.

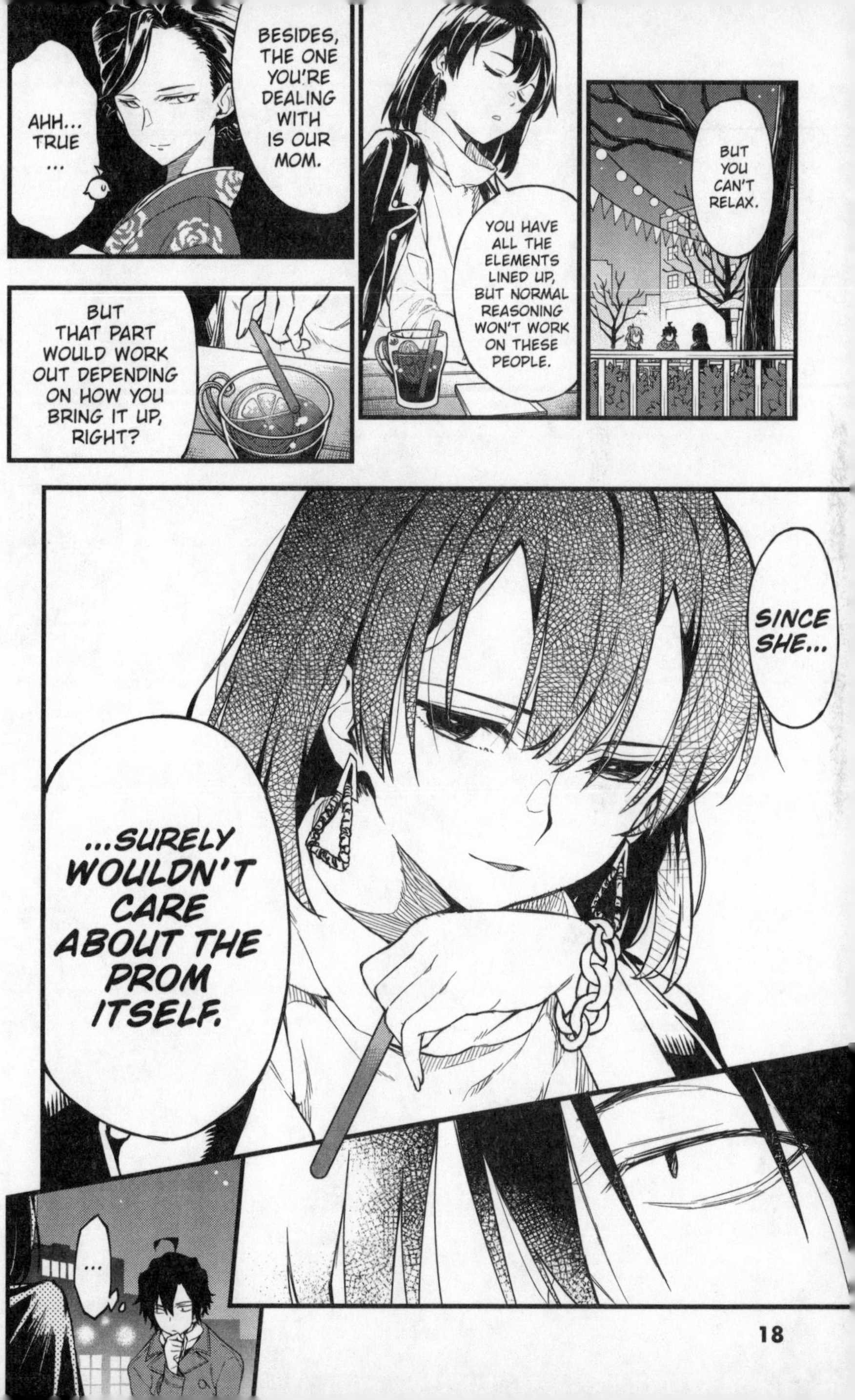
BUT YOU CAN'T RELAX.
YOU HAVE ALL THE ELEMENTS LINED UP, BUT NORMAL REASONING WON'T WORK ON THESE PEOPLE.
BESIDES, THE ONE YOU'RE DEALING WITH IS OUR MOM.
AHH... TRUE ...
BUT THAT PART WOULD WORK OUT DEPENDING ON HOW YOU BRING IT UP, RIGHT?
SINCE SHE...
...SURELY WOULDN'T CARE ABOUT THE PROM ITSELF.
...

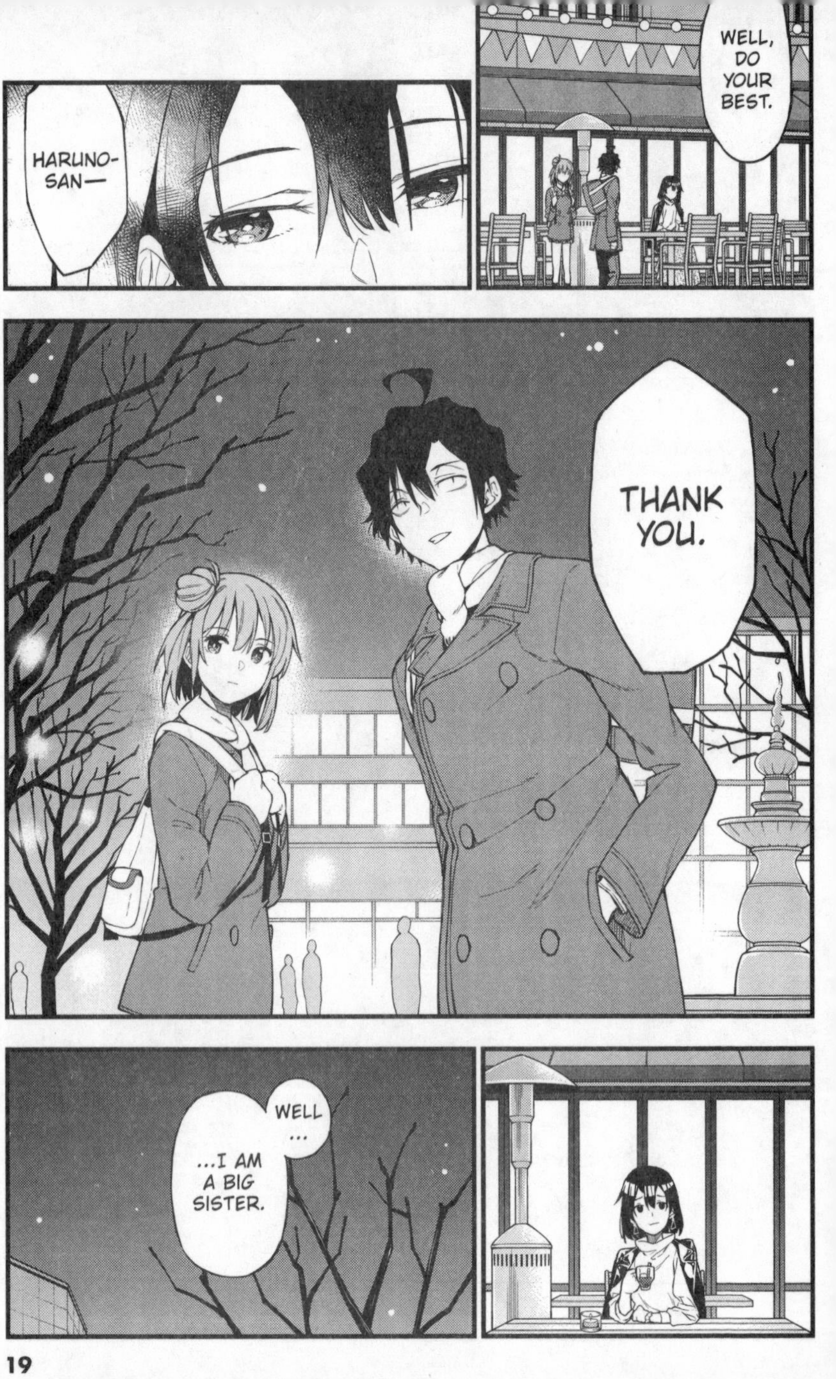
WELL, DO YOUR BEST.
HARUNO-SAN—
THANK YOU.
WELL ...
...I AM A BIG SISTER.

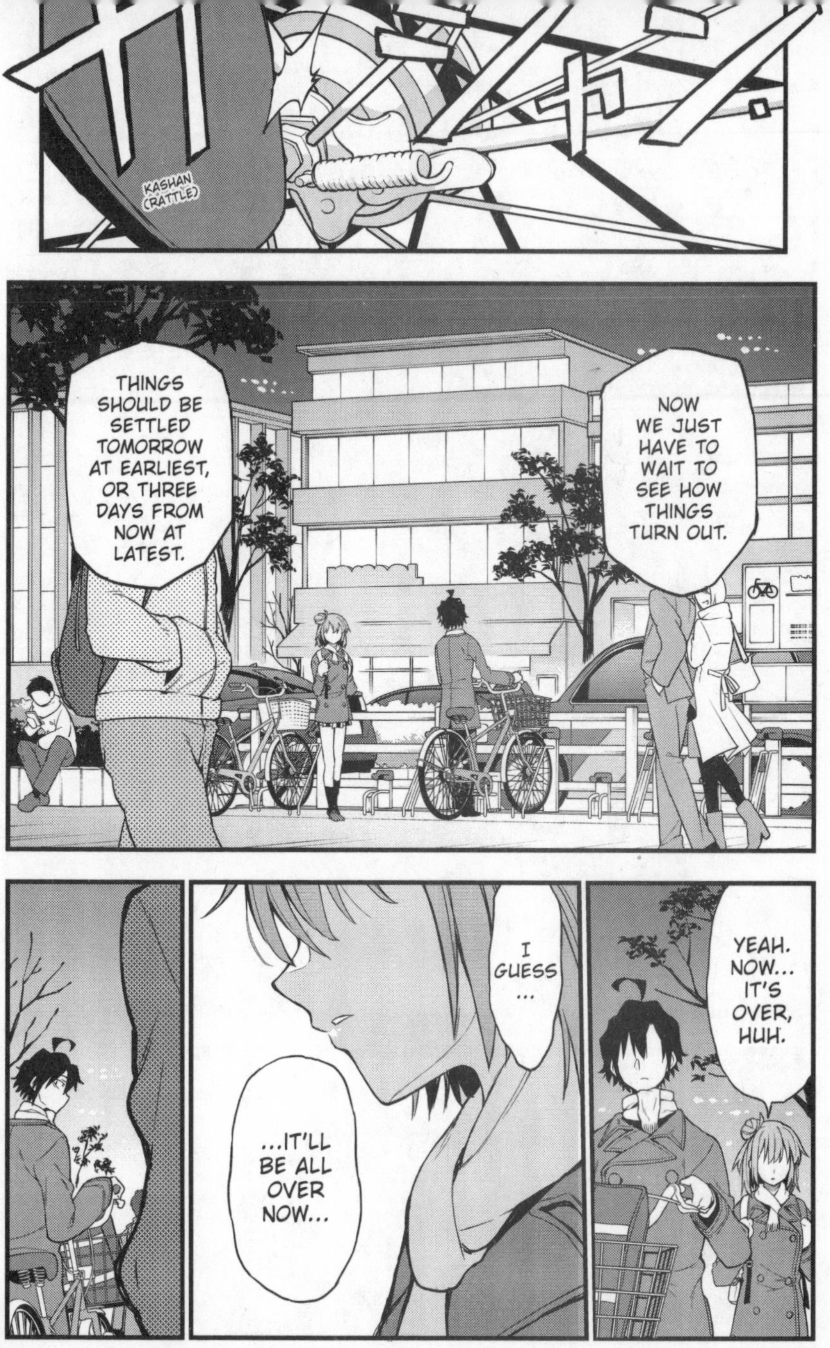
KASHAN (RATTLE)
NOW WE JUST HAVE TO WAIT TO SEE HOW THINGS TURN OUT.
THINGS SHOULD BE SETTLED TOMORROW AT EARLIEST, OR THREE DAYS FROM NOW AT LATEST.
YEAH. NOW... IT'S OVER, HUH.
I GUESS...
...IT'LL BE ALL OVER NOW...

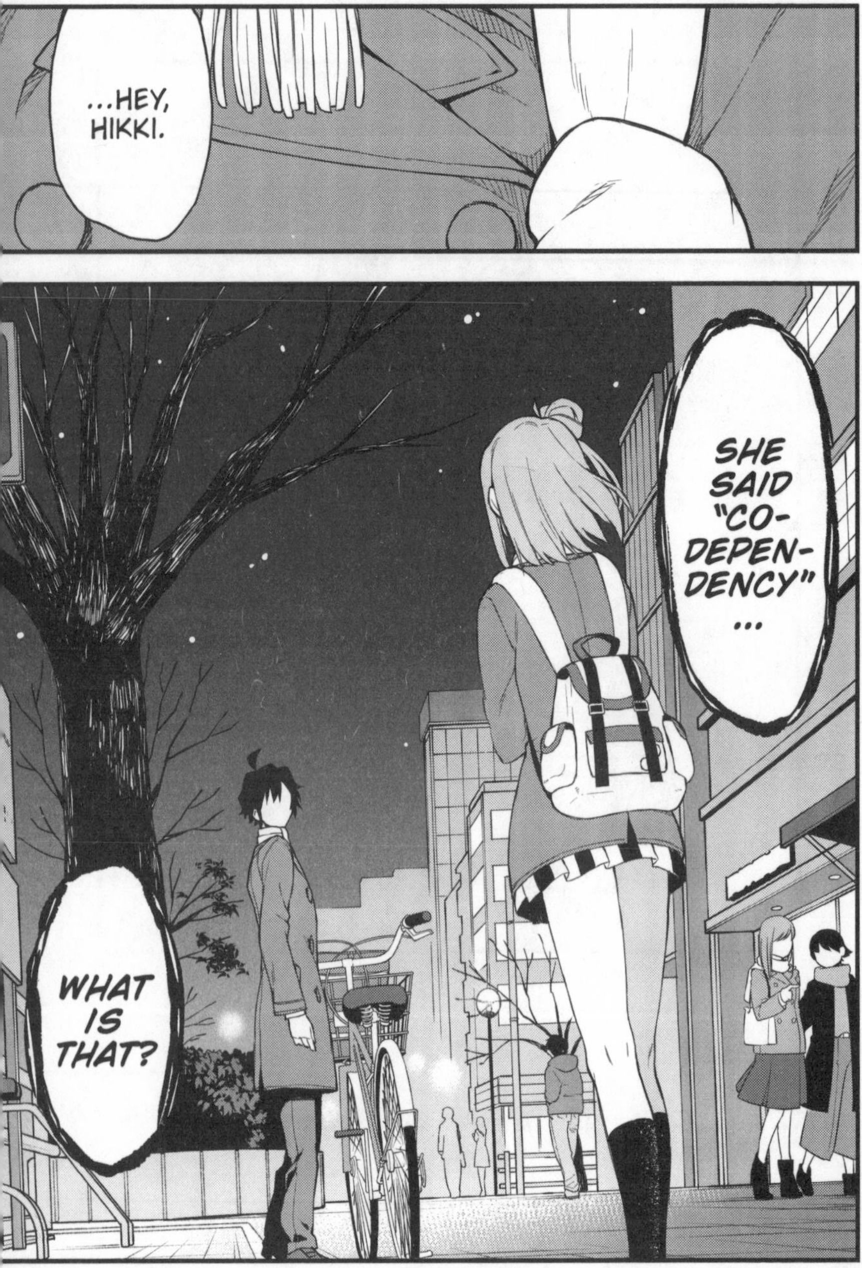
...HEY, HIKKI.
SHE SAID "CO-DEPENDENCY" ...
WHAT IS THAT?

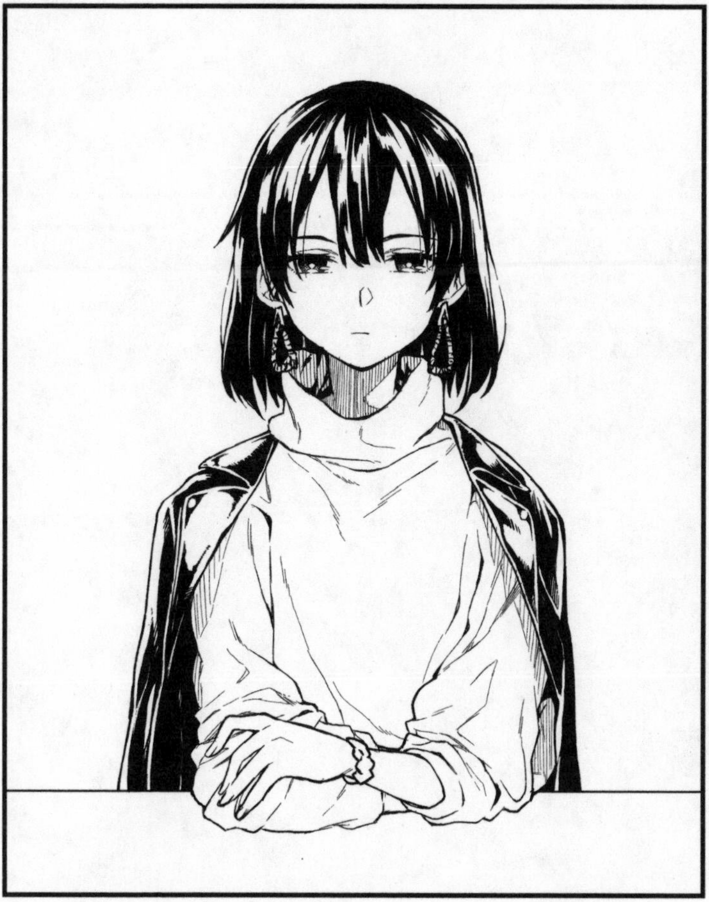

CHAPTER 102.5 … INTERLUDE HARUNO YUKINOSHITA.

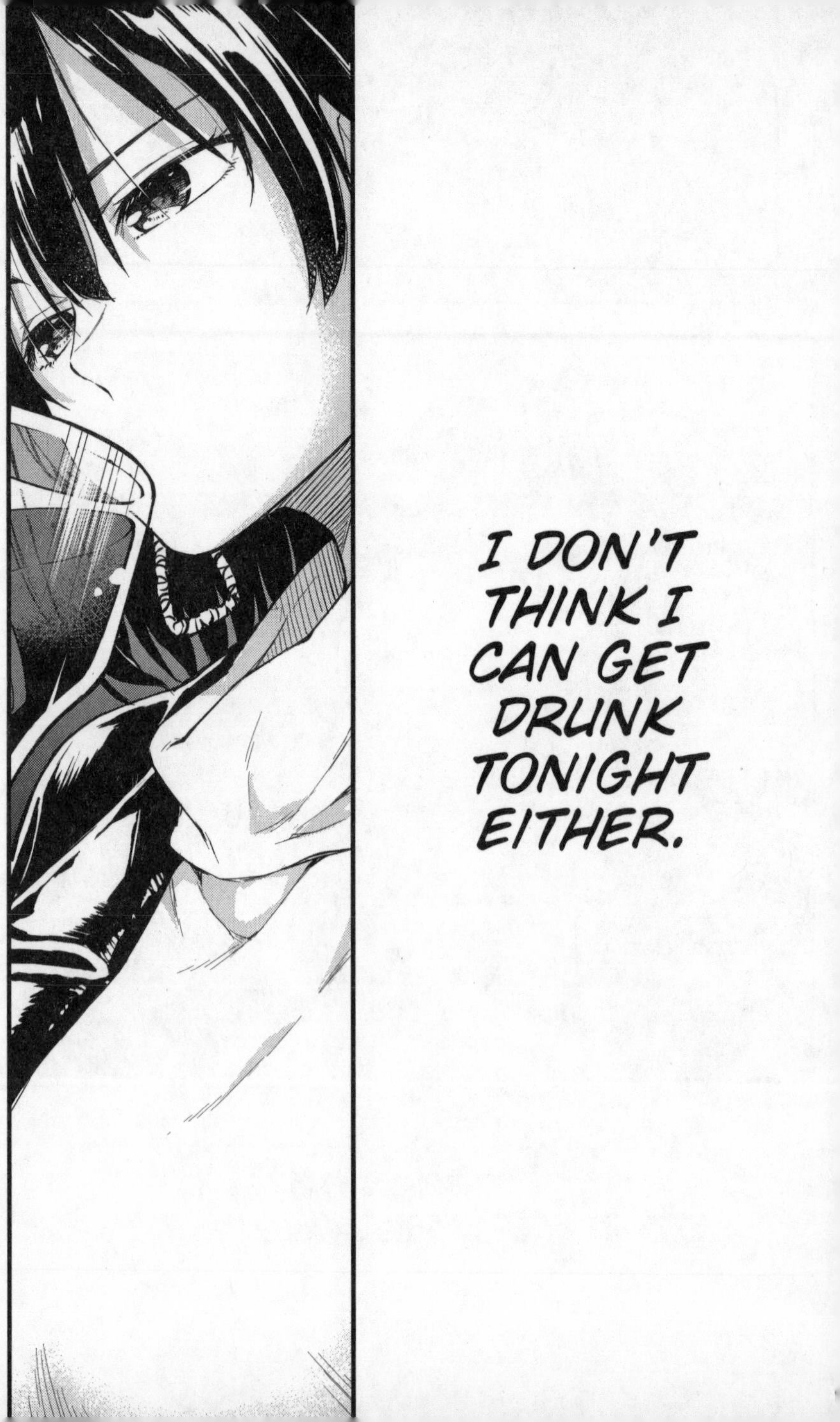
I DON'T THINK I CAN GET DRUNK TONIGHT EITHER.

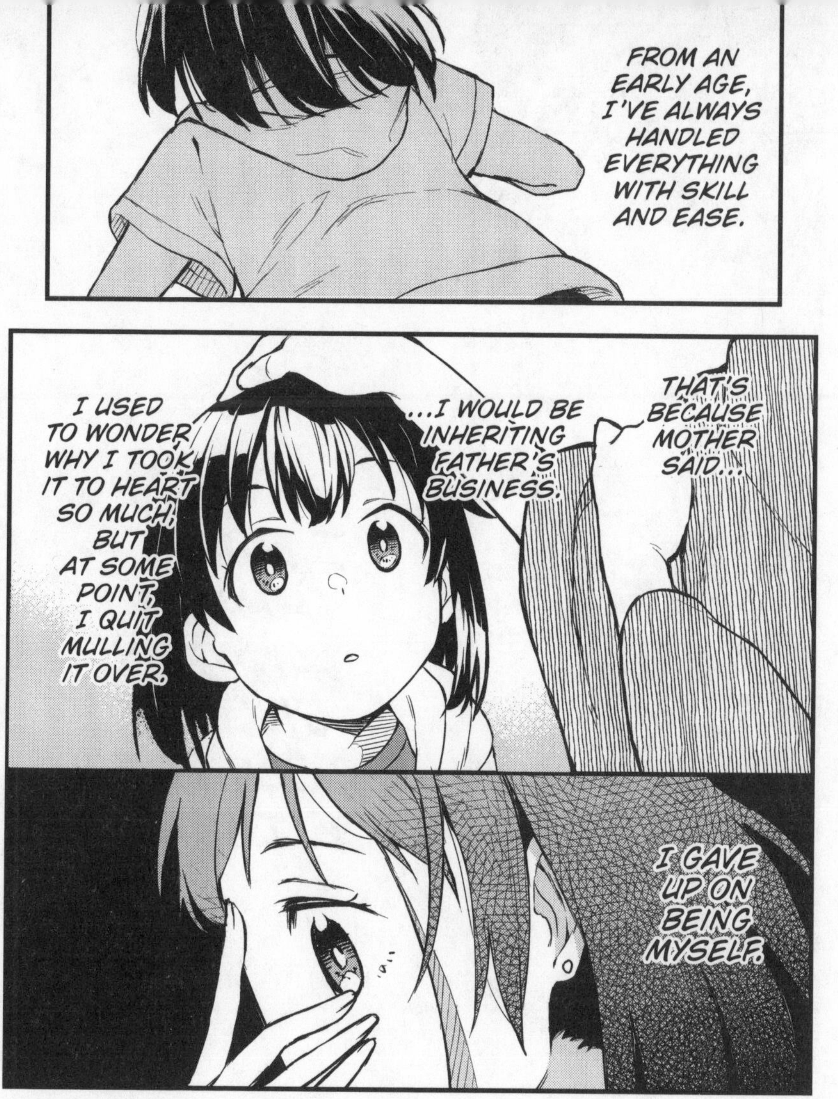
FROM AN EARLY AGE, I'VE ALWAYS HANDLED EVERYTHING WITH SKILL AND EASE.
THAT'S BECAUSE MOTHER SAID...
...I WOULD BE INHERITING FATHER'S BUSINESS.
I USED TO WONDER WHY I TOOK IT TO HEART SO MUCH, BUT AT SOME POINT, I QUIT MULLING IT OVER.
I GAVE UP ON BEING MYSELF.

THAT WAS HOW I STARTED PERFORMING "ME."

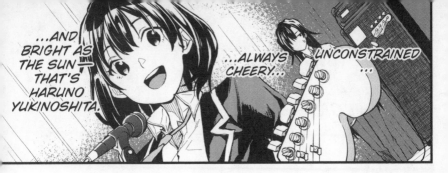

UNCONSTRAINED...
...ALWAYS CHEERY...
...AND BRIGHT AS THE SUN—THAT'S HARUNO YUKINOSHITA.

UNFORTUNATELY, PUTTING ON THAT ACT WASN'T A STRUGGLE FOR ME.

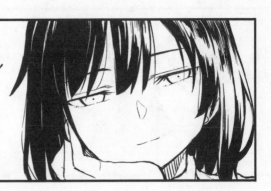

OCCASIONALLY, I'D CONSCIOUSLY PUT ON A COLD SMILE. BUT I DIDN'T EVEN THINK OF THOSE AS MINE ANYMORE.

BEFORE I KNEW IT...

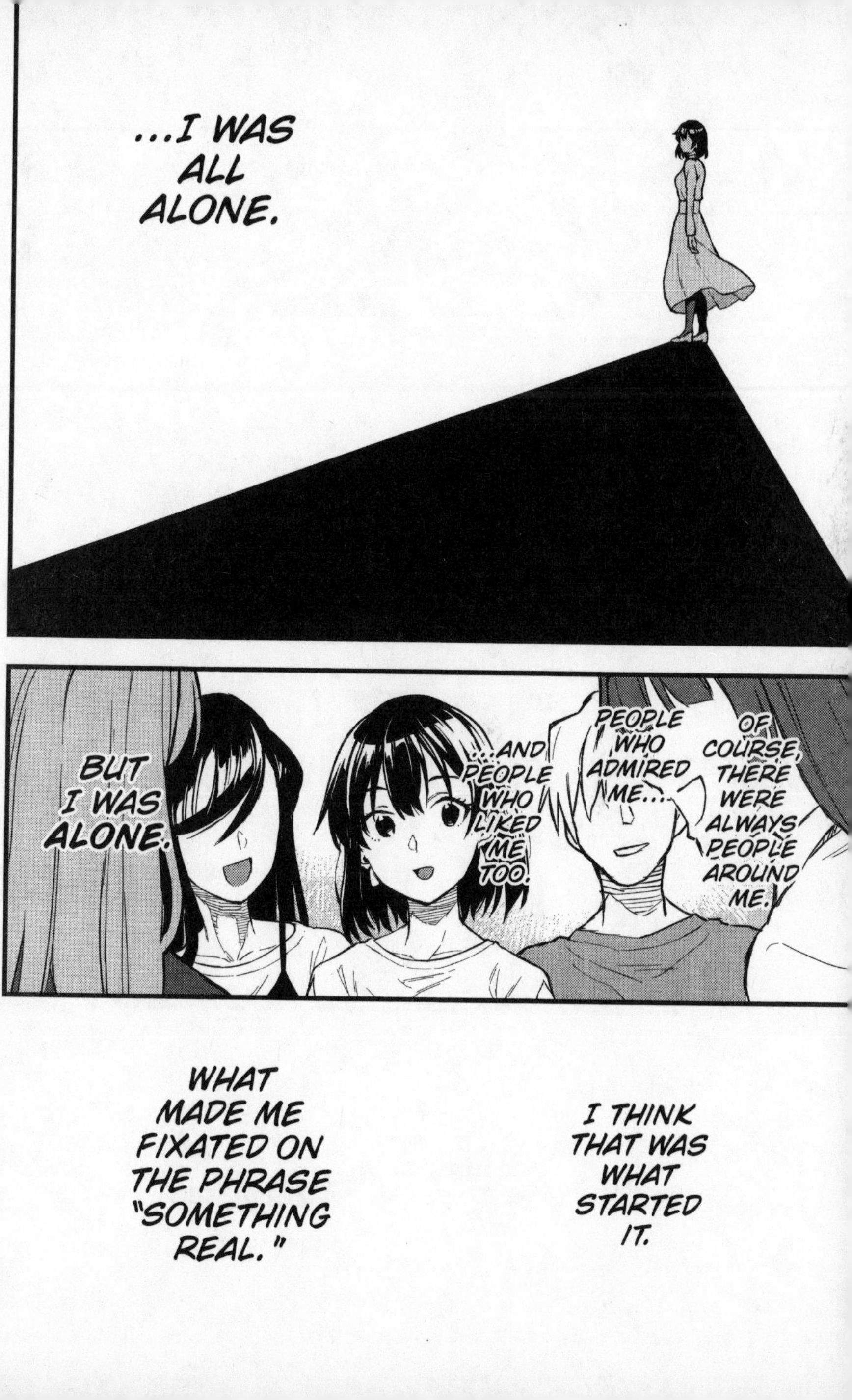

...I WAS ALL ALONE.
OF COURSE, THERE WERE ALWAYS PEOPLE AROUND ME.
PEOPLE WHO ADMIRED ME...
...AND PEOPLE WHO LIKED ME TOO.
BUT I WAS ALONE.
I THINK THAT WAS WHAT STARTED IT.
WHAT MADE ME FIXATED ON THE PHRASE "SOMETHING REAL."

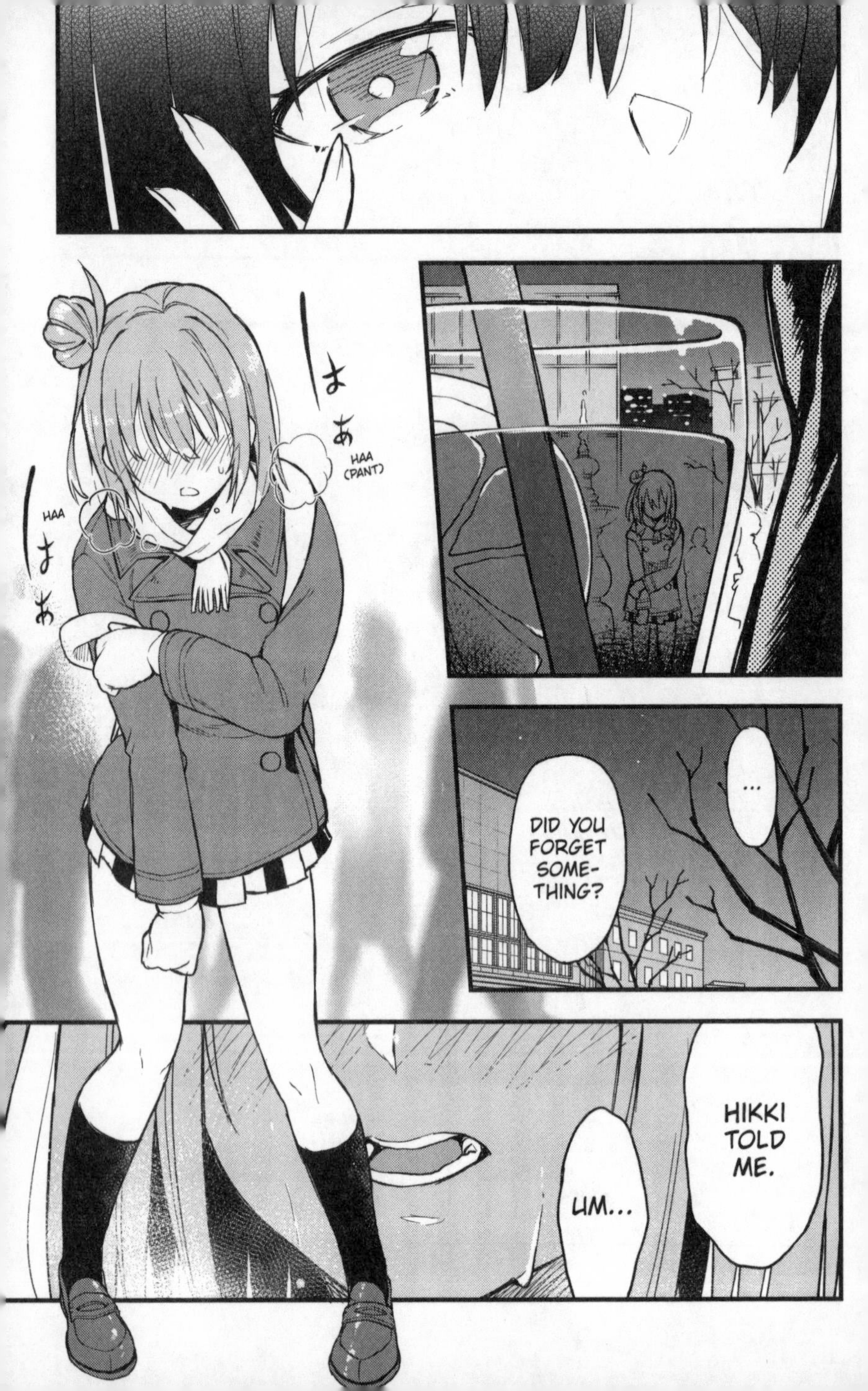

...
DID YOU FORGET SOMETHING?
はぁ
HAA (PANT)
はぁ
HAA
HIKKI TOLD ME.
UM...

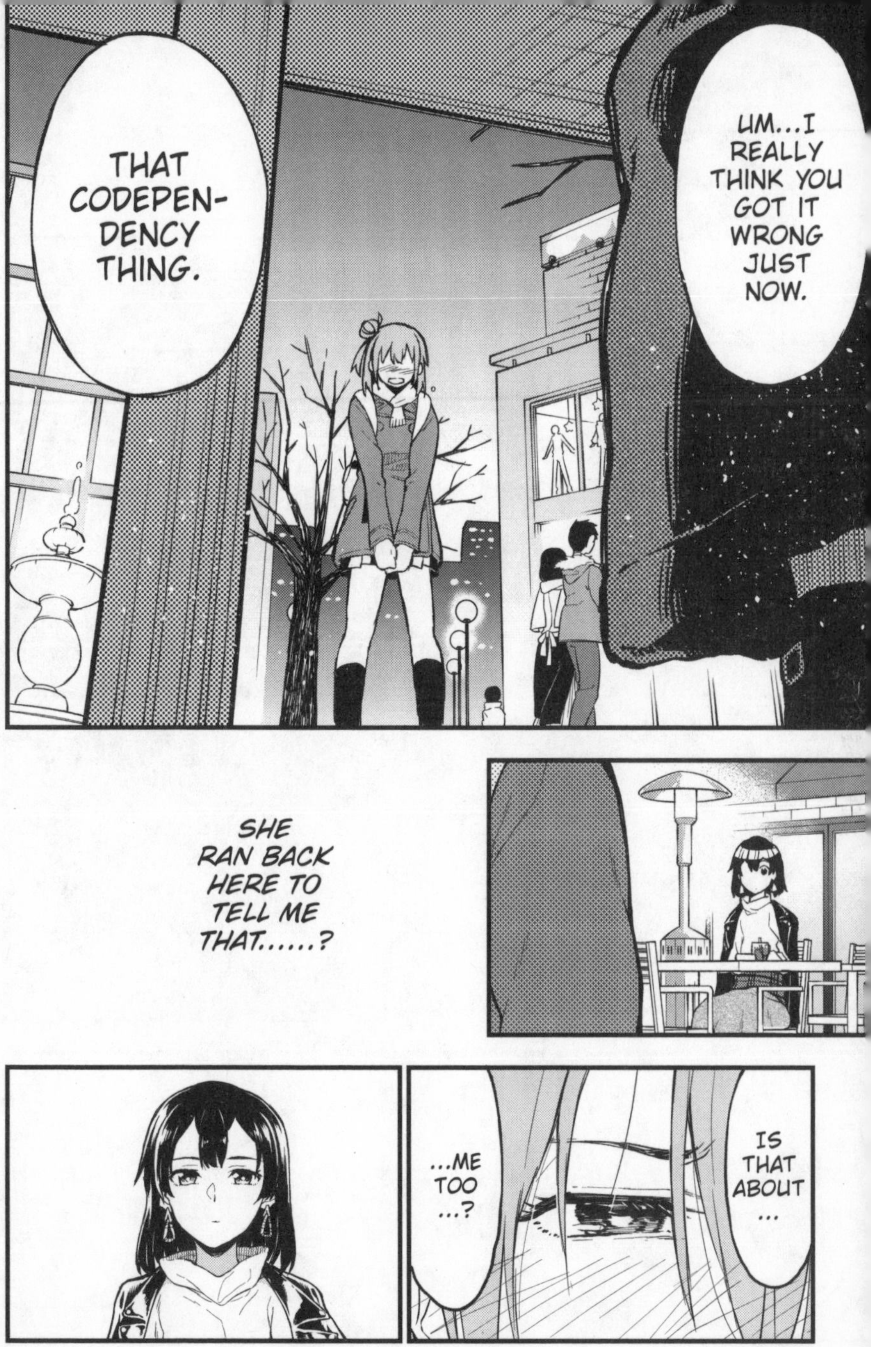
UM...I REALLY THINK YOU GOT IT WRONG JUST NOW.
THAT CODEPEN-DENCY THING.
SHE RAN BACK HERE TO TELL ME THAT......?
IS THAT ABOUT ...
...ME TOO ...?

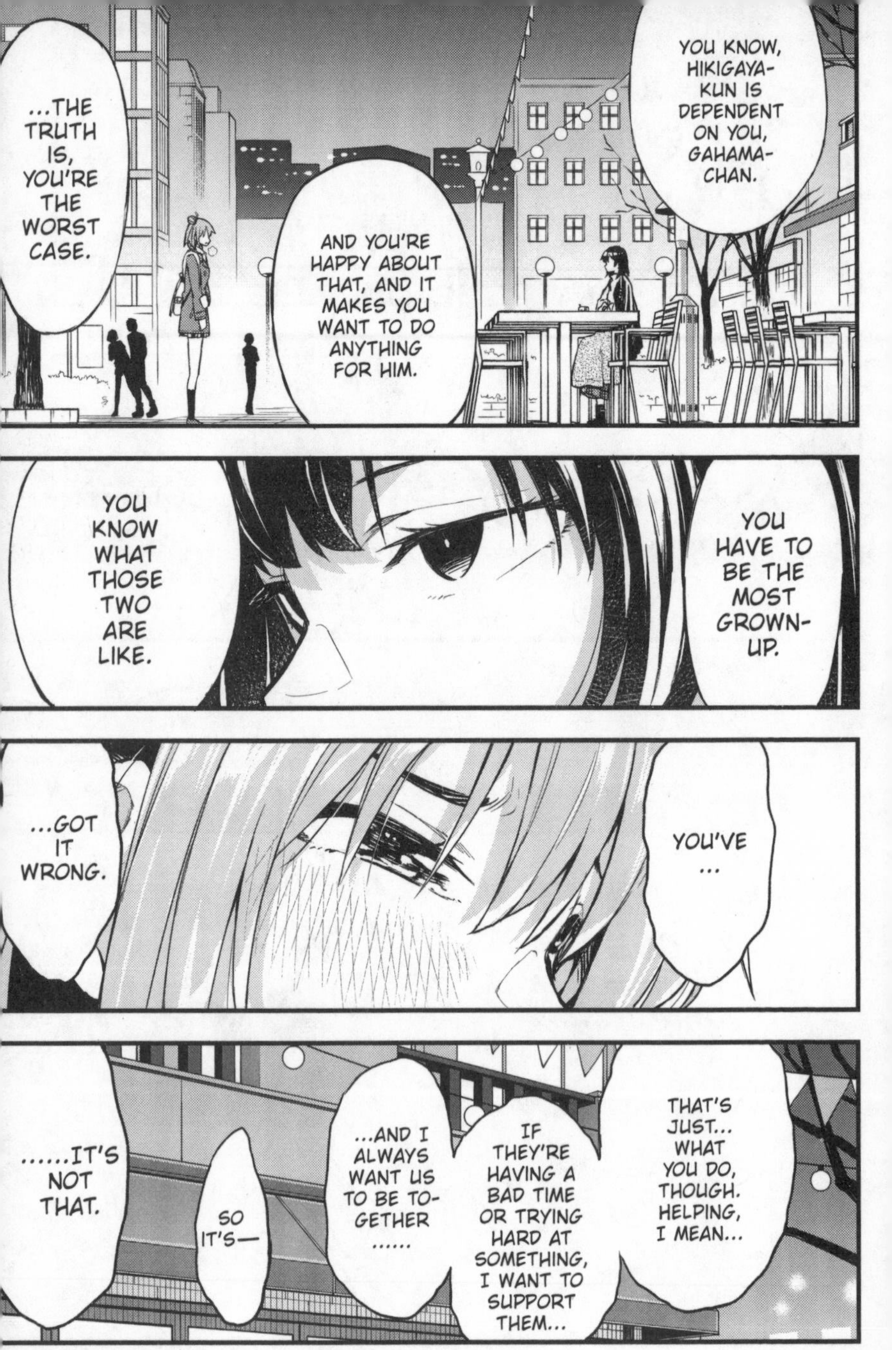
YOU KNOW, HIKIGAYA-KUN IS DEPENDENT ON YOU, GAHAMA-CHAN.
AND YOU'RE HAPPY ABOUT THAT, AND IT MAKES YOU WANT TO DO ANYTHING FOR HIM.
...THE TRUTH IS, YOU'RE THE WORST CASE.
YOU HAVE TO BE THE MOST GROWN-UP.
YOU KNOW WHAT THOSE TWO ARE LIKE.
YOU'VE...
...GOT IT WRONG.
THAT'S JUST... WHAT YOU DO, THOUGH. HELPING, I MEAN...
IF THEY'RE HAVING A BAD TIME OR TRYING HARD AT SOMETHING, I WANT TO SUPPORT THEM...
...AND I ALWAYS WANT US TO BE TOGETHER......
SO IT'S—
......IT'S NOT THAT.

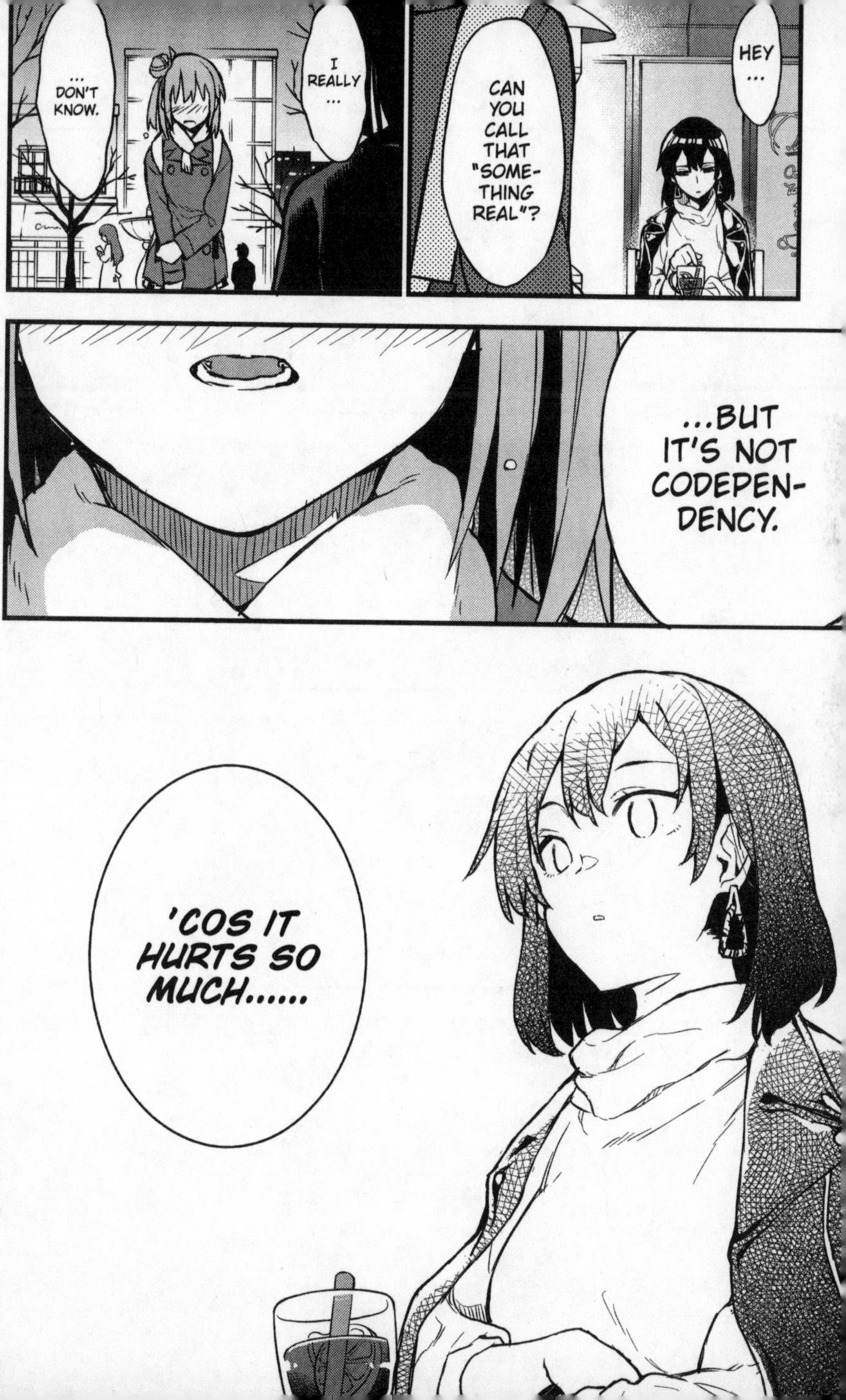
HEY ...
CAN YOU CALL THAT "SOMETHING REAL"?
I REALLY ...
... DON'T KNOW.
...BUT IT'S NOT CODEPENDENCY.
'COS IT HURTS SO MUCH......

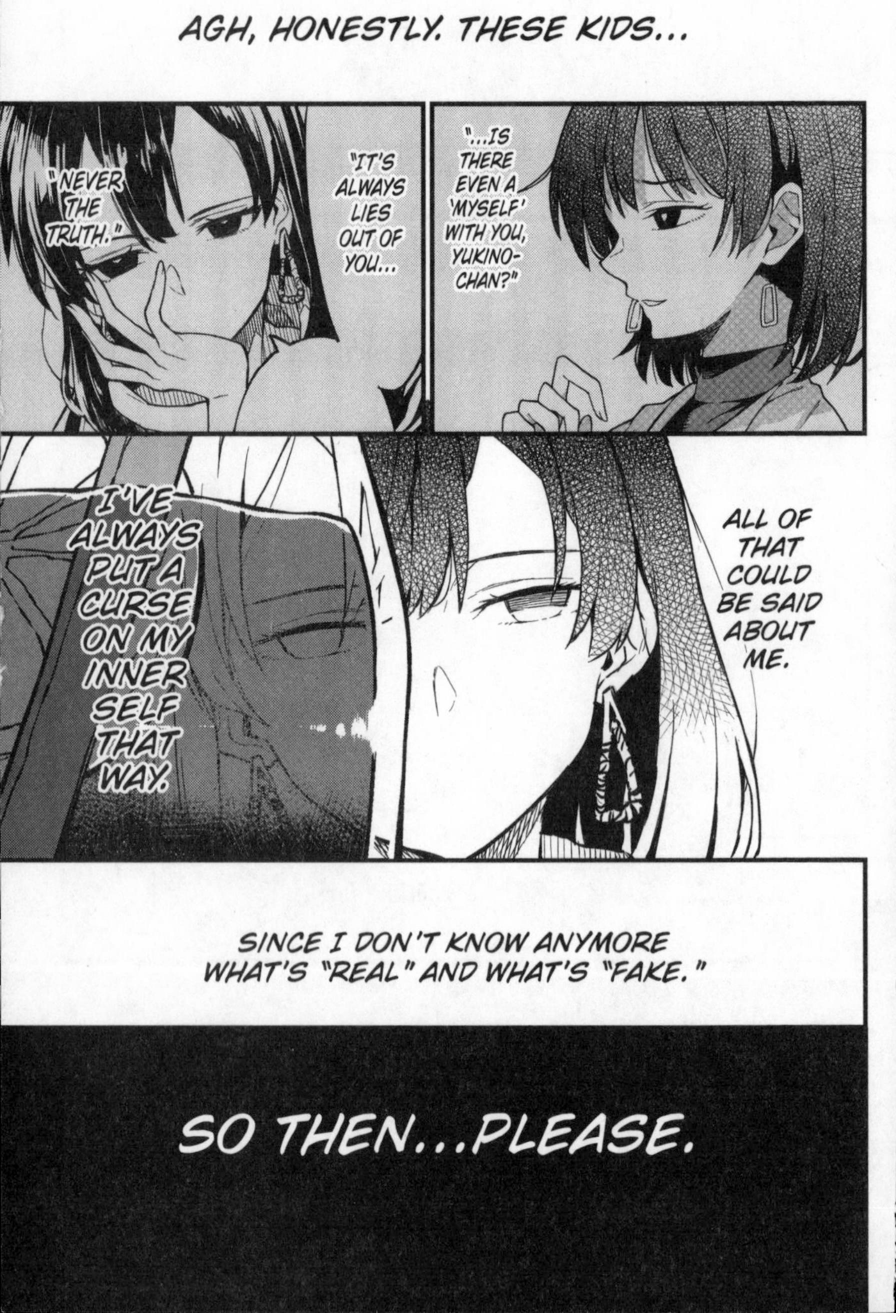
AGH, HONESTLY. THESE KIDS...
"...IS THERE EVEN A 'MYSELF' WITH YOU, YUKINO-CHAN?"
"IT'S ALWAYS LIES OUT OF YOU...
"NEVER THE TRUTH."
ALL OF THAT COULD BE SAID ABOUT ME.
I'VE ALWAYS PUT A CURSE ON MY INNER SELF THAT WAY.
SINCE I DON'T KNOW ANYMORE WHAT'S "REAL" AND WHAT'S "FAKE."
SO THEN...PLEASE.

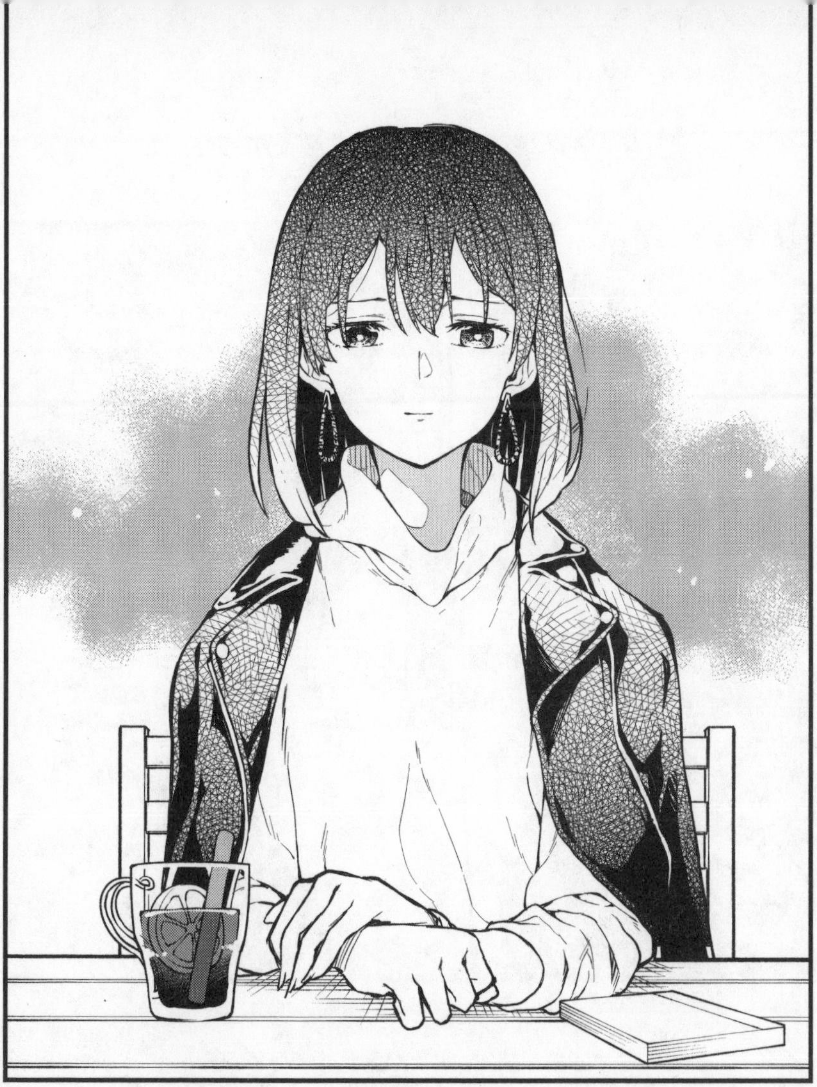

SHOW ME SOMETHING REAL.

MY **YOUTH**
R♥MANTIC C☺MEDY
is **WRØNG,** AS I EXPECTED
@ *comic*

サァァ...
SAAA...
(FSHHH)

HIKI-
GAYA.

DO YOU
HAVE A
MINUTE?

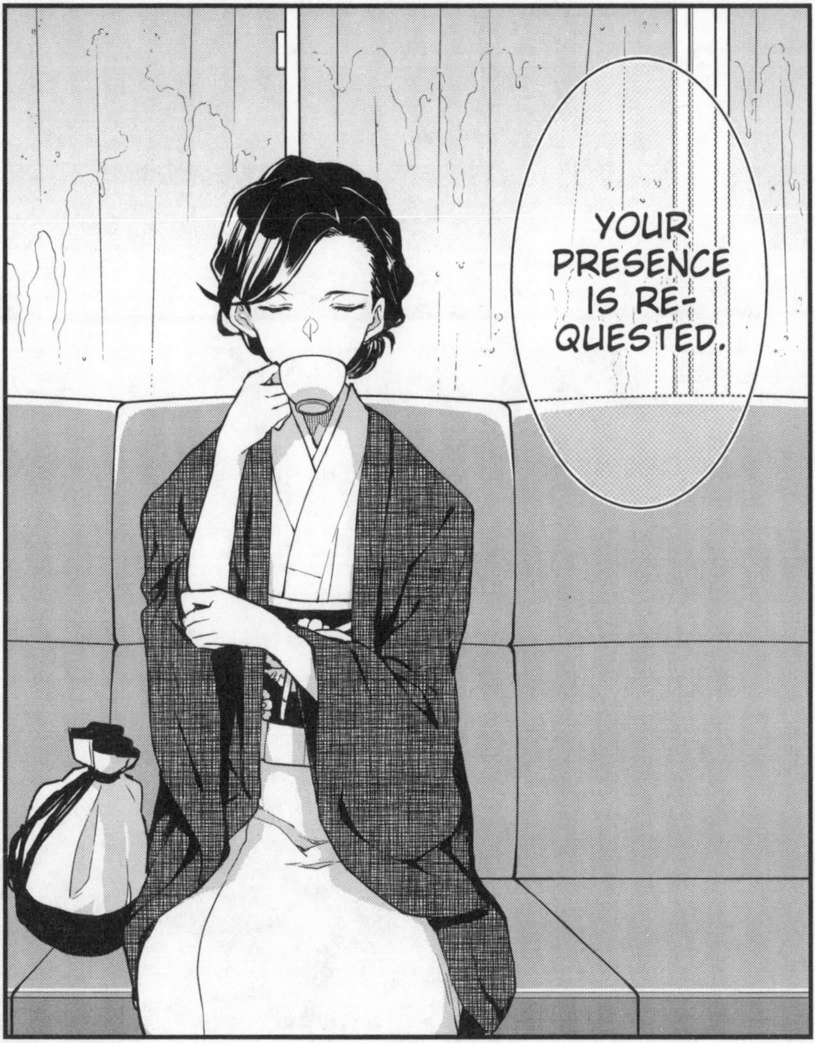
YOUR PRESENCE IS RE-QUESTED.

CHAPTER 103 ··· WHILE WISHING TO NOT GO WRONG AGAIN, AT LEAST... (PART TWO)

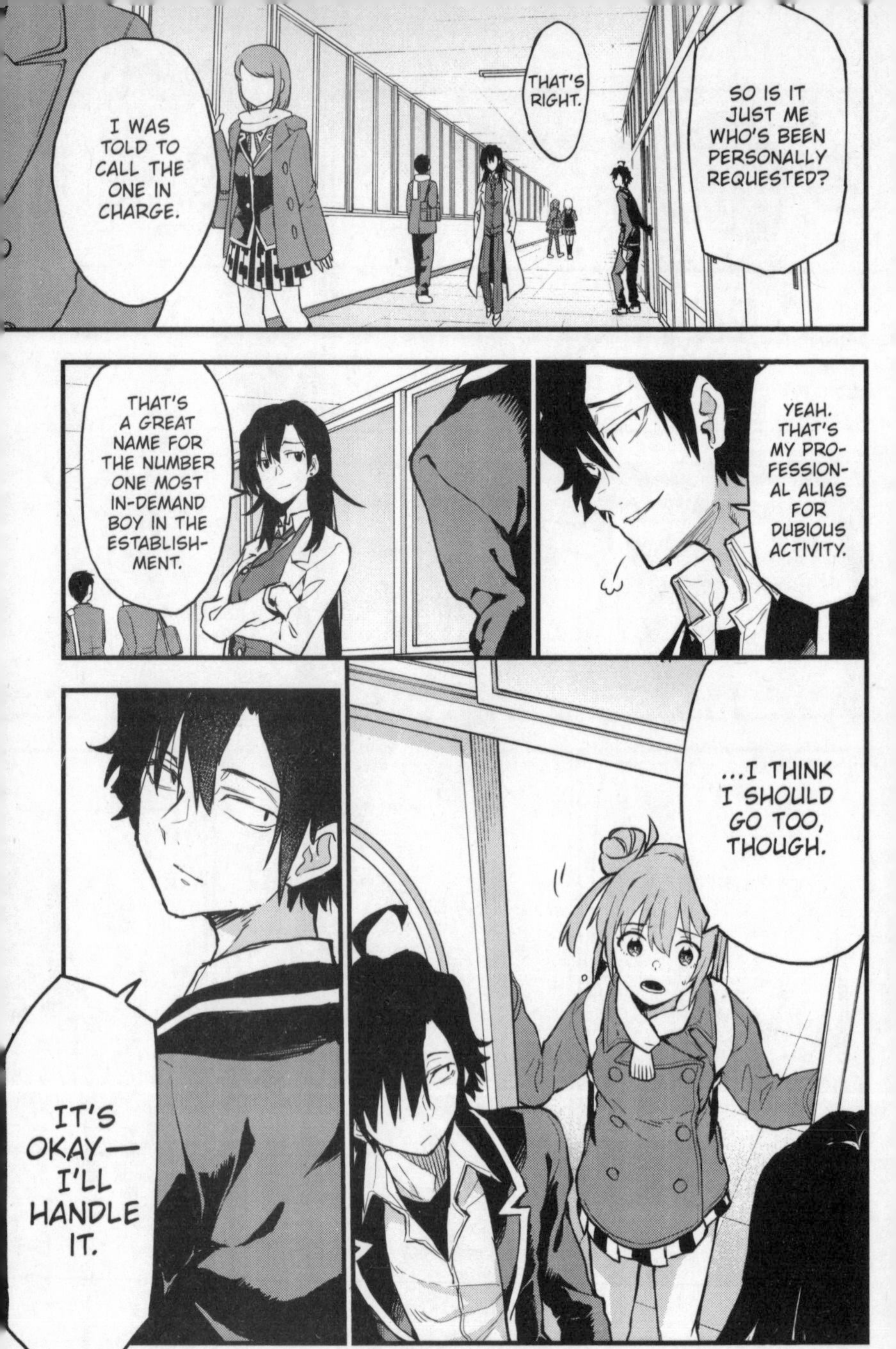
SO IS IT JUST ME WHO'S BEEN PERSONALLY REQUESTED?
THAT'S RIGHT.
I WAS TOLD TO CALL THE ONE IN CHARGE.
YEAH. THAT'S MY PROFESSIONAL ALIAS FOR DUBIOUS ACTIVITY.
THAT'S A GREAT NAME FOR THE NUMBER ONE MOST IN-DEMAND BOY IN THE ESTABLISHMENT.
...I THINK I SHOULD GO TOO, THOUGH.
IT'S OKAY—I'LL HANDLE IT.

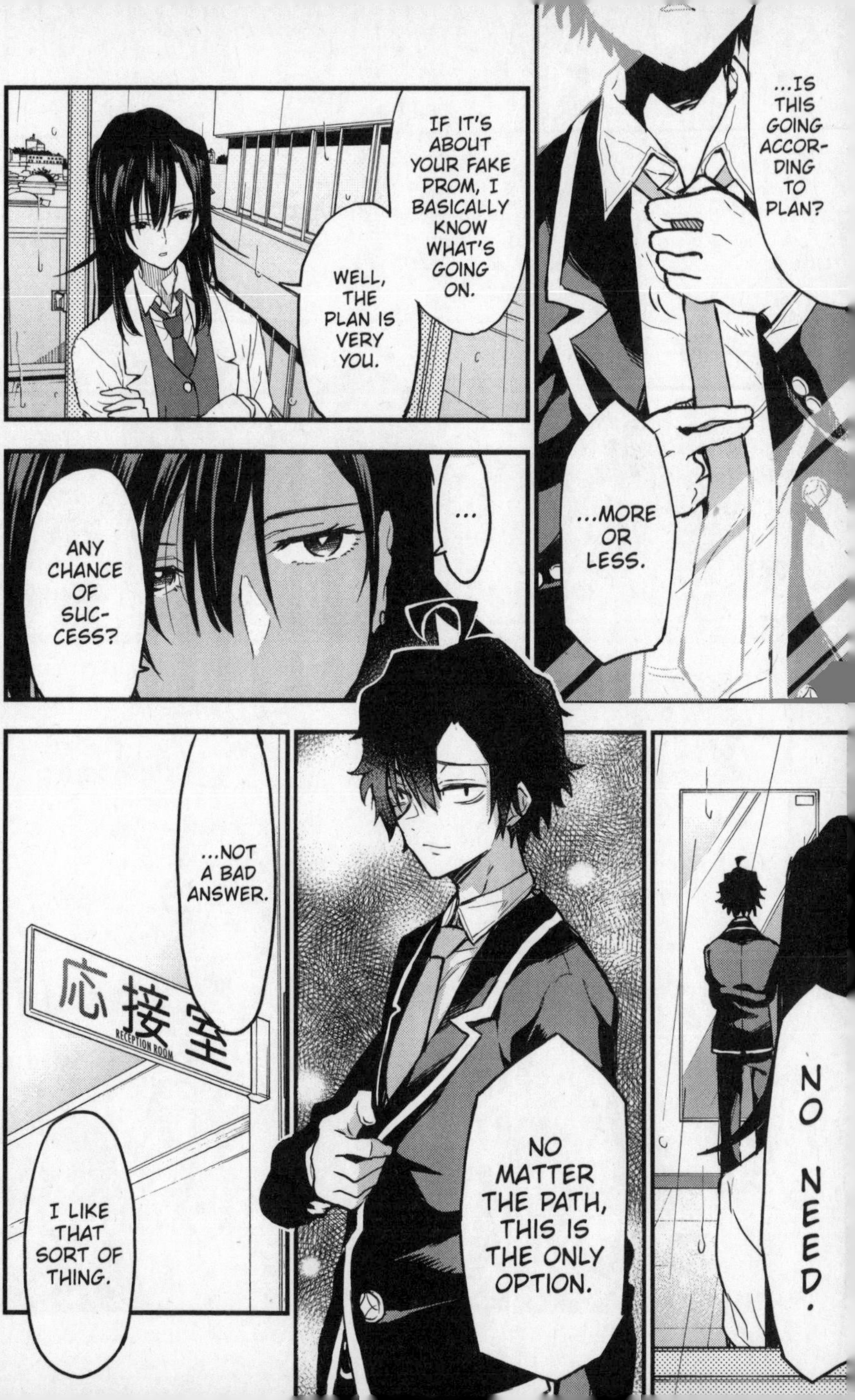
...IS THIS GOING ACCORDING TO PLAN?
...MORE OR LESS.
IF IT'S ABOUT YOUR FAKE PROM, I BASICALLY KNOW WHAT'S GOING ON.
WELL, THE PLAN IS VERY YOU.
...
ANY CHANCE OF SUCCESS?
NO NEED.
NO MATTER THE PATH, THIS IS THE ONLY OPTION.
...NOT A BAD ANSWER.
応接室
RECEPTION ROOM
I LIKE THAT SORT OF THING.

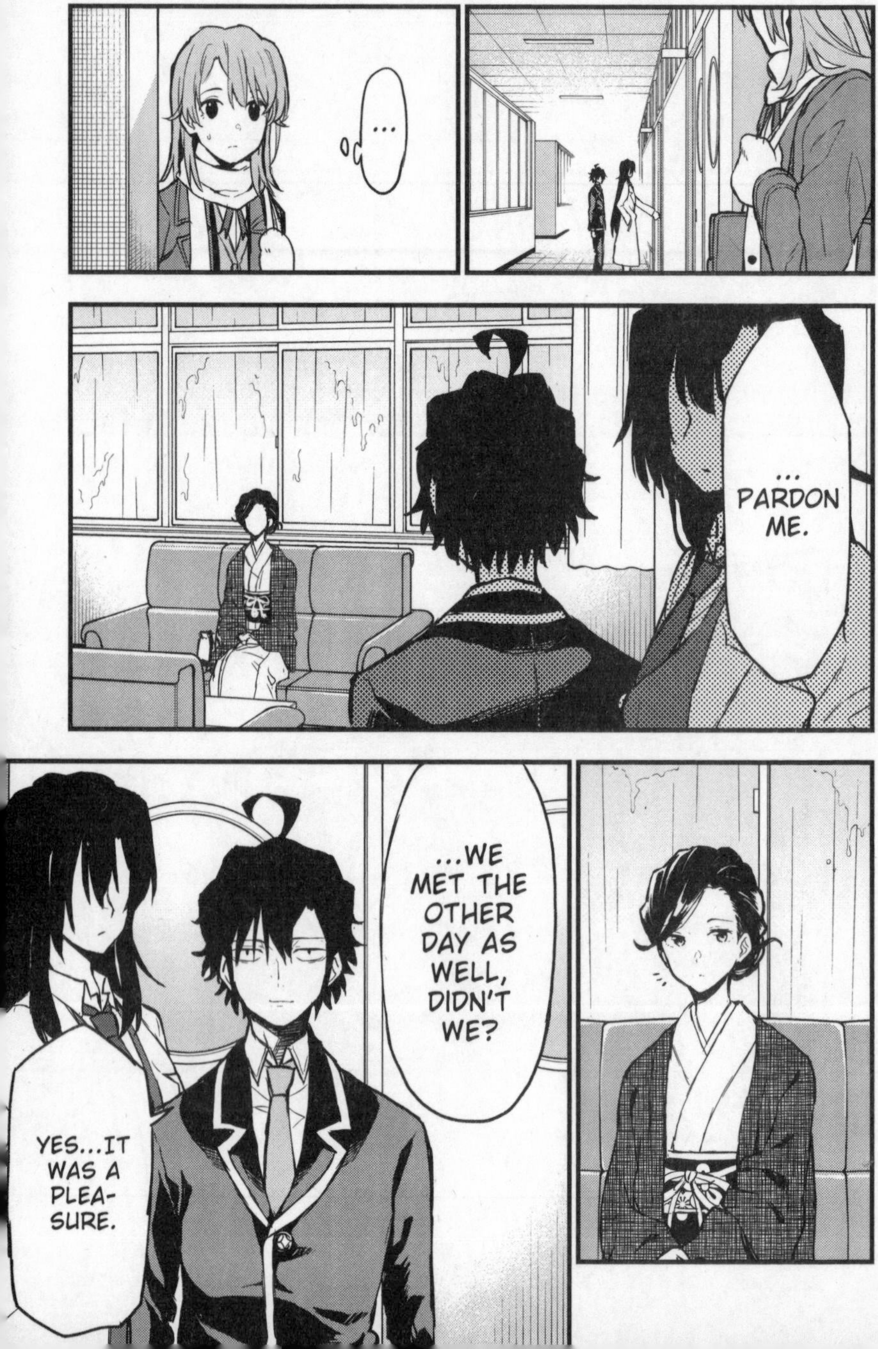
...
... PARDON ME.
...WE MET THE OTHER DAY AS WELL, DIDN'T WE?
YES...IT WAS A PLEA-SURE.

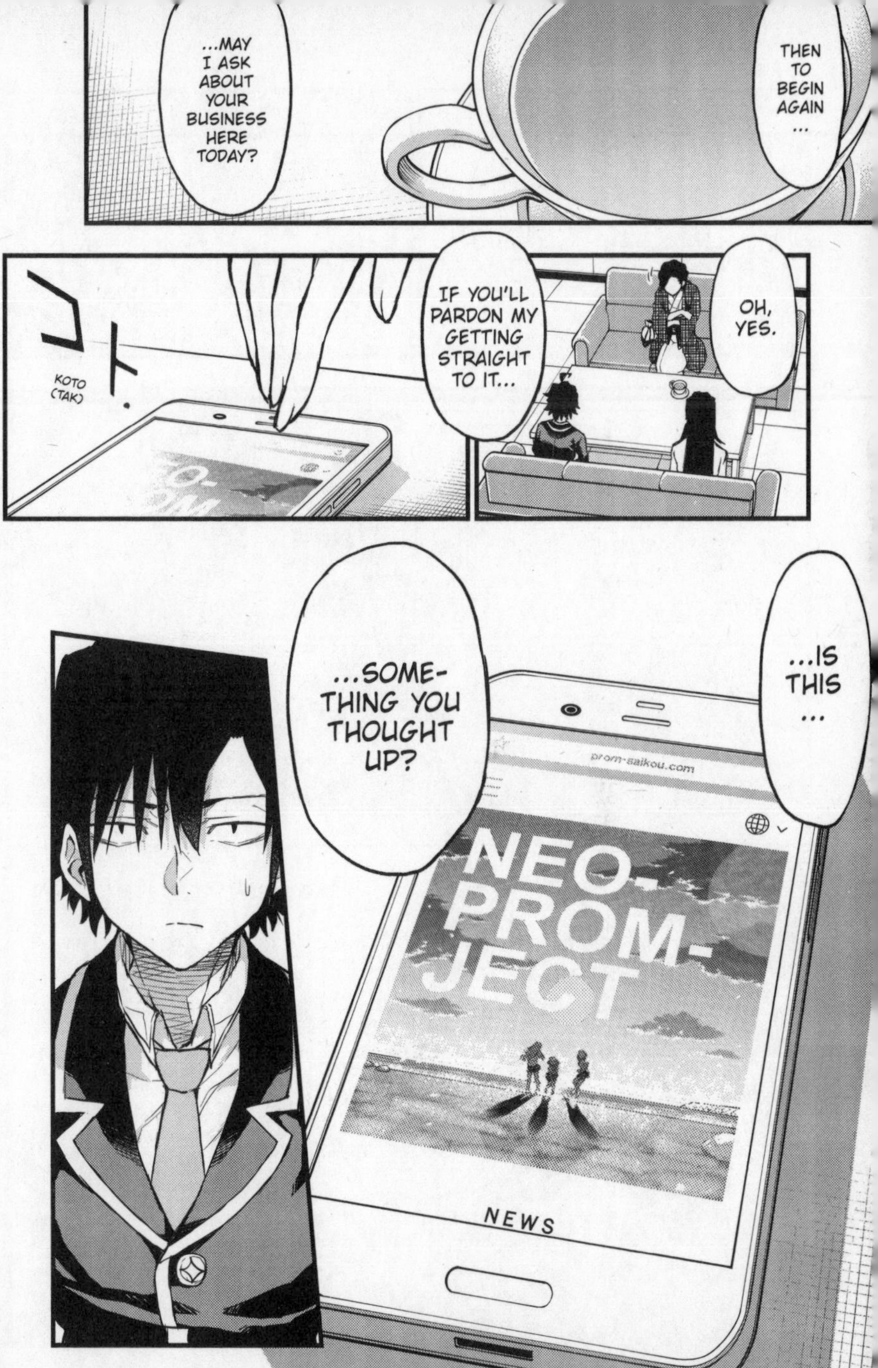
THEN TO BEGIN AGAIN...
...MAY I ASK ABOUT YOUR BUSINESS HERE TODAY?
OH, YES.
IF YOU'LL PARDON MY GETTING STRAIGHT TO IT...
KOTO (TAK)
...IS THIS...
...SOME-THING YOU THOUGHT UP?
prom-saikou.com
NEO-PROM-JECT
NEWS

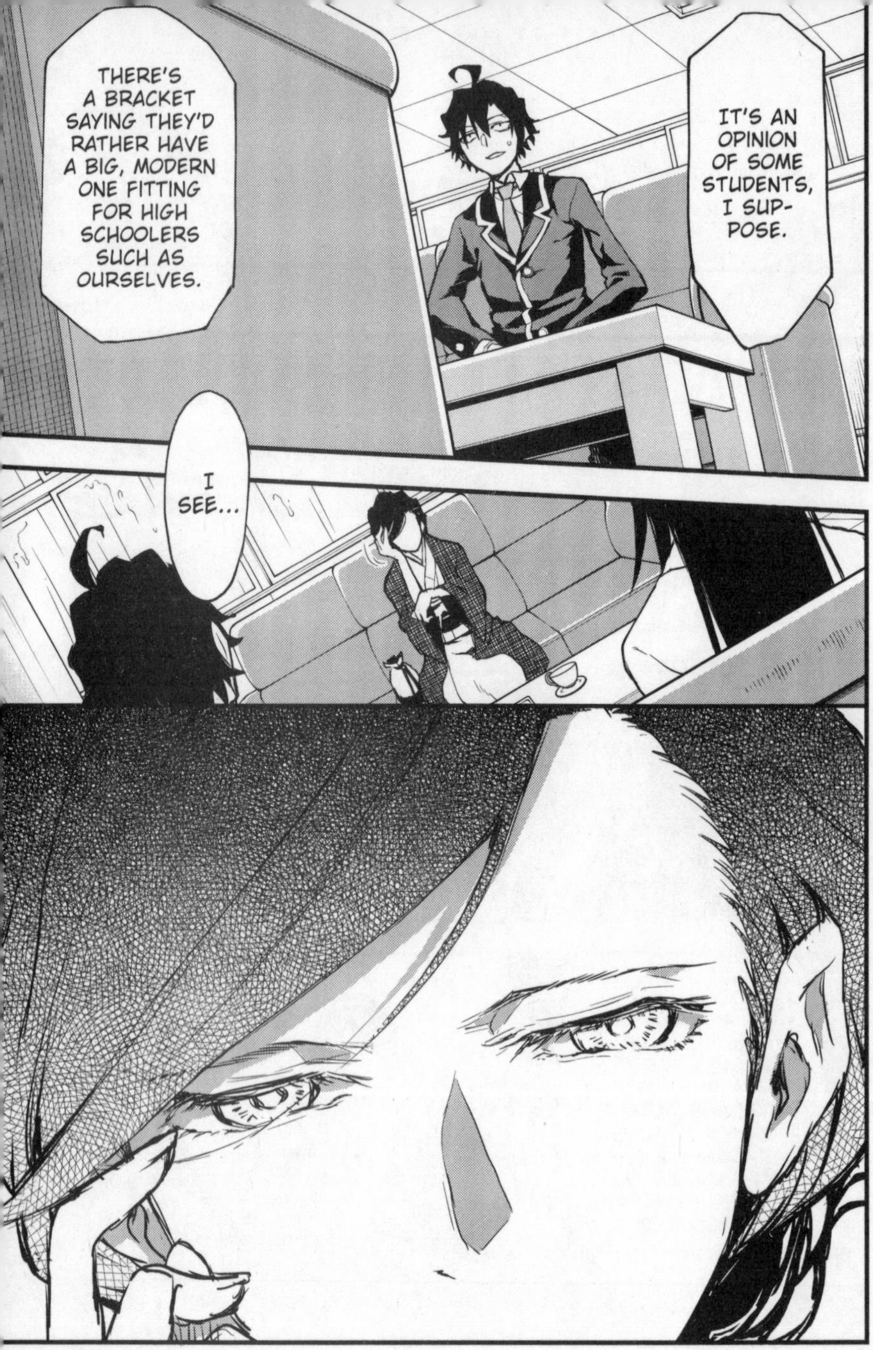
IT'S AN OPINION OF SOME STUDENTS, I SUP-POSE.
THERE'S A BRACKET SAYING THEY'D RATHER HAVE A BIG, MODERN ONE FITTING FOR HIGH SCHOOLERS SUCH AS OURSELVES.
I SEE...

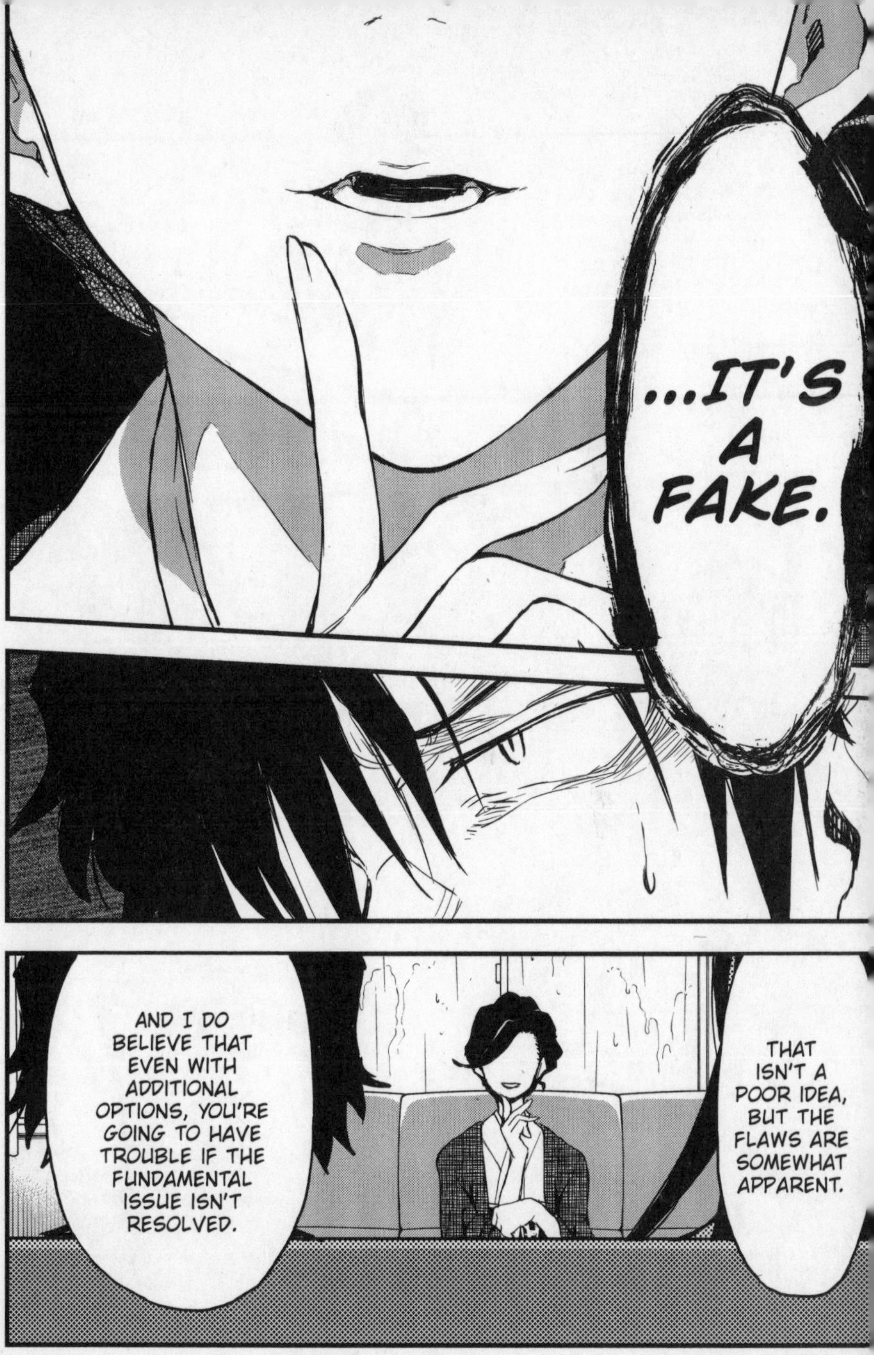
...IT'S A FAKE.
THAT ISN'T A POOR IDEA, BUT THE FLAWS ARE SOMEWHAT APPARENT.
AND I DO BELIEVE THAT EVEN WITH ADDITIONAL OPTIONS, YOU'RE GOING TO HAVE TROUBLE IF THE FUNDAMENTAL ISSUE ISN'T RESOLVED.

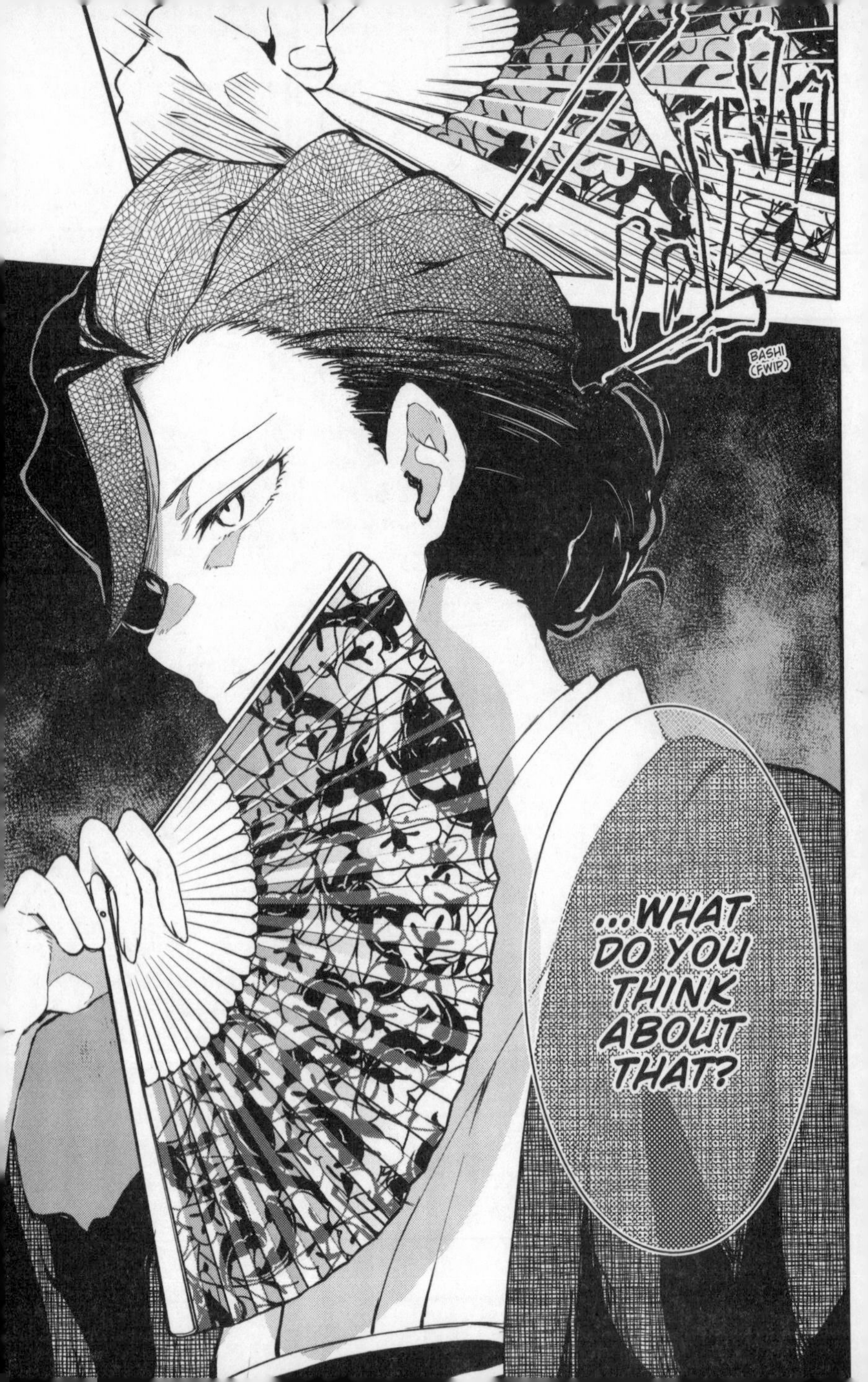
BASHI (FWIP)
...WHAT DO YOU THINK ABOUT THAT?

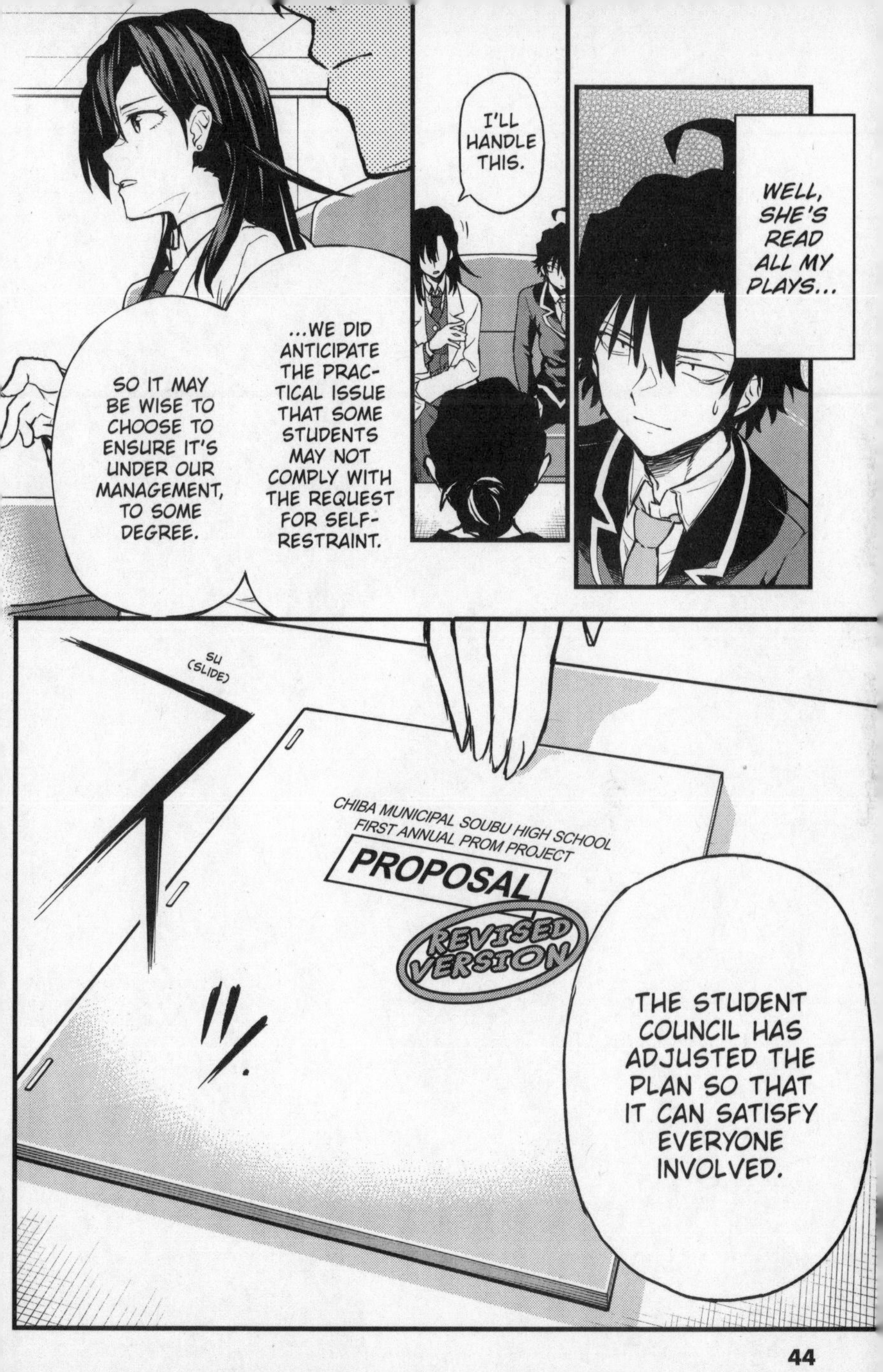
WELL, SHE'S READ ALL MY PLAYS...
I'LL HANDLE THIS.
...WE DID ANTICIPATE THE PRACTICAL ISSUE THAT SOME STUDENTS MAY NOT COMPLY WITH THE REQUEST FOR SELF-RESTRAINT.
SO IT MAY BE WISE TO CHOOSE TO ENSURE IT'S UNDER OUR MANAGEMENT, TO SOME DEGREE.
SU (SLIDE)
CHIBA MUNICIPAL SOUBU HIGH SCHOOL FIRST ANNUAL PROM PROJECT
PROPOSAL
REVISED VERSION
THE STUDENT COUNCIL HAS ADJUSTED THE PLAN SO THAT IT CAN SATISFY EVERYONE INVOLVED.

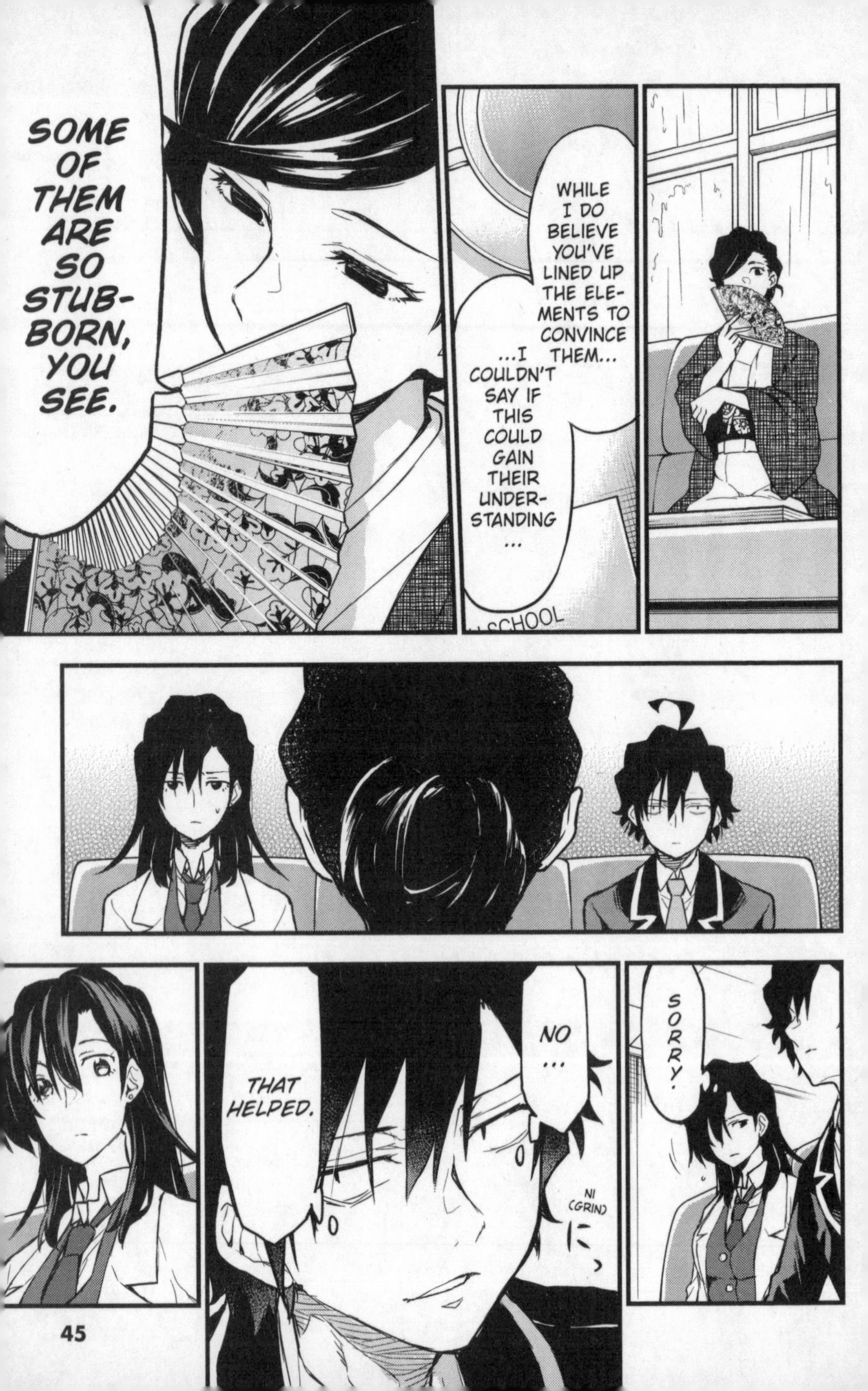
WHILE I DO BELIEVE YOU'VE LINED UP THE ELE-MENTS TO CONVINCE THEM...
...I COULDN'T SAY IF THIS COULD GAIN THEIR UNDER-STANDING...
SCHOOL
SOME OF THEM ARE SO STUB-BORN, YOU SEE.
SORRY.
NO...
THAT HELPED.
NI (GRIN)
に、

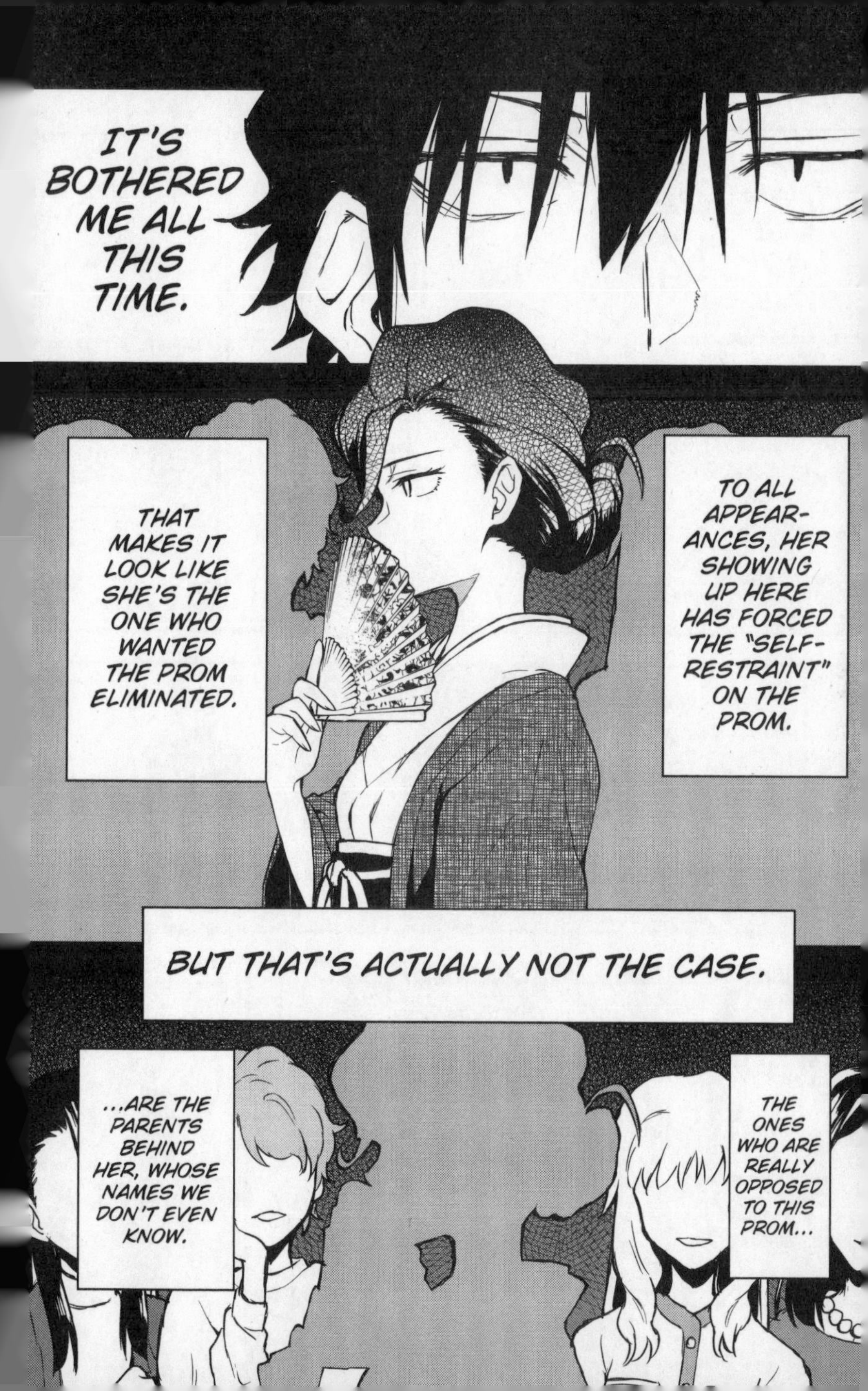
IT'S BOTHERED ME ALL THIS TIME.
TO ALL APPEARANCES, HER SHOWING UP HERE HAS FORCED THE "SELF-RESTRAINT" ON THE PROM.
THAT MAKES IT LOOK LIKE SHE'S THE ONE WHO WANTED THE PROM ELIMINATED.
BUT THAT'S ACTUALLY NOT THE CASE.
THE ONES WHO ARE REALLY OPPOSED TO THIS PROM...
...ARE THE PARENTS BEHIND HER, WHOSE NAMES WE DON'T EVEN KNOW.

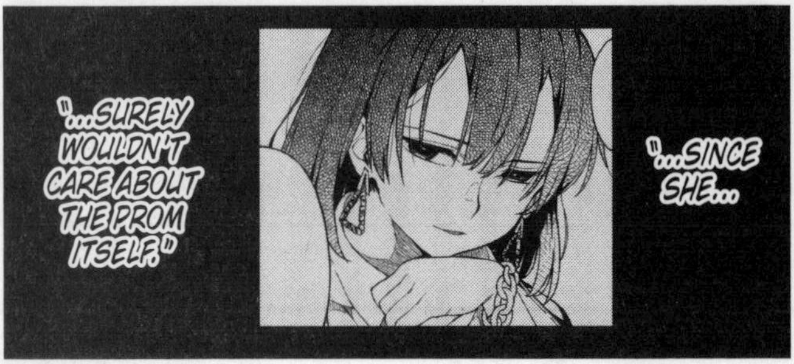
"...SINCE SHE...
"...SURELY WOULDN'T CARE ABOUT THE PROM ITSELF."

AND THAT'S PROVED BY...

...HOW SHE SAID SOMETHING SIMILAR TO HARUNO-SAN, DESPITE BEING IN TOTALLY DIFFERENT POSITIONS.

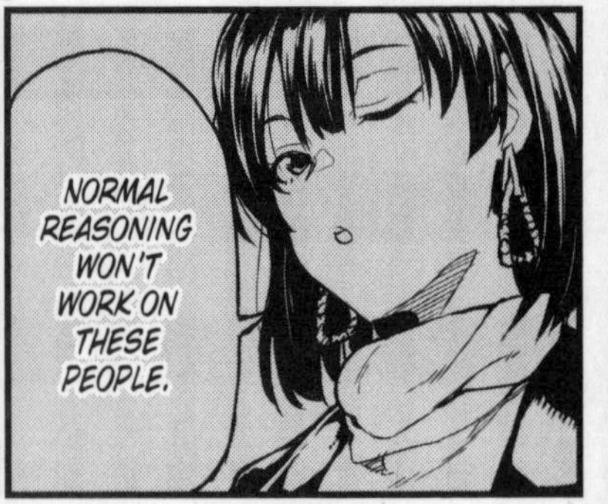
NORMAL REASONING WON'T WORK ON THESE PEOPLE.

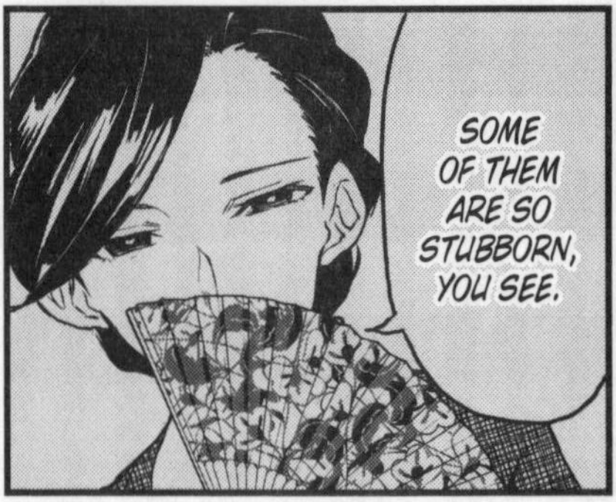
SOME OF THEM ARE SO STUBBORN, YOU SEE.

THANKS TO HIRATSUKA-SENSEI HAVING DRAWN THAT REMARK FROM HER, NOW I'M SURE.

BASICALLY, YUKINOSHITA'S MOTHER...

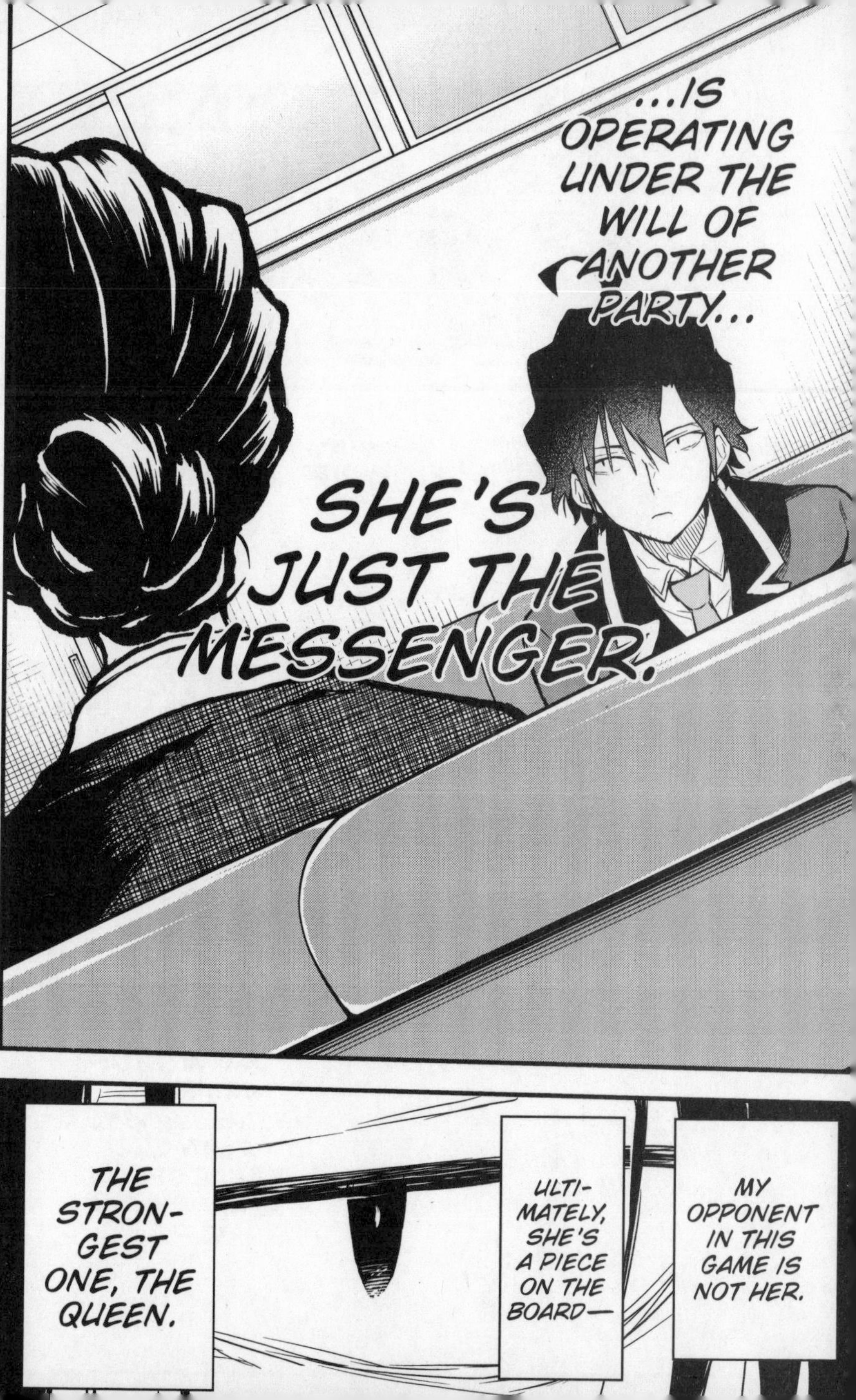
...IS OPERATING UNDER THE WILL OF ANOTHER PARTY...
SHE'S JUST THE MESSENGER.
MY OPPONENT IN THIS GAME IS NOT HER.
ULTI-MATELY, SHE'S A PIECE ON THE BOARD—
THE STRON-GEST ONE, THE QUEEN.

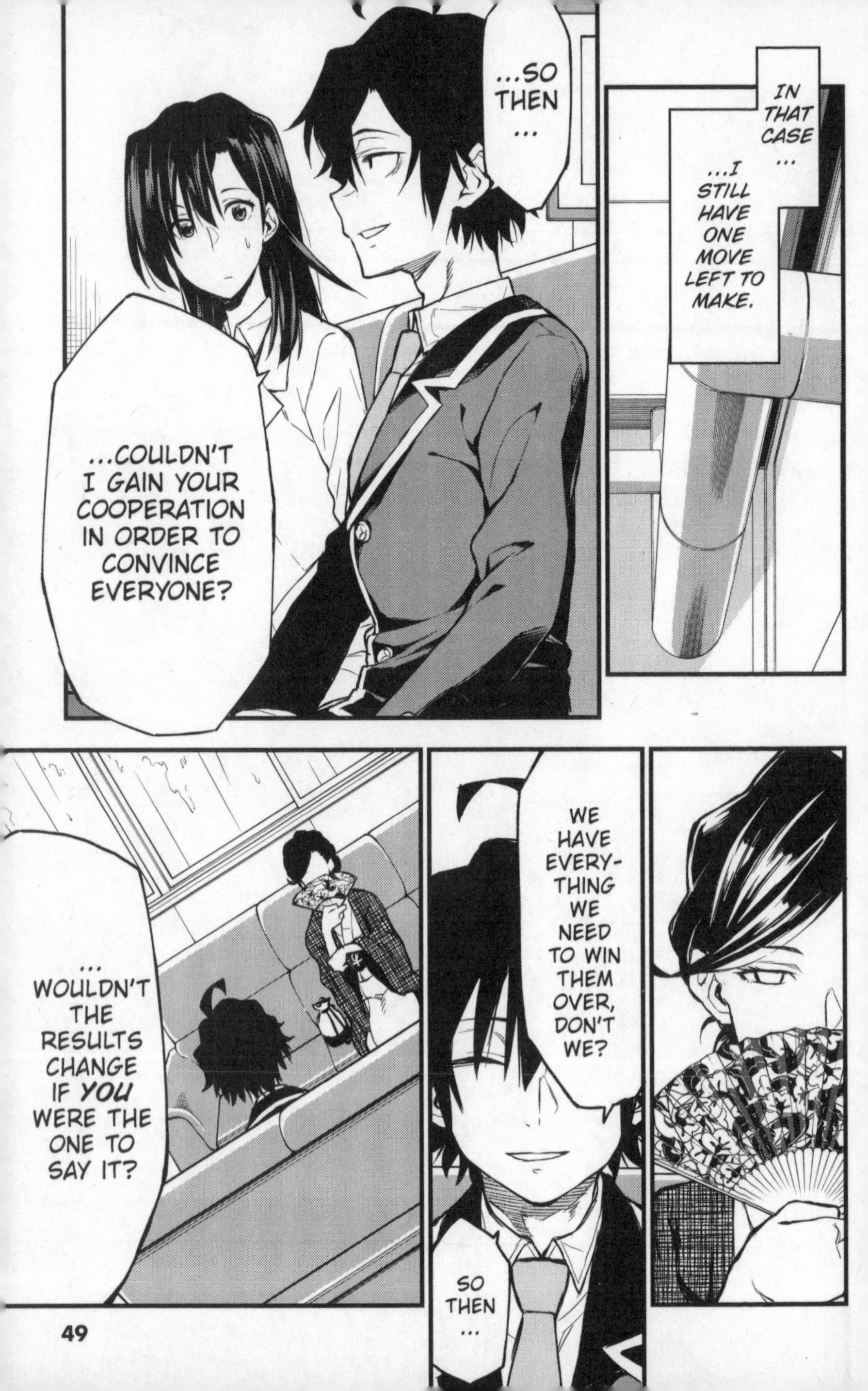
IN THAT CASE ...
...I STILL HAVE ONE MOVE LEFT TO MAKE.
...SO THEN ...
...COULDN'T I GAIN YOUR COOPERATION IN ORDER TO CONVINCE EVERYONE?
WE HAVE EVERY-THING WE NEED TO WIN THEM OVER, DON'T WE?
SO THEN ...
... WOULDN'T THE RESULTS CHANGE IF *YOU* WERE THE ONE TO SAY IT?

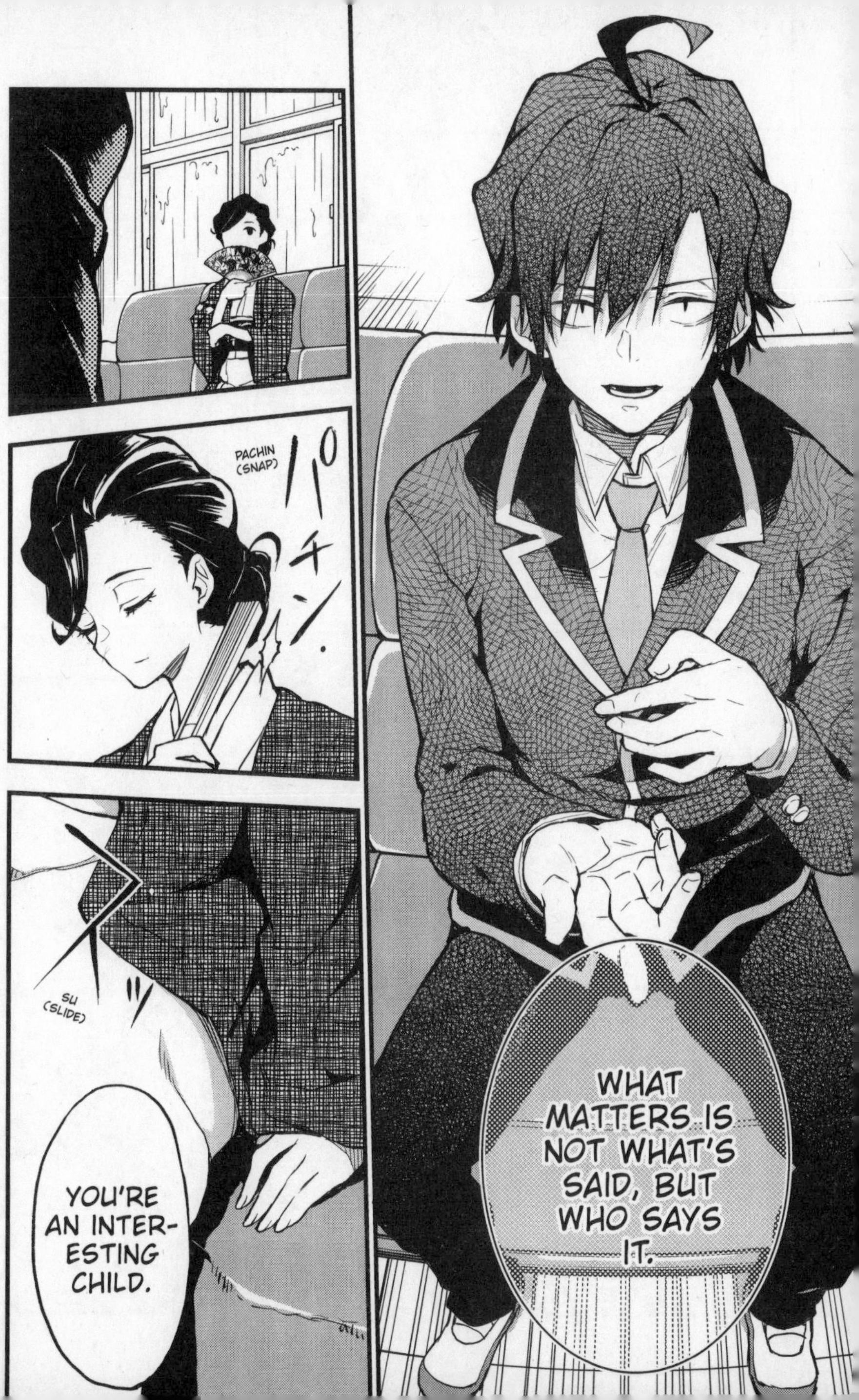
WHAT MATTERS IS NOT WHAT'S SAID, BUT WHO SAYS IT.
PACHIN (SNAP)
SU (SLIDE)
YOU'RE AN INTER-ESTING CHILD.

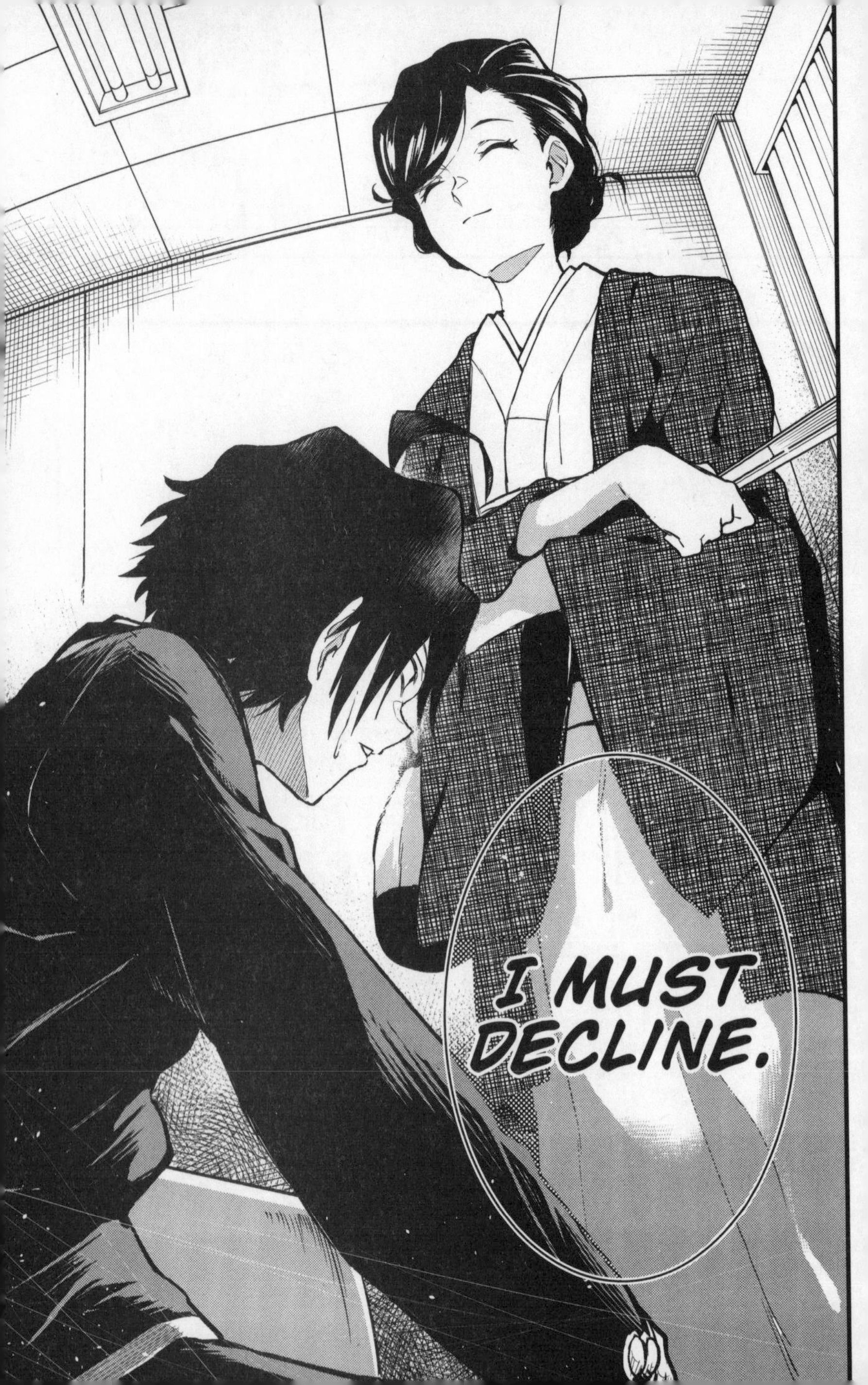
I MUST DECLINE.

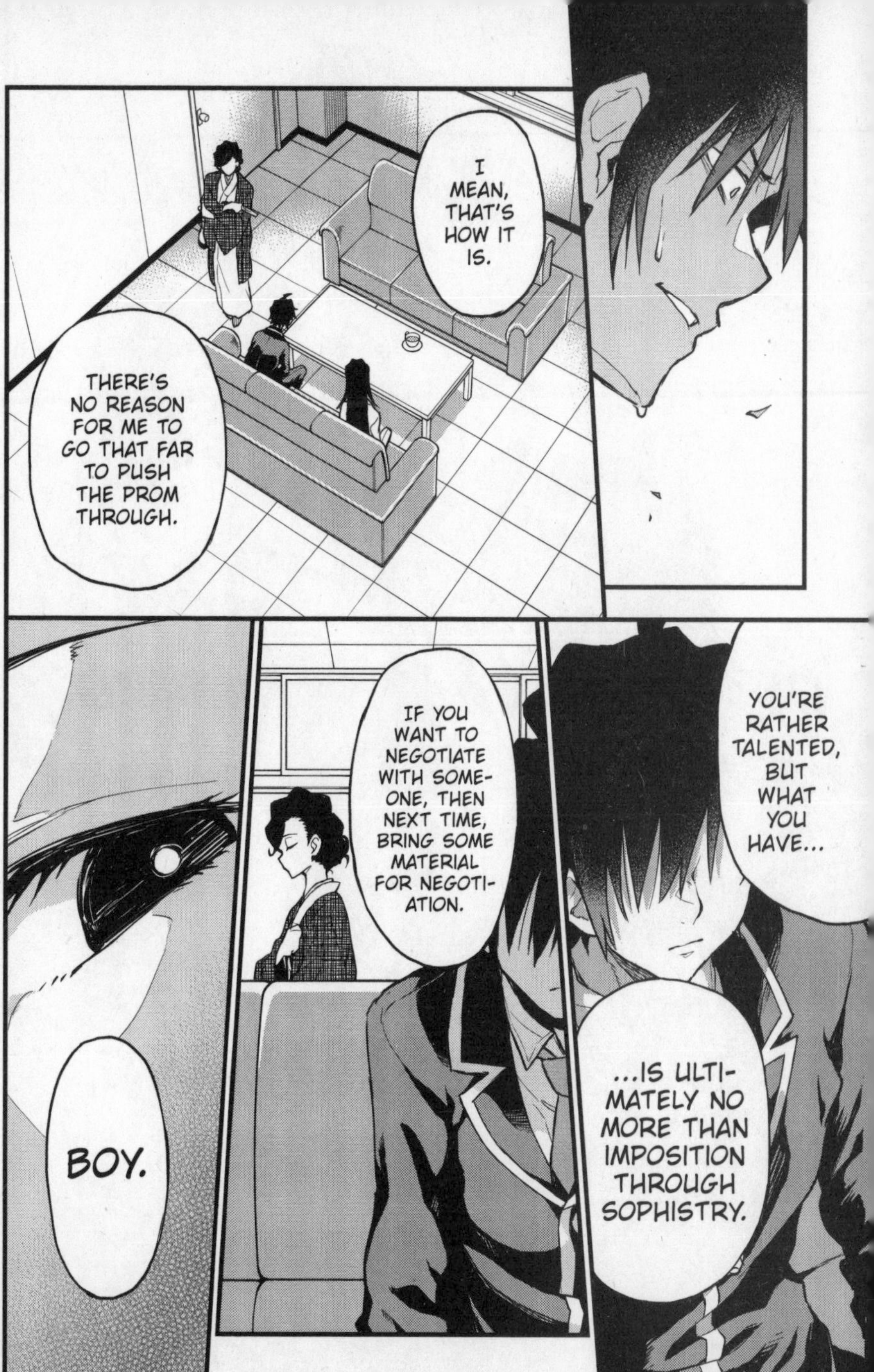
I MEAN, THAT'S HOW IT IS.
THERE'S NO REASON FOR ME TO GO THAT FAR TO PUSH THE PROM THROUGH.
YOU'RE RATHER TALENTED, BUT WHAT YOU HAVE...
...IS ULTIMATELY NO MORE THAN IMPOSITION THROUGH SOPHISTRY.
IF YOU WANT TO NEGOTIATE WITH SOME-ONE, THEN NEXT TIME, BRING SOME MATERIAL FOR NEGOTI-ATION.
BOY.

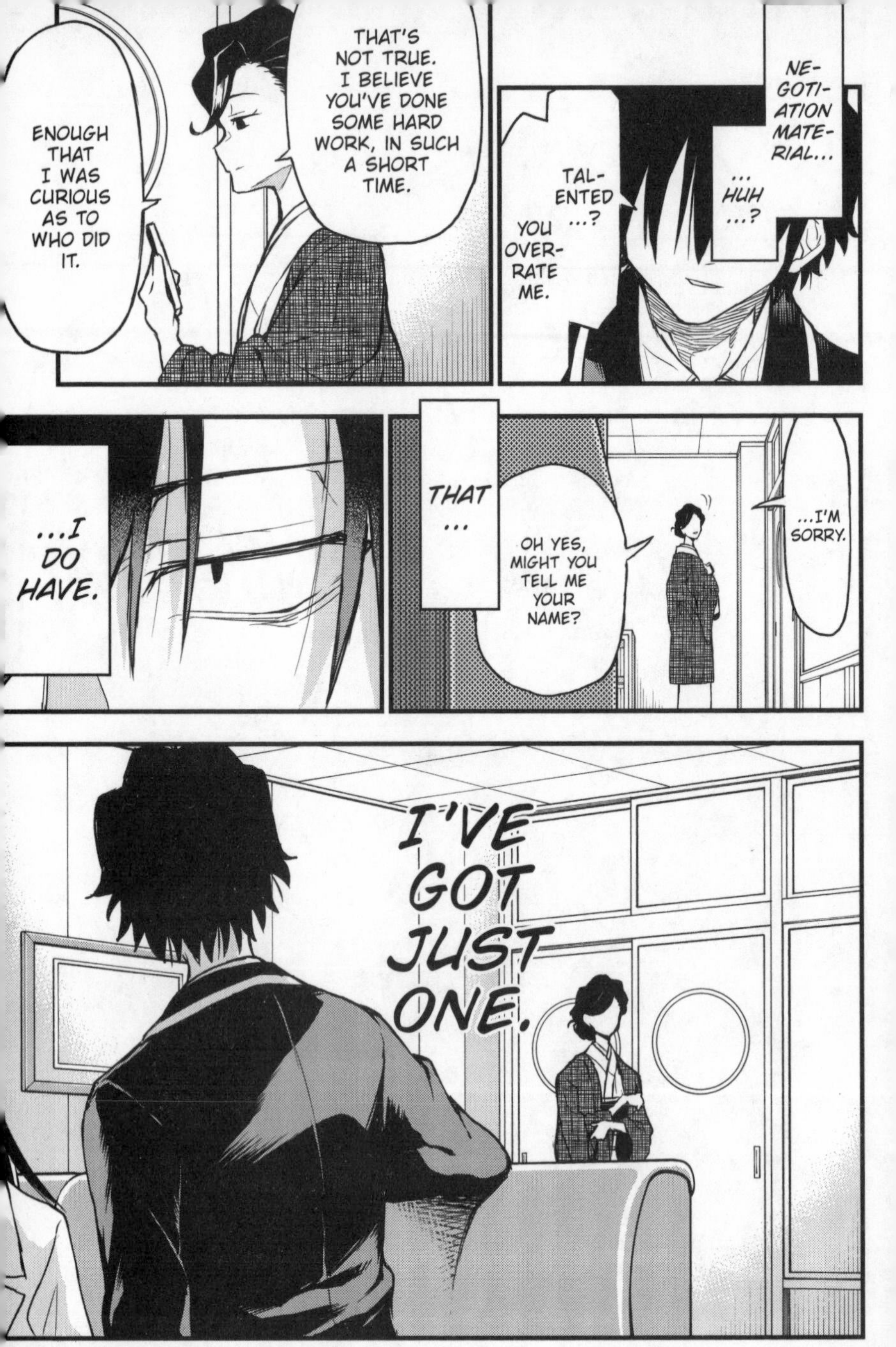
NE-GOTI-ATION MATE-RIAL...
...HUH...?
TAL-ENTED...?
YOU OVER-RATE ME.
THAT'S NOT TRUE. I BELIEVE YOU'VE DONE SOME HARD WORK, IN SUCH A SHORT TIME.
ENOUGH THAT I WAS CURIOUS AS TO WHO DID IT.
...I'M SORRY.
OH YES, MIGHT YOU TELL ME YOUR NAME?
THAT...
...I DO HAVE.
I'VE GOT JUST ONE.

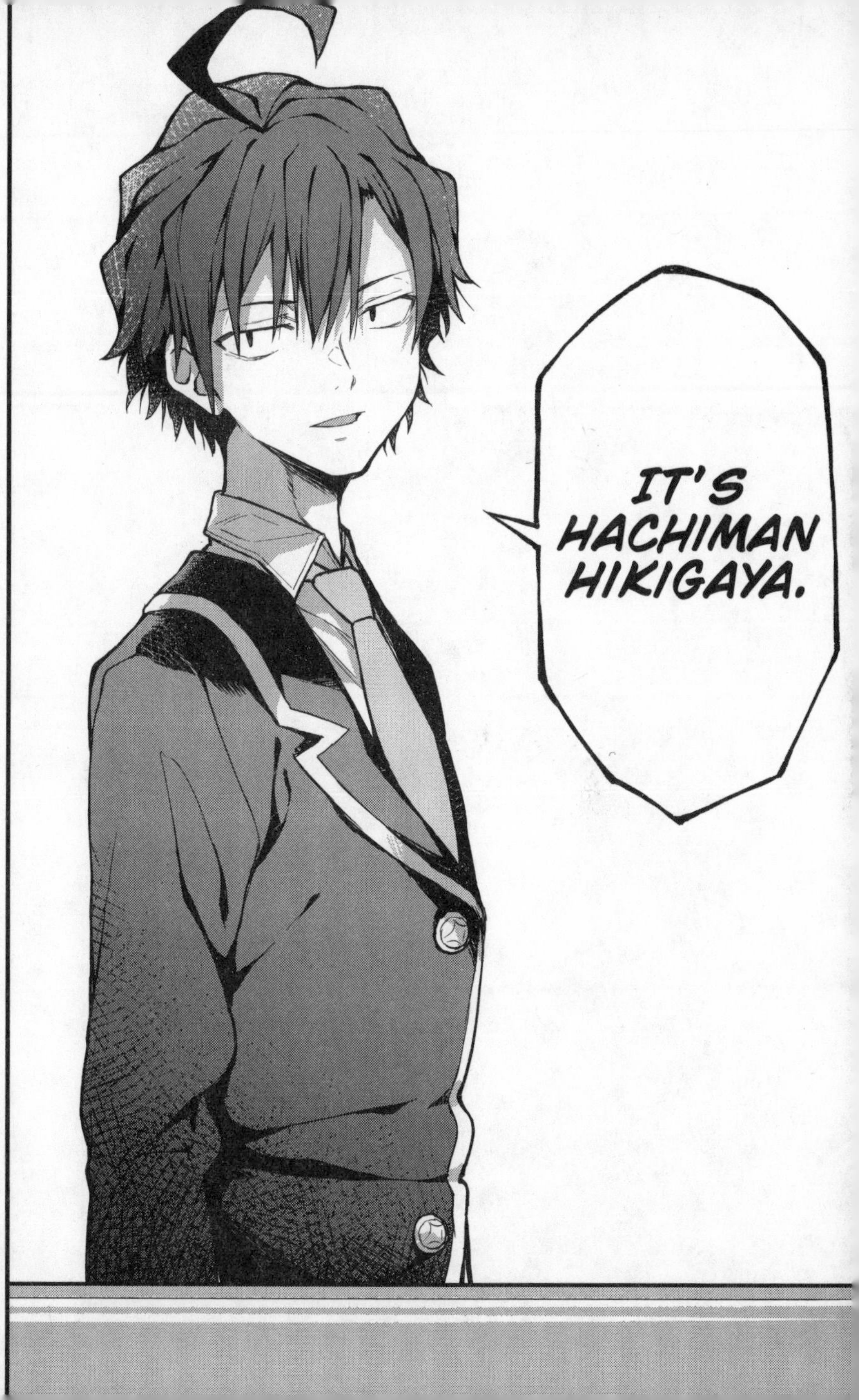
IT'S HACHIMAN HIKIGAYA.

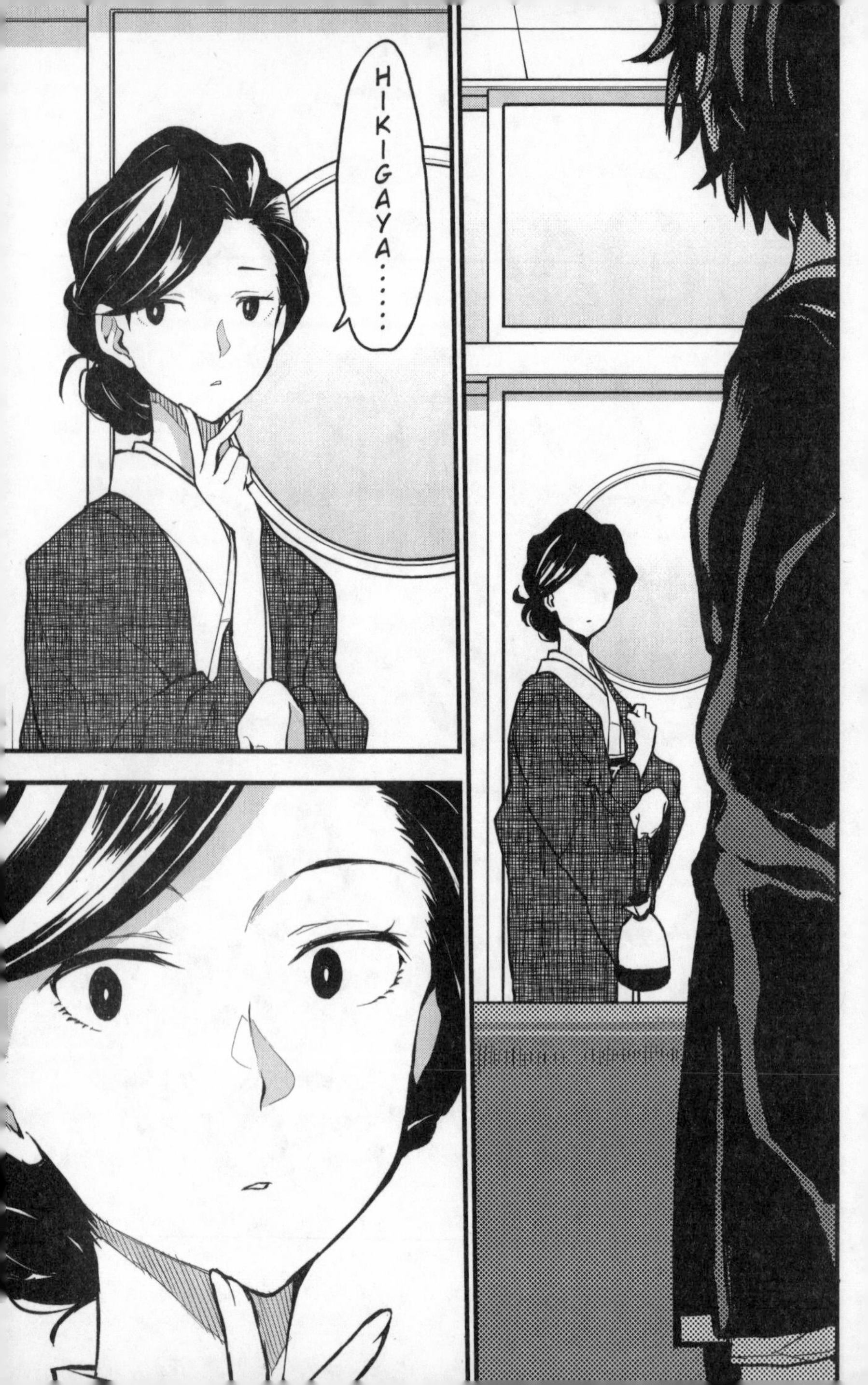
HIKIGAYA......

ON THE
FIRST
DAY OF
SCHOOL, I
WAS IN A
TRAFFIC
ACCIDENT.

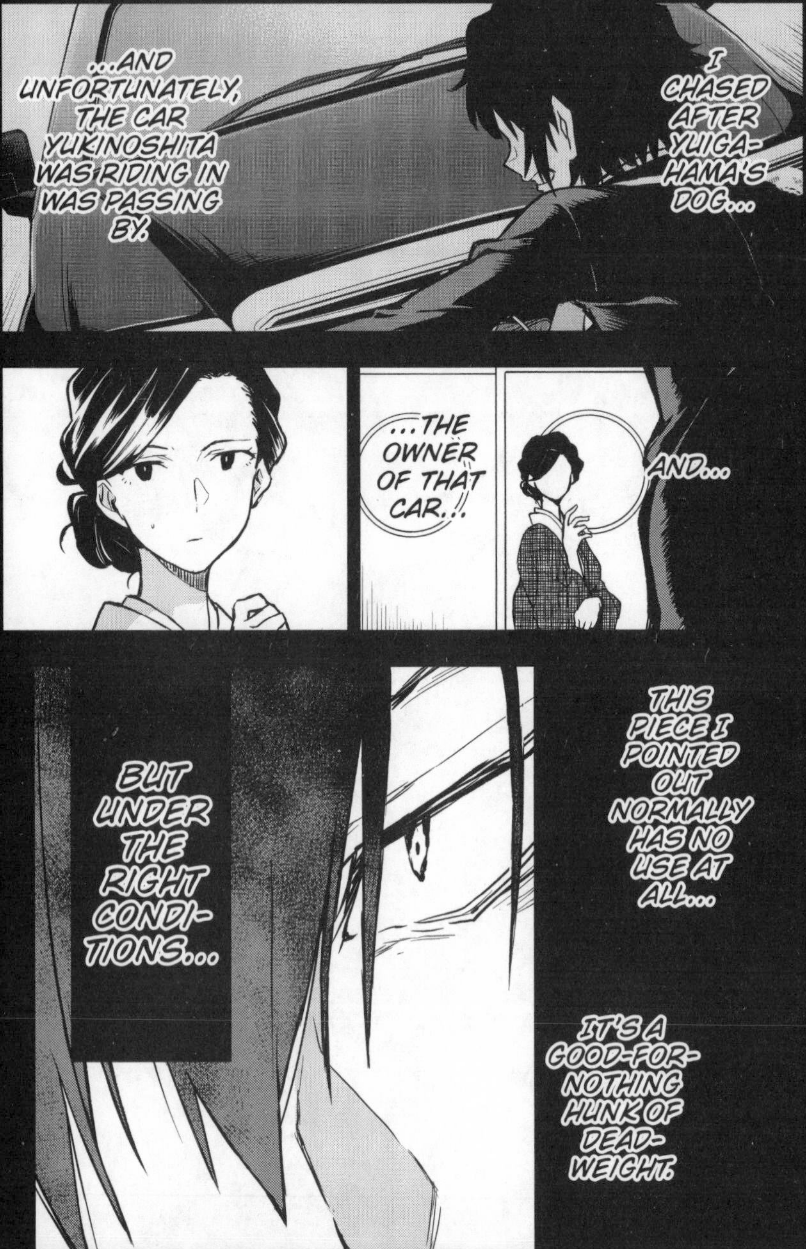
I CHASED AFTER YUIGAHAMA'S DOG...
...AND UNFORTUNATELY, THE CAR YUKINOSHITA WAS RIDING IN WAS PASSING BY.
AND...
...THE OWNER OF THAT CAR...
THIS PIECE I POINTED OUT NORMALLY HAS NO USE AT ALL...
IT'S A GOOD-FOR-NOTHING HUNK OF DEADWEIGHT.
BUT UNDER THE RIGHT CONDITIONS...

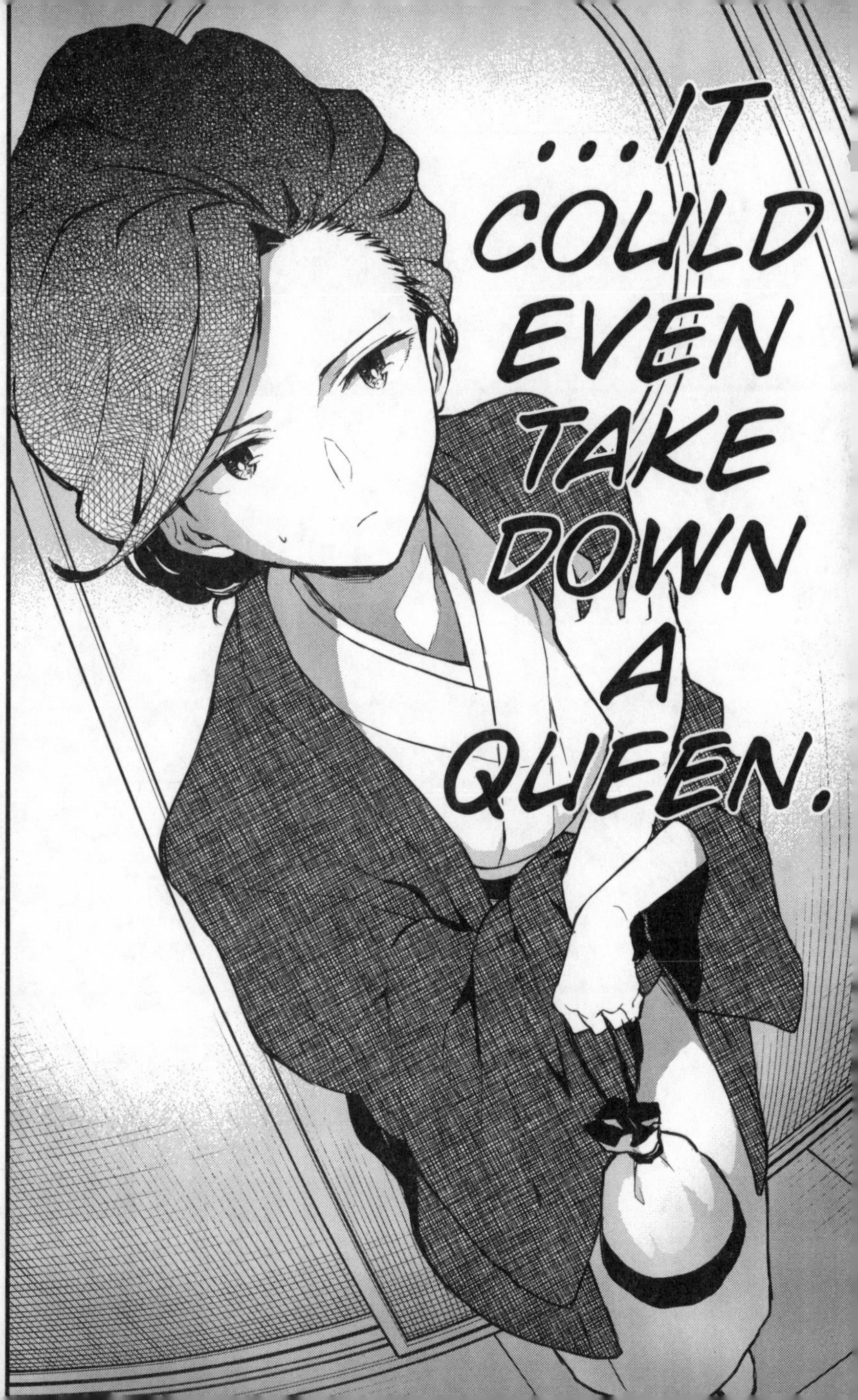
...IT COULD EVEN TAKE DOWN A QUEEN.

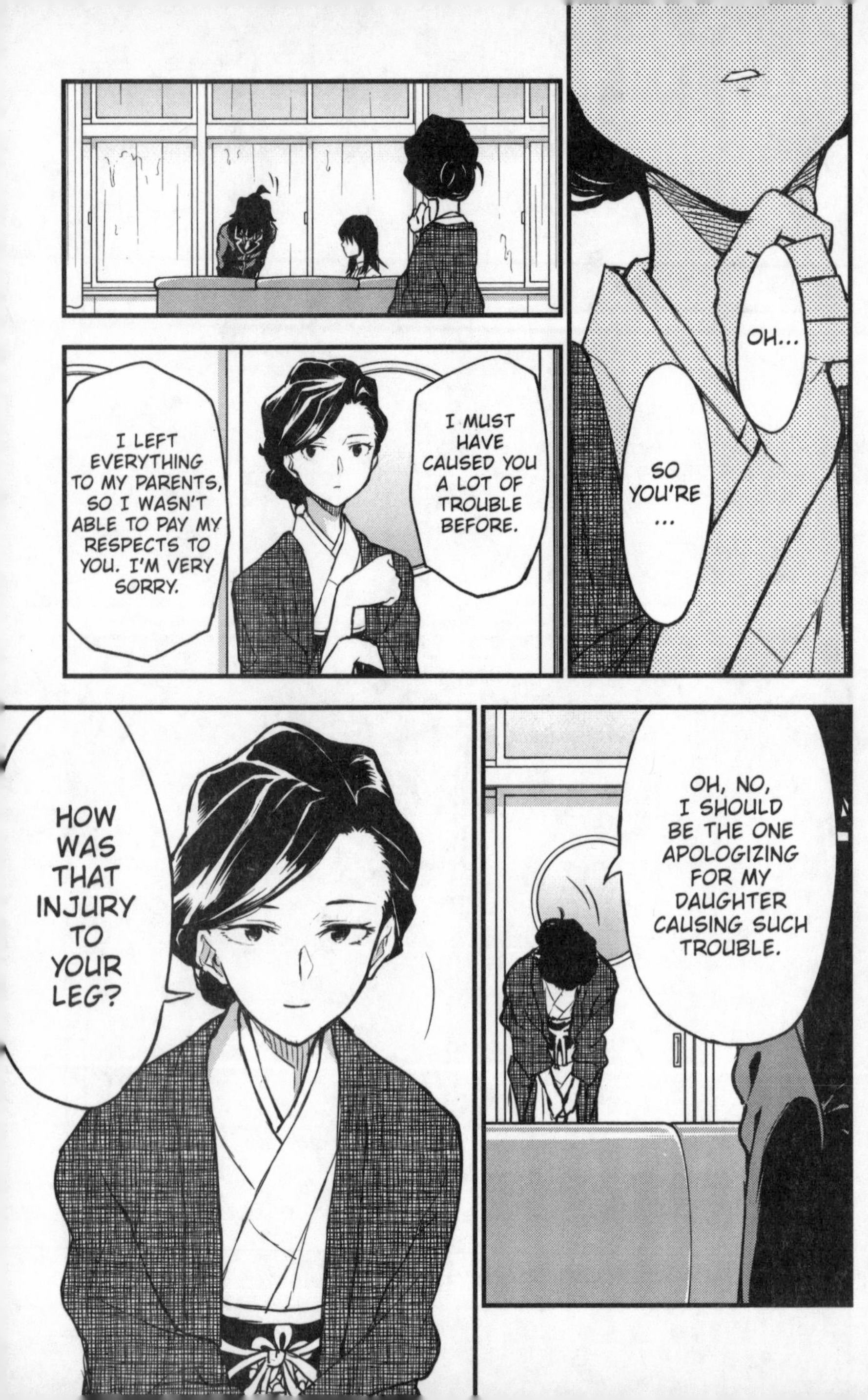
OH...
SO YOU'RE ...
I MUST HAVE CAUSED YOU A LOT OF TROUBLE BEFORE.
I LEFT EVERYTHING TO MY PARENTS, SO I WASN'T ABLE TO PAY MY RESPECTS TO YOU. I'M VERY SORRY.
OH, NO, I SHOULD BE THE ONE APOLOGIZING FOR MY DAUGHTER CAUSING SUCH TROUBLE.
HOW WAS THAT INJURY TO YOUR LEG?

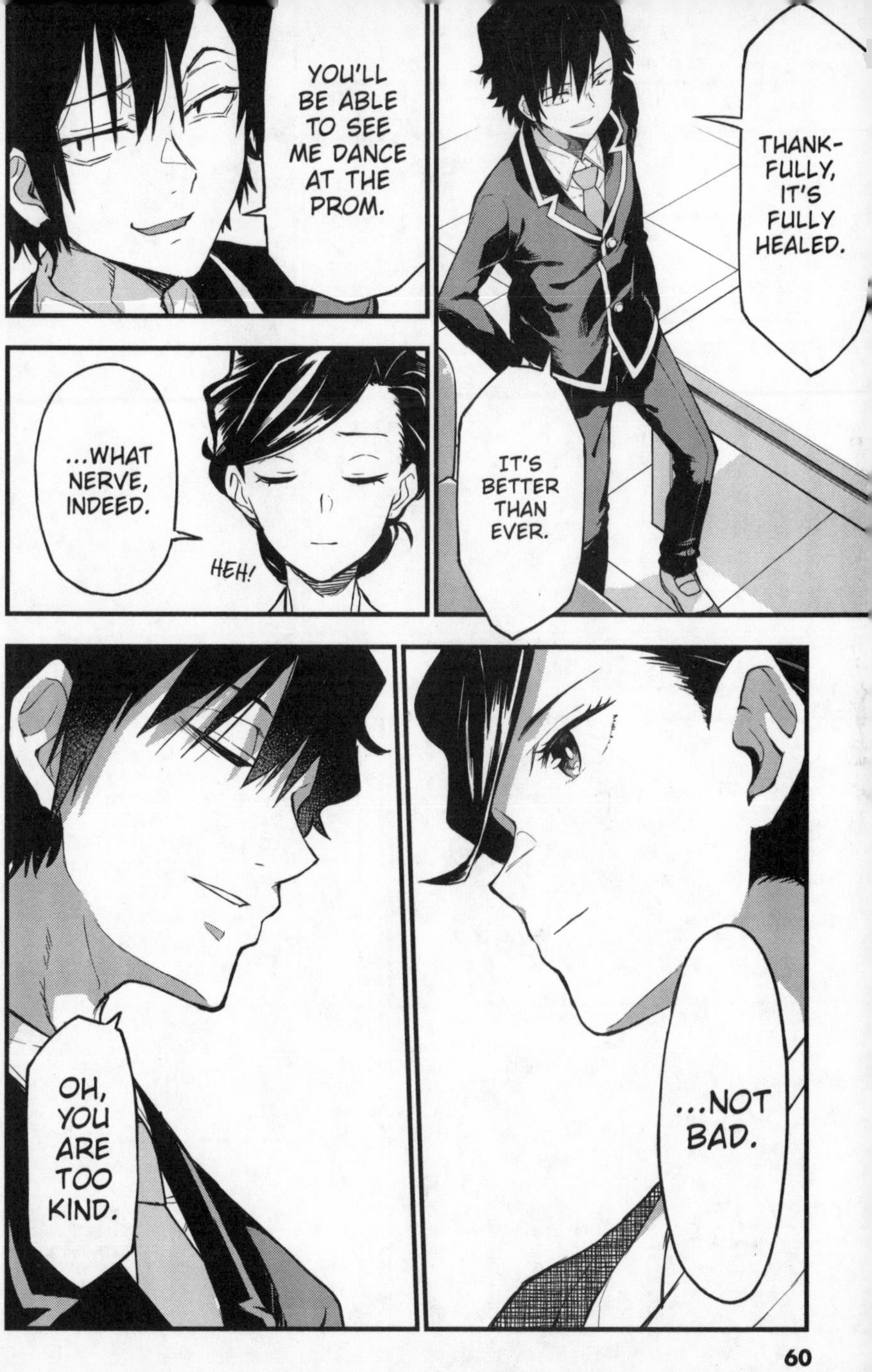
THANK-FULLY, IT'S FULLY HEALED.
IT'S BETTER THAN EVER.
YOU'LL BE ABLE TO SEE ME DANCE AT THE PROM.
...WHAT NERVE, INDEED.
HEH!
...NOT BAD.
OH, YOU ARE TOO KIND.

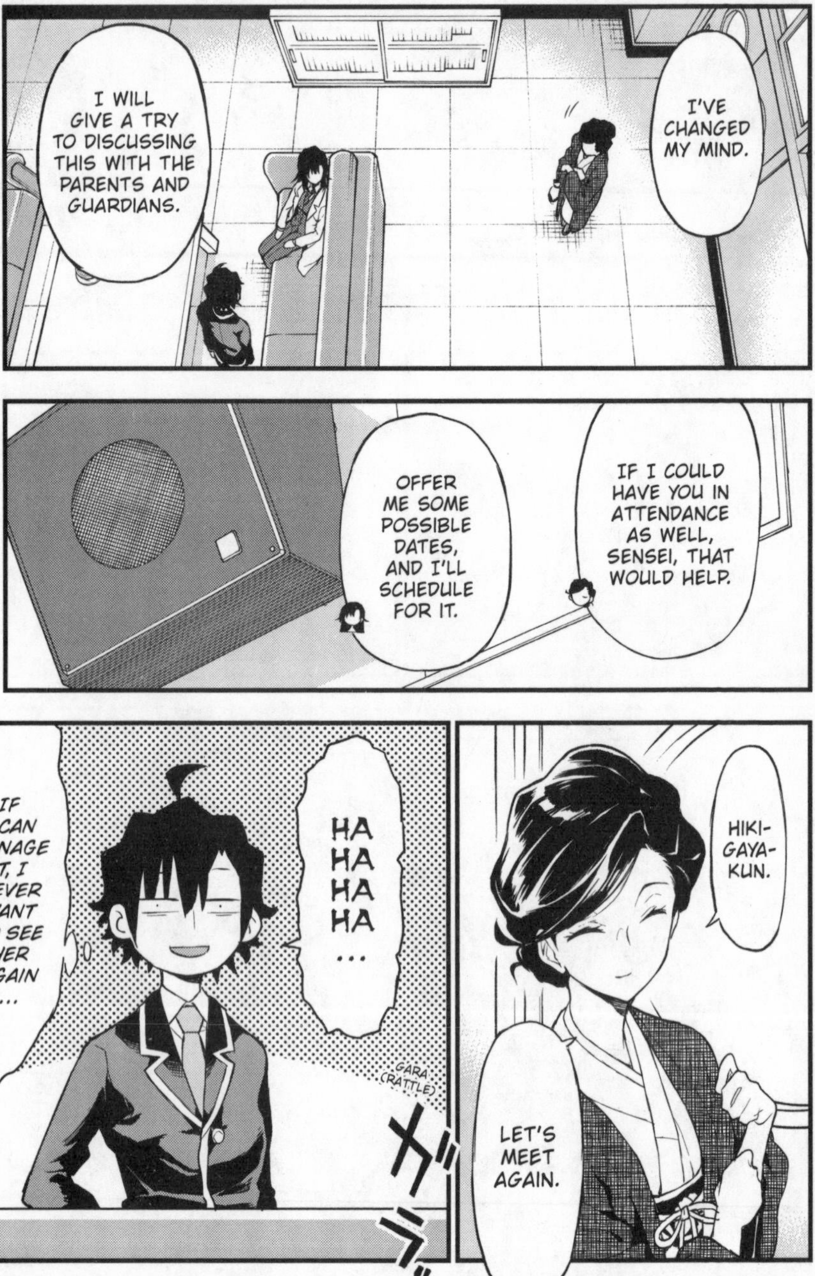
I'VE CHANGED MY MIND.
I WILL GIVE A TRY TO DISCUSSING THIS WITH THE PARENTS AND GUARDIANS.
IF I COULD HAVE YOU IN ATTENDANCE AS WELL, SENSEI, THAT WOULD HELP.
OFFER ME SOME POSSIBLE DATES, AND I'LL SCHEDULE FOR IT.
HIKI-GAYA-KUN.
LET'S MEET AGAIN.
GARA (RATTLE)
HA HA HA HA ...
IF I CAN MANAGE IT, I NEVER WANT TO SEE HER AGAIN ...

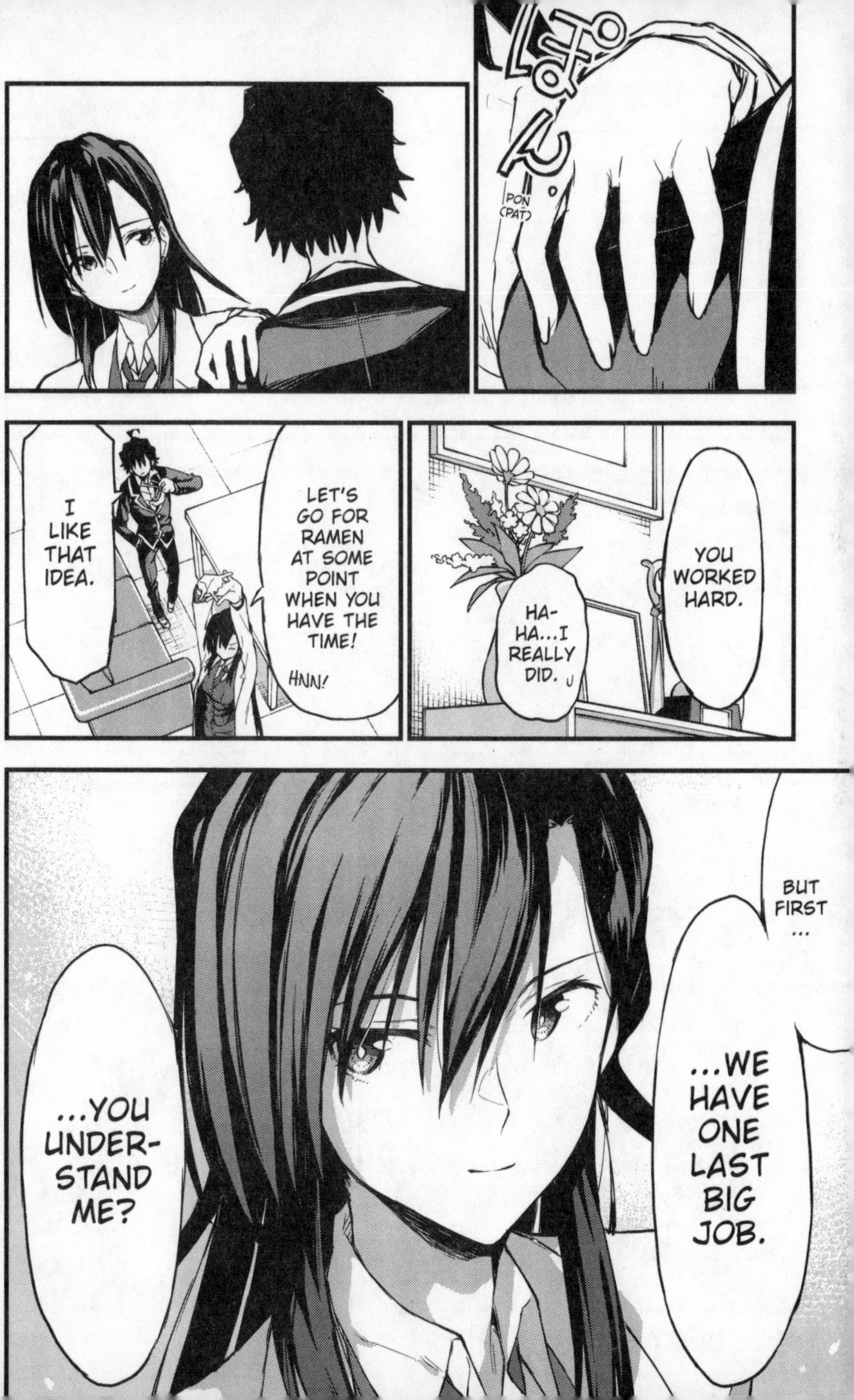
ぽん
PON (PAT)
YOU WORKED HARD.
HA-HA...I REALLY DID.
LET'S GO FOR RAMEN AT SOME POINT WHEN YOU HAVE THE TIME!
HNN!
I LIKE THAT IDEA.
BUT FIRST...
...WE HAVE ONE LAST BIG JOB.
...YOU UNDER-STAND ME?

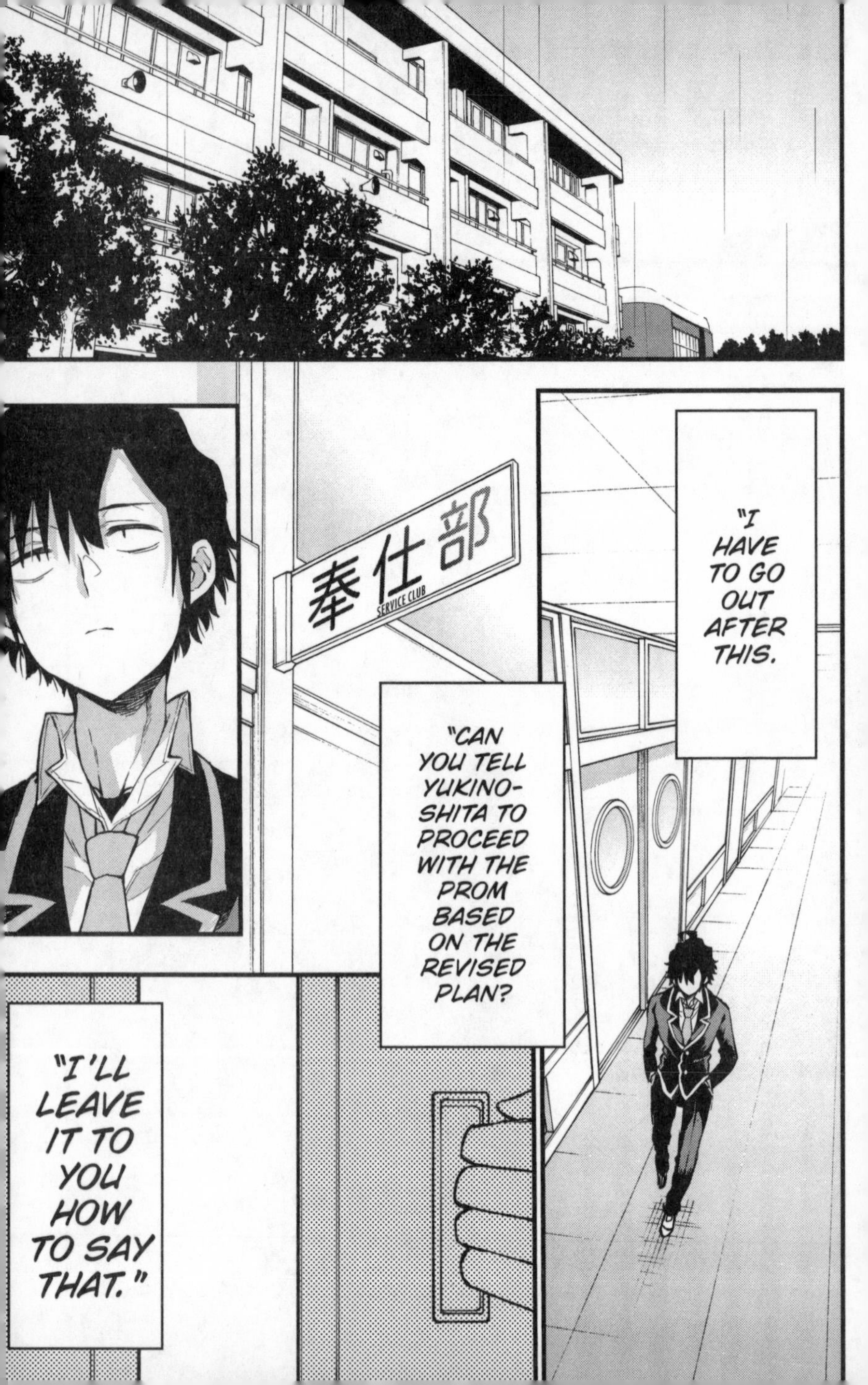
"I HAVE TO GO OUT AFTER THIS.
"CAN YOU TELL YUKINO-SHITA TO PROCEED WITH THE PROM BASED ON THE REVISED PLAN?
奉仕部
SERVICE CLUB
"I'LL LEAVE IT TO YOU HOW TO SAY THAT."

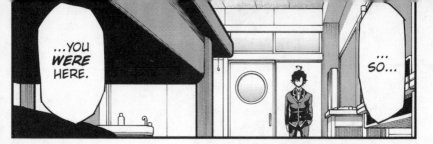

...YOU WERE HERE.

...SO...

...

HELLO.

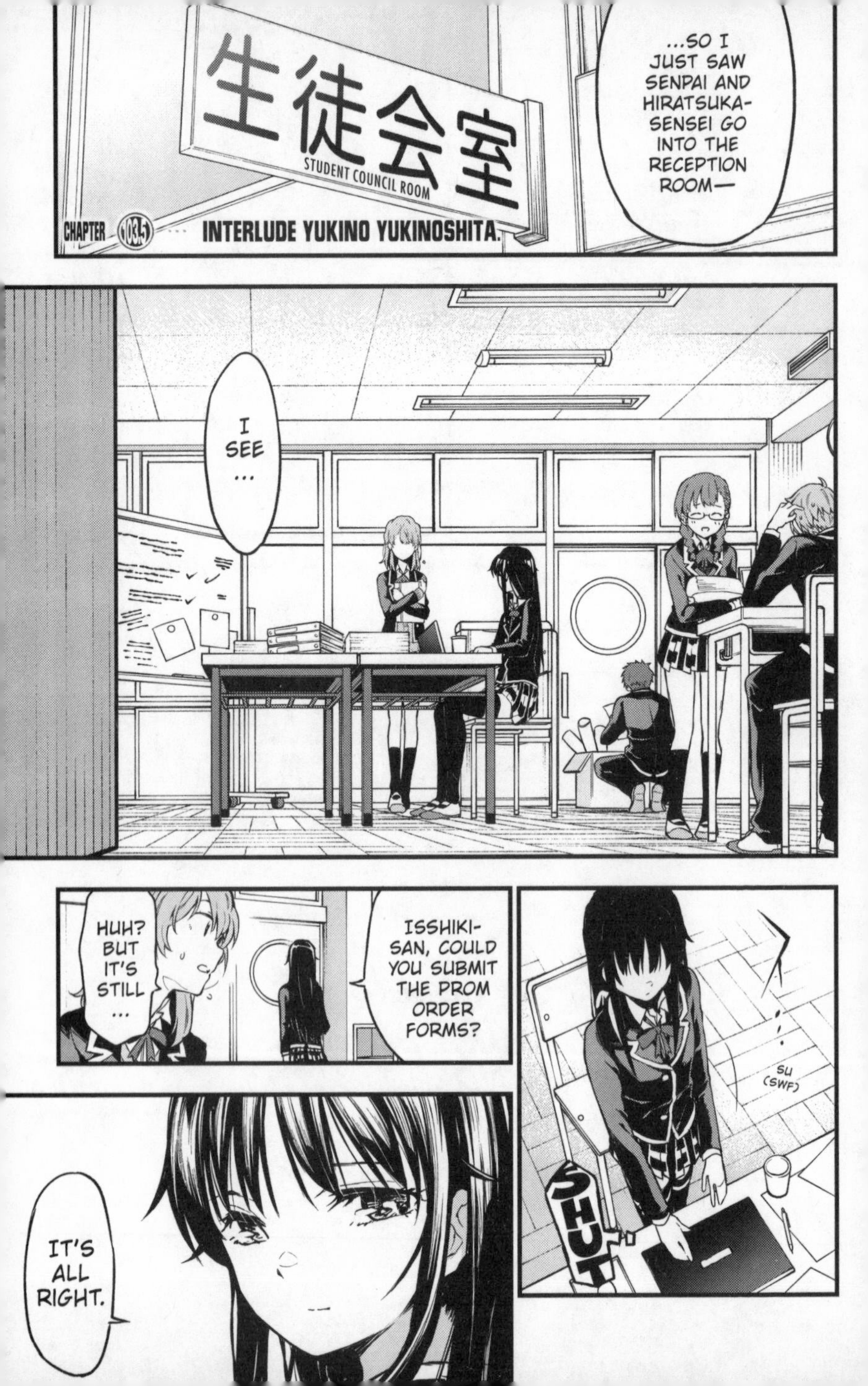
...SO I JUST SAW SENPAI AND HIRATSUKA-SENSEI GO INTO THE RECEPTION ROOM—
生徒会室
STUDENT COUNCIL ROOM
CHAPTER 103.5 ... INTERLUDE YUKINO YUKINOSHITA.
I SEE ...
SU (SWF)
SHUT
ISSHIKI-SAN, COULD YOU SUBMIT THE PROM ORDER FORMS?
HUH? BUT IT'S STILL ...
IT'S ALL RIGHT.

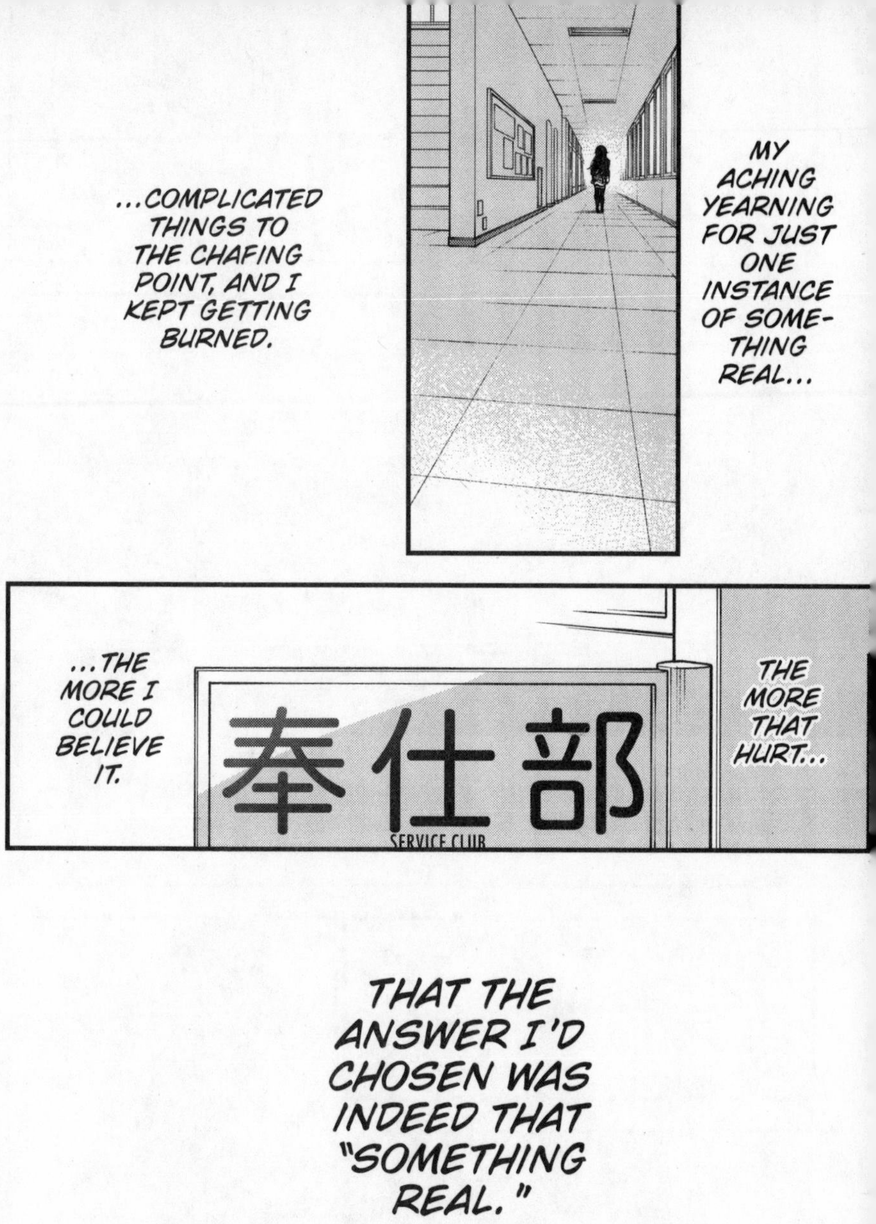
MY ACHING YEARNING FOR JUST ONE INSTANCE OF SOME-THING REAL...
...COMPLICATED THINGS TO THE CHAFING POINT, AND I KEPT GETTING BURNED.
THE MORE THAT HURT...
奉仕部
SERVICE CLUB
...THE MORE I COULD BELIEVE IT.
THAT THE ANSWER I'D CHOSEN WAS INDEED THAT "SOMETHING REAL."

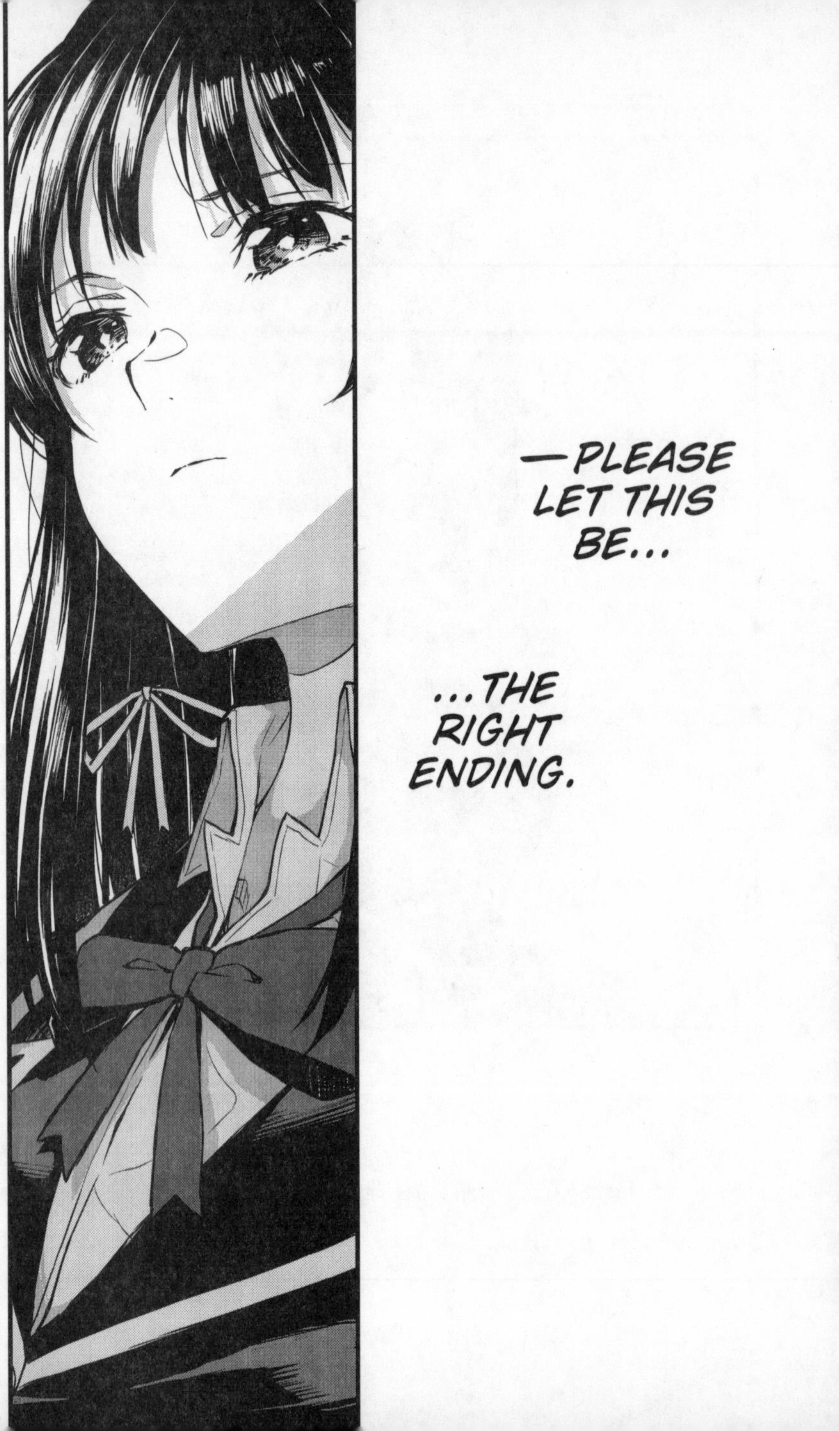
—PLEASE LET THIS BE...
...THE RIGHT ENDING.

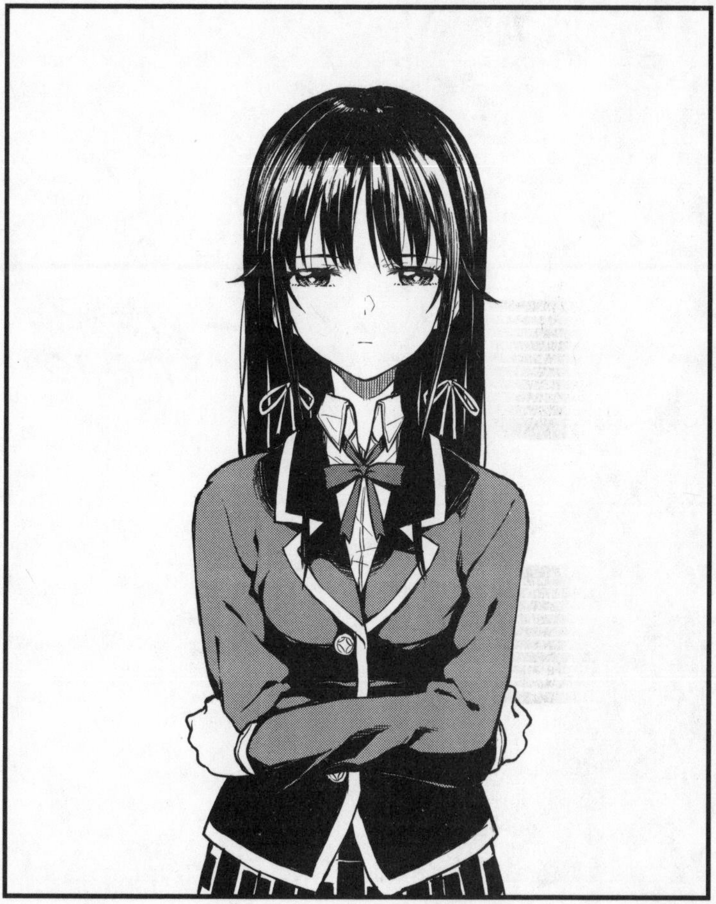

CHAPTER 103.5 ··· INTERLUDE YUKINO YUKINOSHITA.

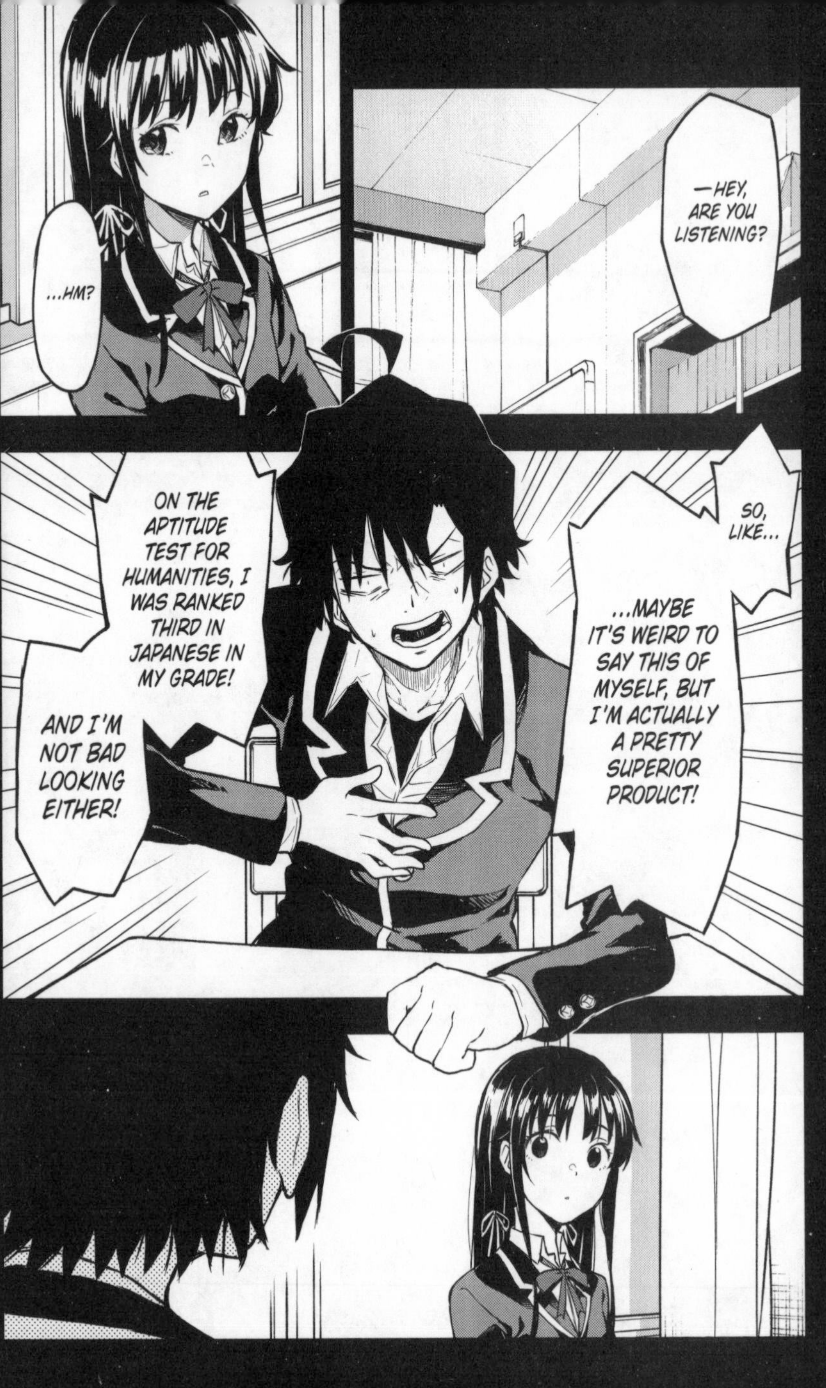
—HEY, ARE YOU LISTENING?
...HM?
SO, LIKE...
...MAYBE IT'S WEIRD TO SAY THIS OF MYSELF, BUT I'M ACTUALLY A PRETTY SUPERIOR PRODUCT!
ON THE APTITUDE TEST FOR HUMANITIES, I WAS RANKED THIRD IN JAPANESE IN MY GRADE!
AND I'M NOT BAD LOOKING EITHER!

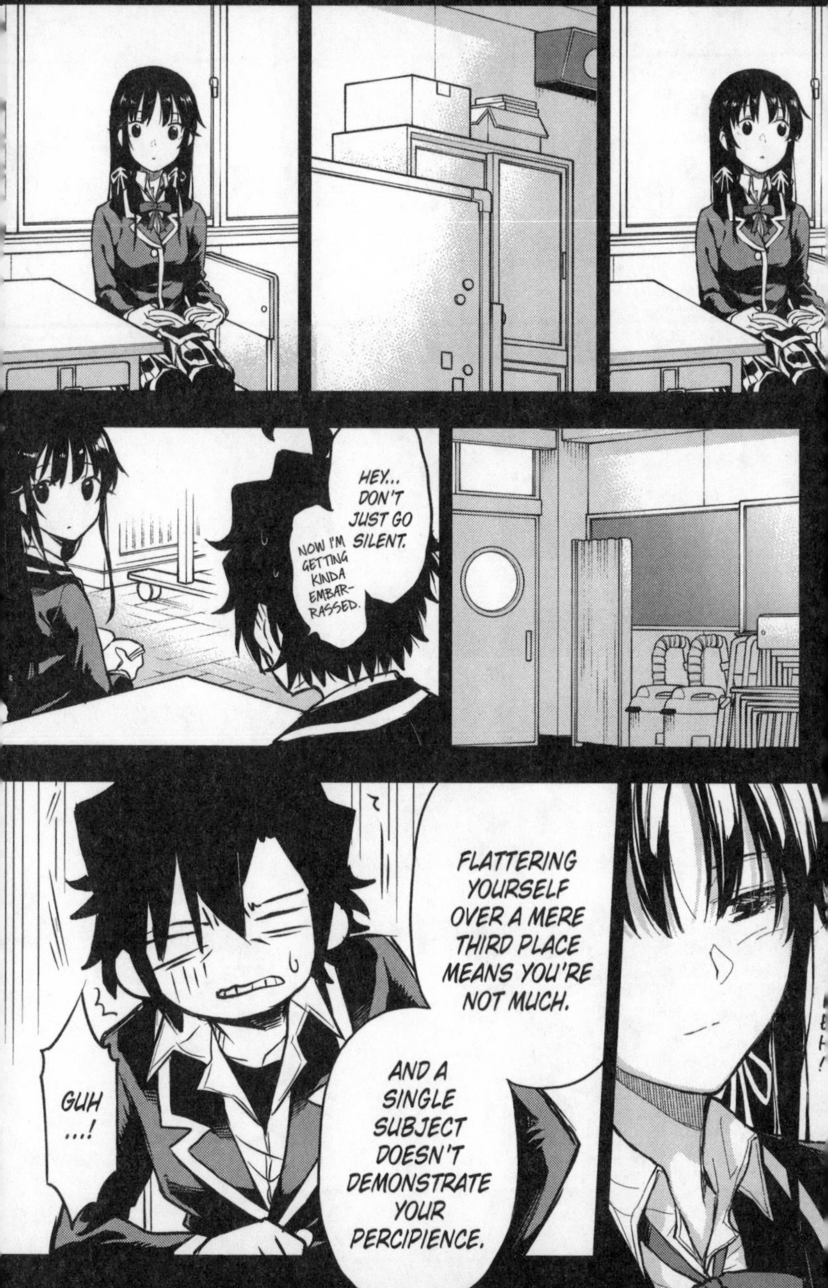
HEY... DON'T JUST GO SILENT.
NOW I'M GETTING KINDA EMBARRASSED.
FLATTERING YOURSELF OVER A MERE THIRD PLACE MEANS YOU'RE NOT MUCH.
AND A SINGLE SUBJECT DOESN'T DEMONSTRATE YOUR PERCIPIENCE.
GUH ...!

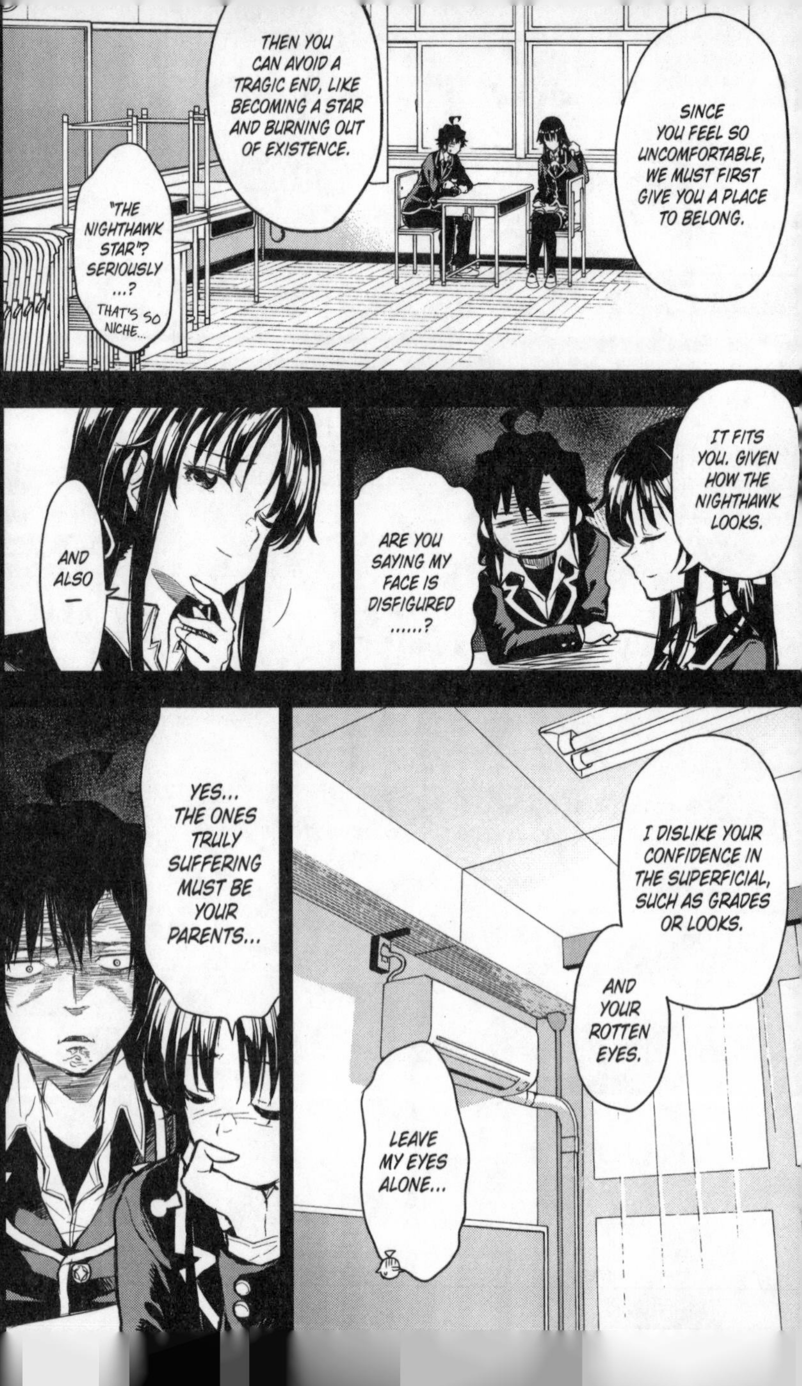
SINCE YOU FEEL SO UNCOMFORTABLE, WE MUST FIRST GIVE YOU A PLACE TO BELONG.
THEN YOU CAN AVOID A TRAGIC END, LIKE BECOMING A STAR AND BURNING OUT OF EXISTENCE.
"THE NIGHTHAWK STAR"? SERIOUSLY ...?
THAT'S SO NICHE...
IT FITS YOU. GIVEN HOW THE NIGHTHAWK LOOKS.
ARE YOU SAYING MY FACE IS DISFIGURED ......?
AND ALSO —
I DISLIKE YOUR CONFIDENCE IN THE SUPERFICIAL, SUCH AS GRADES OR LOOKS.
AND YOUR ROTTEN EYES.
LEAVE MY EYES ALONE...
YES... THE ONES TRULY SUFFERING MUST BE YOUR PARENTS...

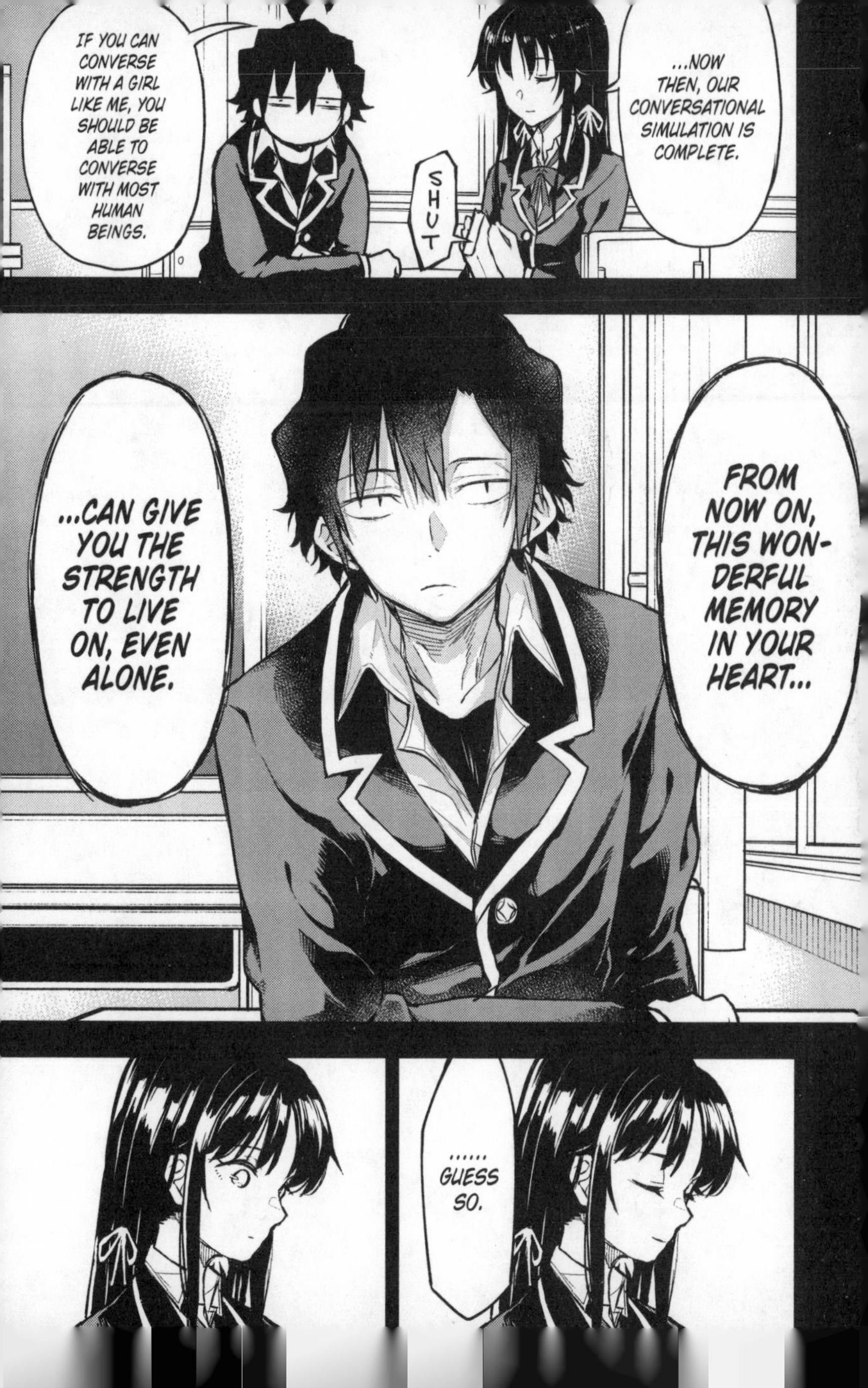
...NOW THEN, OUR CONVERSATIONAL SIMULATION IS COMPLETE.
SHUT
IF YOU CAN CONVERSE WITH A GIRL LIKE ME, YOU SHOULD BE ABLE TO CONVERSE WITH MOST HUMAN BEINGS.
FROM NOW ON, THIS WON-DERFUL MEMORY IN YOUR HEART...
...CAN GIVE YOU THE STRENGTH TO LIVE ON, EVEN ALONE.
......GUESS SO.

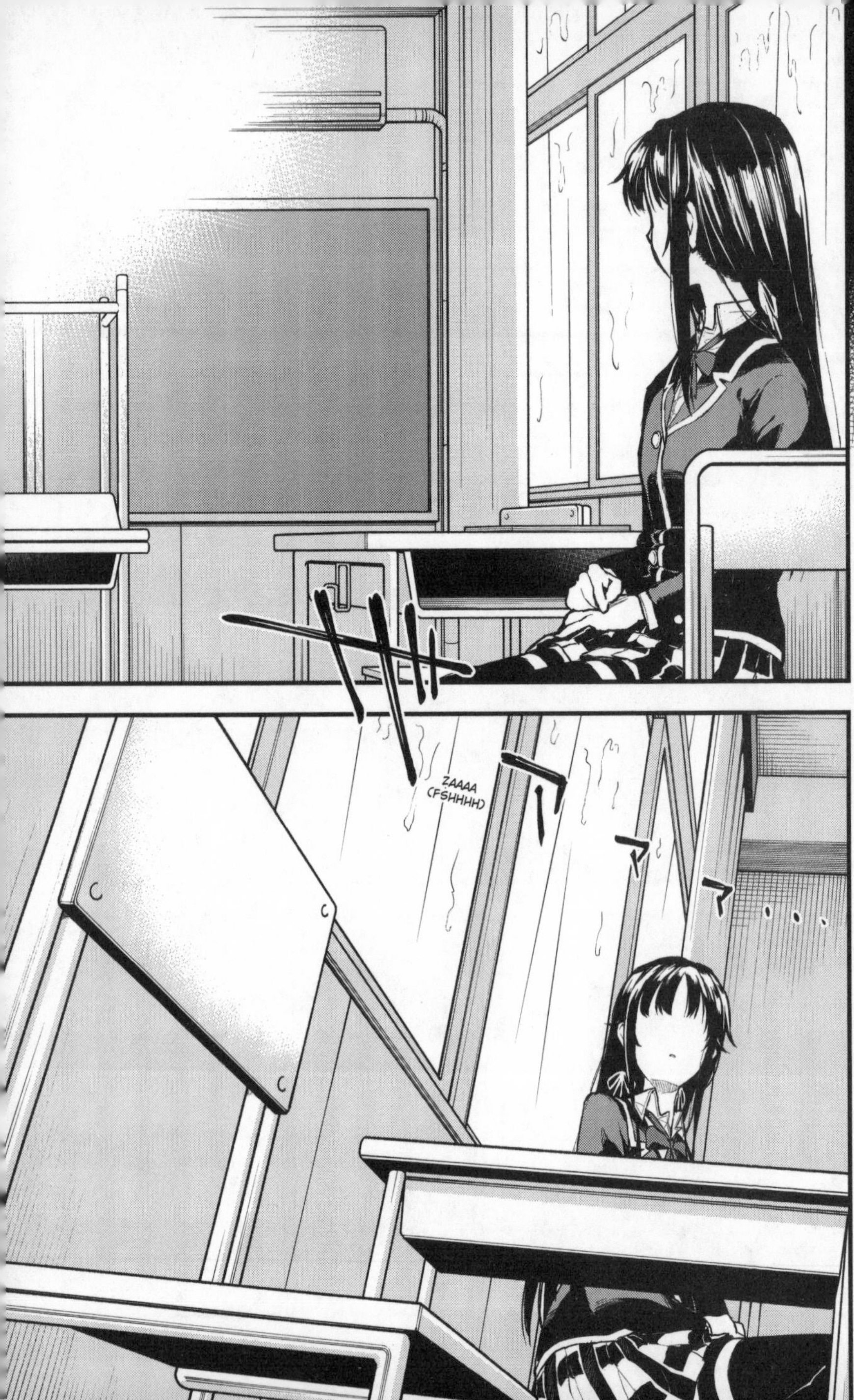
ZAAAA
(FSHHHH)

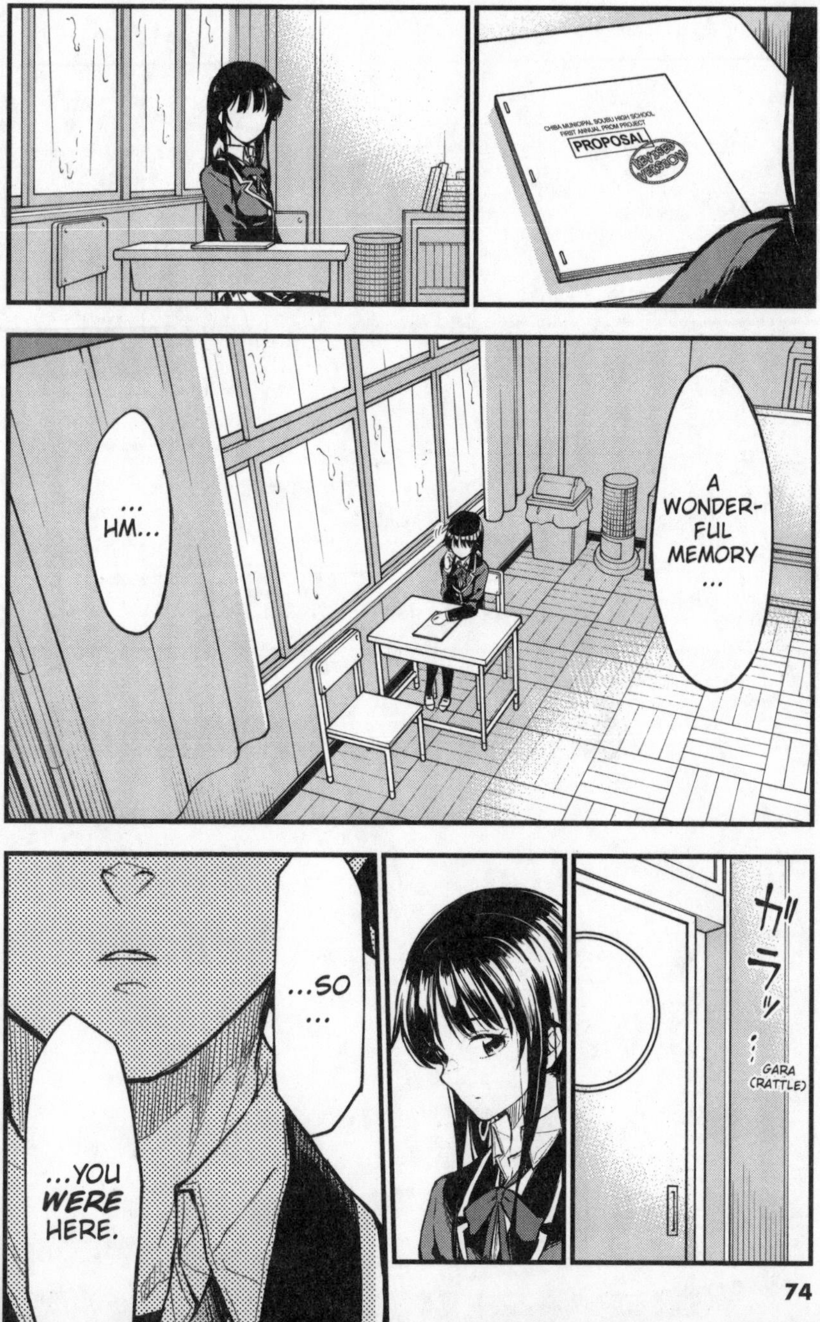
CHIBA MUNICIPAL SOUBU HIGH SCHOOL
FIRST ANNUAL PROM PROJECT
PROPOSAL
REVISED VERSION
A WONDERFUL MEMORY ...
... HM...
ガラッ…
GARA (RATTLE)
...SO ...
...YOU WERE HERE.

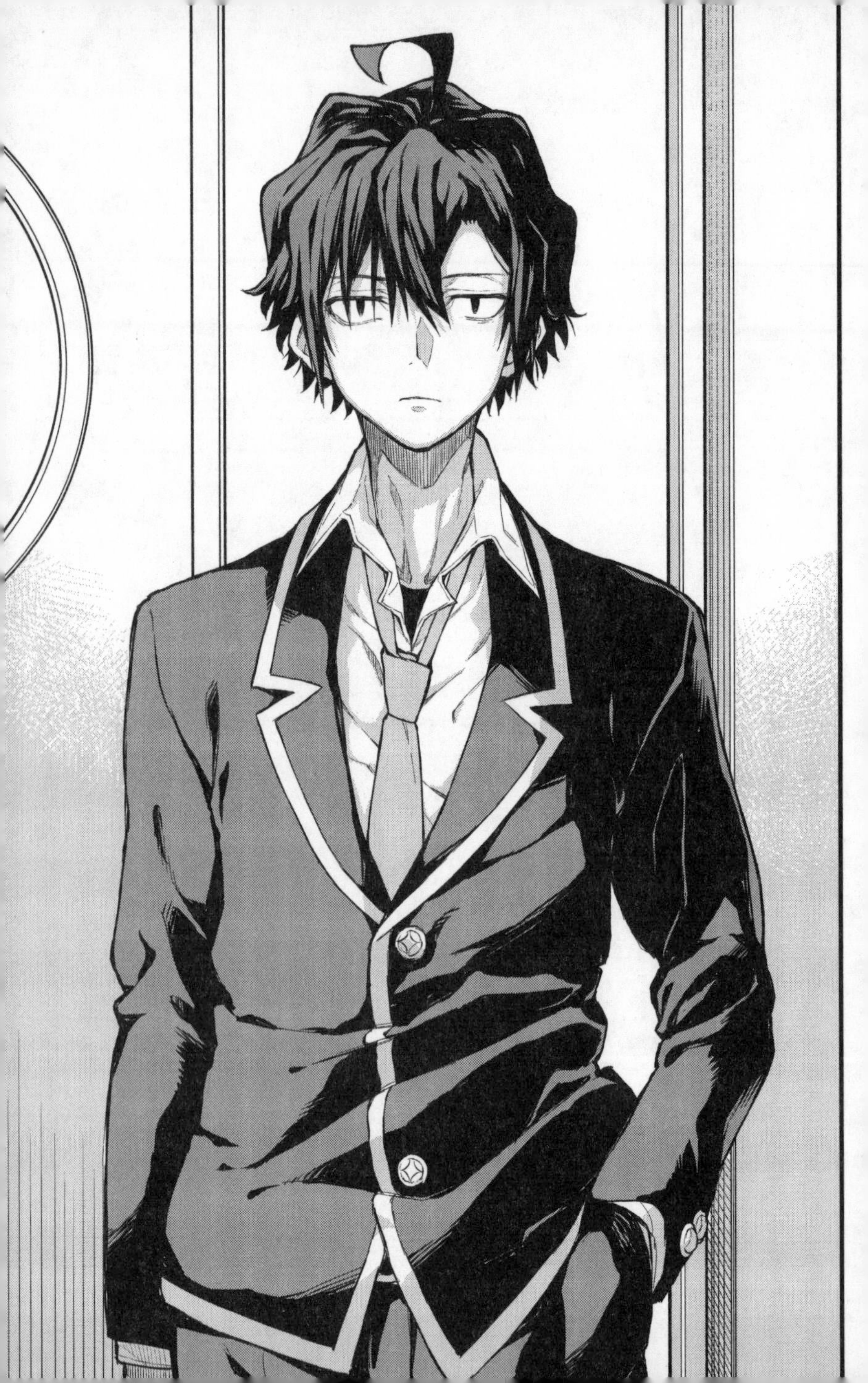

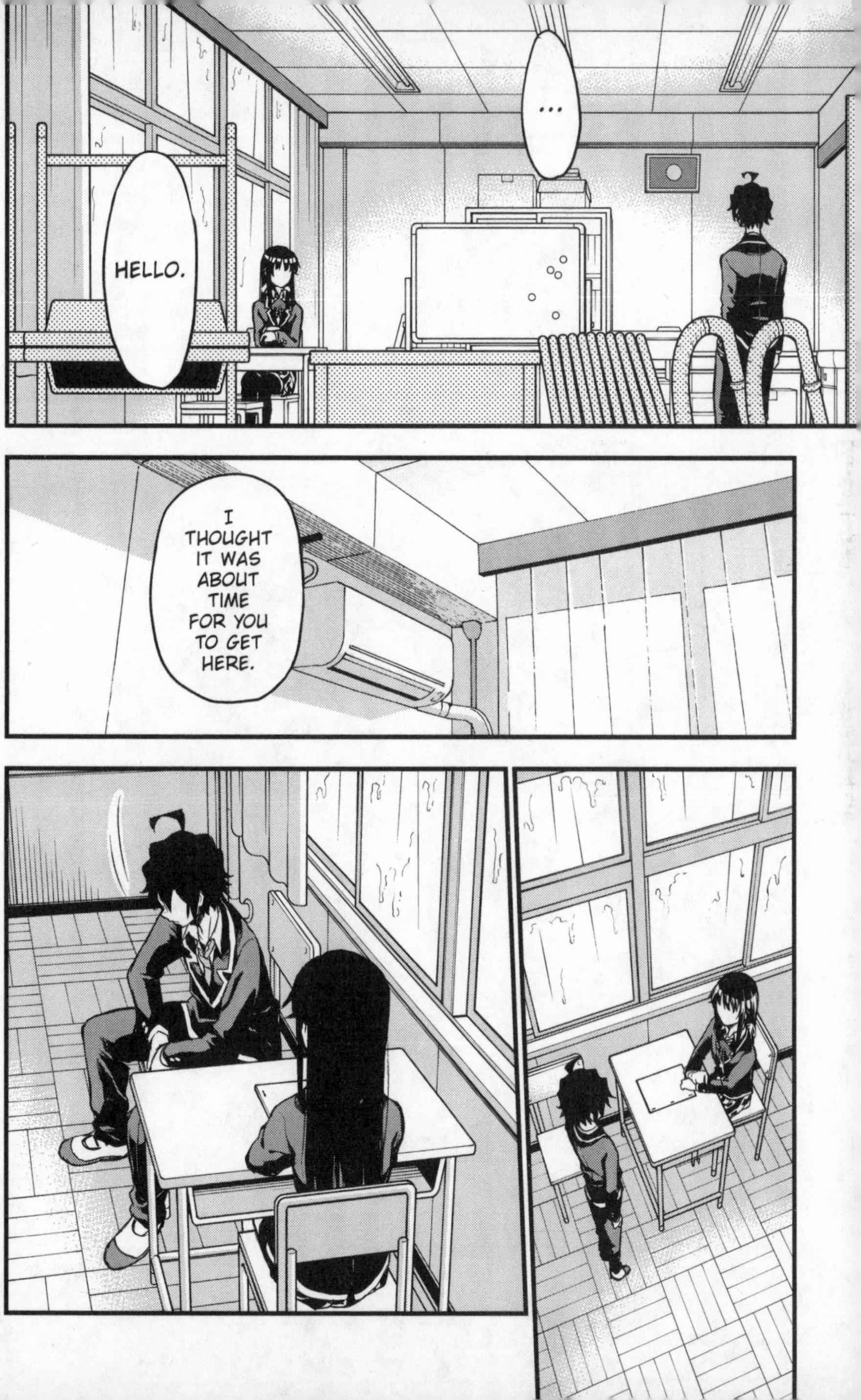
...
HELLO.
I THOUGHT IT WAS ABOUT TIME FOR YOU TO GET HERE.

...ABOUT THE PROM— ULTIMATELY, YOUR PLAN WENT THROUGH.

SHE'S GONNA EXPLAIN TO THE PARENTS WHO OPPOSED IT TO WIN THEM OVER.

NO.

IT'S YOUR WIN.

SO, WELL...

...THIS IS MY LOSS.

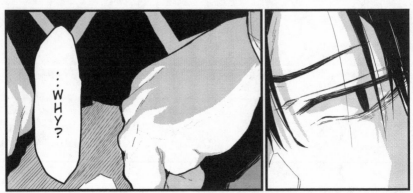

...WHY?

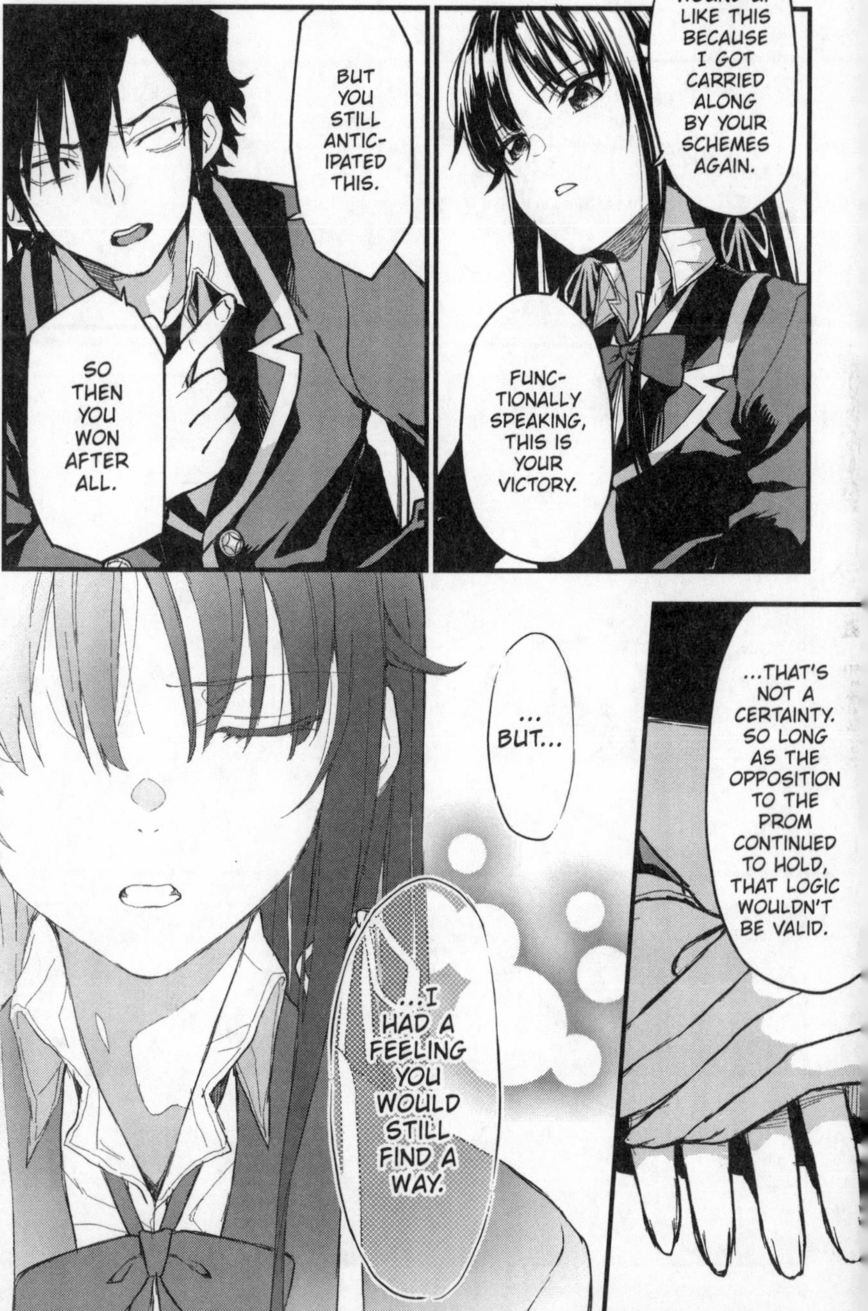
THINGS WOUND UP LIKE THIS BECAUSE I GOT CARRIED ALONG BY YOUR SCHEMES AGAIN.
FUNCTIONALLY SPEAKING, THIS IS YOUR VICTORY.
BUT YOU STILL ANTICIPATED THIS.
SO THEN YOU WON AFTER ALL.
...THAT'S NOT A CERTAINTY. SO LONG AS THE OPPOSITION TO THE PROM CONTINUED TO HOLD, THAT LOGIC WOULDN'T BE VALID.
... BUT...
...I HAD A FEELING YOU WOULD STILL FIND A WAY.

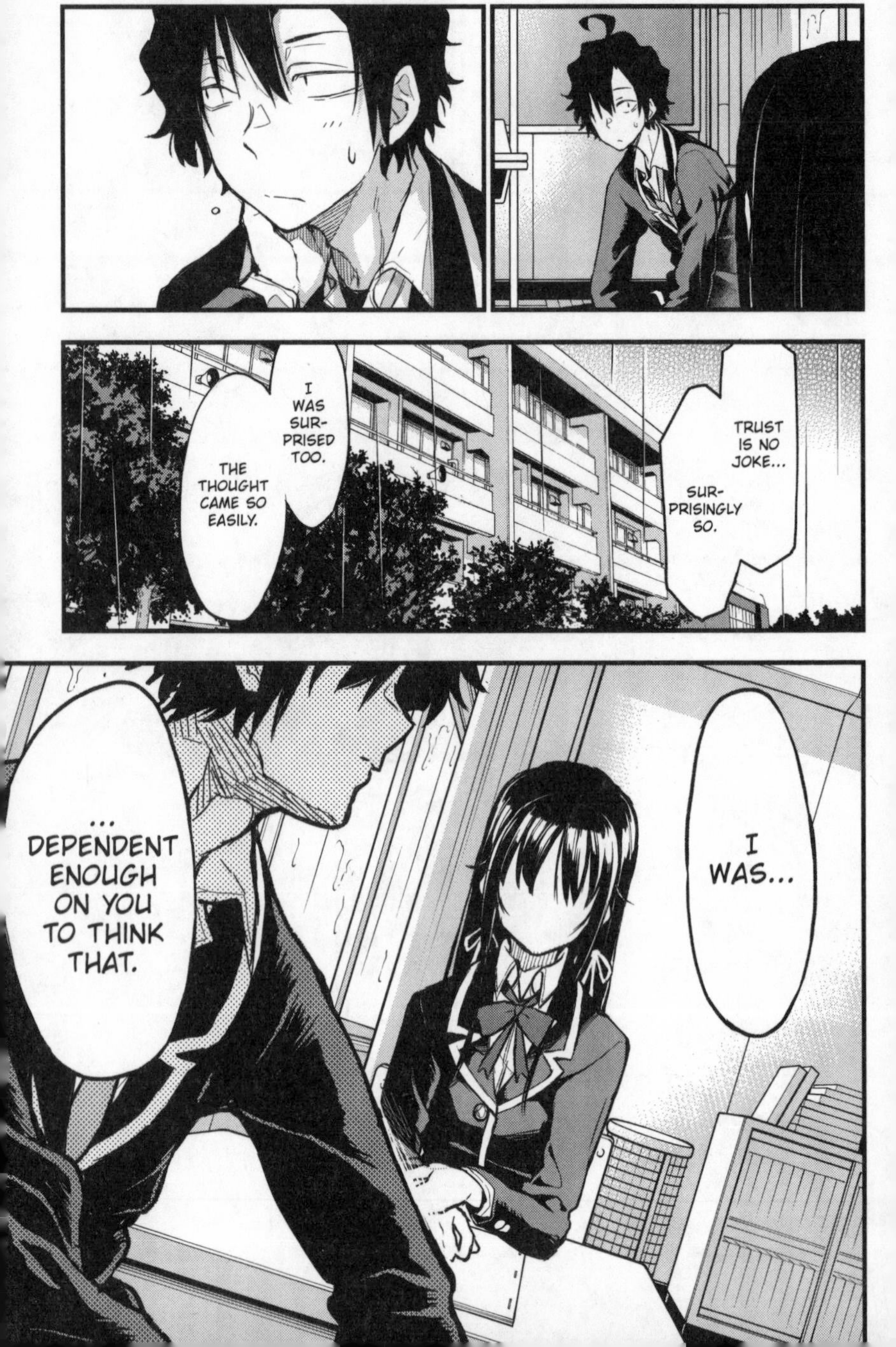
TRUST IS NO JOKE...
SURPRISINGLY SO.
I WAS SURPRISED TOO.
THE THOUGHT CAME SO EASILY.
I WAS...
...DEPENDENT ENOUGH ON YOU TO THINK THAT.

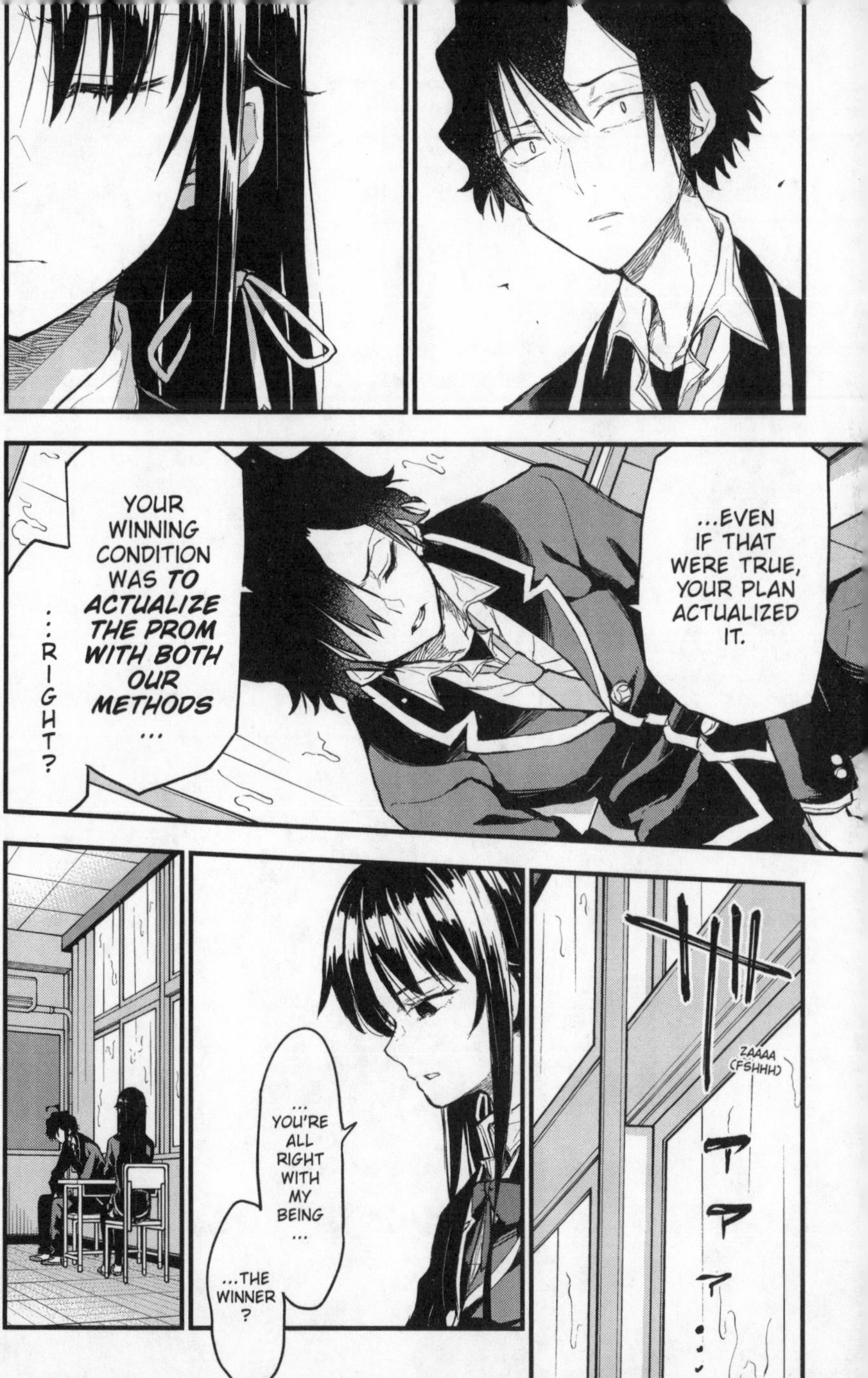
...EVEN IF THAT WERE TRUE, YOUR PLAN ACTUALIZED IT.
YOUR WINNING CONDITION WAS TO ACTUALIZE THE PROM WITH BOTH OUR METHODS...
...RIGHT?
ZAAAA (FSHHH)
...YOU'RE ALL RIGHT WITH MY BEING...
...THE WINNER?

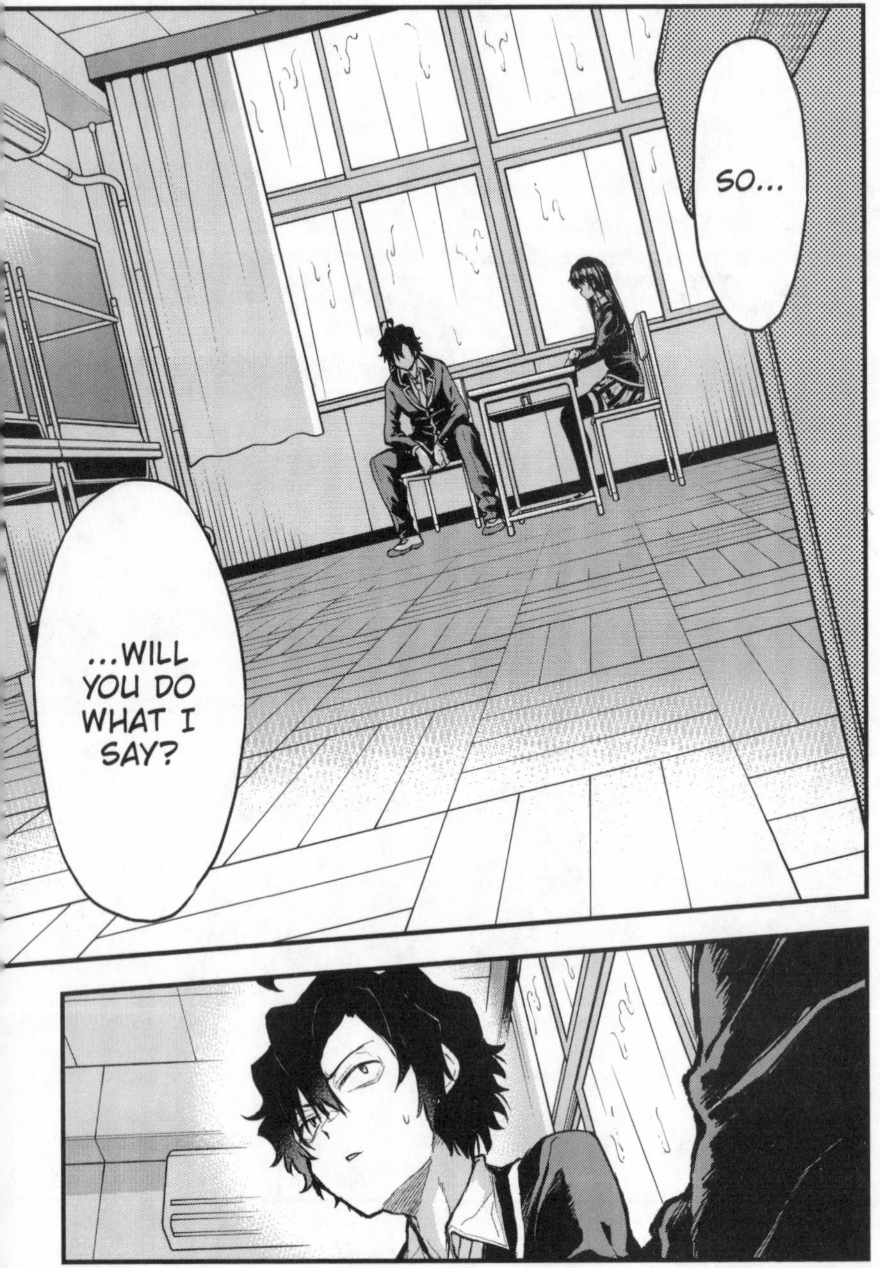
SO...
...WILL YOU DO WHAT I SAY?

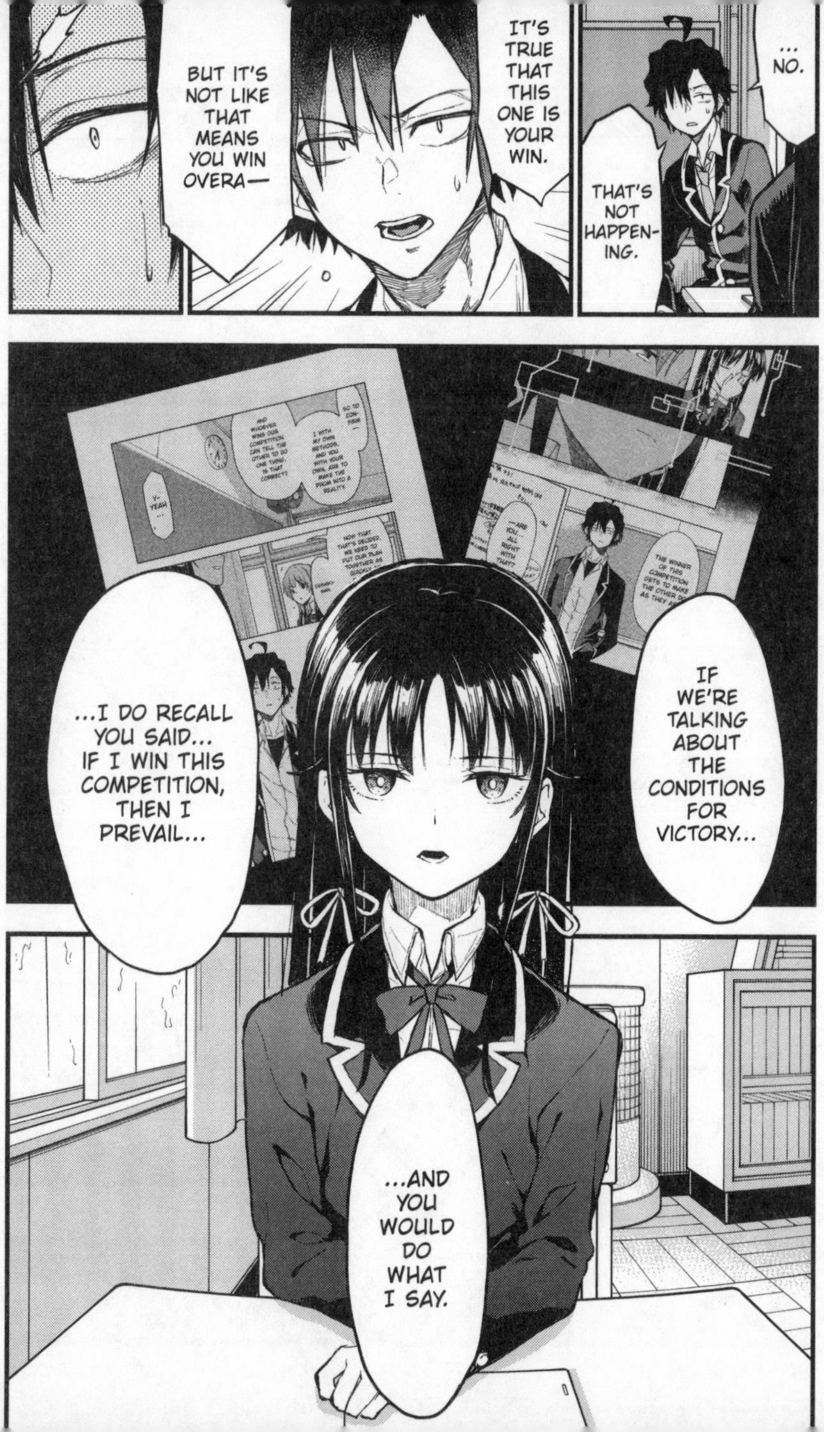
...NO.
THAT'S NOT HAPPENING.
IT'S TRUE THAT THIS ONE IS YOUR WIN.
BUT IT'S NOT LIKE THAT MEANS YOU WIN OVERA—
IF WE'RE TALKING ABOUT THE CONDITIONS FOR VICTORY...
...I DO RECALL YOU SAID... IF I WIN THIS COMPETITION, THEN I PREVAIL...
...AND YOU WOULD DO WHAT I SAY.

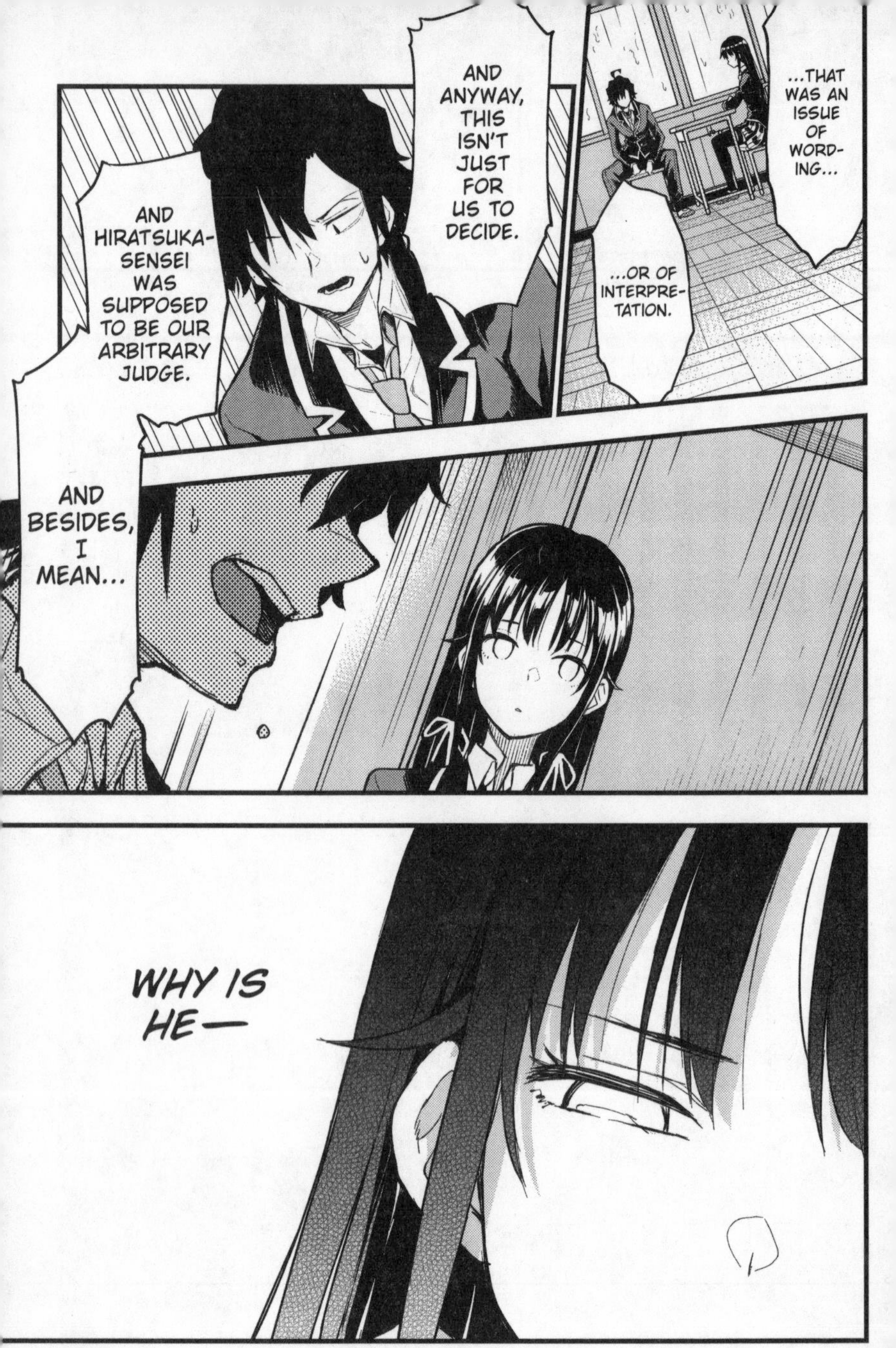
...THAT WAS AN ISSUE OF WORD-ING...
...OR OF INTERPRE-TATION.
AND ANYWAY, THIS ISN'T JUST FOR US TO DECIDE.
AND HIRATSUKA-SENSEI WAS SUPPOSED TO BE OUR ARBITRARY JUDGE.
AND BESIDES, I MEAN...
WHY IS HE—

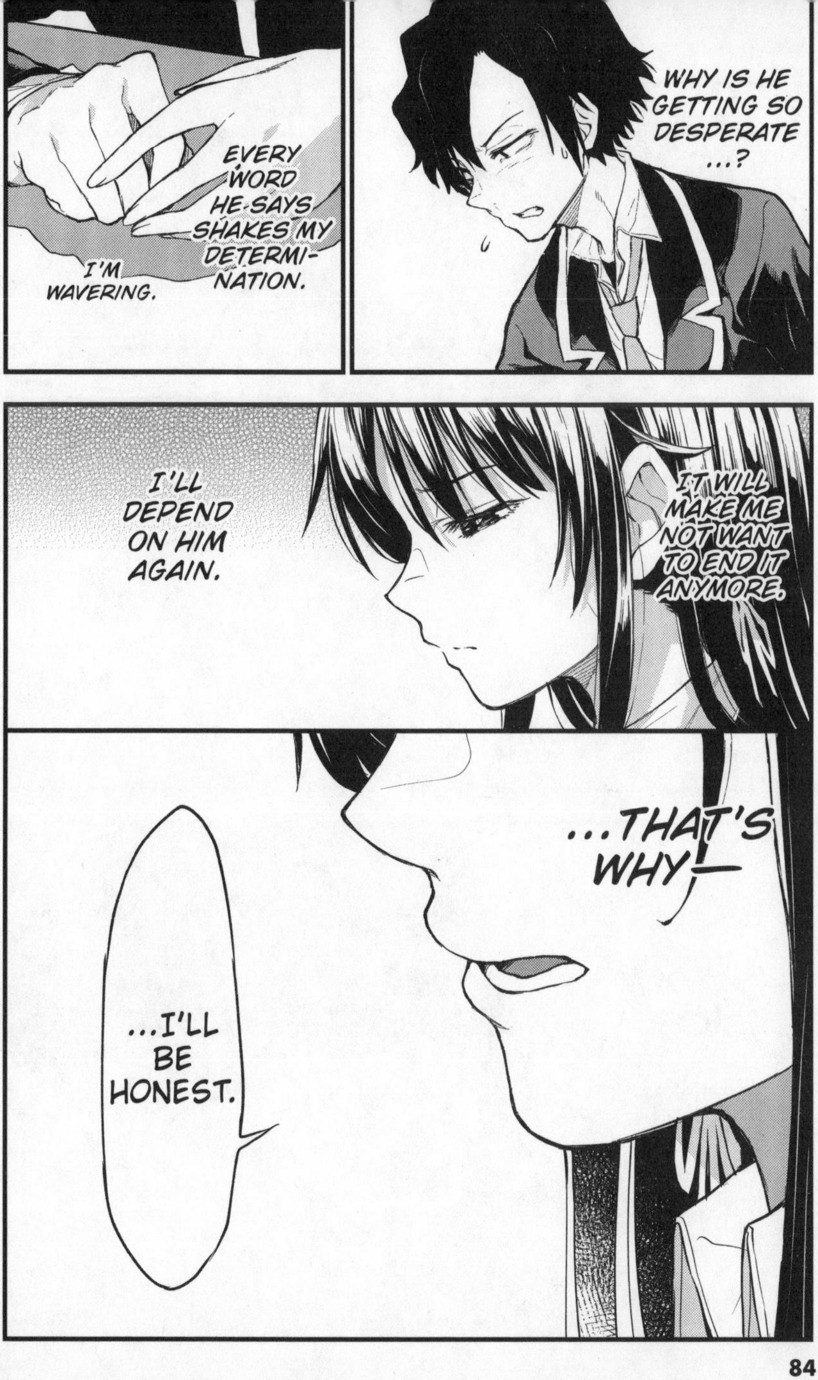
WHY IS HE GETTING SO DESPERATE ...?
EVERY WORD HE SAYS SHAKES MY DETERMI-NATION.
I'M WAVERING.
IT WILL MAKE ME NOT WANT TO END IT ANYMORE.
I'LL DEPEND ON HIM AGAIN.
...THAT'S WHY—
...I'LL BE HONEST.

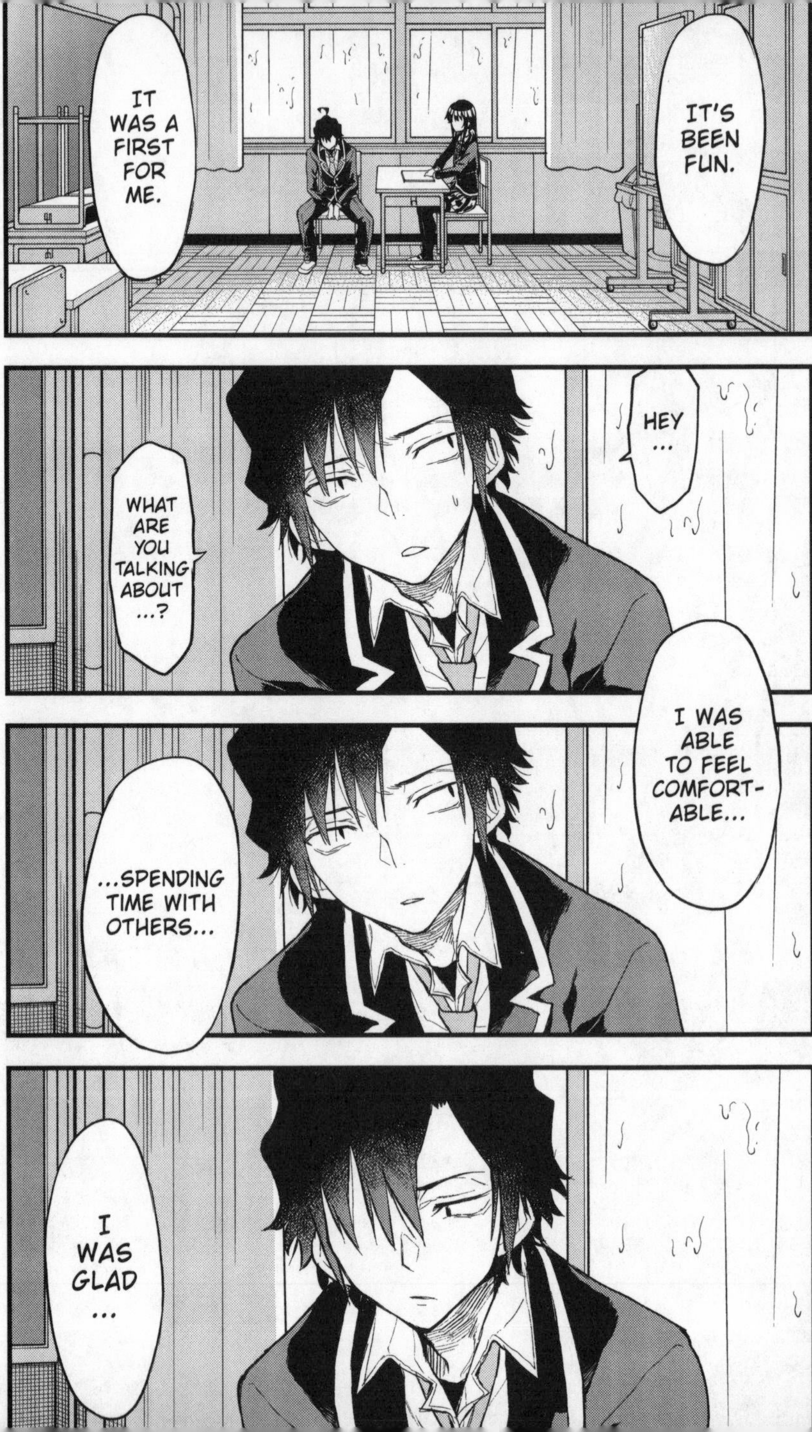
IT'S BEEN FUN.
IT WAS A FIRST FOR ME.
HEY ...
WHAT ARE YOU TALKING ABOUT ...?
I WAS ABLE TO FEEL COMFORT-ABLE...
...SPENDING TIME WITH OTHERS...
I WAS GLAD ...

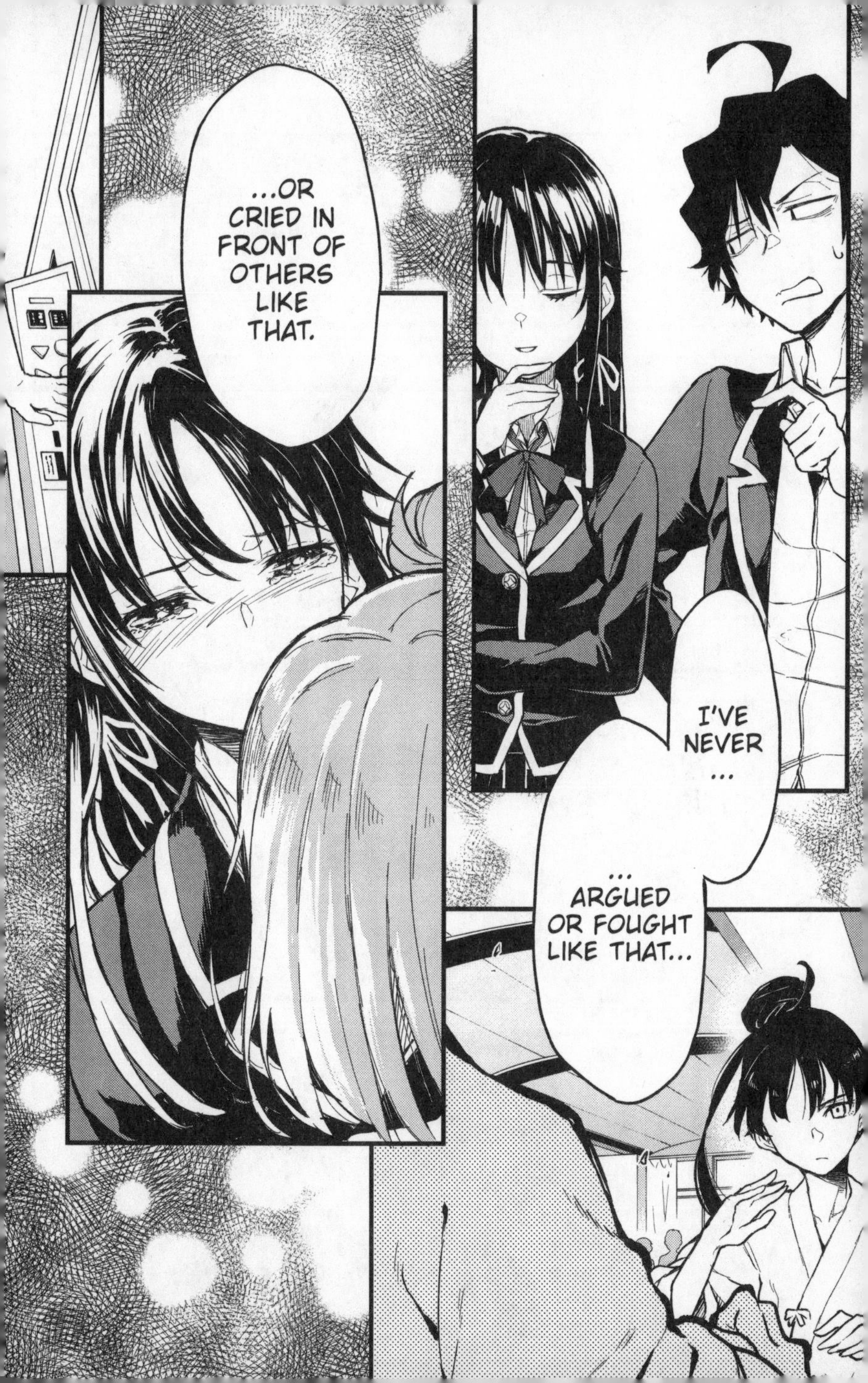
I'VE NEVER ...
... ARGUED OR FOUGHT LIKE THAT...
...OR CRIED IN FRONT OF OTHERS LIKE THAT.

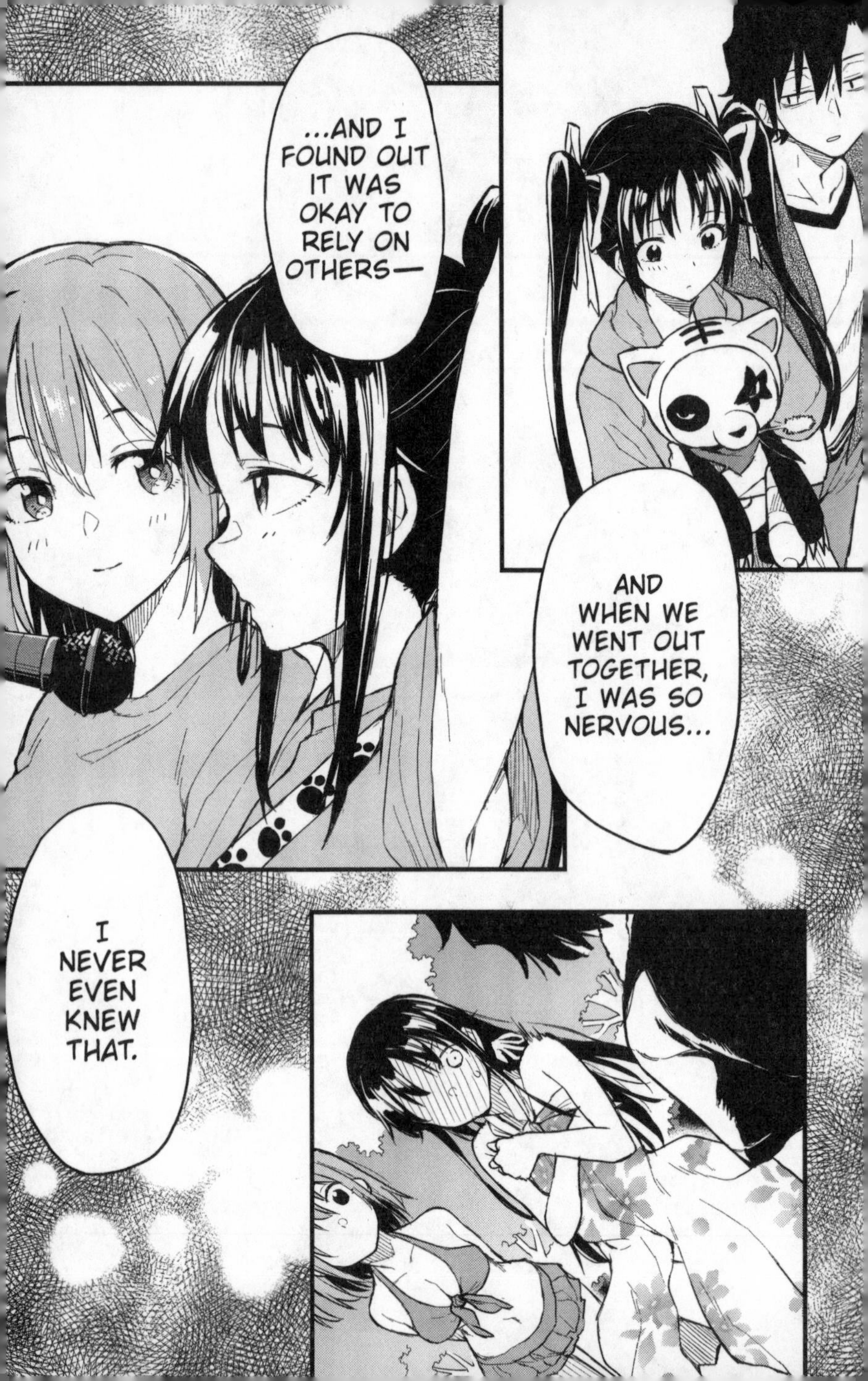
...AND I FOUND OUT IT WAS OKAY TO RELY ON OTHERS—
AND WHEN WE WENT OUT TOGETHER, I WAS SO NERVOUS...
I NEVER EVEN KNEW THAT.

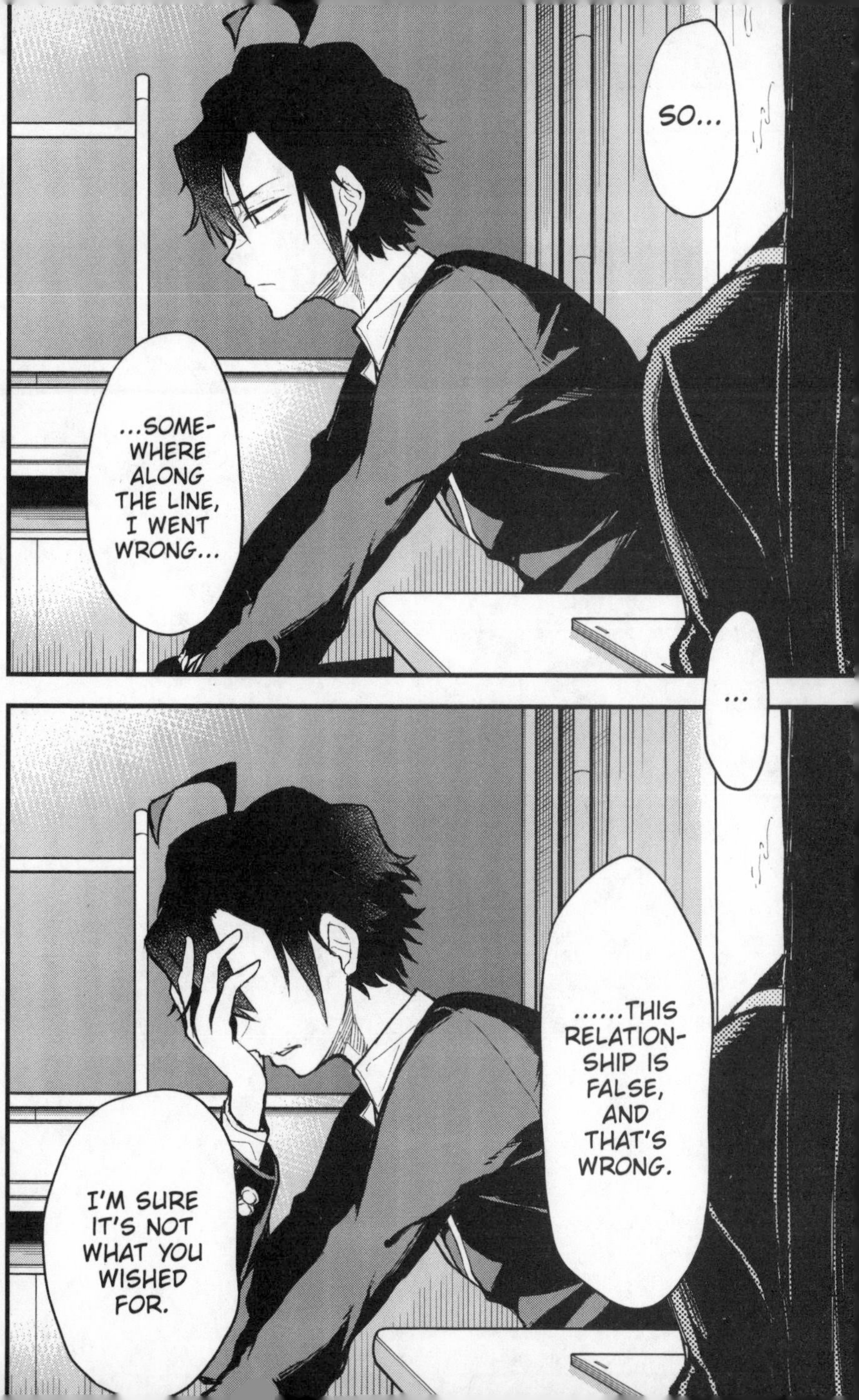
SO...
...SOME-WHERE ALONG THE LINE, I WENT WRONG...
...
......THIS RELATION-SHIP IS FALSE, AND THAT'S WRONG.
I'M SURE IT'S NOT WHAT YOU WISHED FOR.

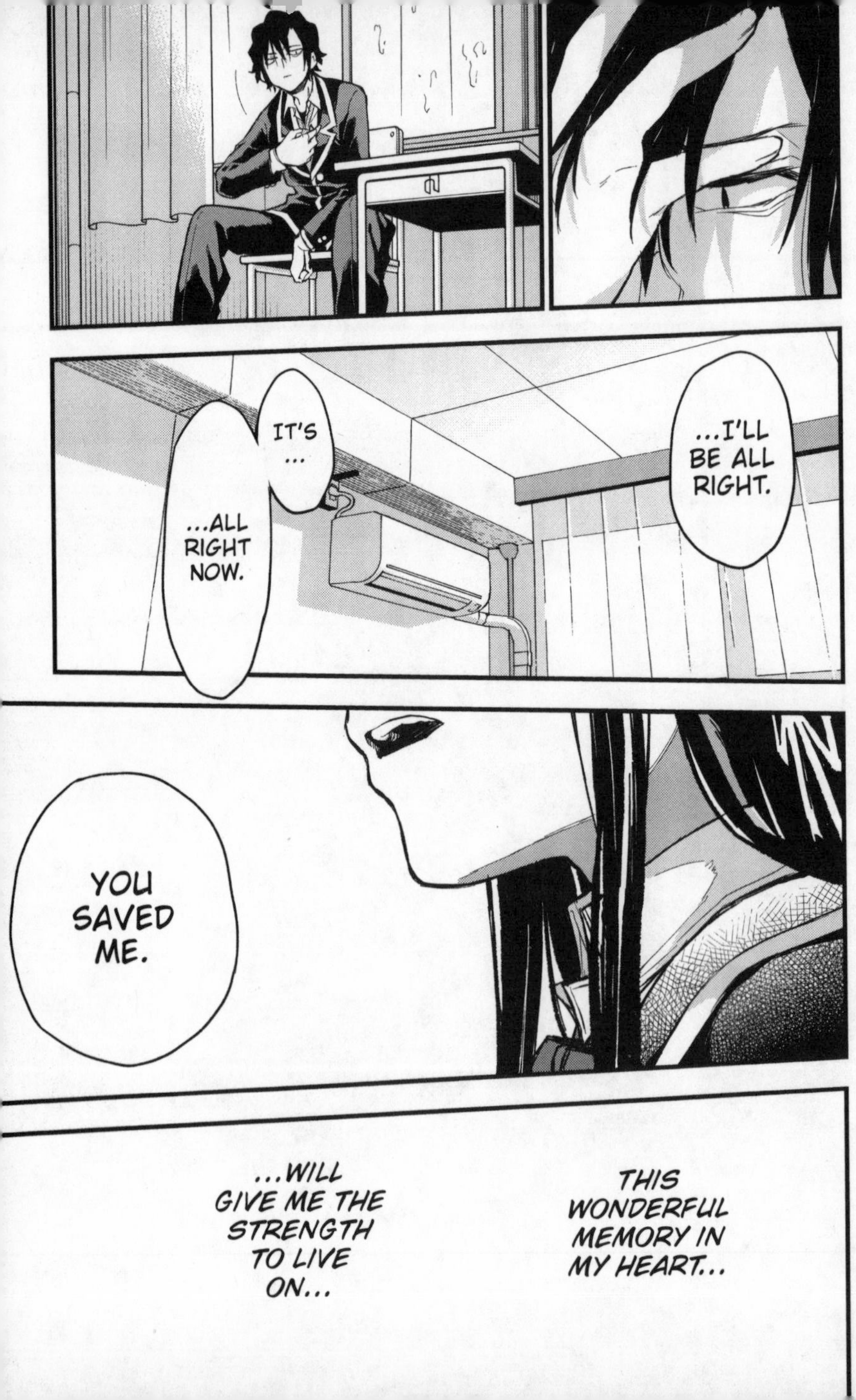
...I'LL BE ALL RIGHT.
IT'S...
...ALL RIGHT NOW.
YOU SAVED ME.
THIS WONDERFUL MEMORY IN MY HEART...
...WILL GIVE ME THE STRENGTH TO LIVE ON...

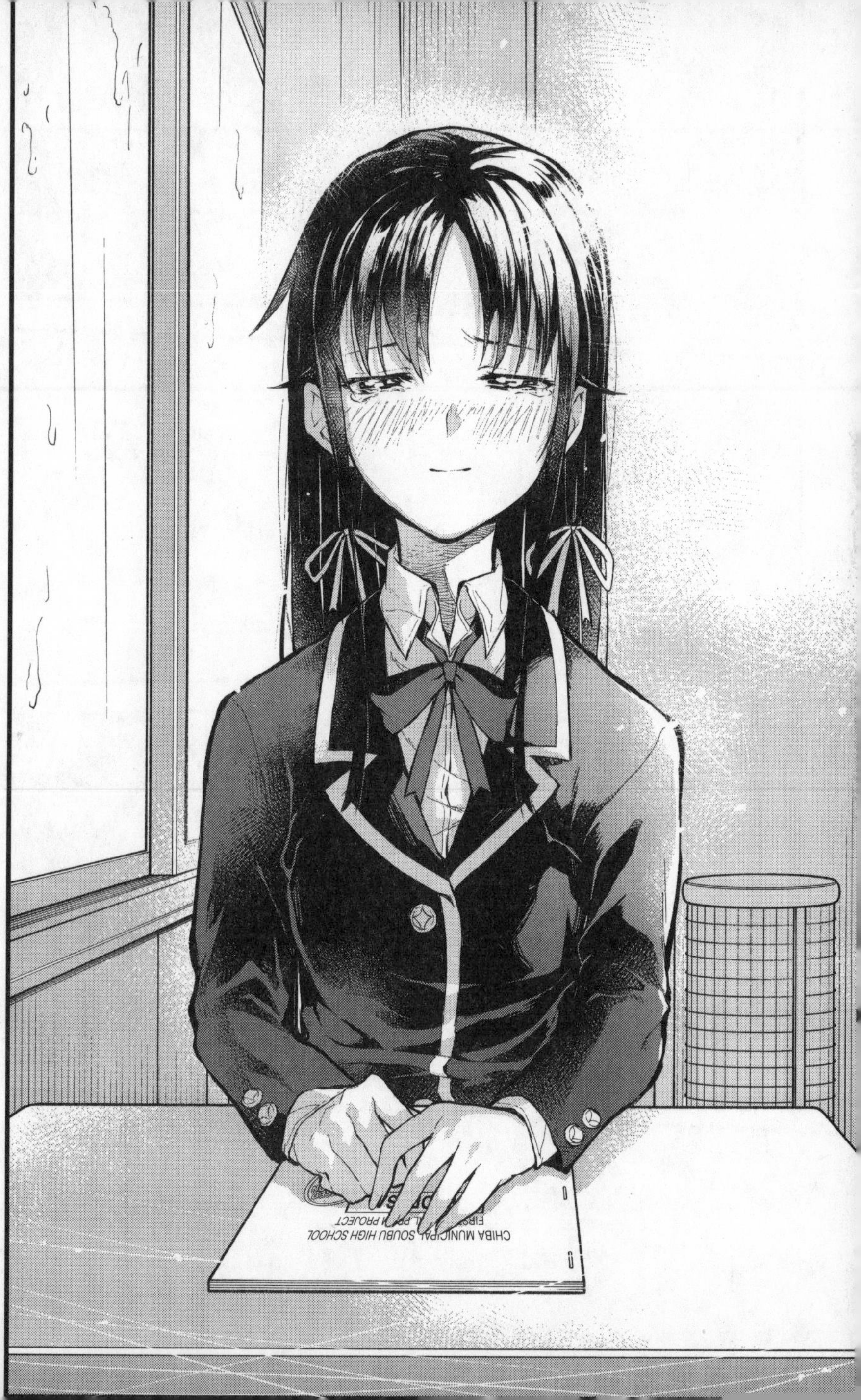
CHIBA MUNICIPAL SOUBU HIGH SCHOOL

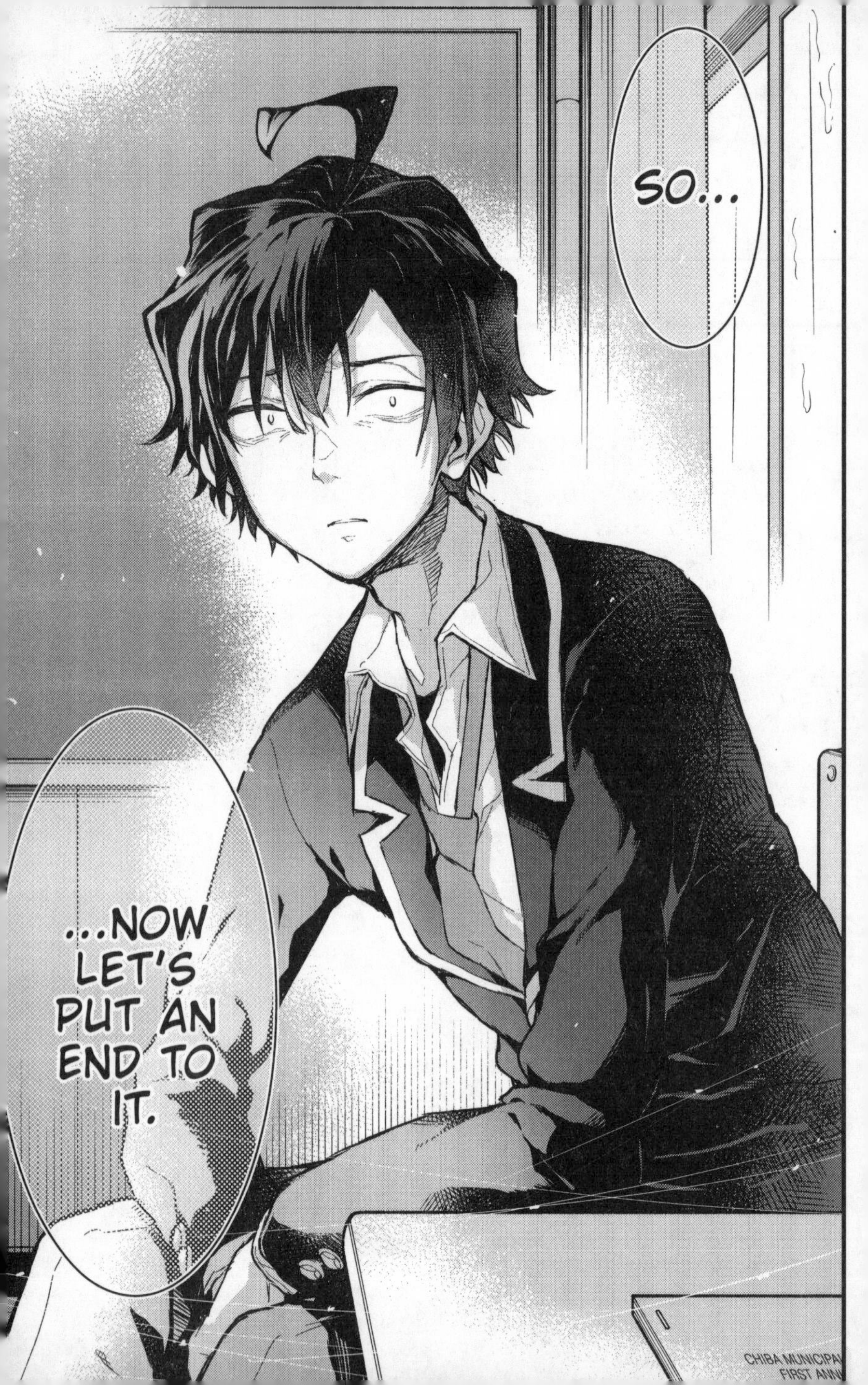
SO...
...NOW LET'S PUT AN END TO IT.
CHIBA MUNICIPA
FIRST ANN

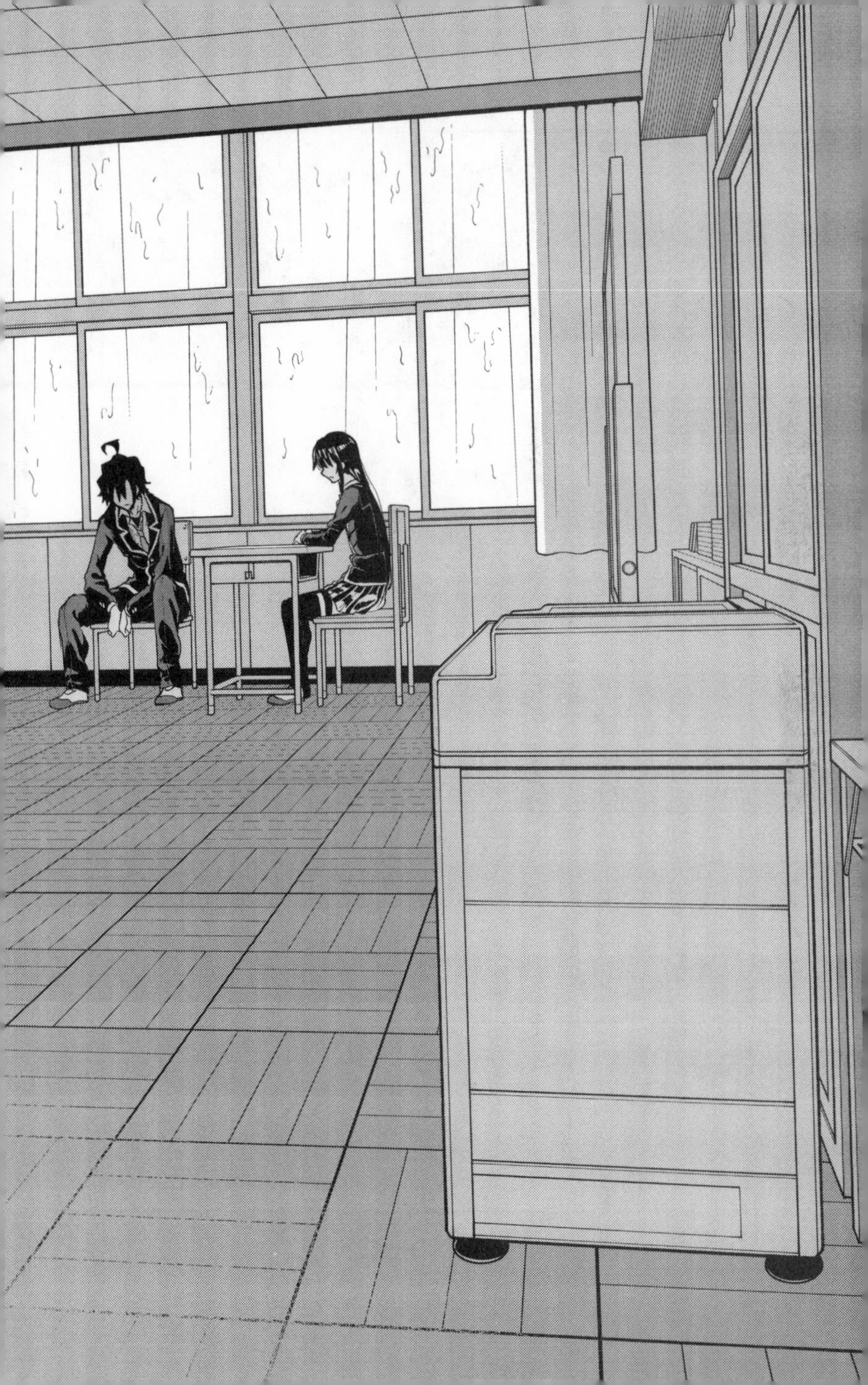

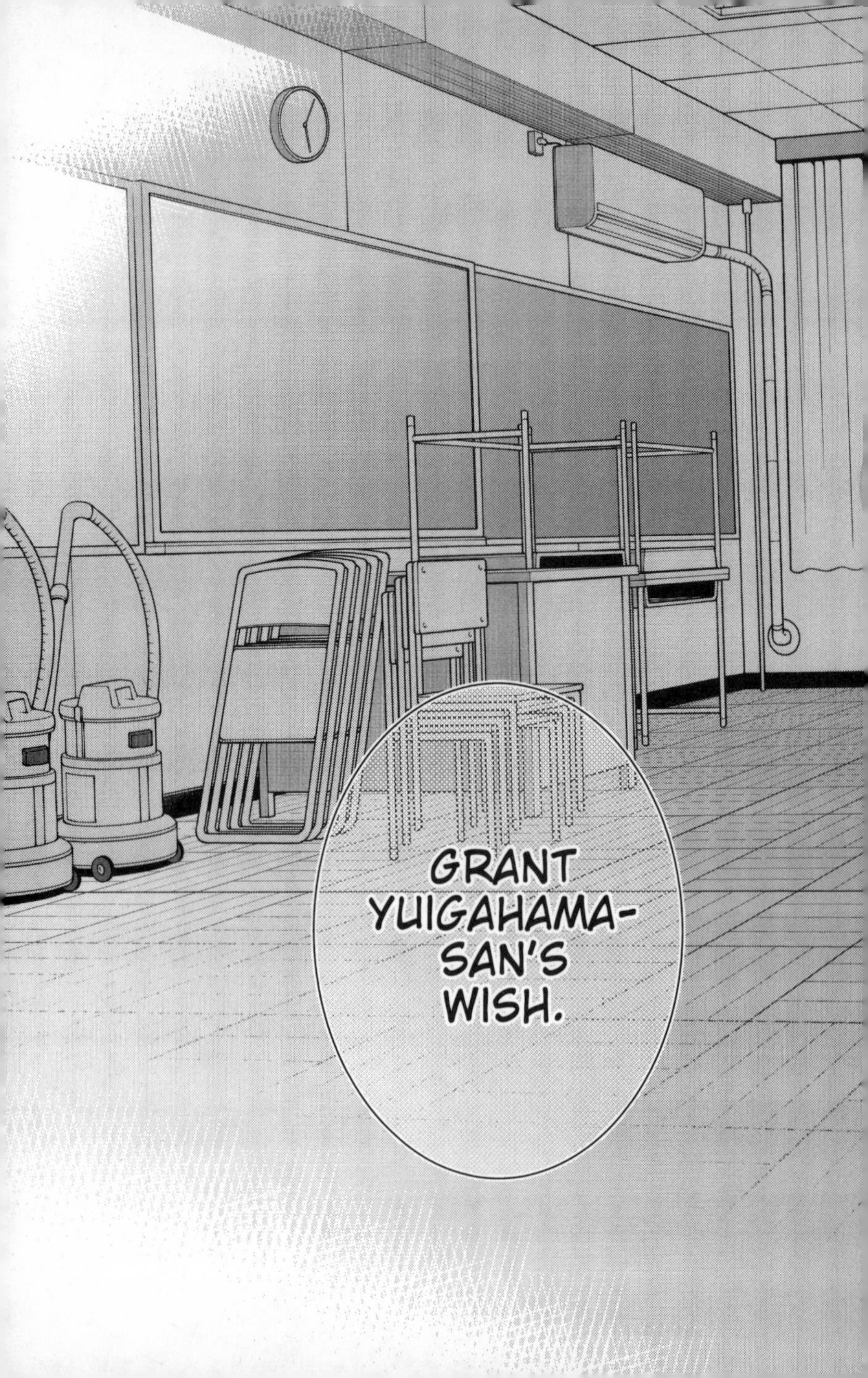
GRANT YUIGAHAMA-SAN'S WISH.

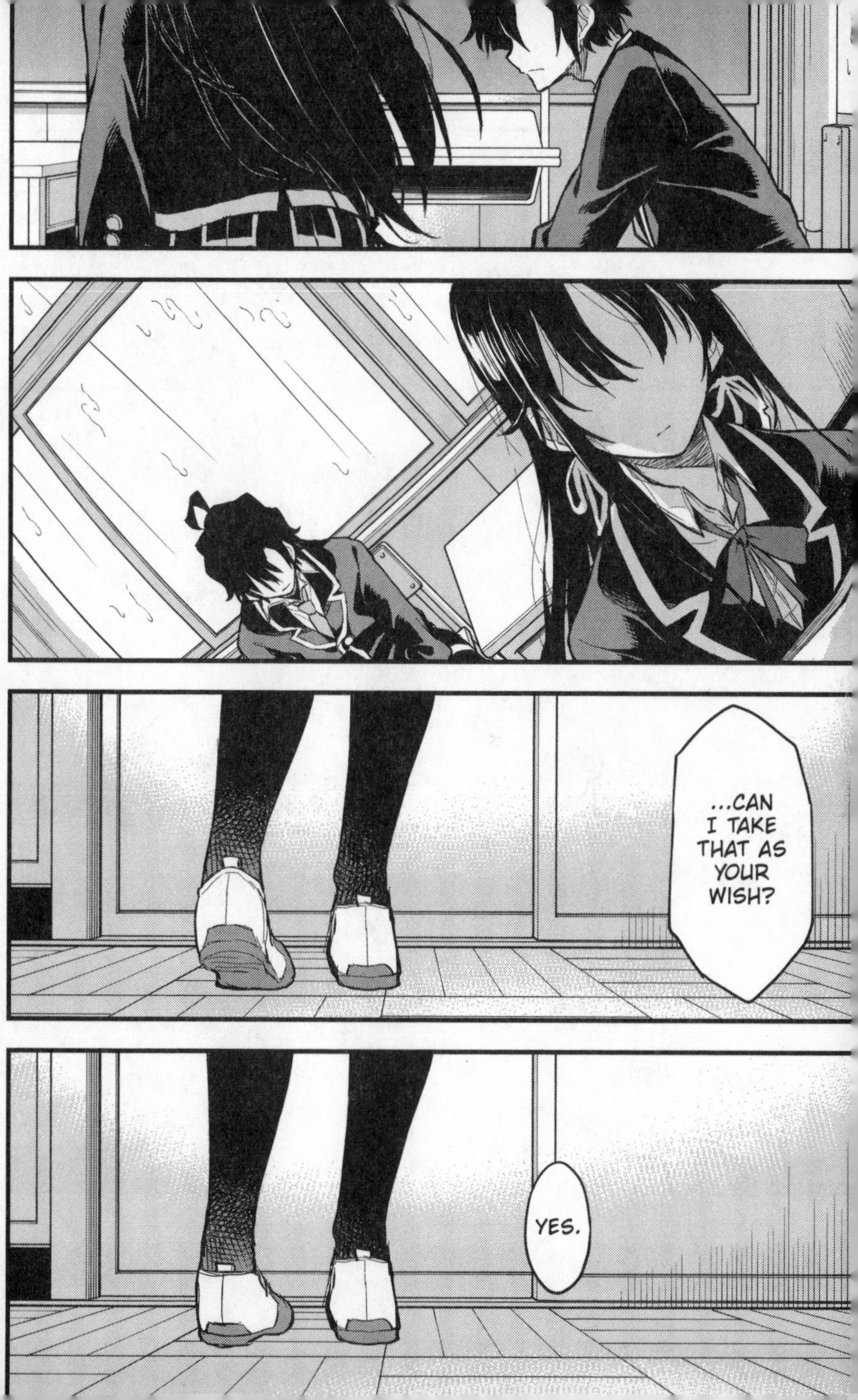
...CAN I TAKE THAT AS YOUR WISH?
YES.

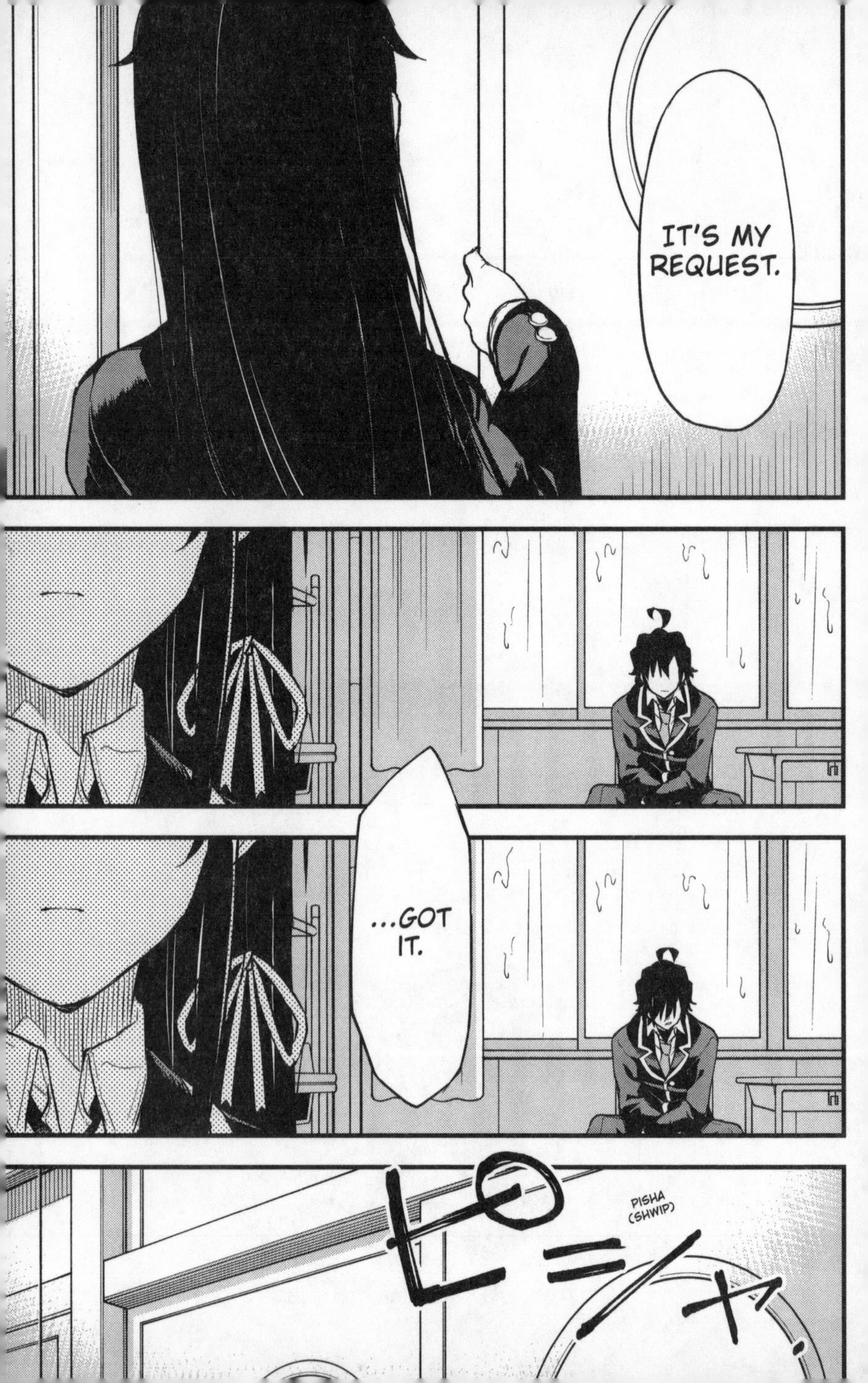
IT'S MY REQUEST.
...GOT IT.
PISHA (SHWIP)

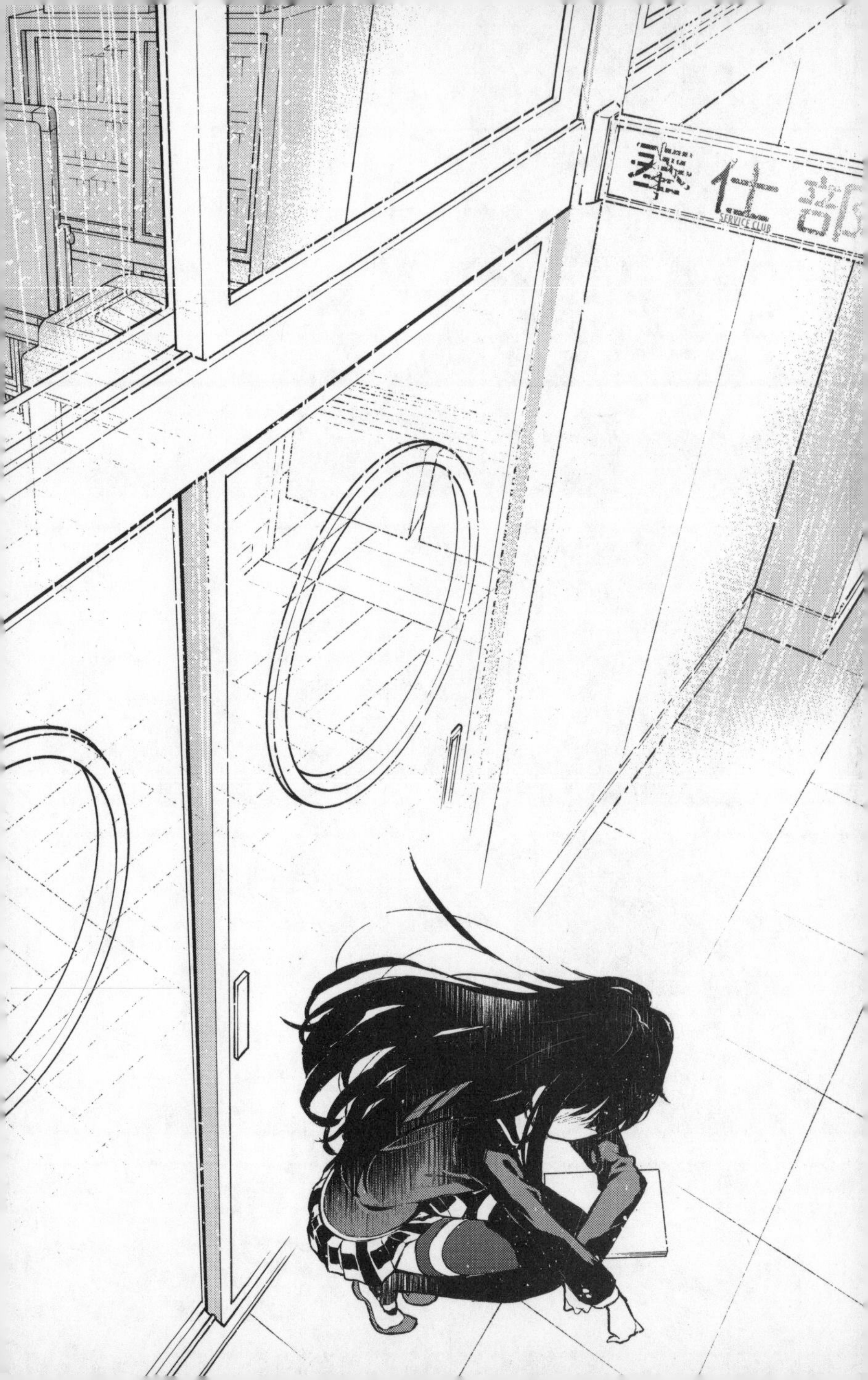
奉仕部
SERVICE CLUB

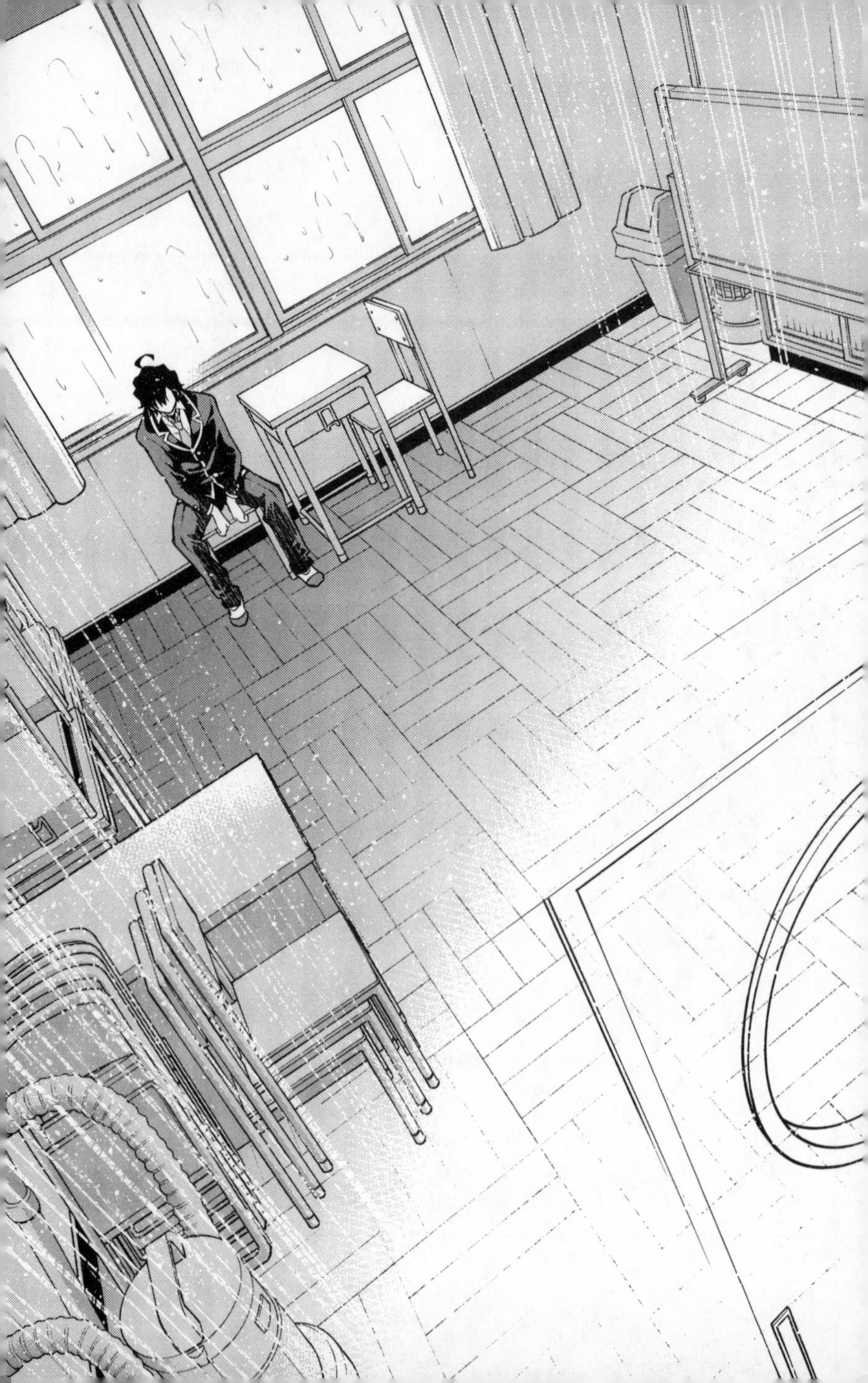

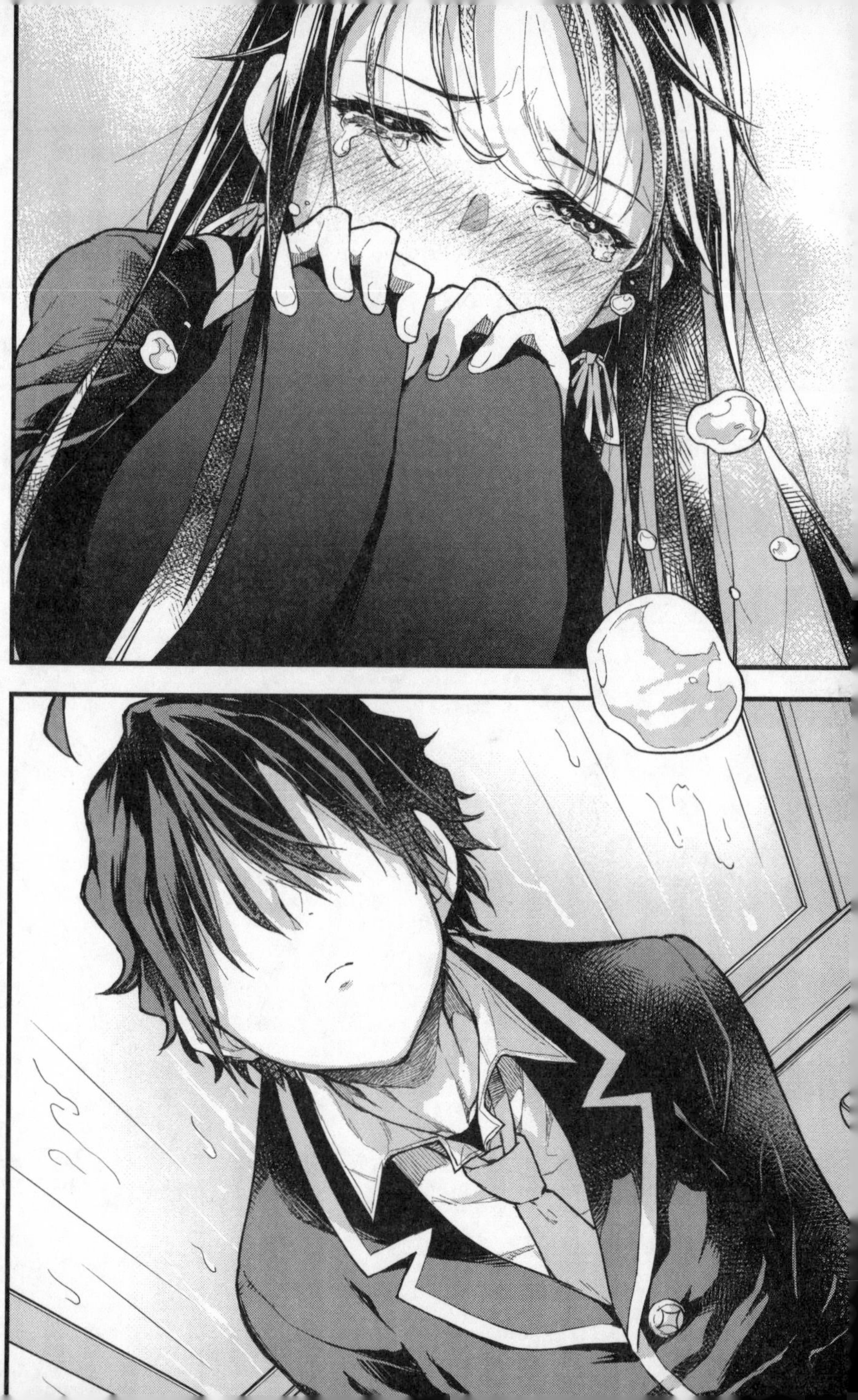

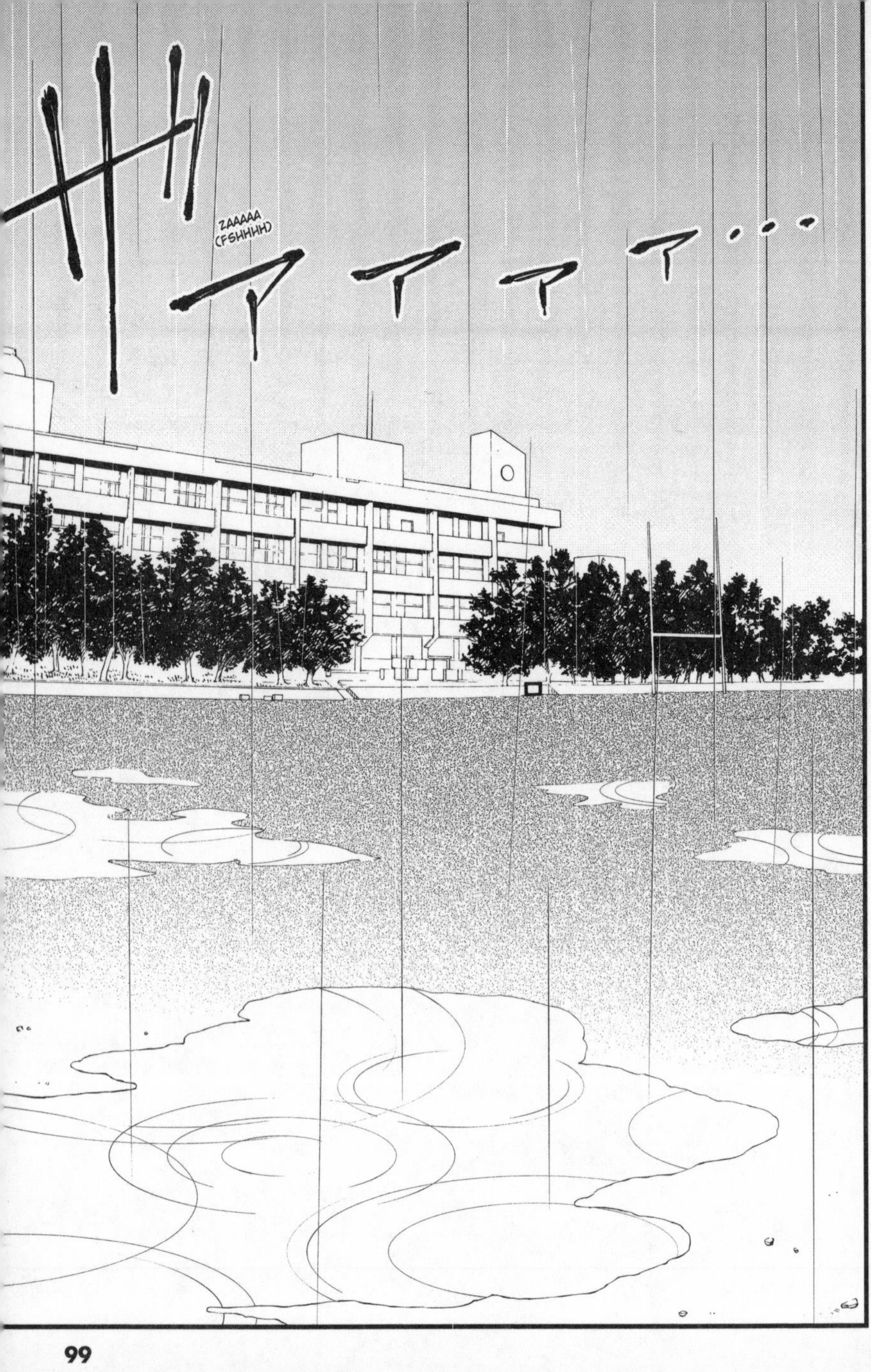
ザアアアア…
ZAAAAA (FSHHHH)

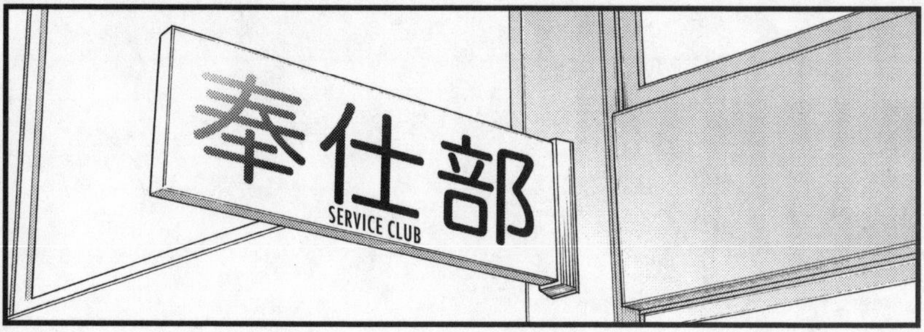
奉仕部
SERVICE CLUB

—PLEASE LET THIS BE...

...THE RIGHT ENDING.

Today

Can we meet now?

Read

ka sa

ke space

...YUKI-NON.

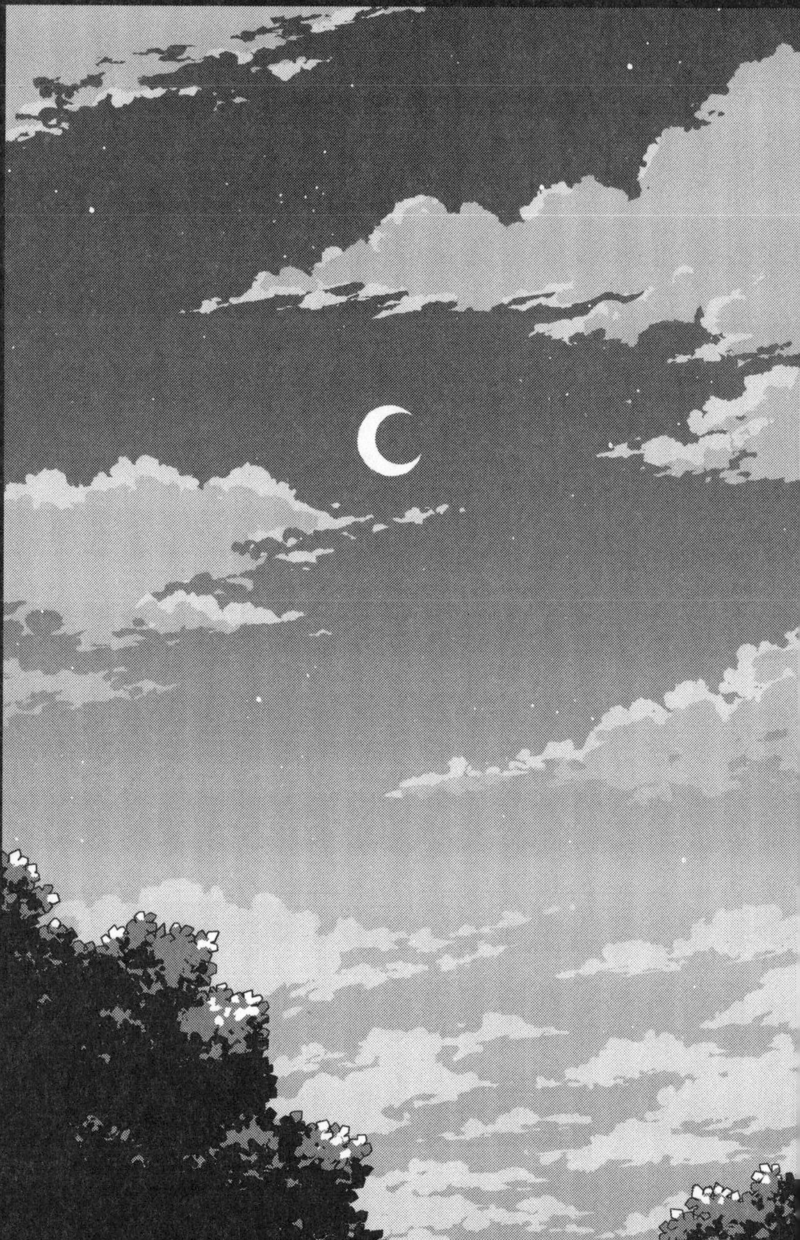

CHAPTER 104 — NEVERTHELESS, HACHIMAN HIKIGAYA'S LIFE GOES ON.

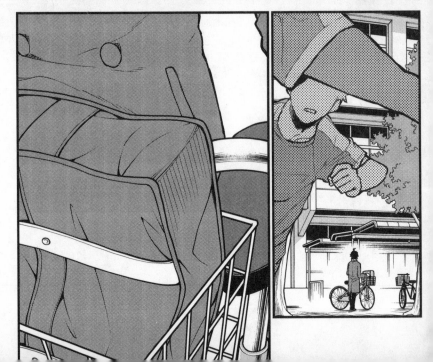

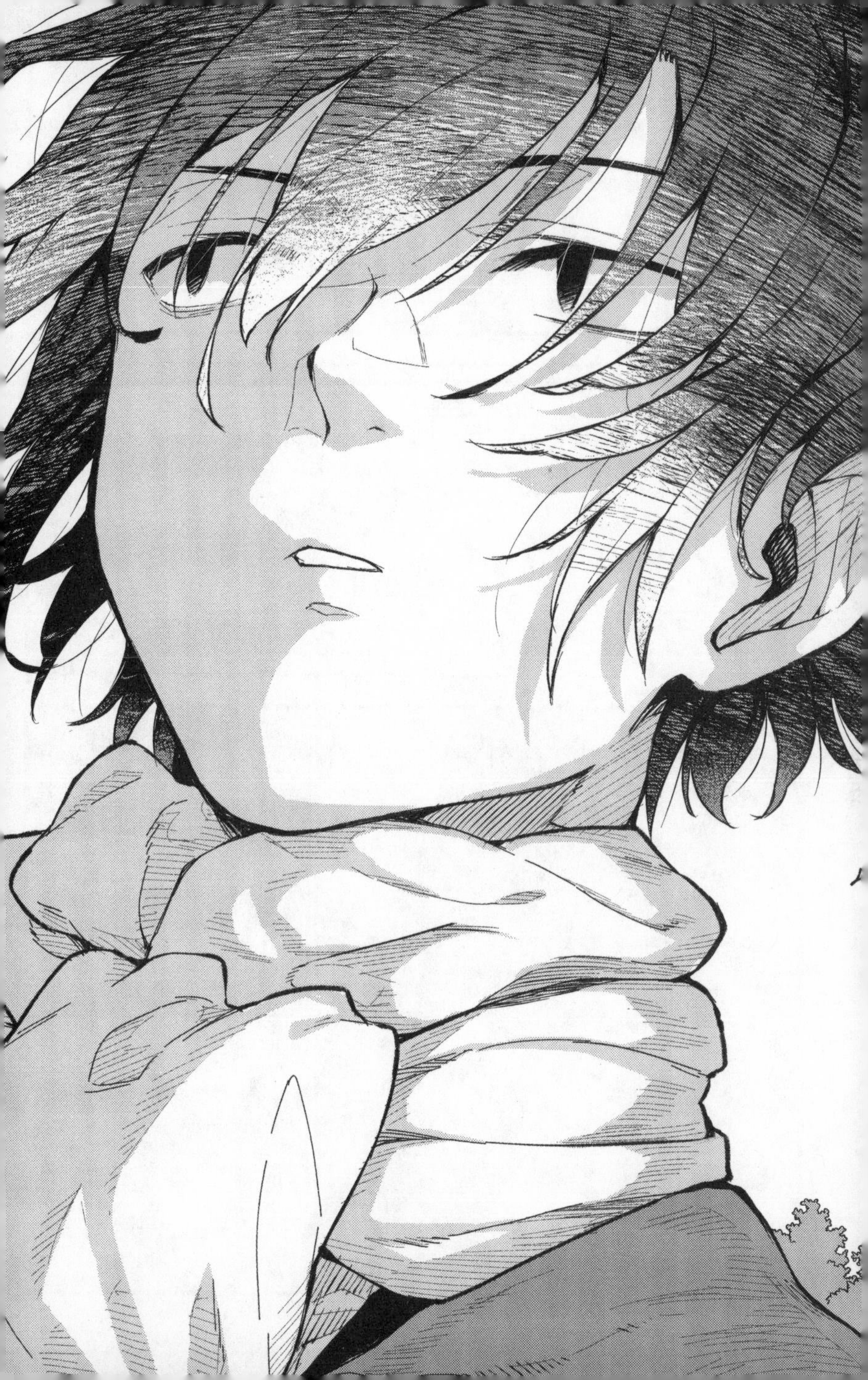

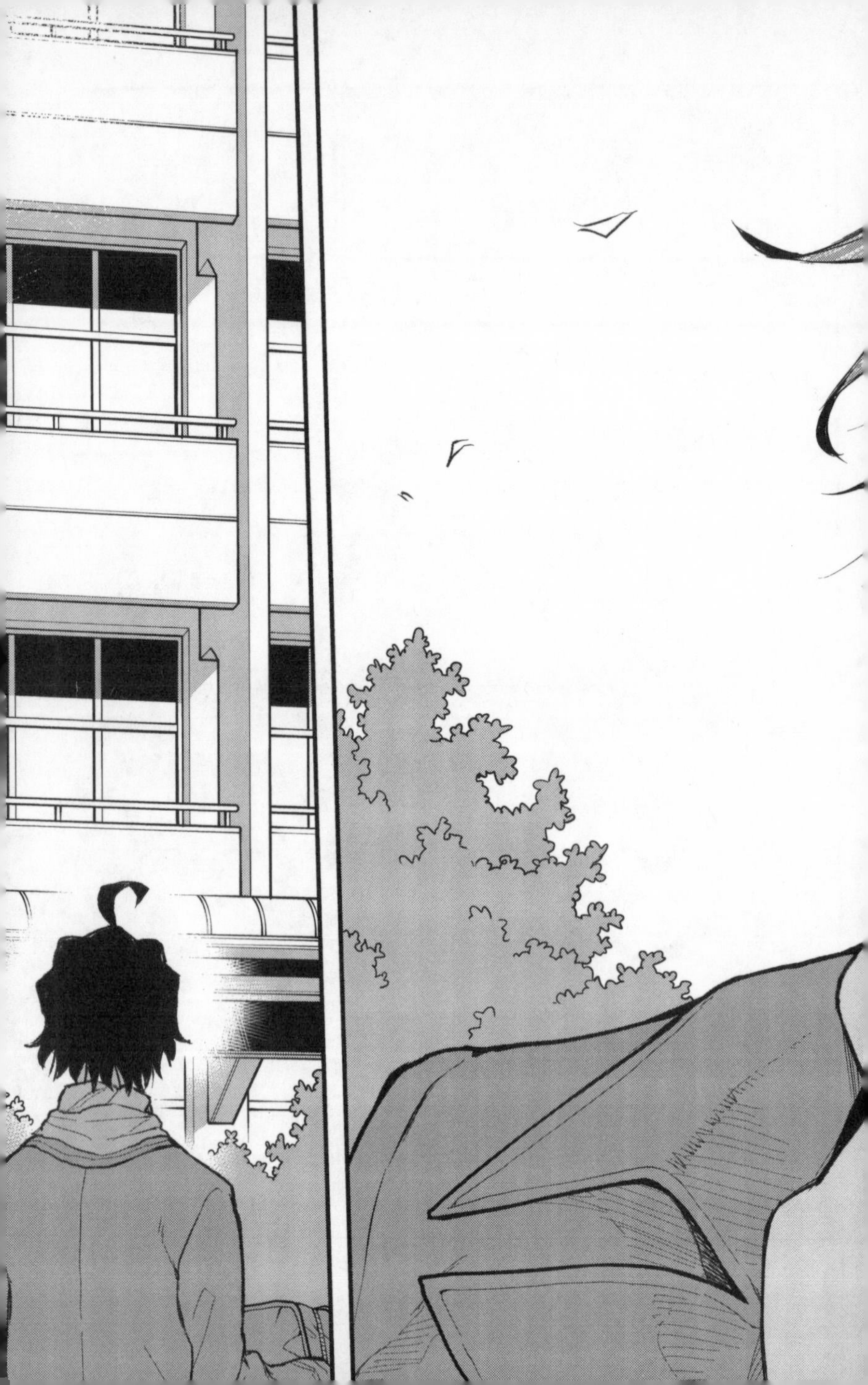

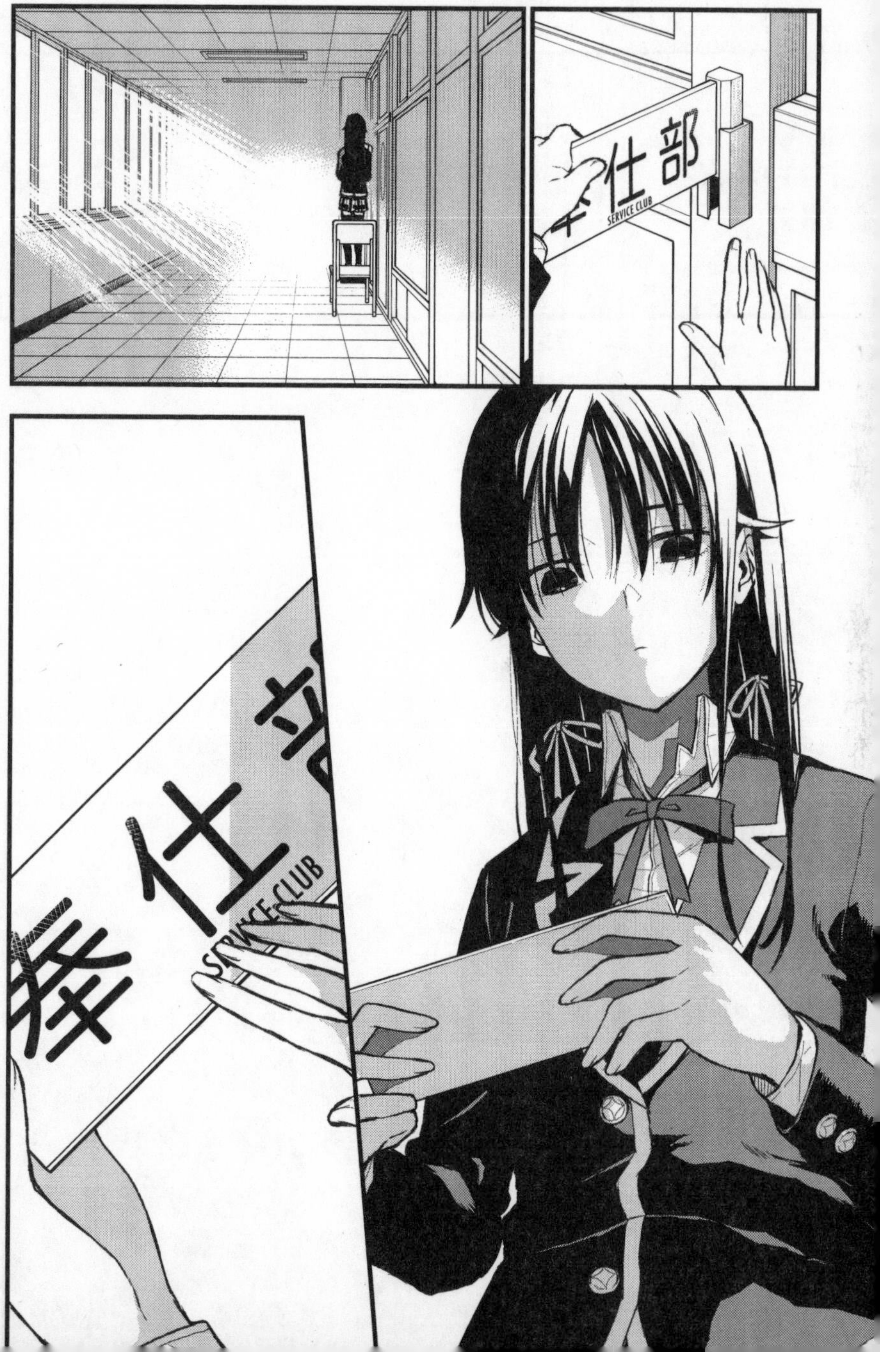
仕部
SERVICE CLUB

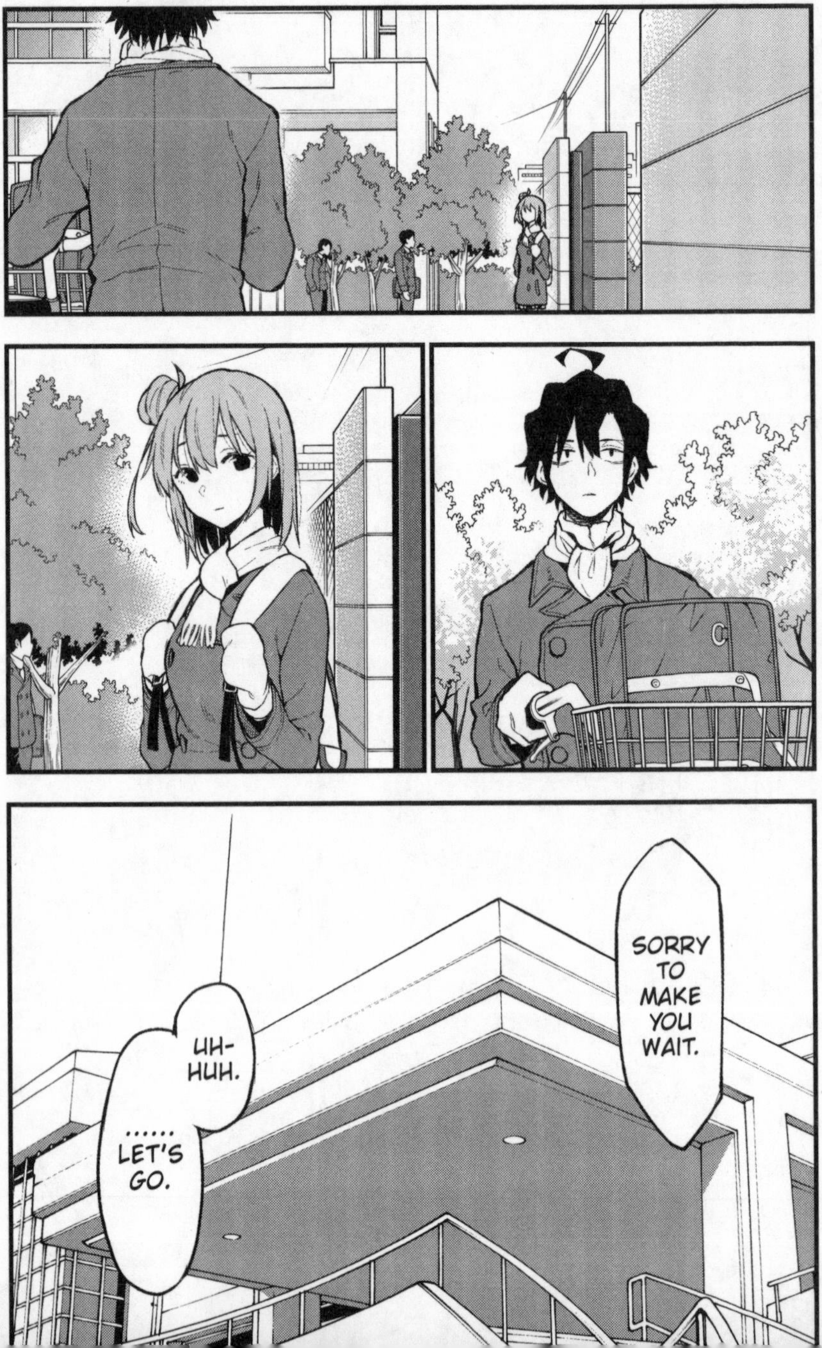
SORRY TO MAKE YOU WAIT.
UH-HUH.
...... LET'S GO.

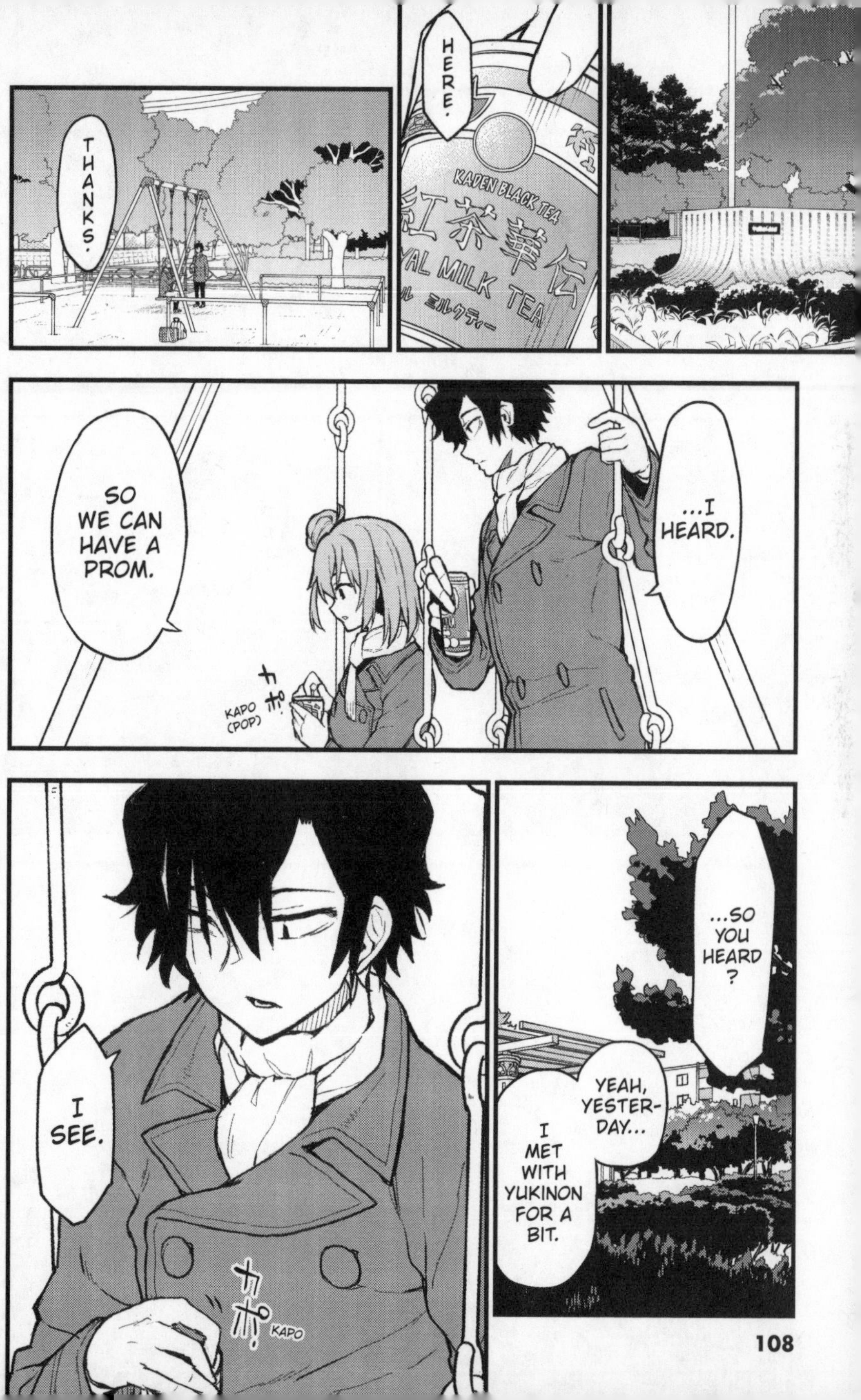
HERE.
KADEN BLACK TEA
紅茶華伝
YAL MILK TEA
ミルクティー
THANKS.
...I HEARD.
SO WE CAN HAVE A PROM.
カポ
KAPO (POP)
...SO YOU HEARD?
YEAH, YESTERDAY...
I MET WITH YUKINON FOR A BIT.
I SEE.
カポ
KAPO

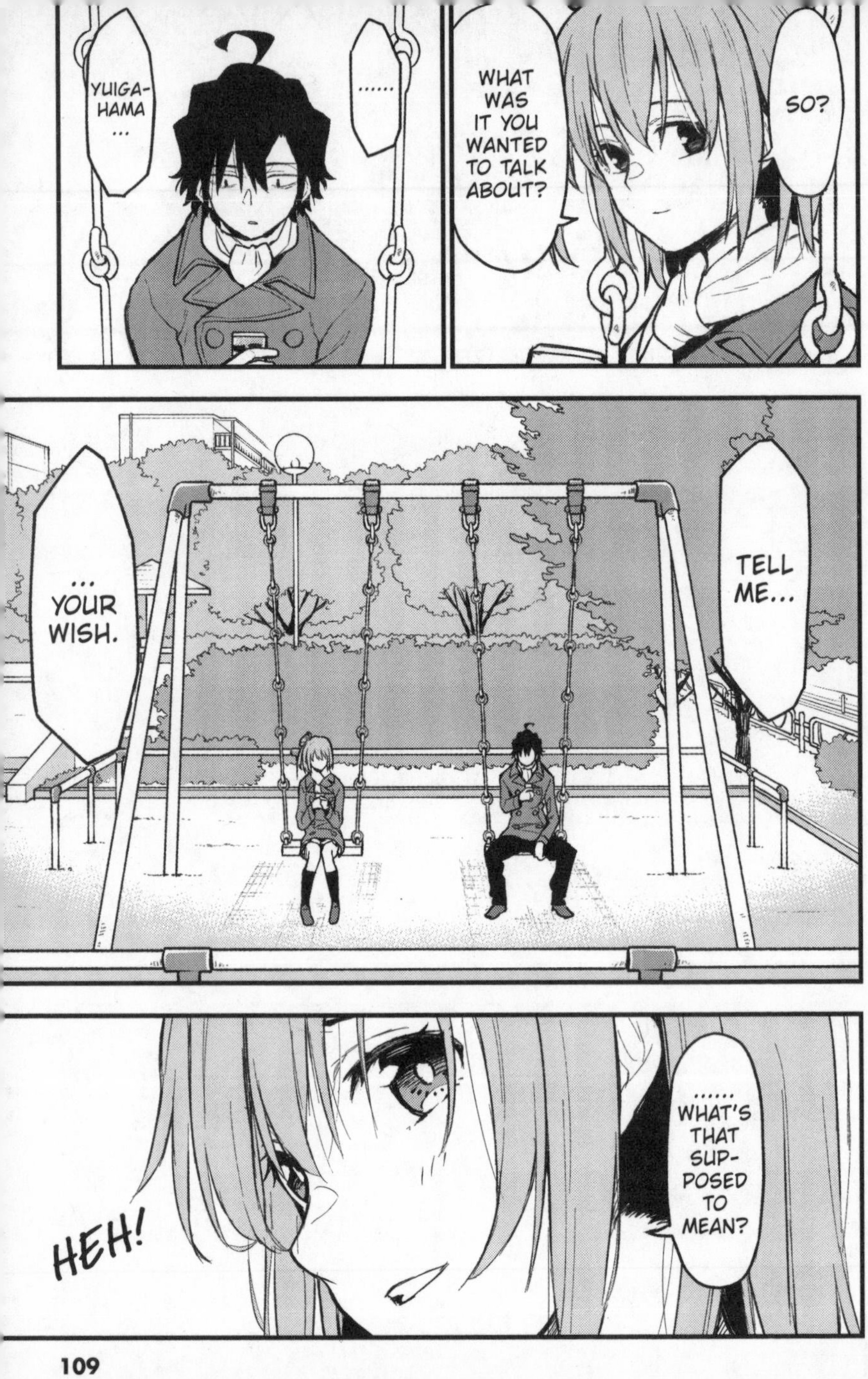
SO?
WHAT WAS IT YOU WANTED TO TALK ABOUT?
......
YUIGA-HAMA...
TELL ME...
...YOUR WISH.
......WHAT'S THAT SUP-POSED TO MEAN?
HEH!

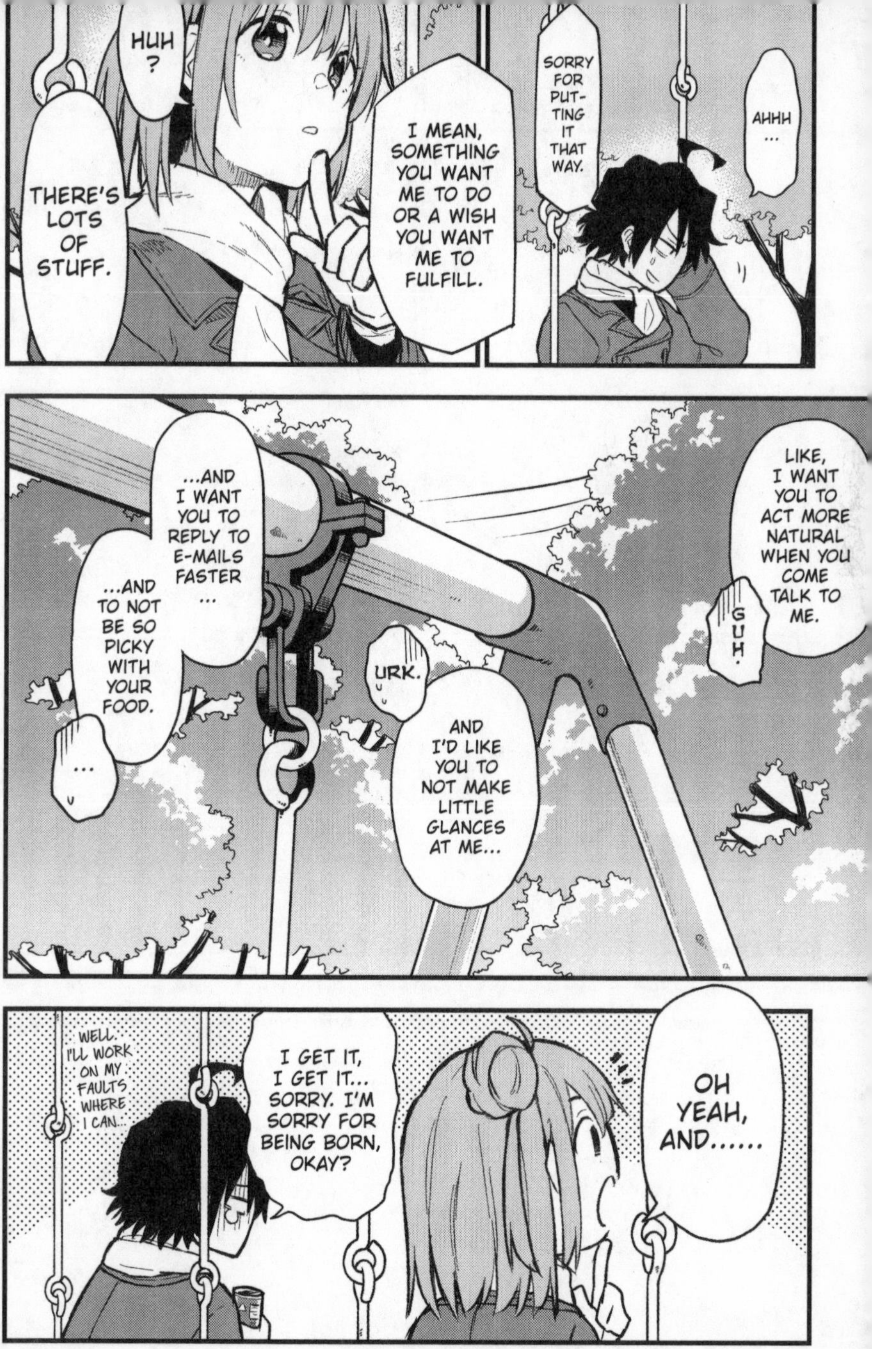
AHHH...
SORRY FOR PUT-TING IT THAT WAY.
I MEAN, SOMETHING YOU WANT ME TO DO OR A WISH YOU WANT ME TO FULFILL.
HUH?
THERE'S LOTS OF STUFF.
LIKE, I WANT YOU TO ACT MORE NATURAL WHEN YOU COME TALK TO ME.
GUH.
AND I'D LIKE YOU TO NOT MAKE LITTLE GLANCES AT ME...
URK.
...AND I WANT YOU TO REPLY TO E-MAILS FASTER...
...AND TO NOT BE SO PICKY WITH YOUR FOOD.
...
OH YEAH, AND......
I GET IT, I GET IT... SORRY. I'M SORRY FOR BEING BORN, OKAY?
WELL. I'LL WORK ON MY FAULTS WHERE I CAN...

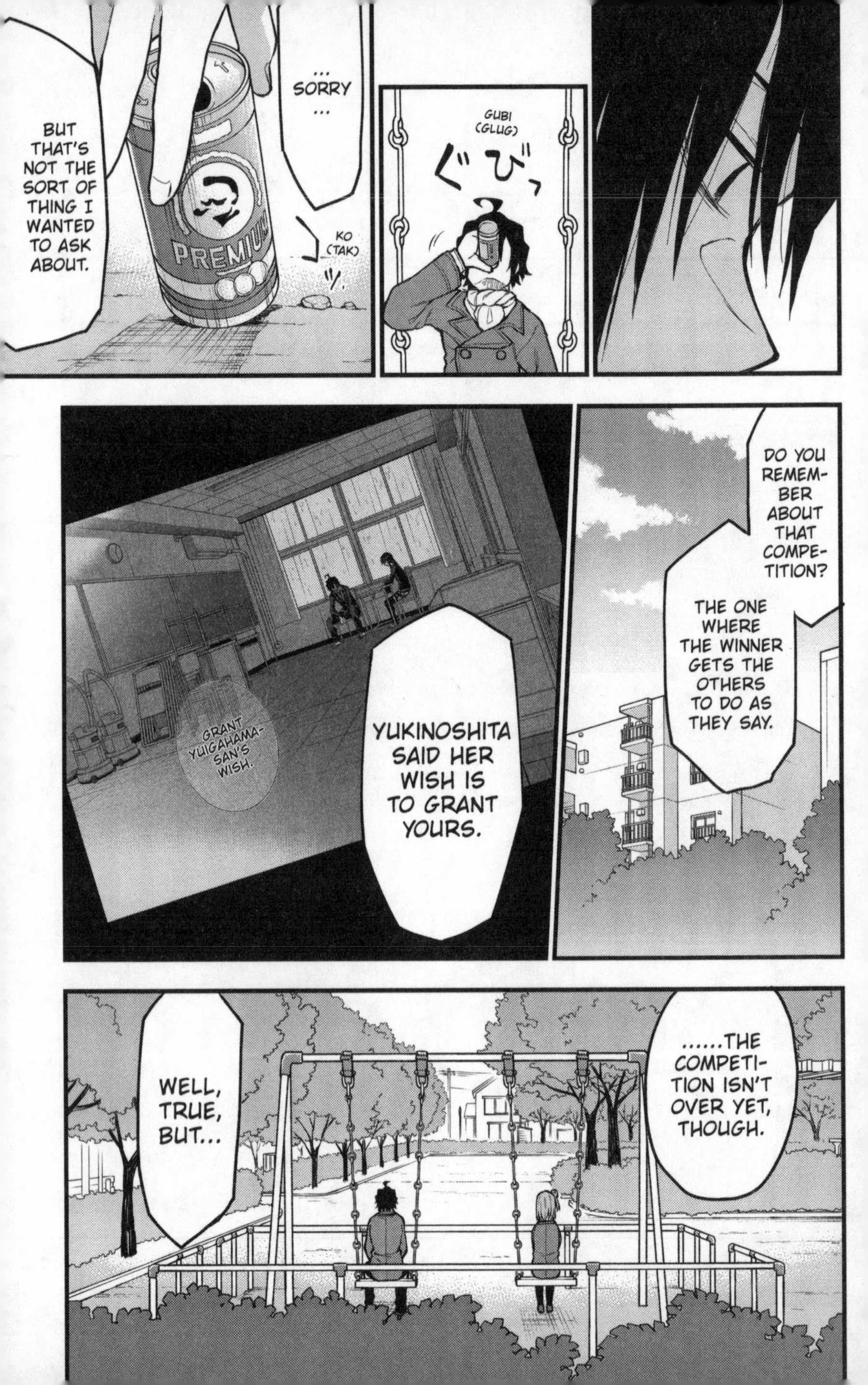
GUBI (GLUG)
ぐびっ
...SORRY...
BUT THAT'S NOT THE SORT OF THING I WANTED TO ASK ABOUT.
KO (TAK)
DO YOU REMEMBER ABOUT THAT COMPETITION?
THE ONE WHERE THE WINNER GETS THE OTHERS TO DO AS THEY SAY.
YUKINOSHITA SAID HER WISH IS TO GRANT YOURS.
GRANT YUIGAHAMA-SAN'S WISH.
......THE COMPETITION ISN'T OVER YET, THOUGH.
WELL, TRUE, BUT...

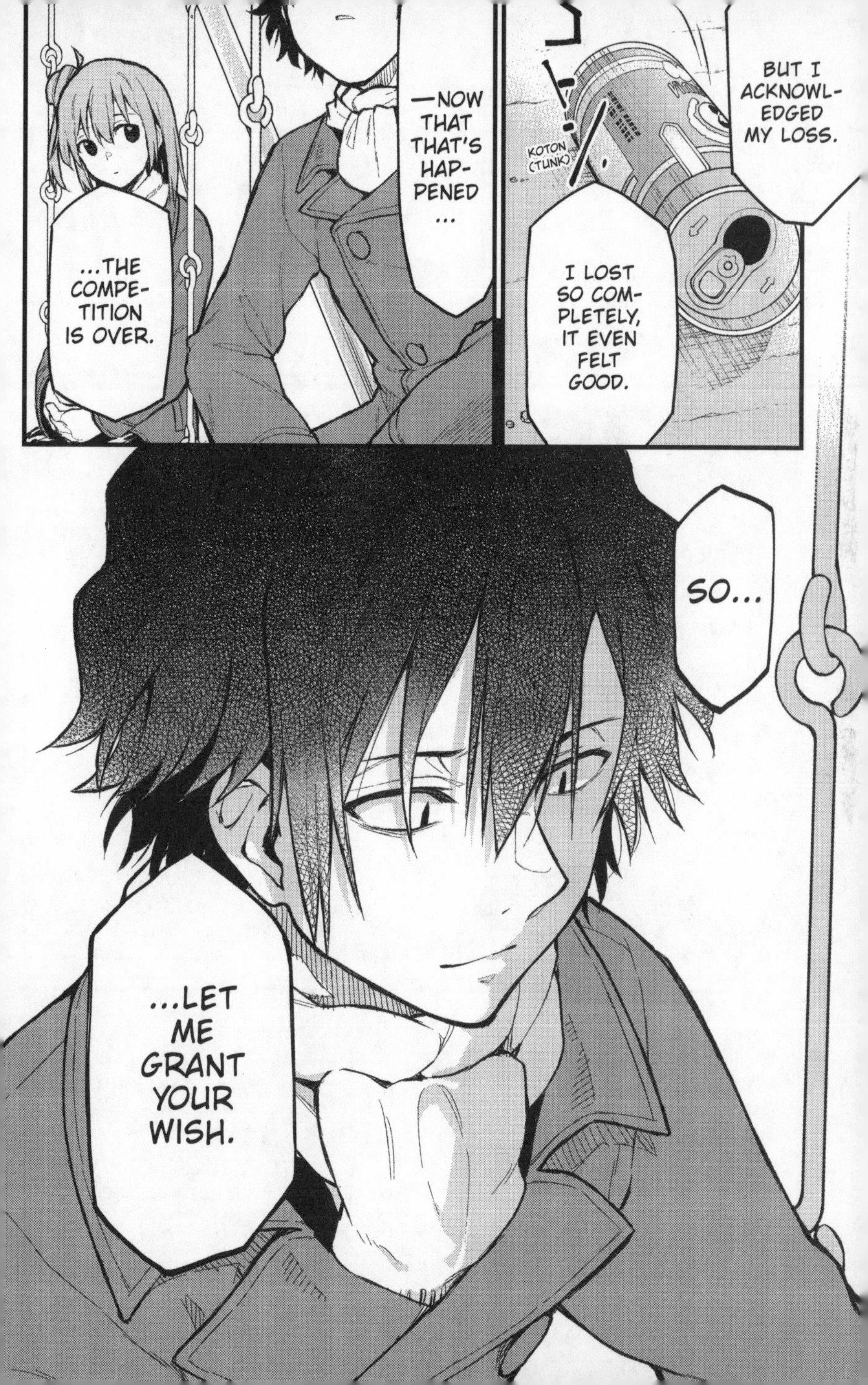
BUT I ACKNOWLEDGED MY LOSS.
KOTON (TUNK)
I LOST SO COMPLETELY, IT EVEN FELT GOOD.
—NOW THAT THAT'S HAPPENED...
...THE COMPETITION IS OVER.
SO...
...LET ME GRANT YOUR WISH.

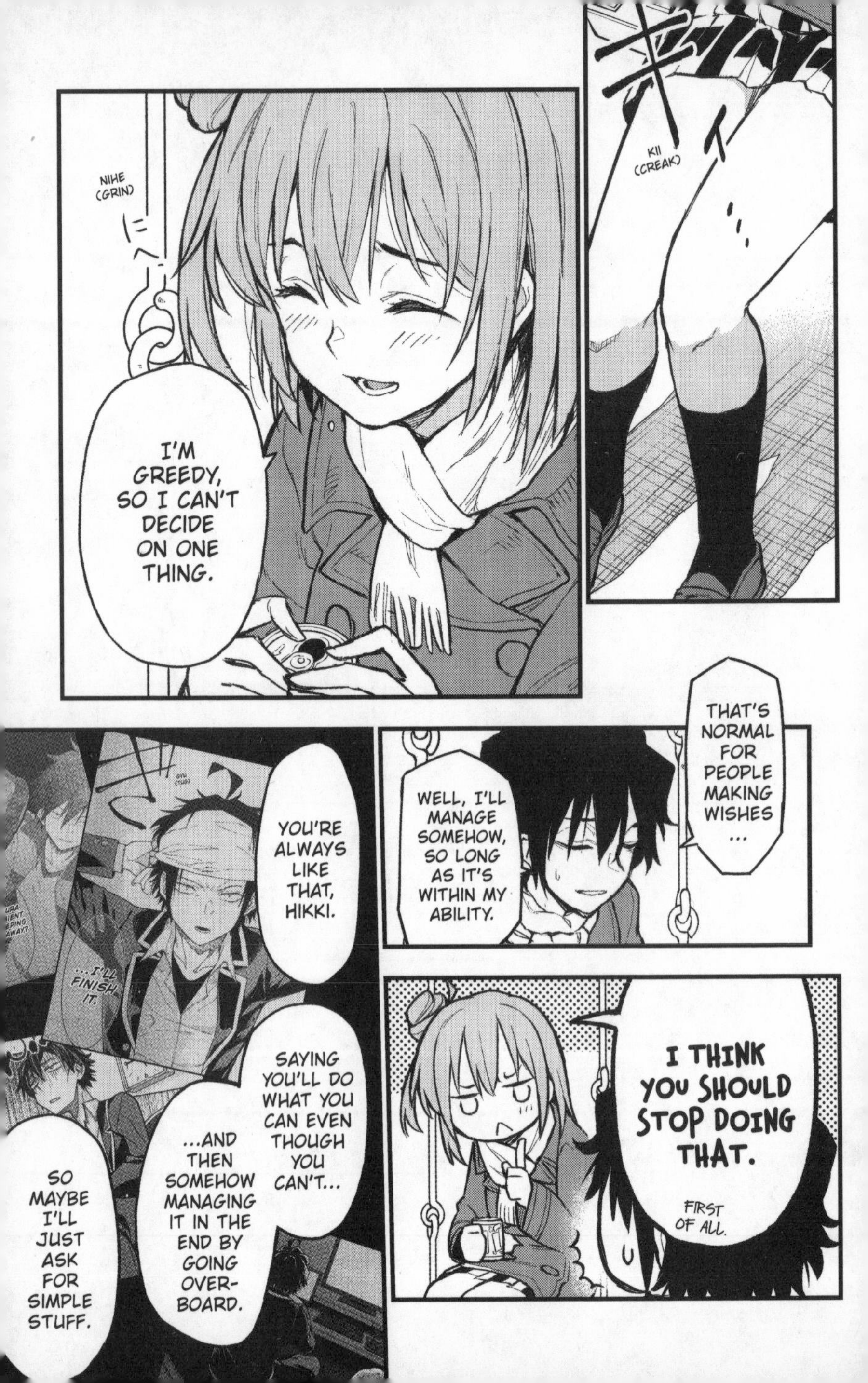
KII
(CREAK)
NIHE
(GRIN)
I'M GREEDY, SO I CAN'T DECIDE ON ONE THING.
THAT'S NORMAL FOR PEOPLE MAKING WISHES...
WELL, I'LL MANAGE SOMEHOW, SO LONG AS IT'S WITHIN MY ABILITY.
I THINK YOU SHOULD STOP DOING THAT.
FIRST OF ALL.
GYU
(TUG)
YOU'RE ALWAYS LIKE THAT, HIKKI.
...I'LL FINISH IT.
SAYING YOU'LL DO WHAT YOU CAN EVEN THOUGH YOU CAN'T...
...AND THEN SOMEHOW MANAGING IT IN THE END BY GOING OVER-BOARD.
SO MAYBE I'LL JUST ASK FOR SIMPLE STUFF.

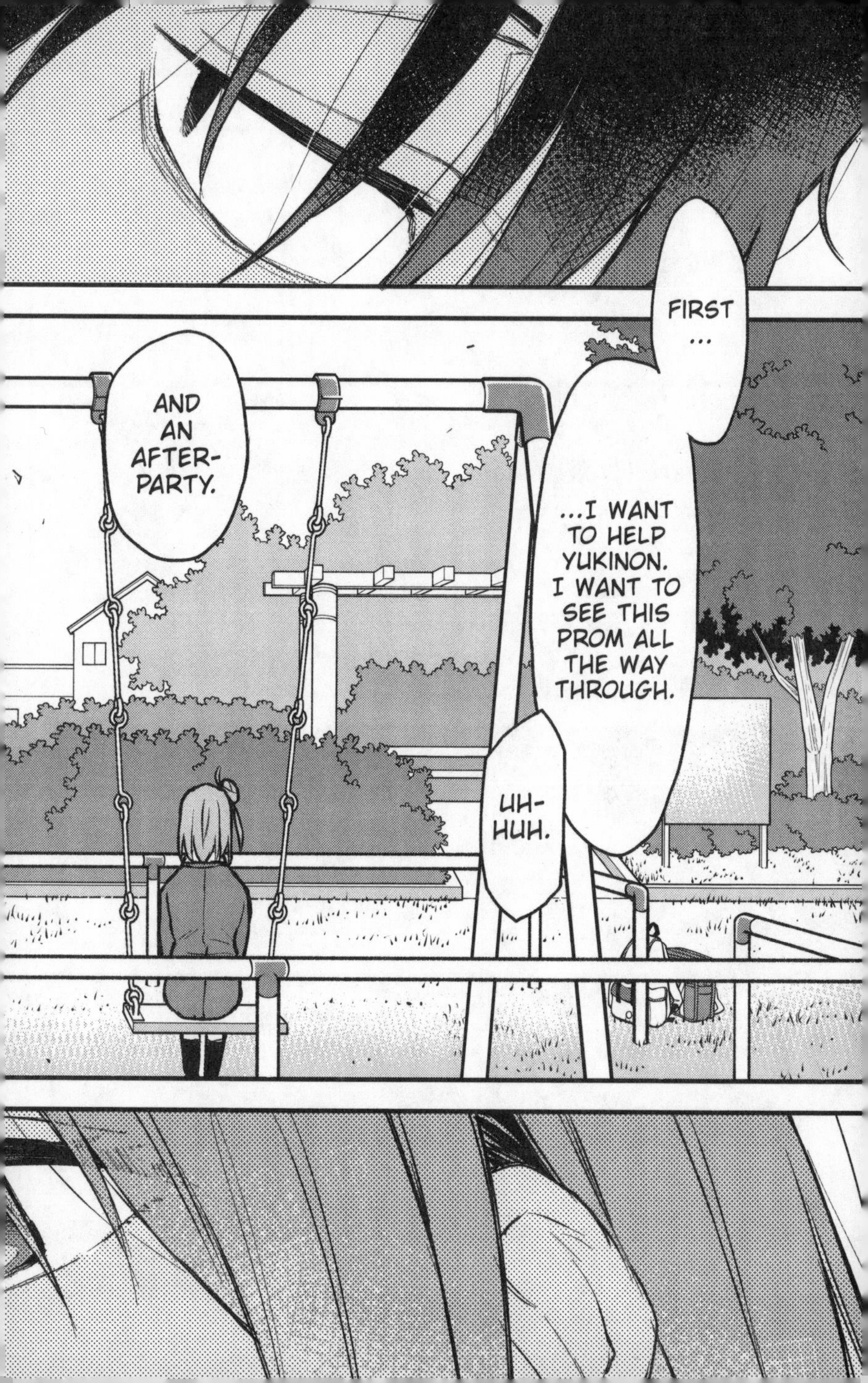
FIRST...
...I WANT TO HELP YUKINON. I WANT TO SEE THIS PROM ALL THE WAY THROUGH.
UH-HUH.
AND AN AFTER-PARTY.

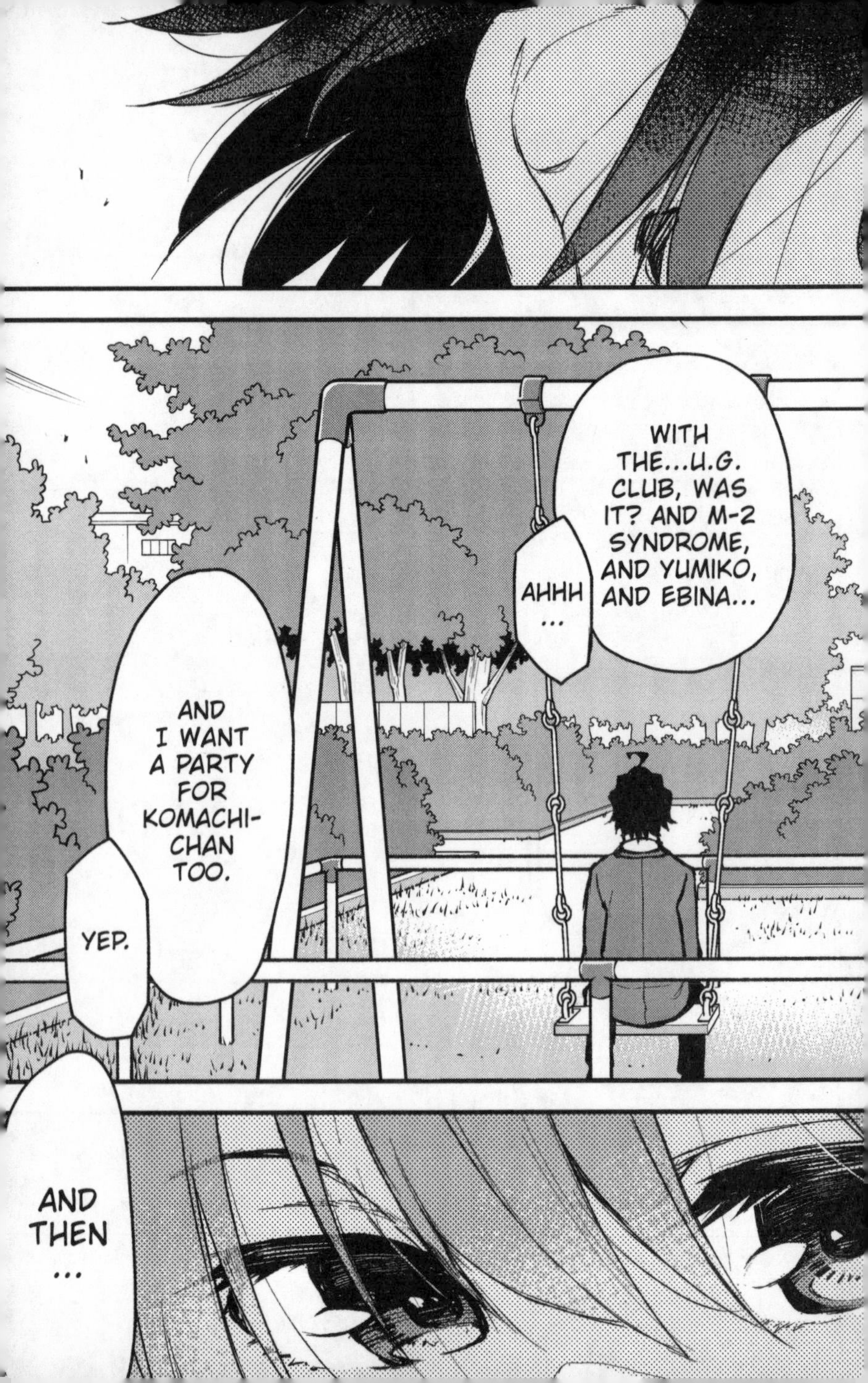
WITH THE...U.G. CLUB, WAS IT? AND M-2 SYNDROME, AND YUMIKO, AND EBINA...
AHHH...
AND I WANT A PARTY FOR KOMACHI-CHAN TOO.
YEP.
AND THEN...

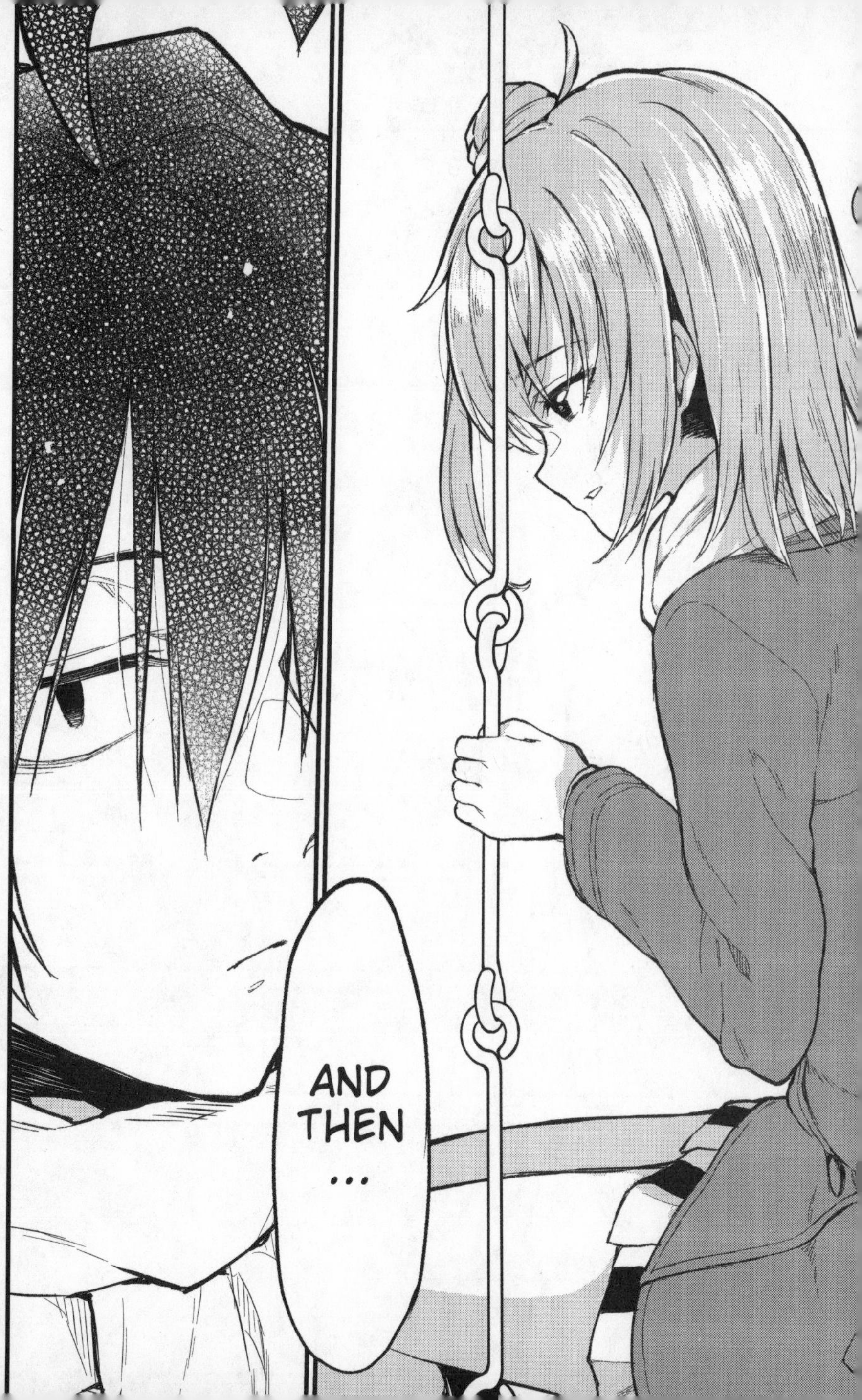
AND THEN ...

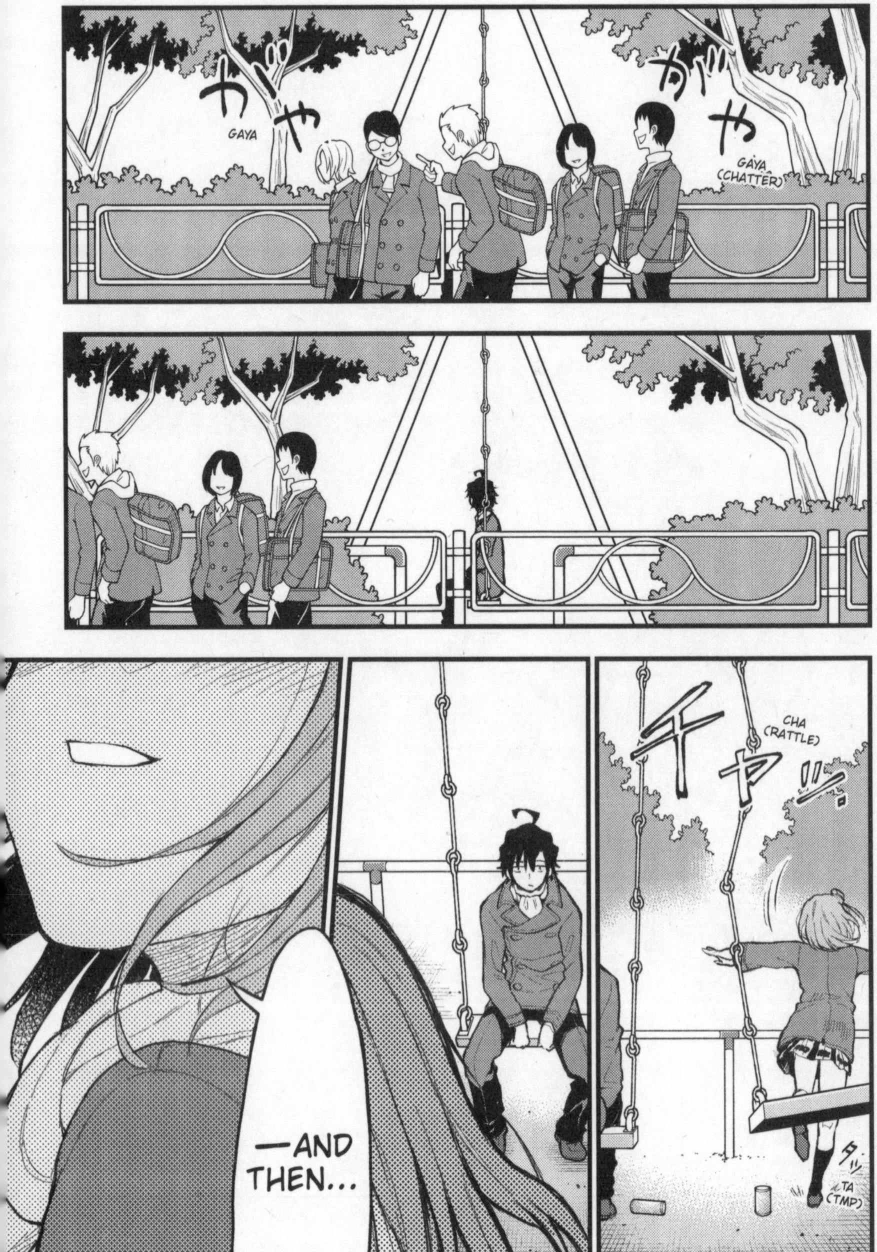
GAYA (CHATTER)
GAYA
CHA (RATTLE)
TA (TMP)
—AND THEN…

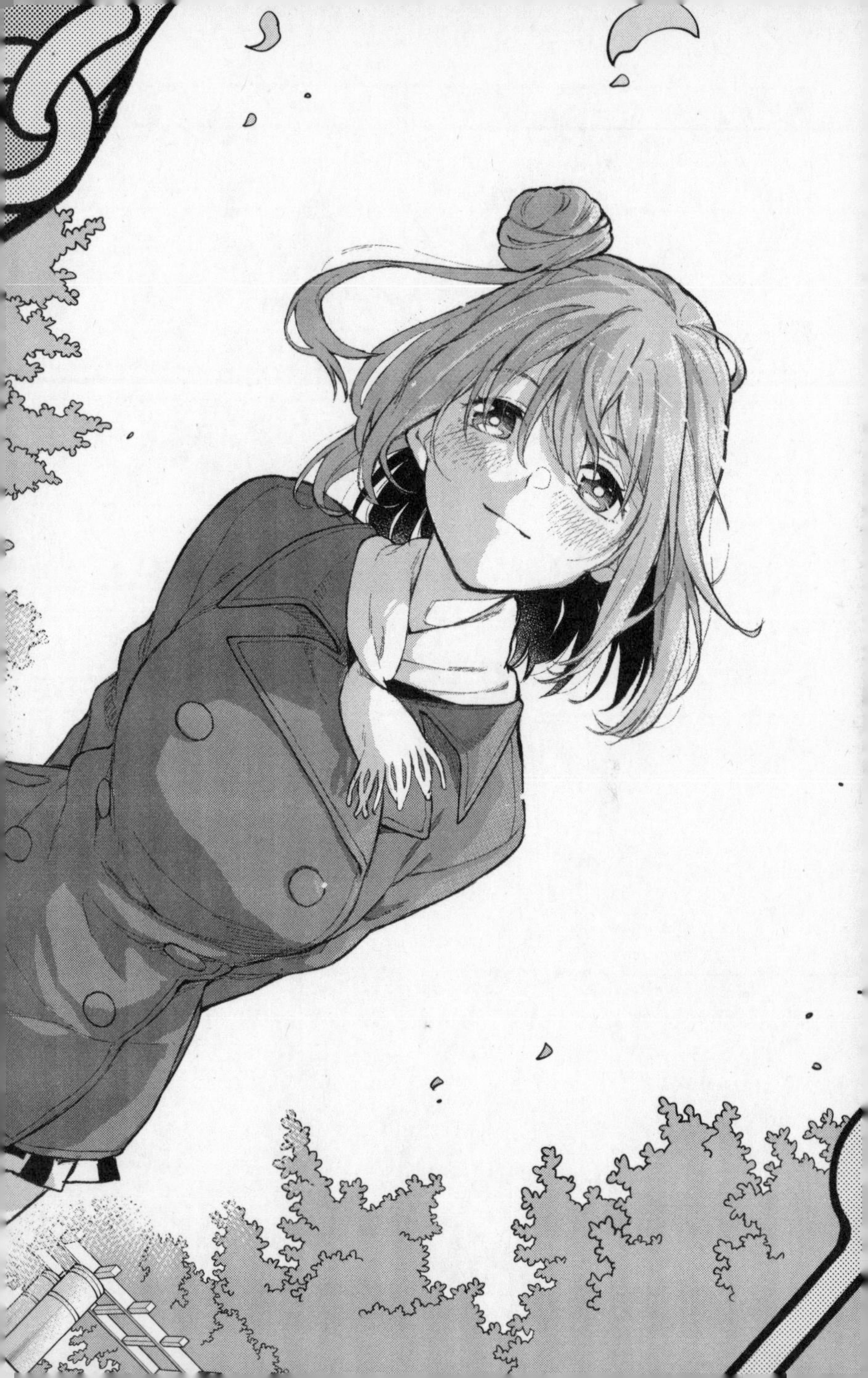

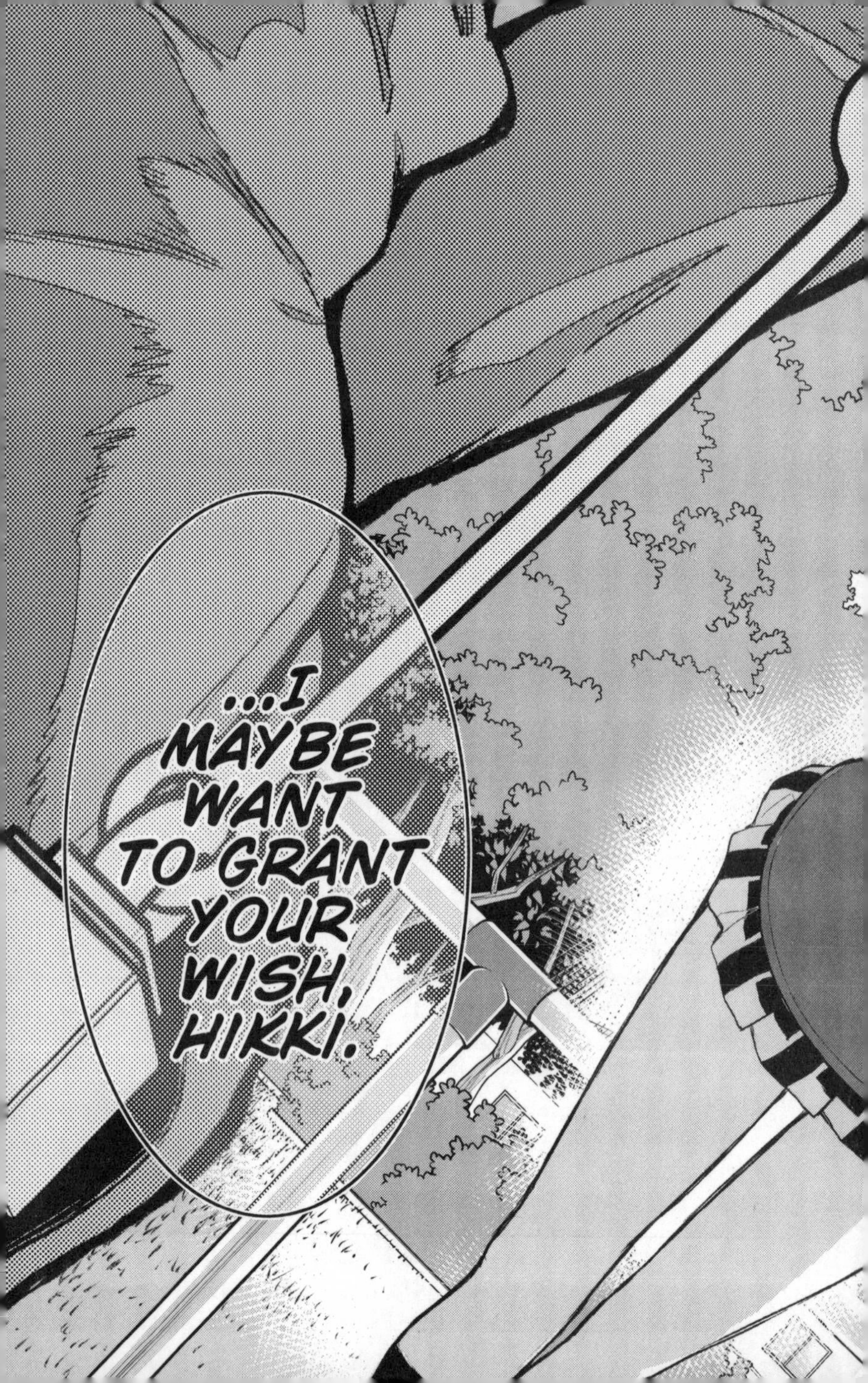
...I MAYBE WANT TO GRANT YOUR WISH, HIKKI.

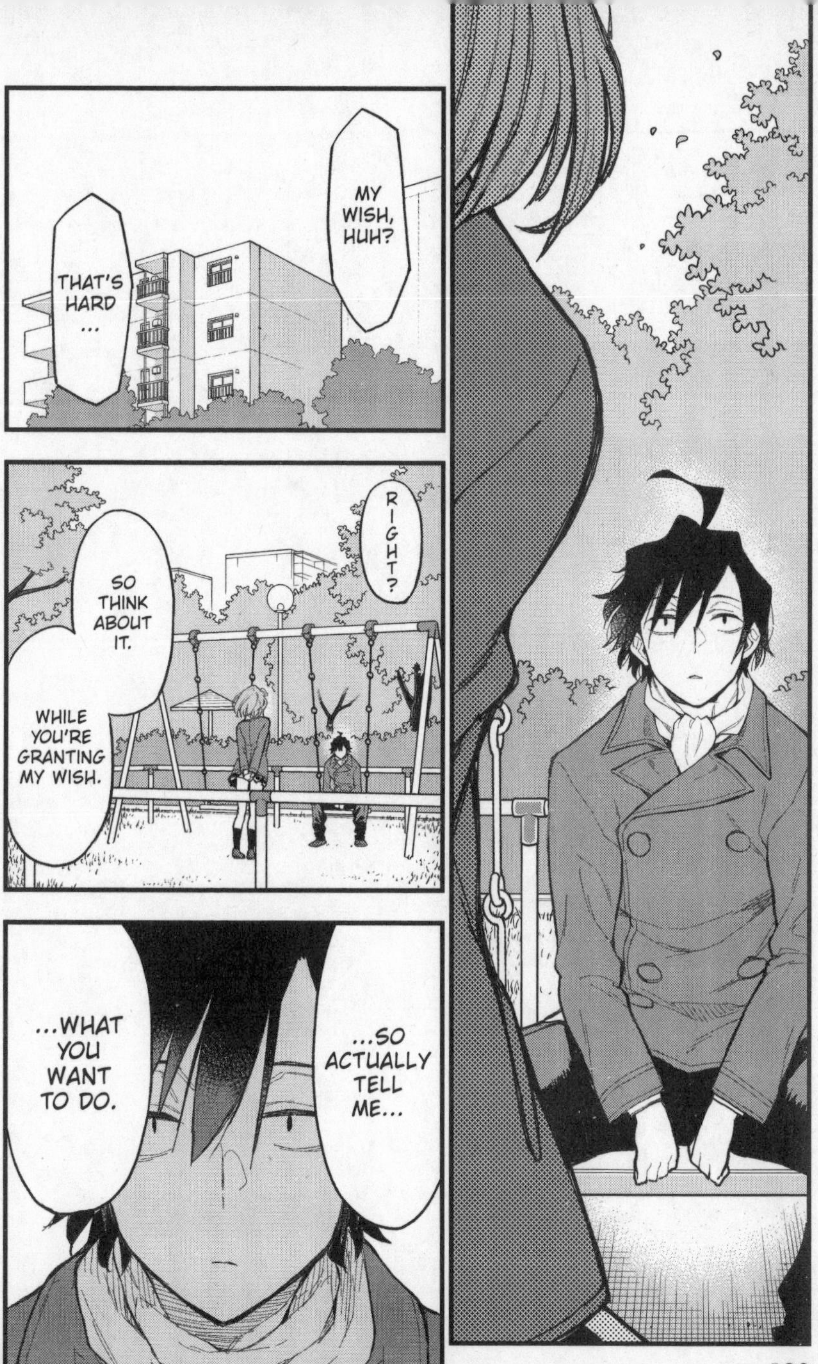
MY WISH, HUH?
THAT'S HARD ...
RIGHT?
SO THINK ABOUT IT.
WHILE YOU'RE GRANTING MY WISH.
...SO ACTUALLY TELL ME...
...WHAT YOU WANT TO DO.

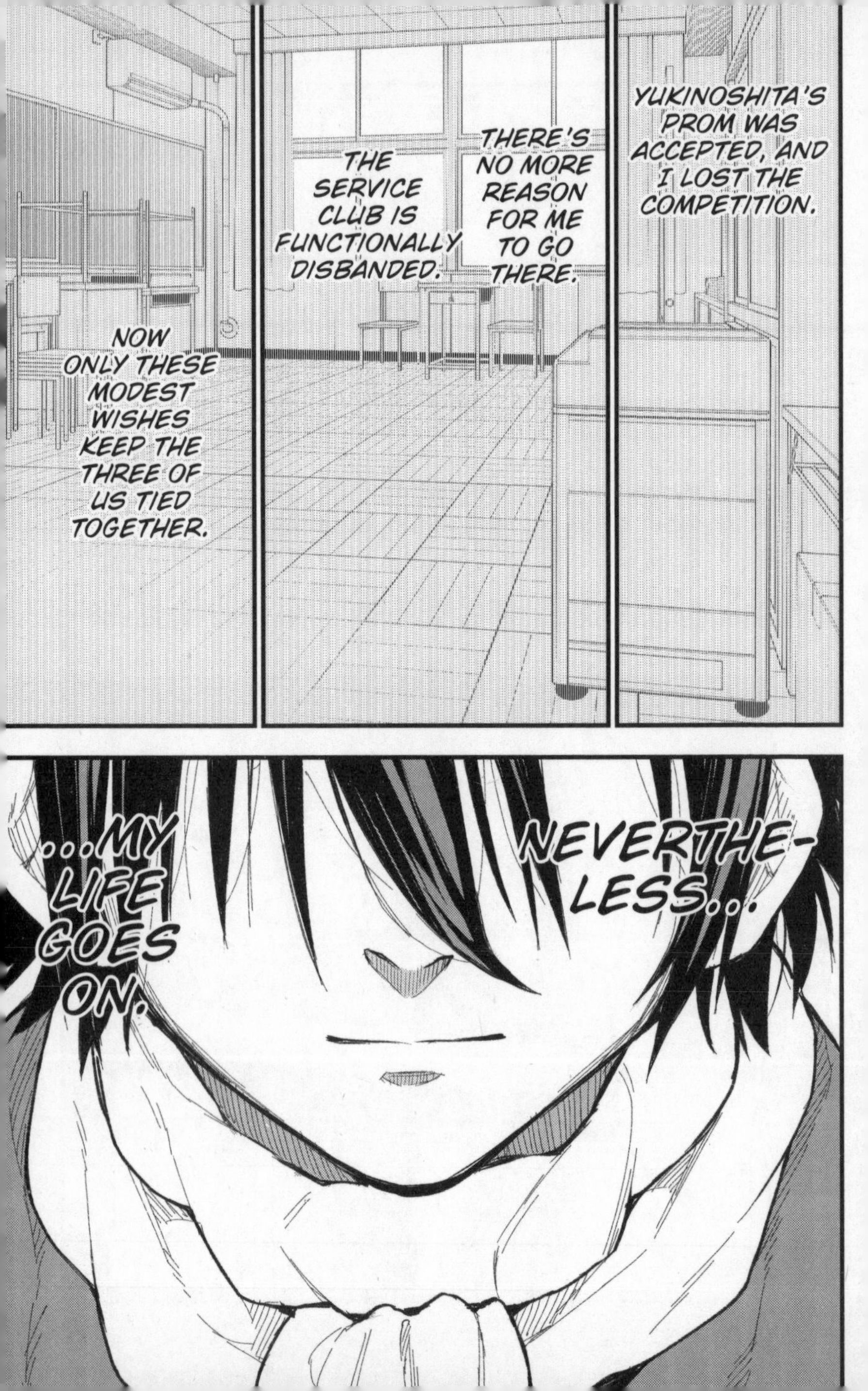
YUKINOSHITA'S PROM WAS ACCEPTED, AND I LOST THE COMPETITION.
THERE'S NO MORE REASON FOR ME TO GO THERE.
THE SERVICE CLUB IS FUNCTIONALLY DISBANDED.
NOW ONLY THESE MODEST WISHES KEEP THE THREE OF US TIED TOGETHER.
NEVERTHE-LESS...
...MY LIFE GOES ON.

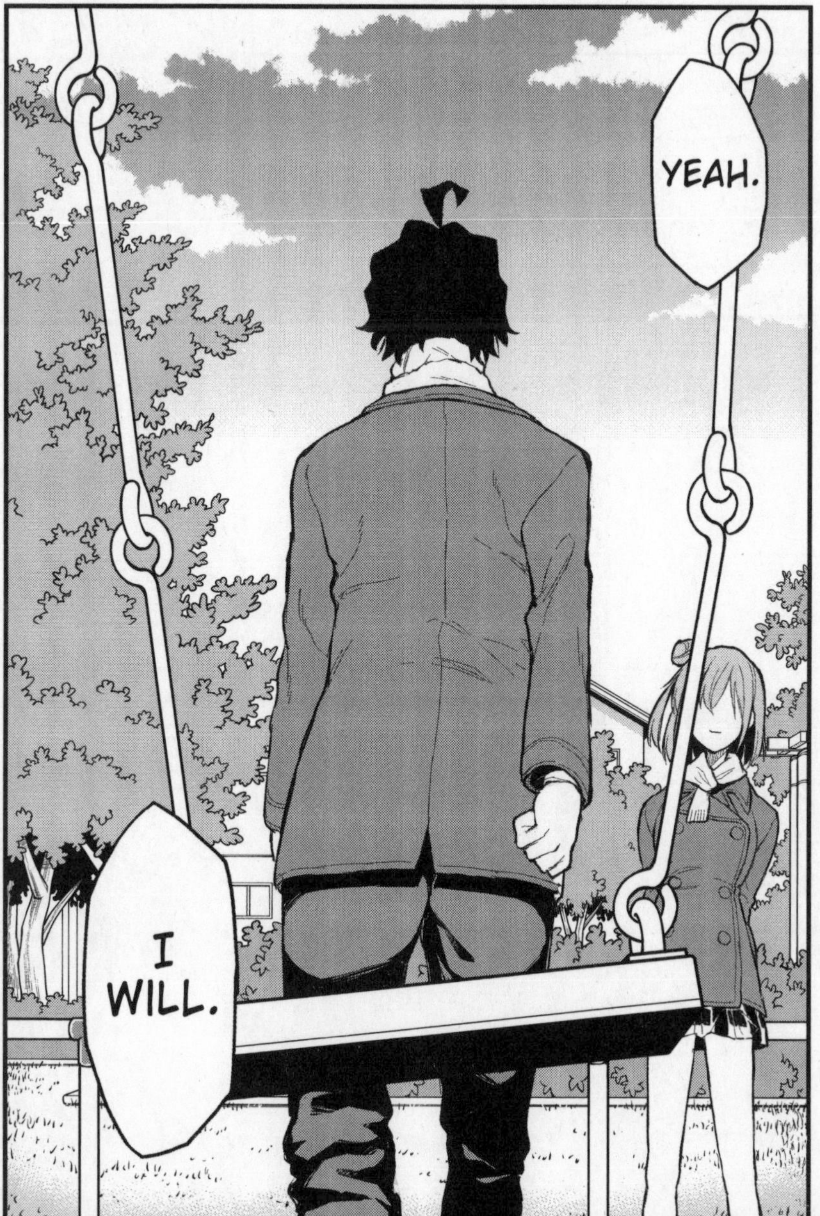
YEAH.
I WILL.

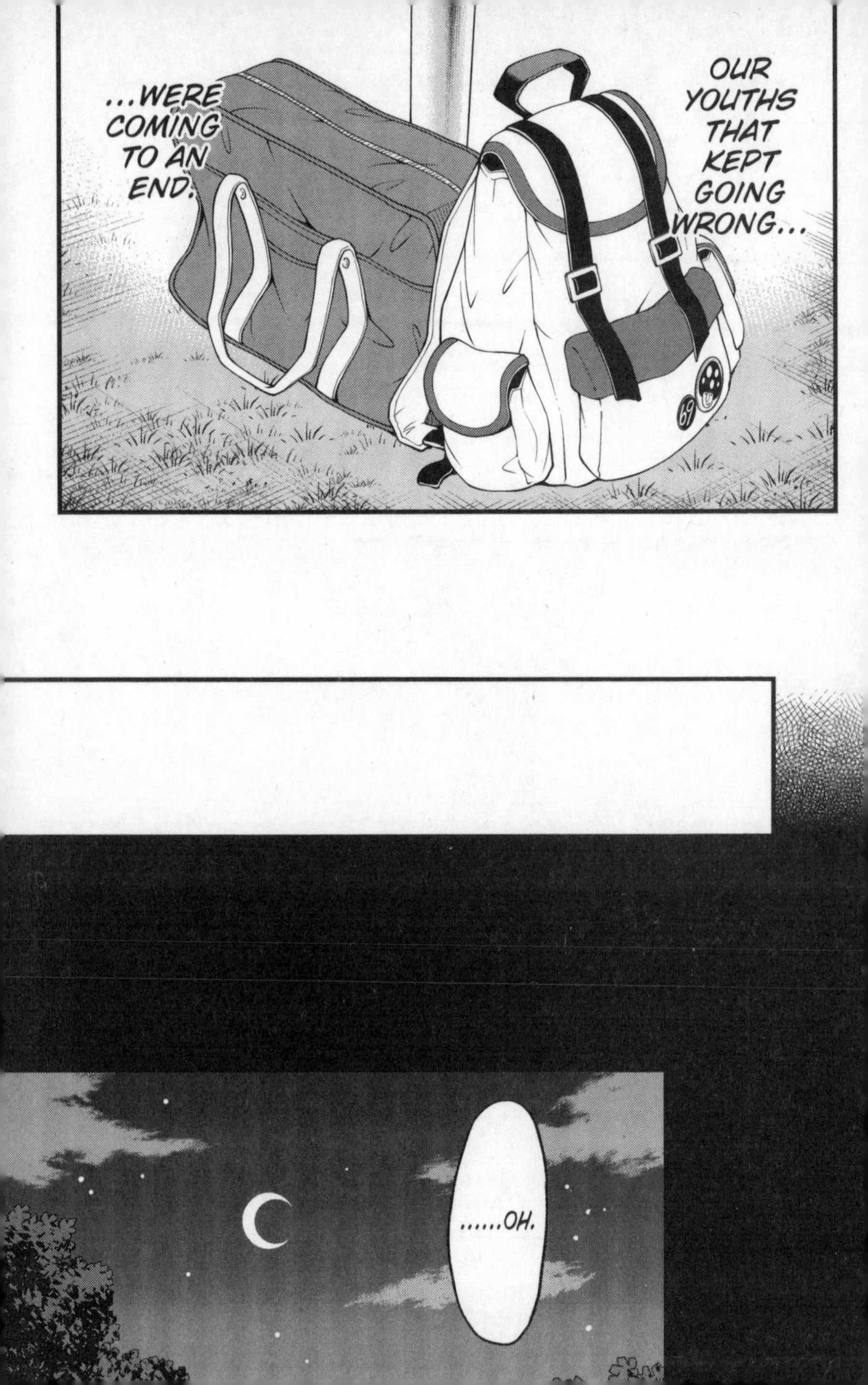
OUR YOUTHS THAT KEPT GOING WRONG...
...WERE COMING TO AN END.
......OH.

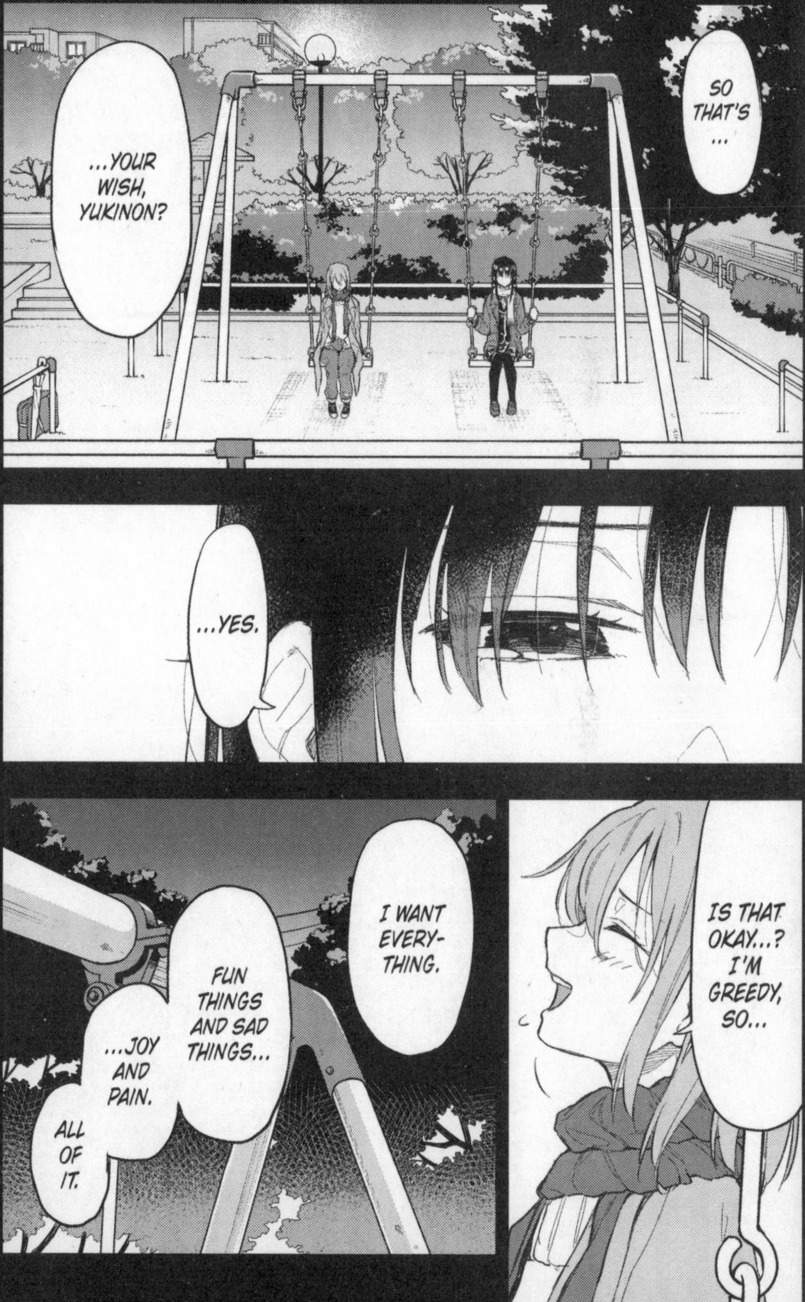
SO THAT'S ...
...YOUR WISH, YUKINON?
...YES.
IS THAT OKAY...? I'M GREEDY, SO...
I WANT EVERY-THING.
FUN THINGS AND SAD THINGS...
...JOY AND PAIN.
ALL OF IT.

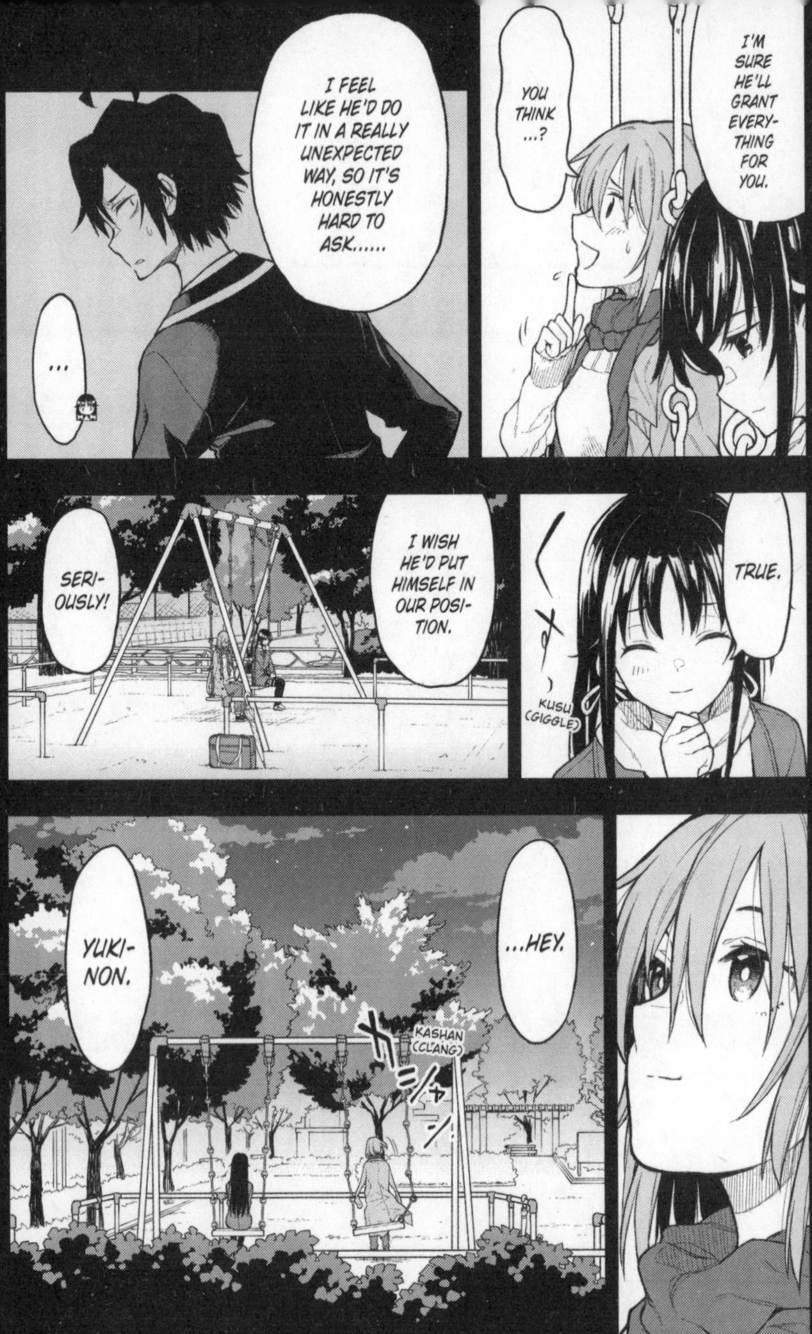
I'M SURE HE'LL GRANT EVERY-THING FOR YOU.
YOU THINK ...?
I FEEL LIKE HE'D DO IT IN A REALLY UNEXPECTED WAY, SO IT'S HONESTLY HARD TO ASK......
...
TRUE.
KUSU (GIGGLE)
I WISH HE'D PUT HIMSELF IN OUR POSI-TION.
SERI-OUSLY!
...HEY.
KASHAN (CLANG)
YUKI-NON.

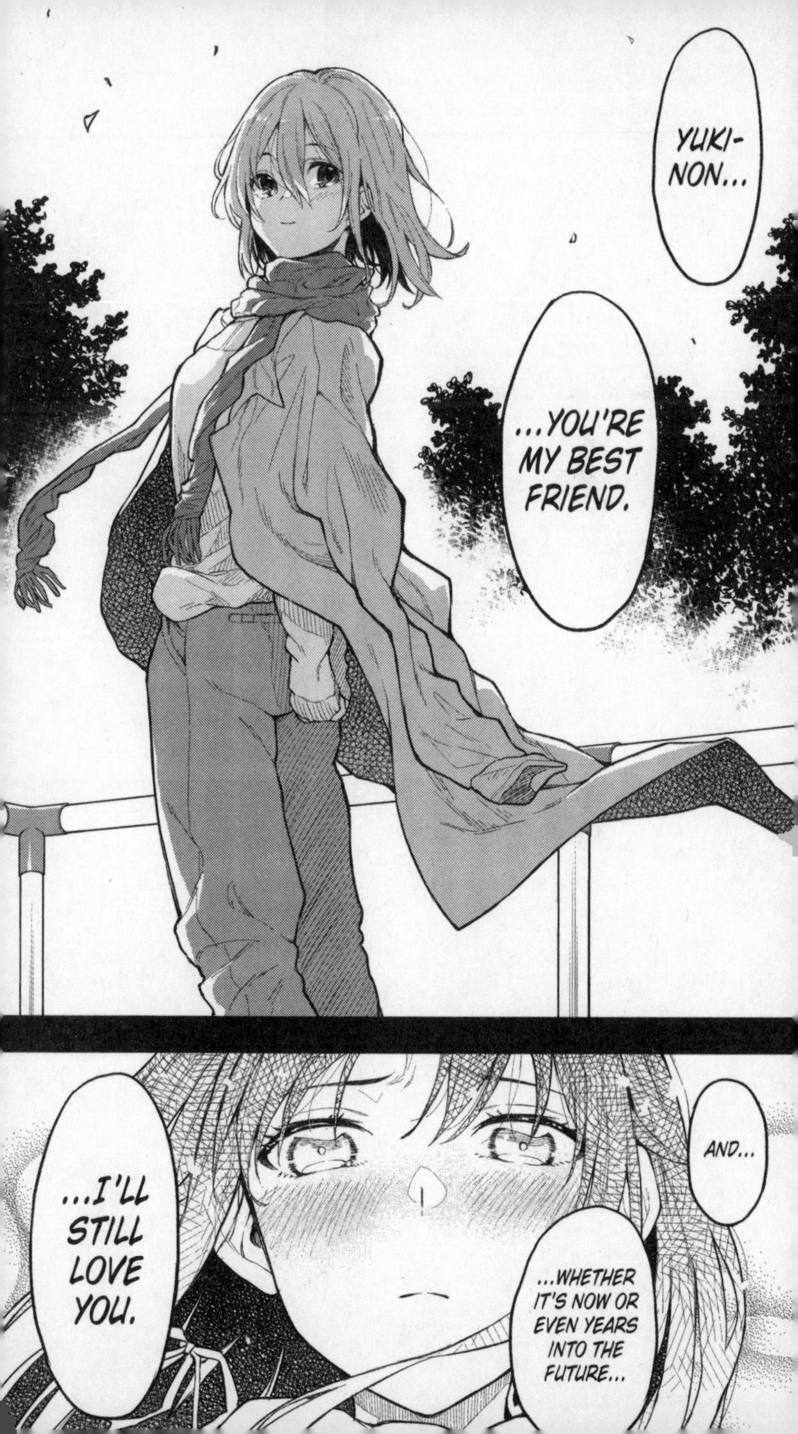
YUKI-NON...
...YOU'RE MY BEST FRIEND.
AND...
...WHETHER IT'S NOW OR EVEN YEARS INTO THE FUTURE...
...I'LL STILL LOVE YOU.

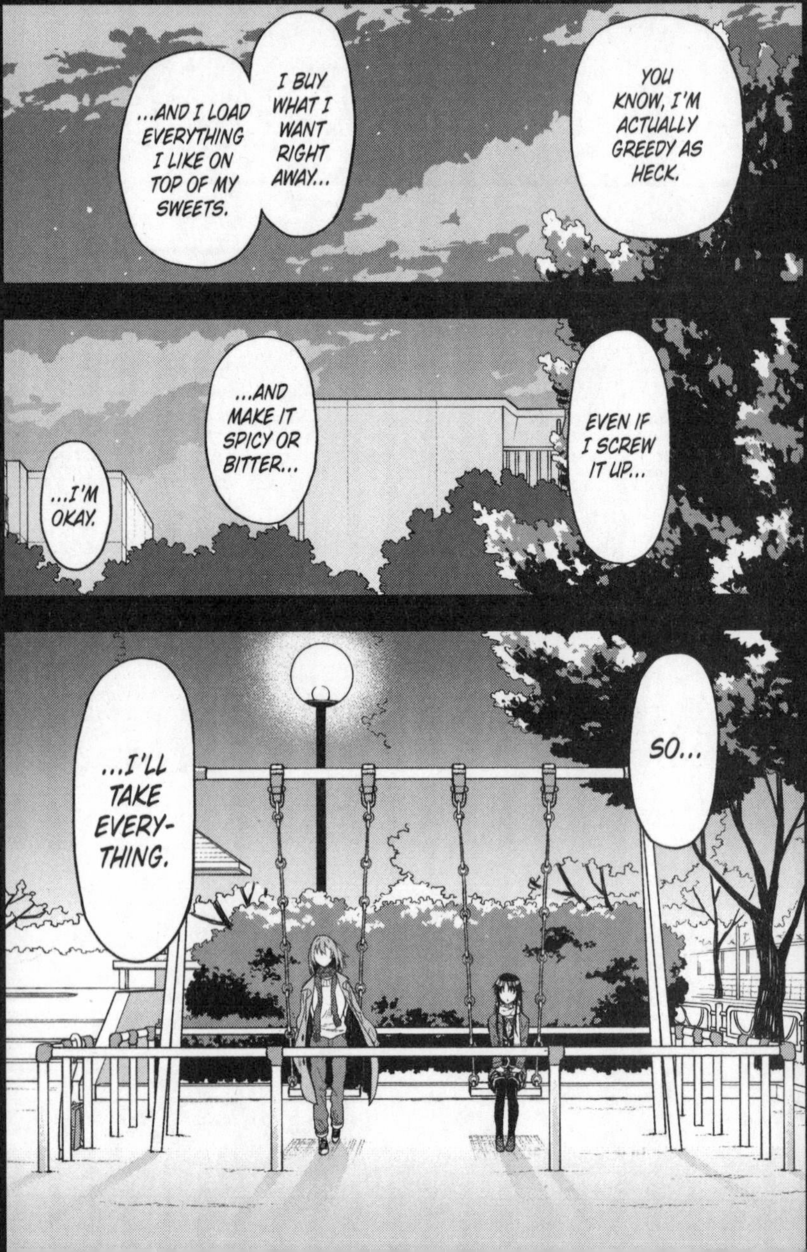
YOU KNOW, I'M ACTUALLY GREEDY AS HECK.
I BUY WHAT I WANT RIGHT AWAY...
...AND I LOAD EVERYTHING I LIKE ON TOP OF MY SWEETS.
EVEN IF I SCREW IT UP...
...AND MAKE IT SPICY OR BITTER...
...I'M OKAY.
SO...
...I'LL TAKE EVERY-THING.

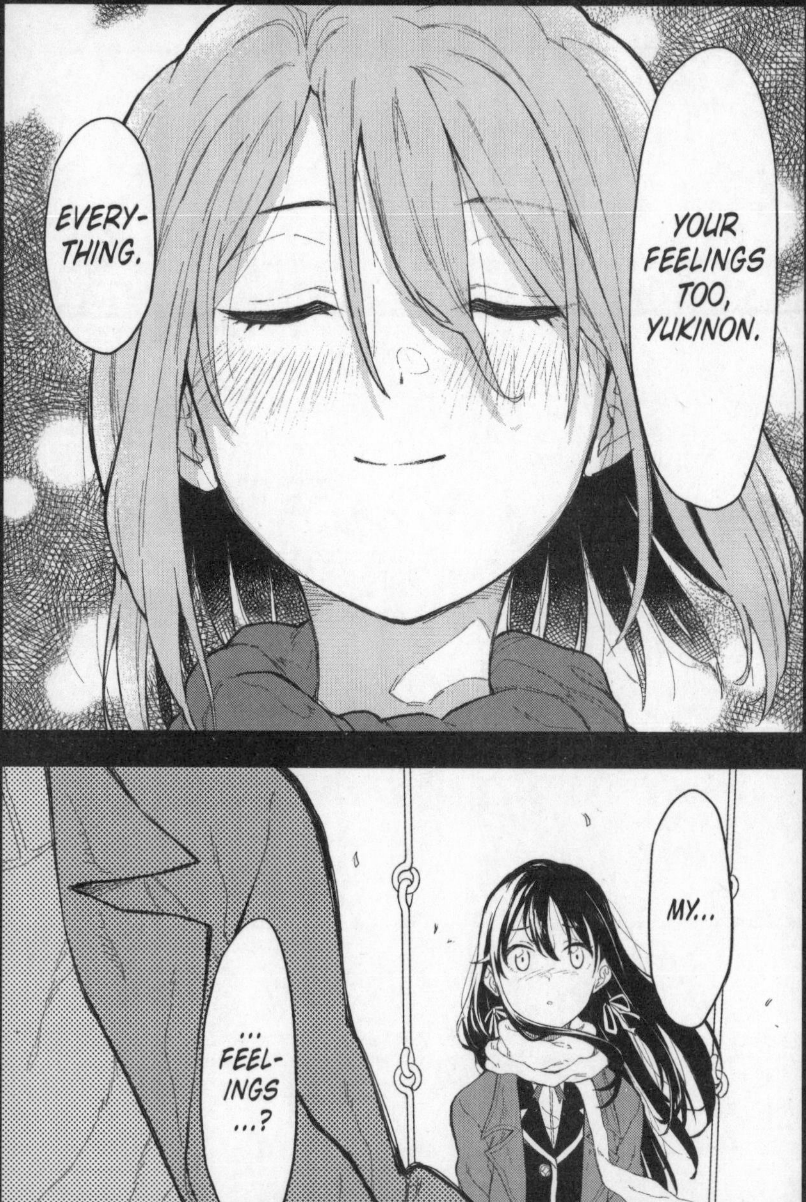
YOUR FEELINGS TOO, YUKINON.
EVERY-THING.
MY...
... FEEL-INGS ...?

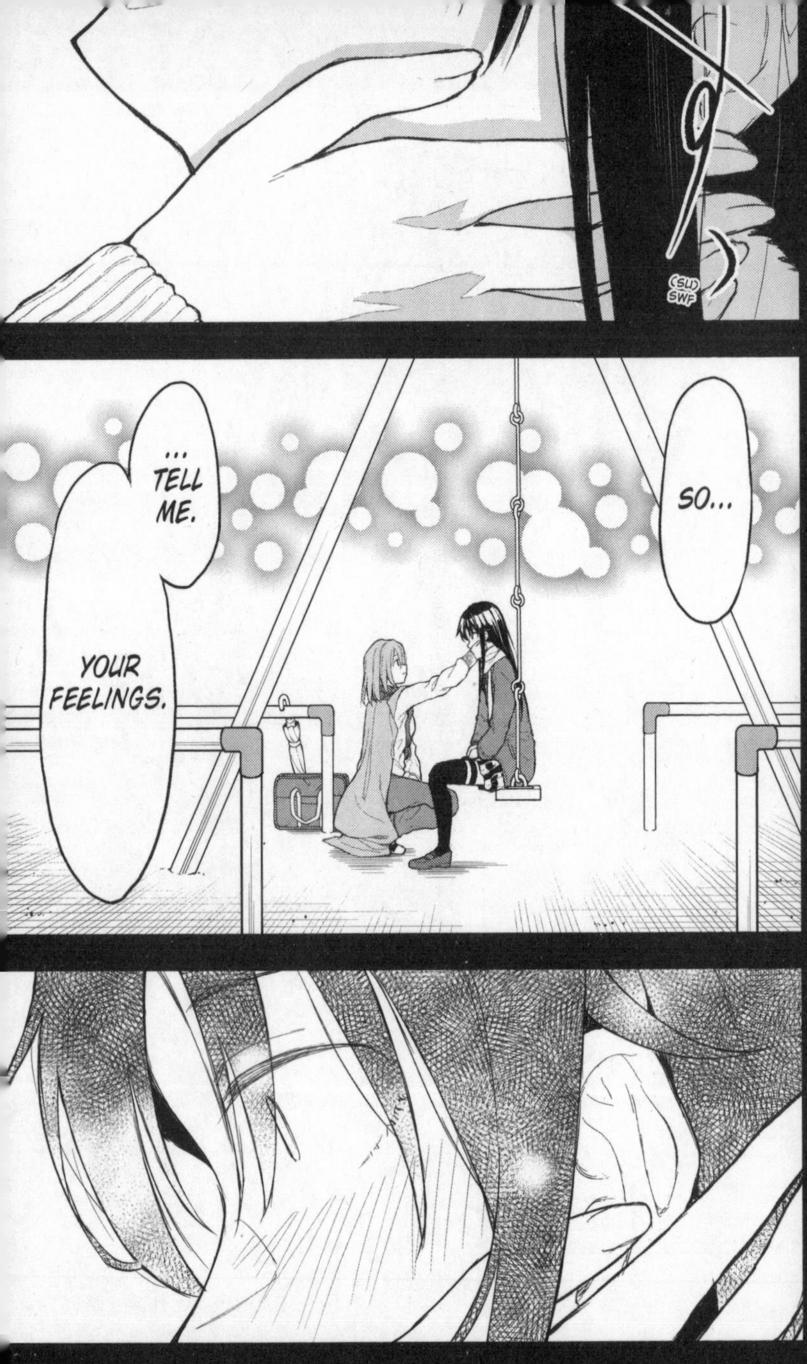
(SU) SWF
SO...
...TELL ME.
YOUR FEELINGS.

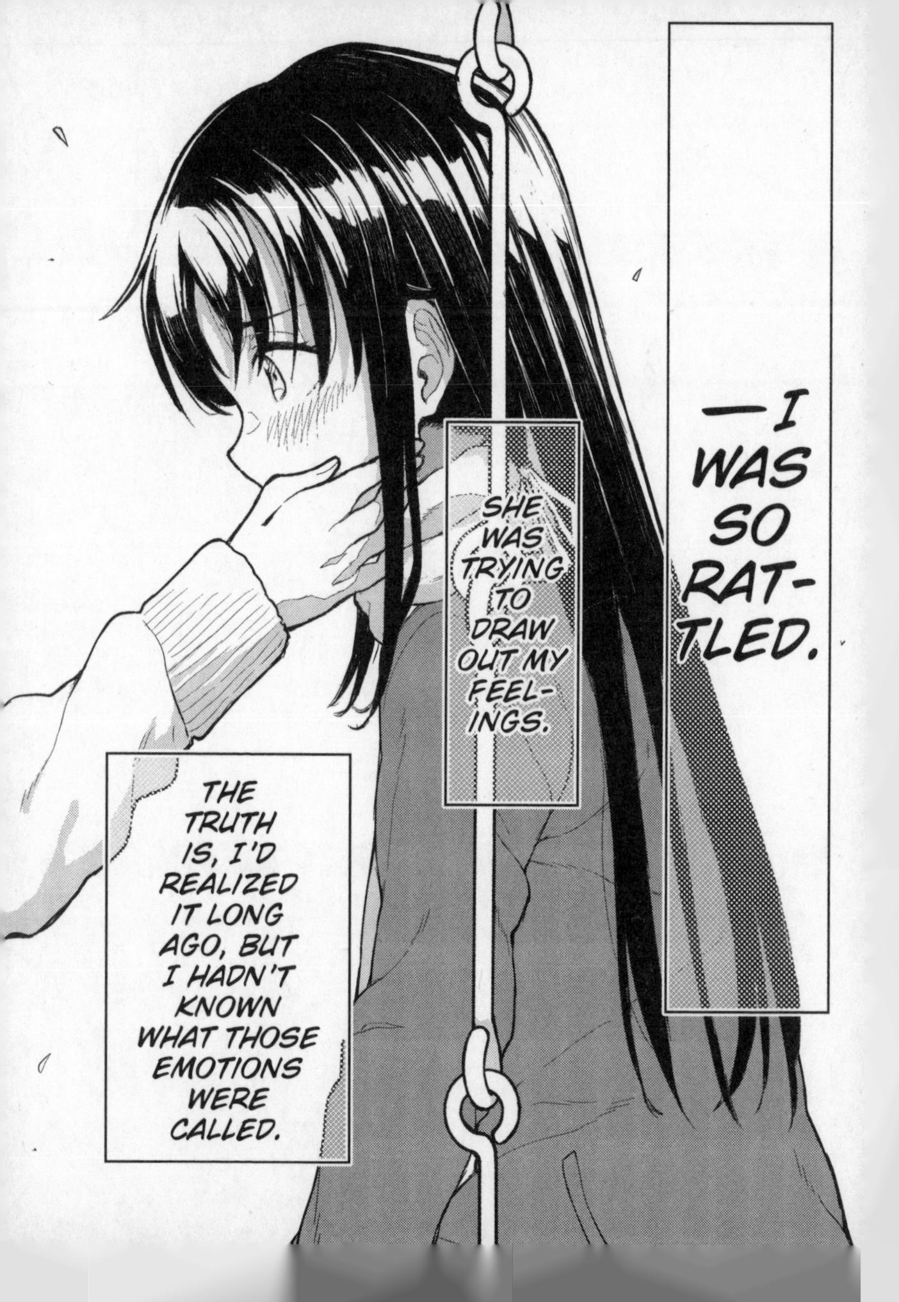
—I WAS SO RAT-TLED.
SHE WAS TRYING TO DRAW OUT MY FEEL-INGS.
THE TRUTH IS, I'D REALIZED IT LONG AGO, BUT I HADN'T KNOWN WHAT THOSE EMOTIONS WERE CALLED.

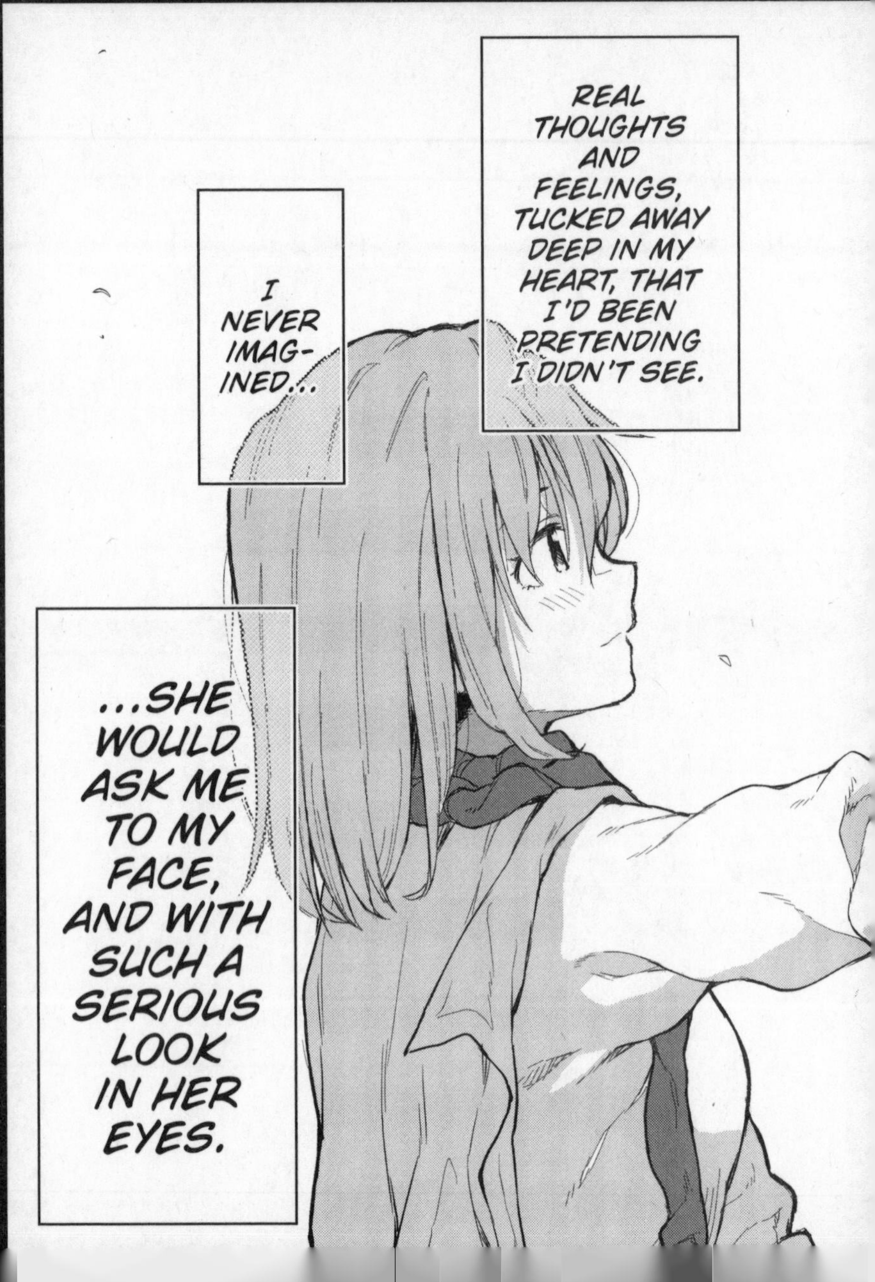
REAL THOUGHTS AND FEELINGS, TUCKED AWAY DEEP IN MY HEART, THAT I'D BEEN PRETENDING I DIDN'T SEE.
I NEVER IMAG-INED...
...SHE WOULD ASK ME TO MY FACE, AND WITH SUCH A SERIOUS LOOK IN HER EYES.

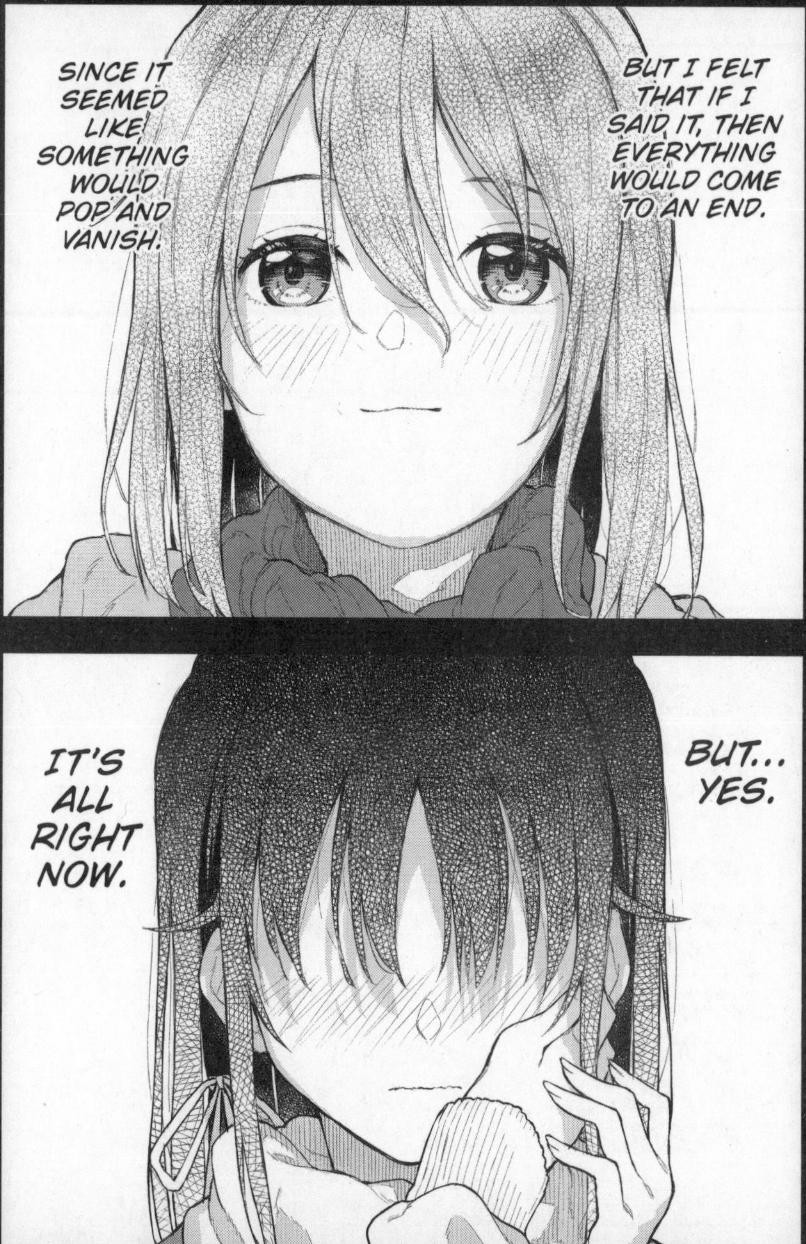
BUT I FELT THAT IF I SAID IT, THEN EVERYTHING WOULD COME TO AN END.
SINCE IT SEEMED LIKE SOMETHING WOULD POP AND VANISH.
BUT... YES.
IT'S ALL RIGHT NOW.

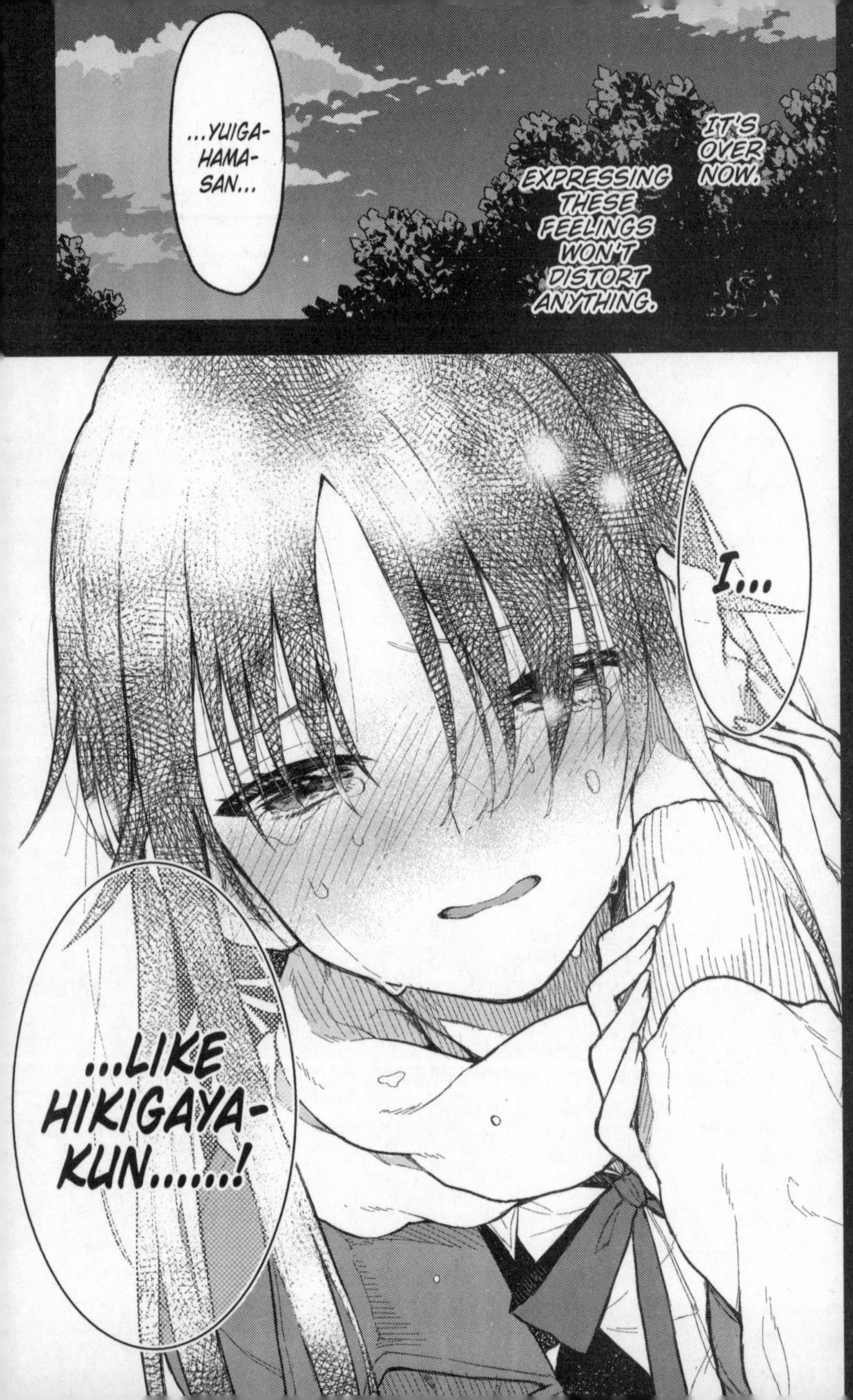
IT'S OVER NOW.
EXPRESSING THESE FEELINGS WON'T DISTORT ANYTHING.
...YUIGA-HAMA-SAN...
I...
...LIKE HIKIGAYA-KUN......!

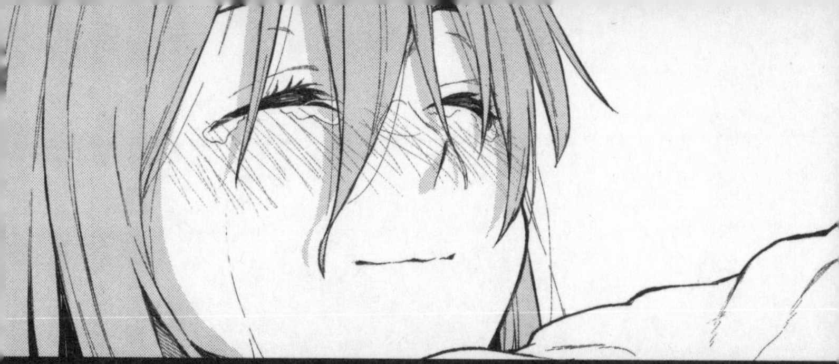

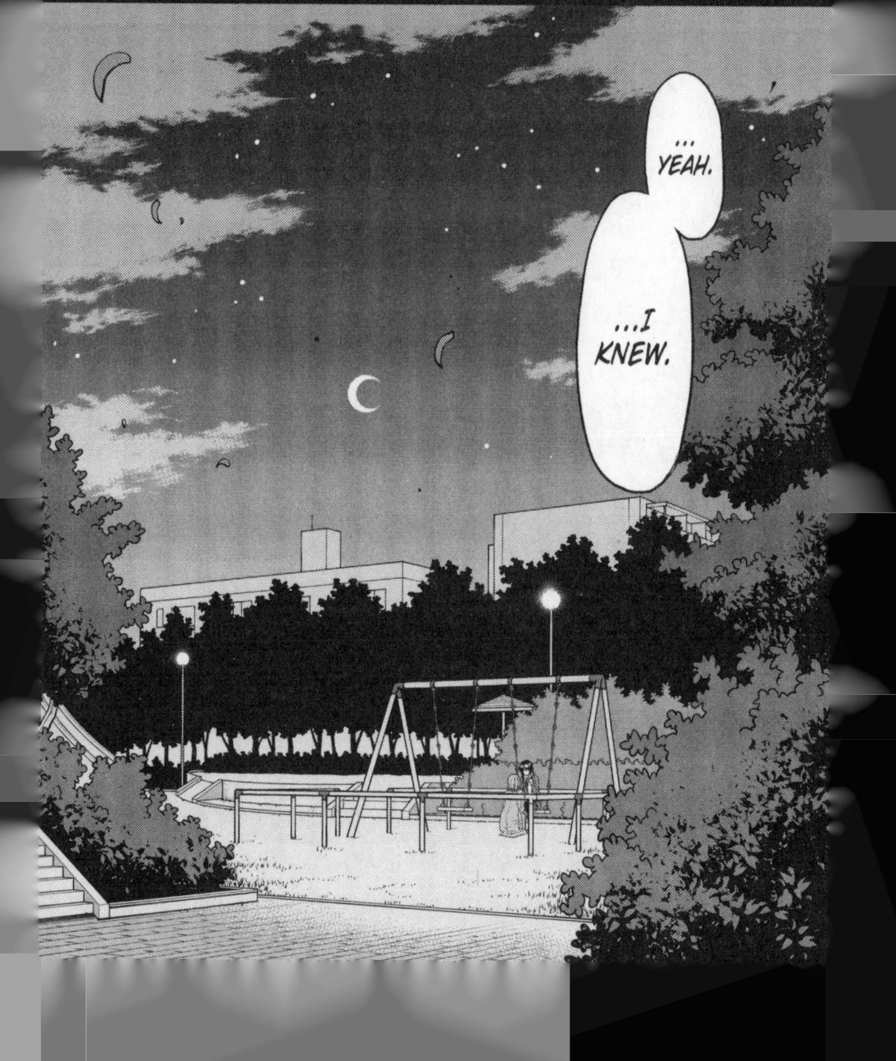
...YEAH.
...I KNEW.

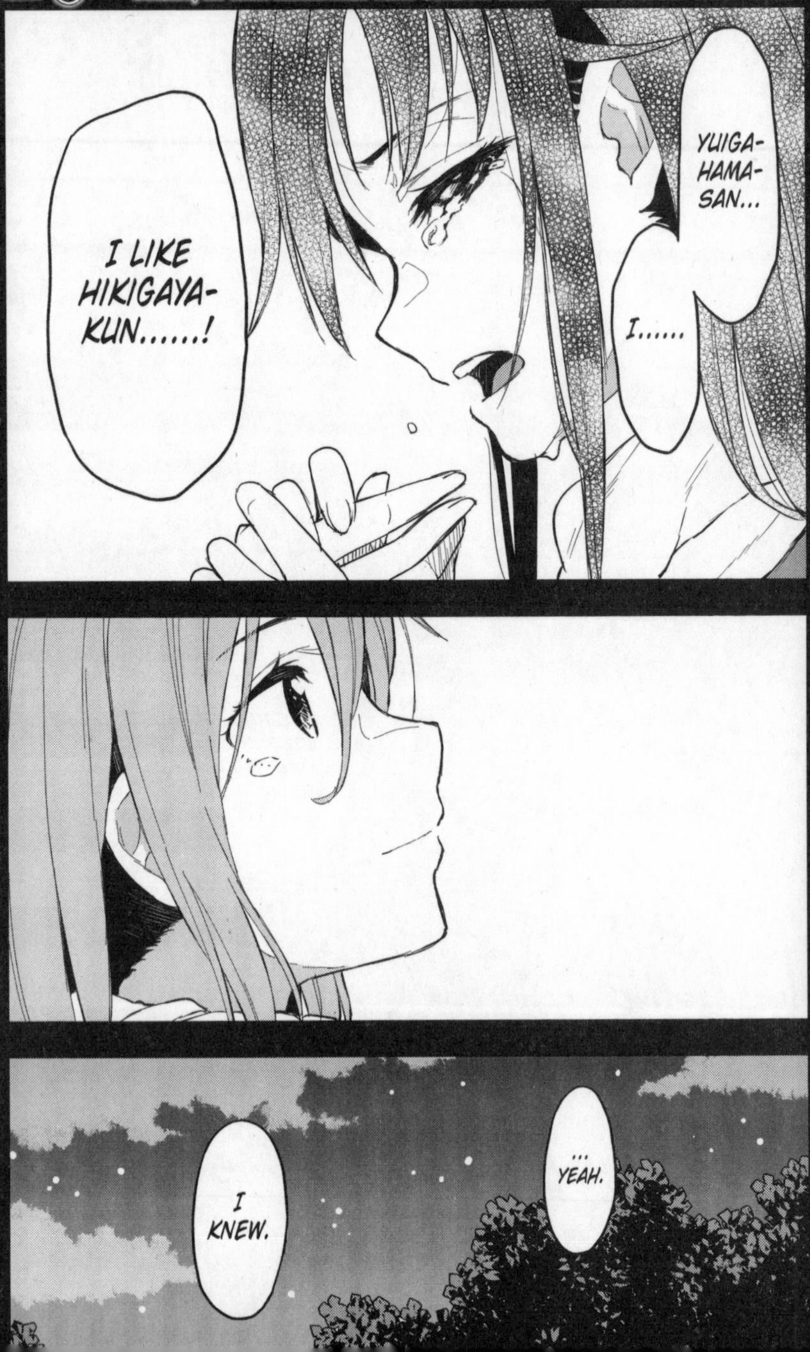
YUIGA-HAMA-SAN...
I......
I LIKE HIKIGAYA-KUN......!
... YEAH.
I KNEW.

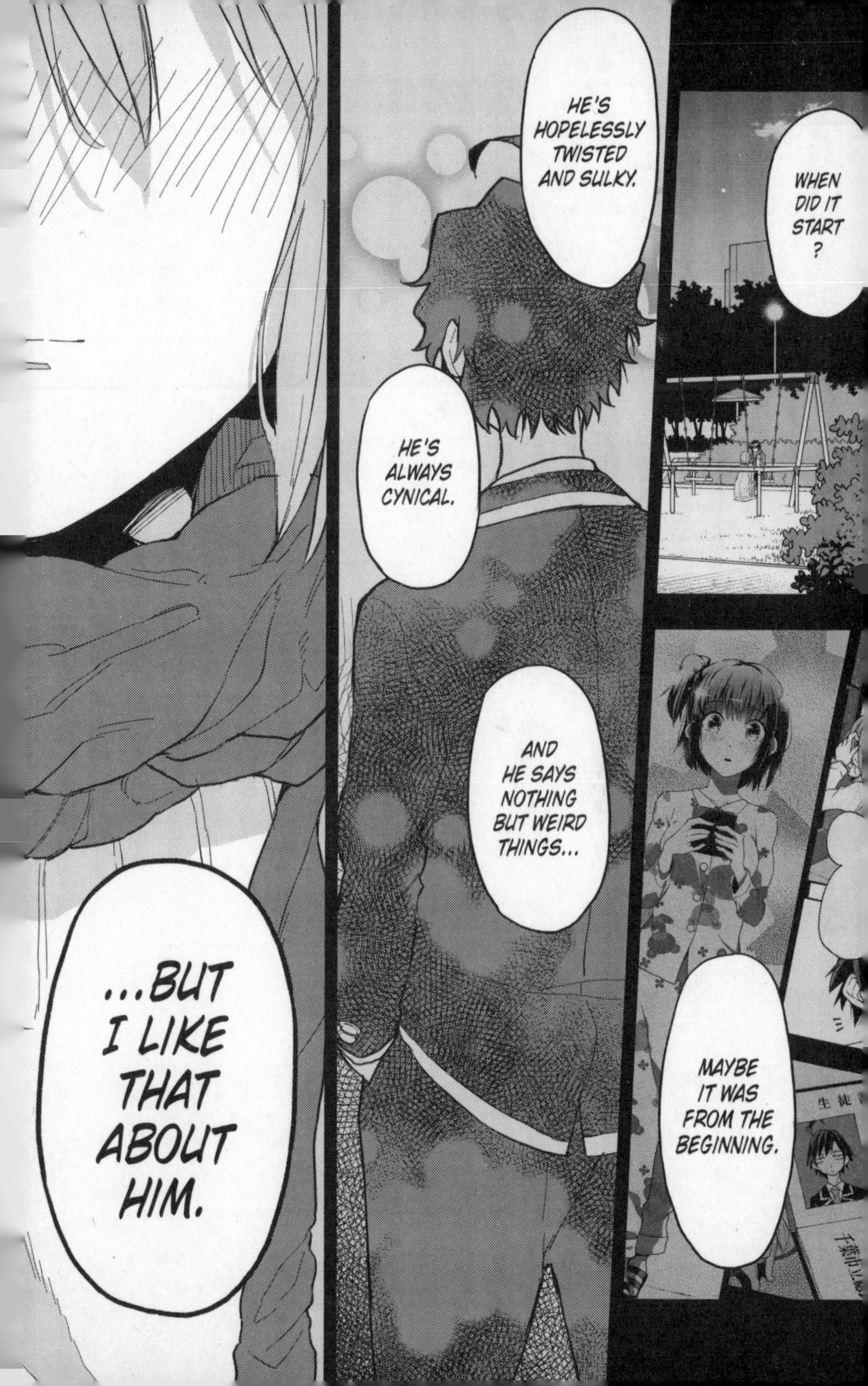
WHEN DID IT START?
MAYBE IT WAS FROM THE BEGINNING.
HE'S HOPELESSLY TWISTED AND SULKY.
HE'S ALWAYS CYNICAL.
AND HE SAYS NOTHING BUT WEIRD THINGS...
...BUT I LIKE THAT ABOUT HIM.

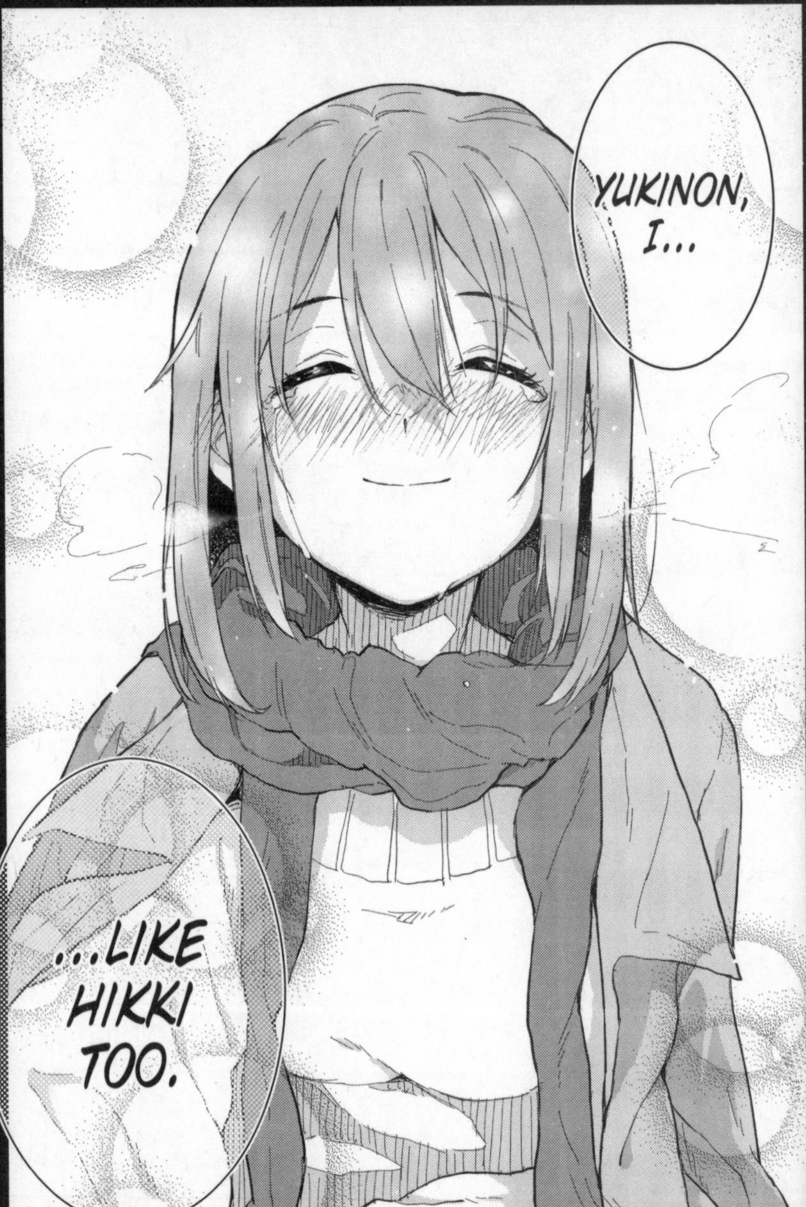
YUKINON, I...
...LIKE HIKKI TOO.

CHAPTER 105 — SURELY, HE WILL REMEMBER THAT SEASON EVERY TIME HE SMELLS THAT SCENT.

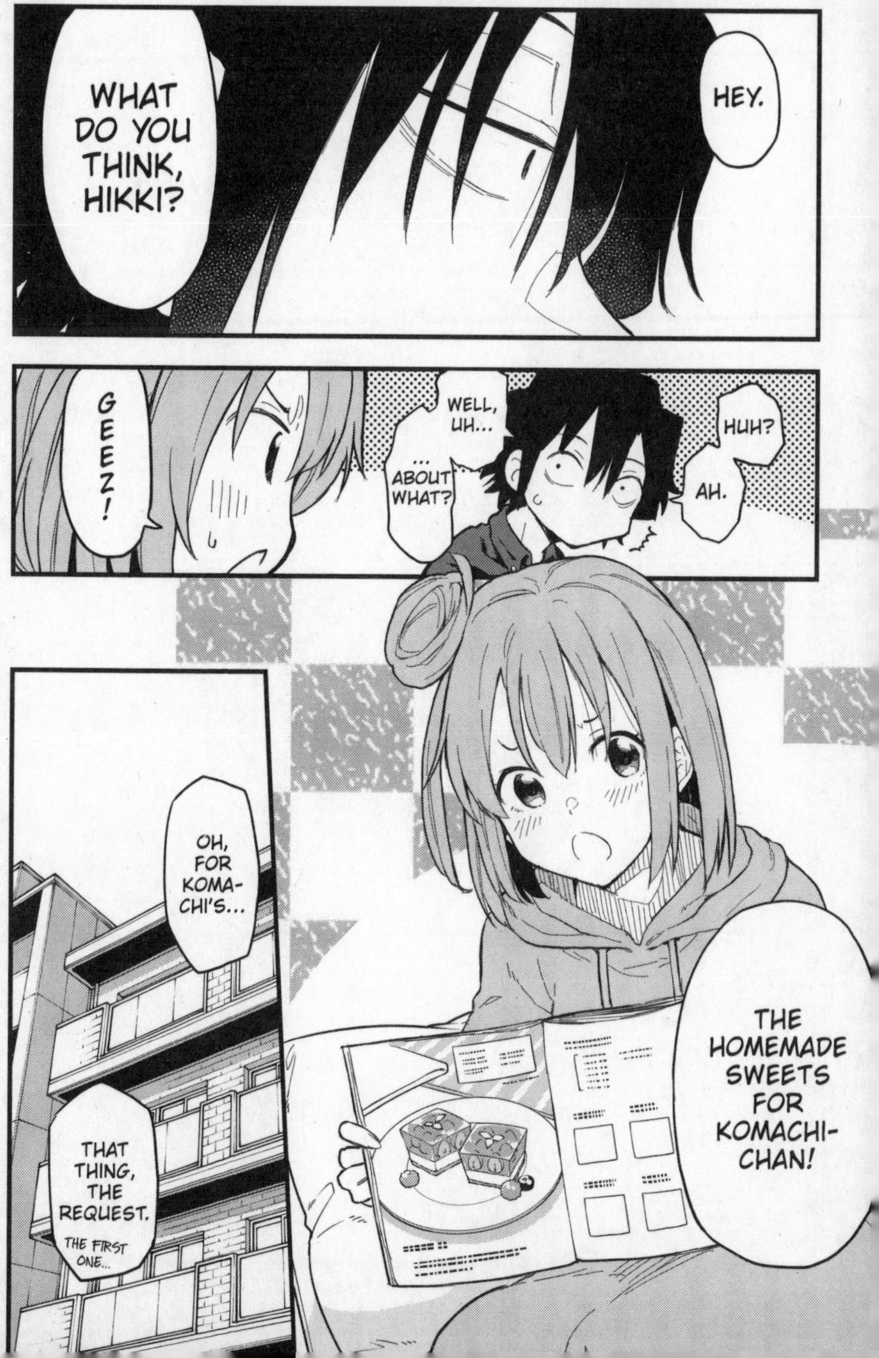
HEY.
WHAT DO YOU THINK, HIKKI?
HUH?
AH.
WELL, UH...
... ABOUT WHAT?
GEEZ!
THE HOMEMADE SWEETS FOR KOMACHI-CHAN!
OH, FOR KOMA-CHI'S...
THAT THING, THE REQUEST.
THE FIRST ONE...

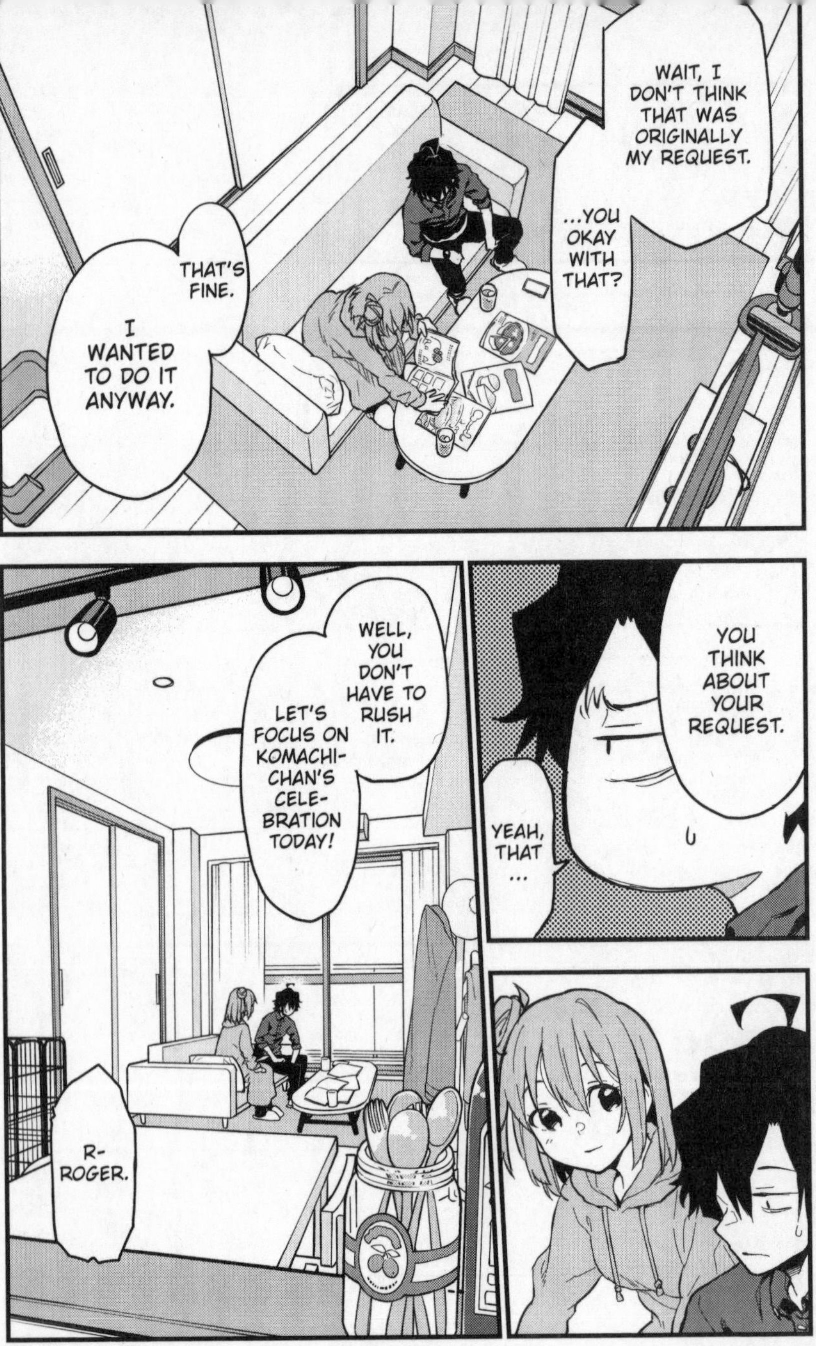
WAIT, I DON'T THINK THAT WAS ORIGINALLY MY REQUEST.
...YOU OKAY WITH THAT?
THAT'S FINE.
I WANTED TO DO IT ANYWAY.
YOU THINK ABOUT YOUR REQUEST.
YEAH, THAT ...
WELL, YOU DON'T HAVE TO RUSH IT.
LET'S FOCUS ON KOMACHI-CHAN'S CELE-BRATION TODAY!
R-ROGER.

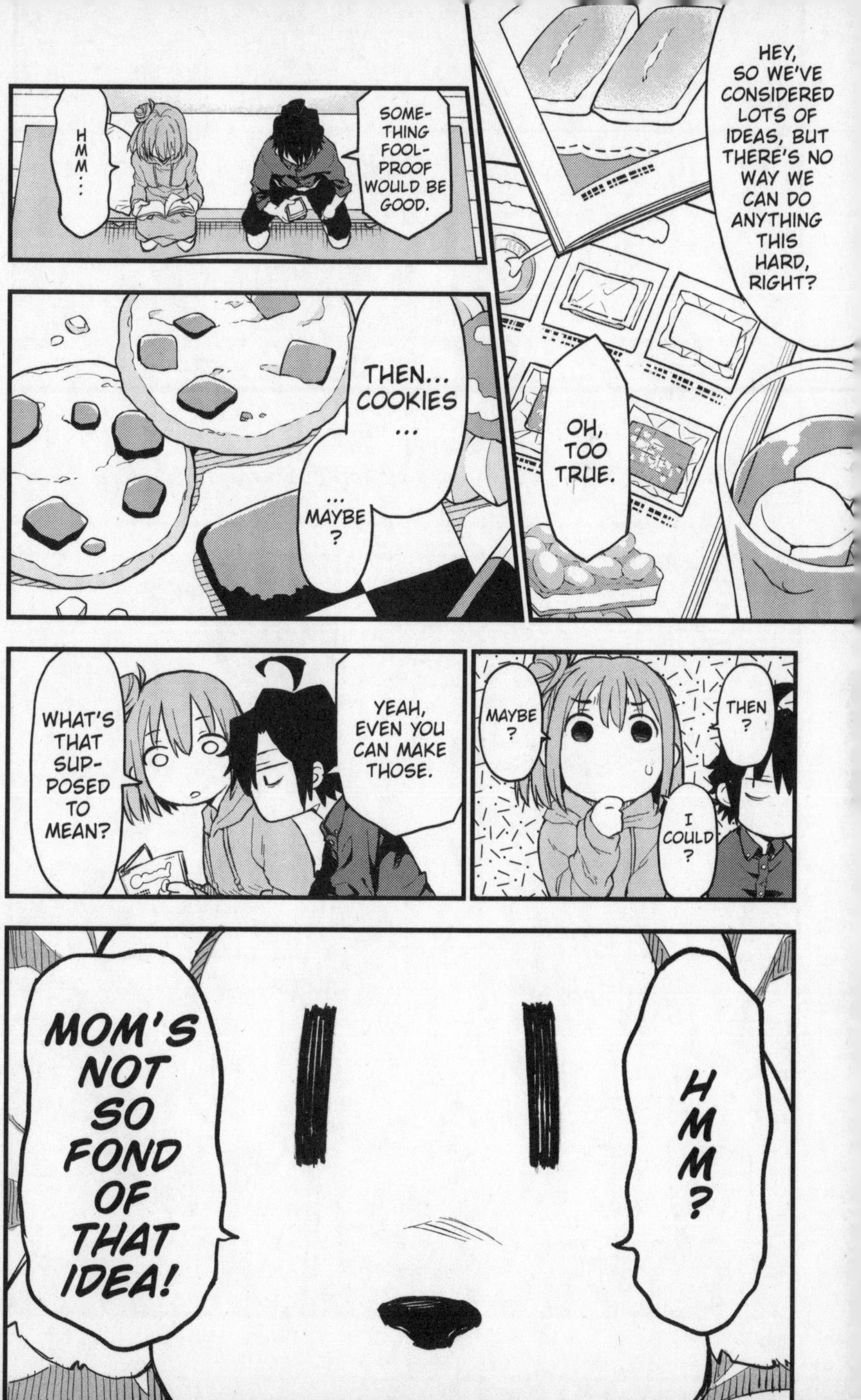
HEY, SO WE'VE CONSIDERED LOTS OF IDEAS, BUT THERE'S NO WAY WE CAN DO ANYTHING THIS HARD, RIGHT?
OH, TOO TRUE.
SOME-THING FOOL-PROOF WOULD BE GOOD.
HMM...
THEN... COOKIES...
...MAYBE?
THEN?
I COULD?
MAYBE?
YEAH, EVEN YOU CAN MAKE THOSE.
WHAT'S THAT SUP-POSED TO MEAN?
HMM?
MOM'S NOT SO FOND OF THAT IDEA!

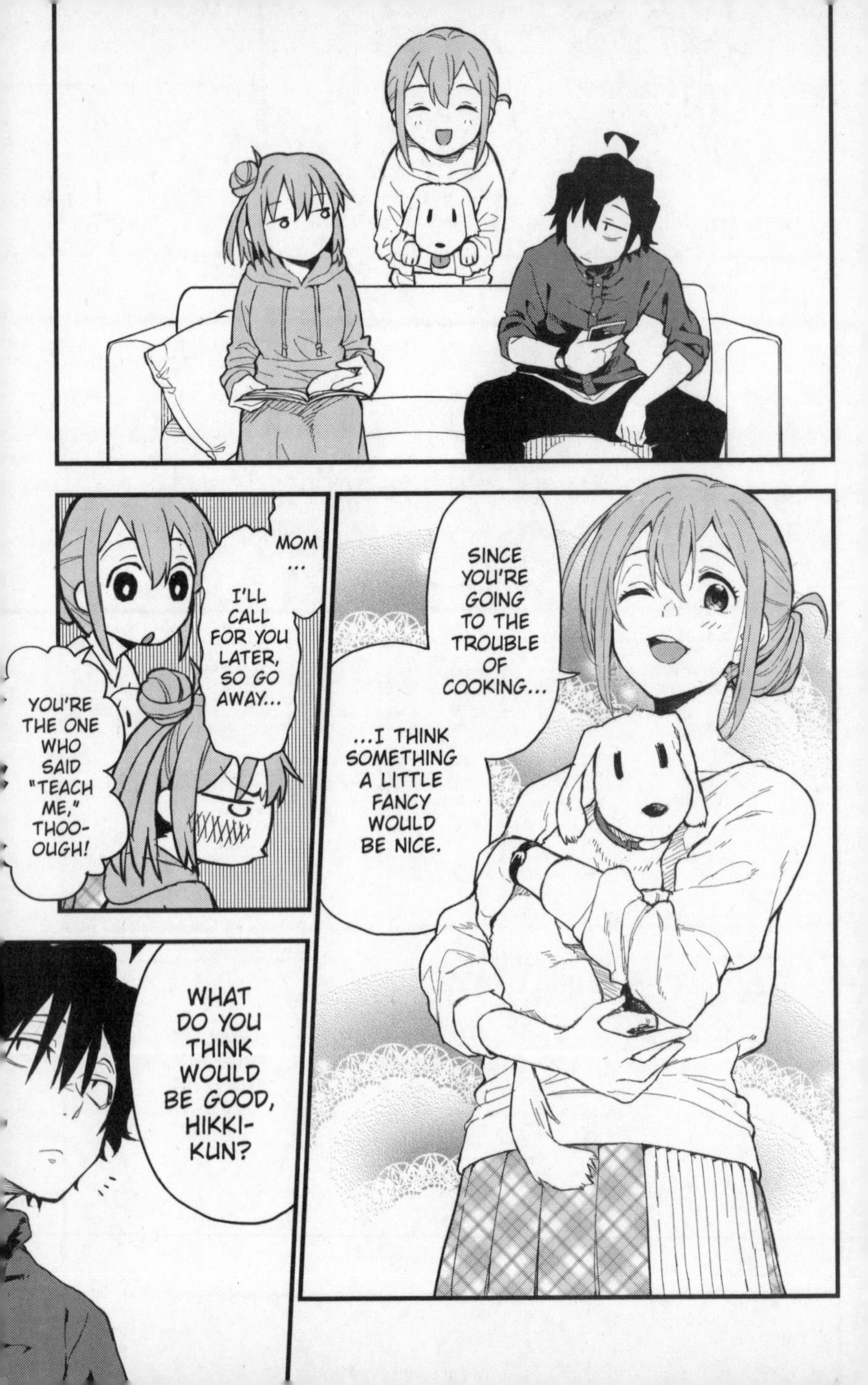
SINCE YOU'RE GOING TO THE TROUBLE OF COOKING...
...I THINK SOMETHING A LITTLE FANCY WOULD BE NICE.
MOM ...
I'LL CALL FOR YOU LATER, SO GO AWAY...
YOU'RE THE ONE WHO SAID "TEACH ME," THOO-OUGH!
WHAT DO YOU THINK WOULD BE GOOD, HIKKI-KUN?

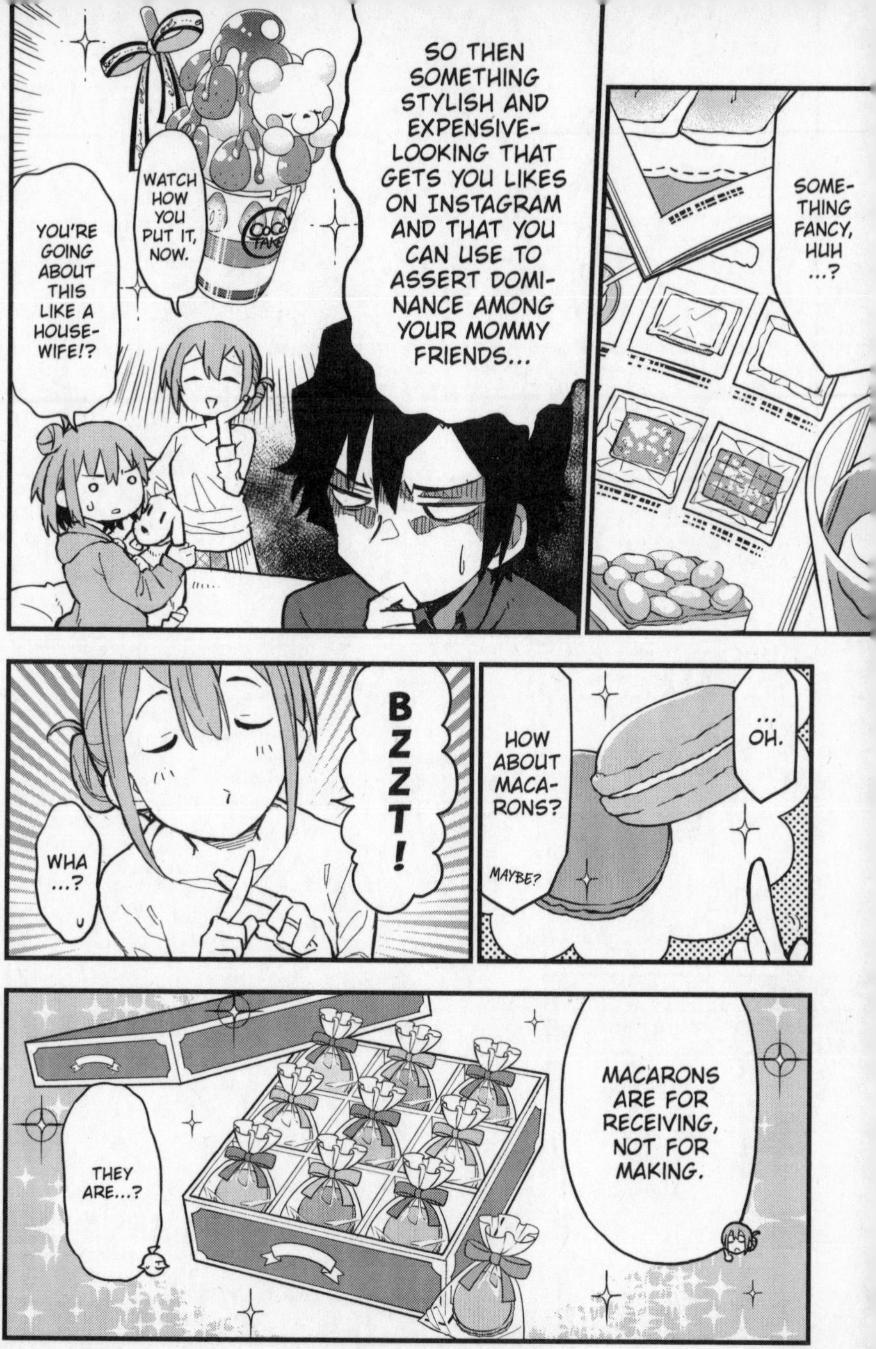
SOME-THING FANCY, HUH ...?
SO THEN SOMETHING STYLISH AND EXPENSIVE-LOOKING THAT GETS YOU LIKES ON INSTAGRAM AND THAT YOU CAN USE TO ASSERT DOMI-NANCE AMONG YOUR MOMMY FRIENDS...
WATCH HOW YOU PUT IT, NOW.
YOU'RE GOING ABOUT THIS LIKE A HOUSE-WIFE!?
... OH.
HOW ABOUT MACA-RONS?
MAYBE?
BZZZT!
WHA ...?
MACARONS ARE FOR RECEIVING, NOT FOR MAKING.
THEY ARE...?

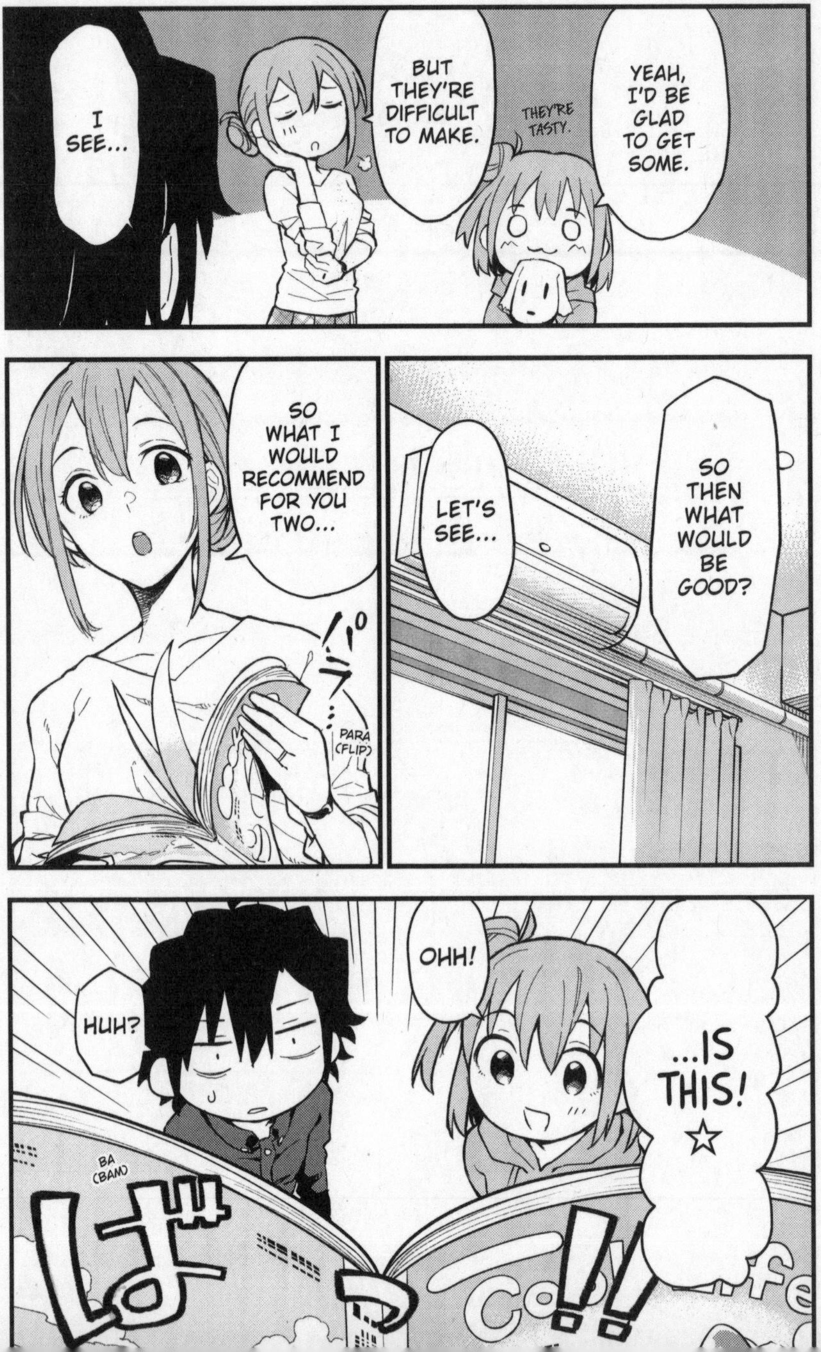
YEAH, I'D BE GLAD TO GET SOME.
THEY'RE TASTY.
BUT THEY'RE DIFFICULT TO MAKE.
I SEE...
SO THEN WHAT WOULD BE GOOD?
LET'S SEE...
SO WHAT I WOULD RECOMMEND FOR YOU TWO...
PARA (FLIP)
...IS THIS! ☆
OHH!
HUH?
BA (BAM)
ばっ!!

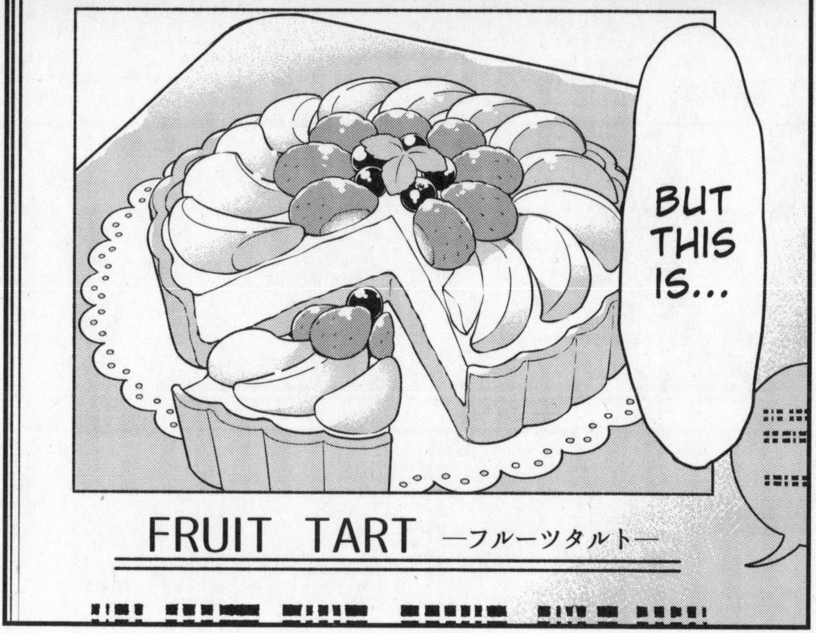
BUT THIS IS...
FRUIT TART —フルーツタルト—

PACKAGES: TASTY MILK / MIRIN RICE WINE / FLOUR

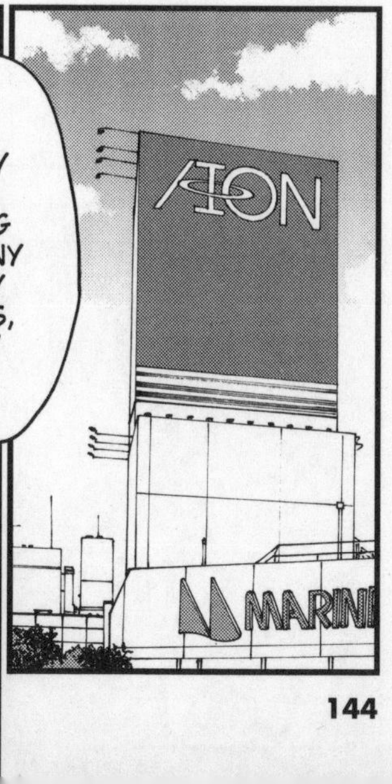
AEON
MARINI

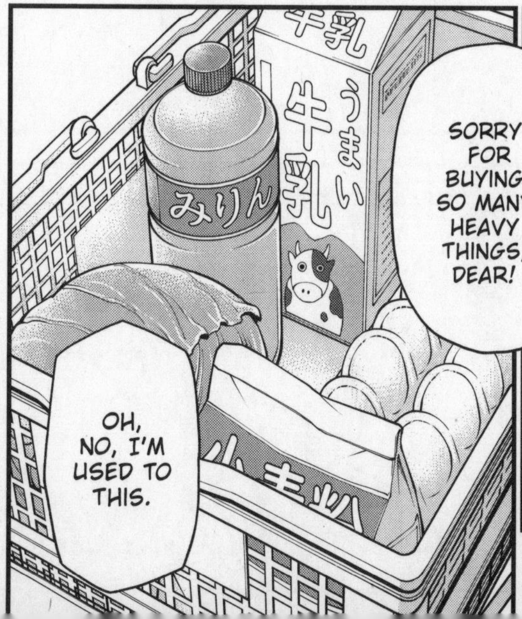
牛乳
うまい牛乳
みりん
小麦粉
SORRY FOR BUYING SO MANY HEAVY THINGS, DEAR!
OH, NO, I'M USED TO THIS.

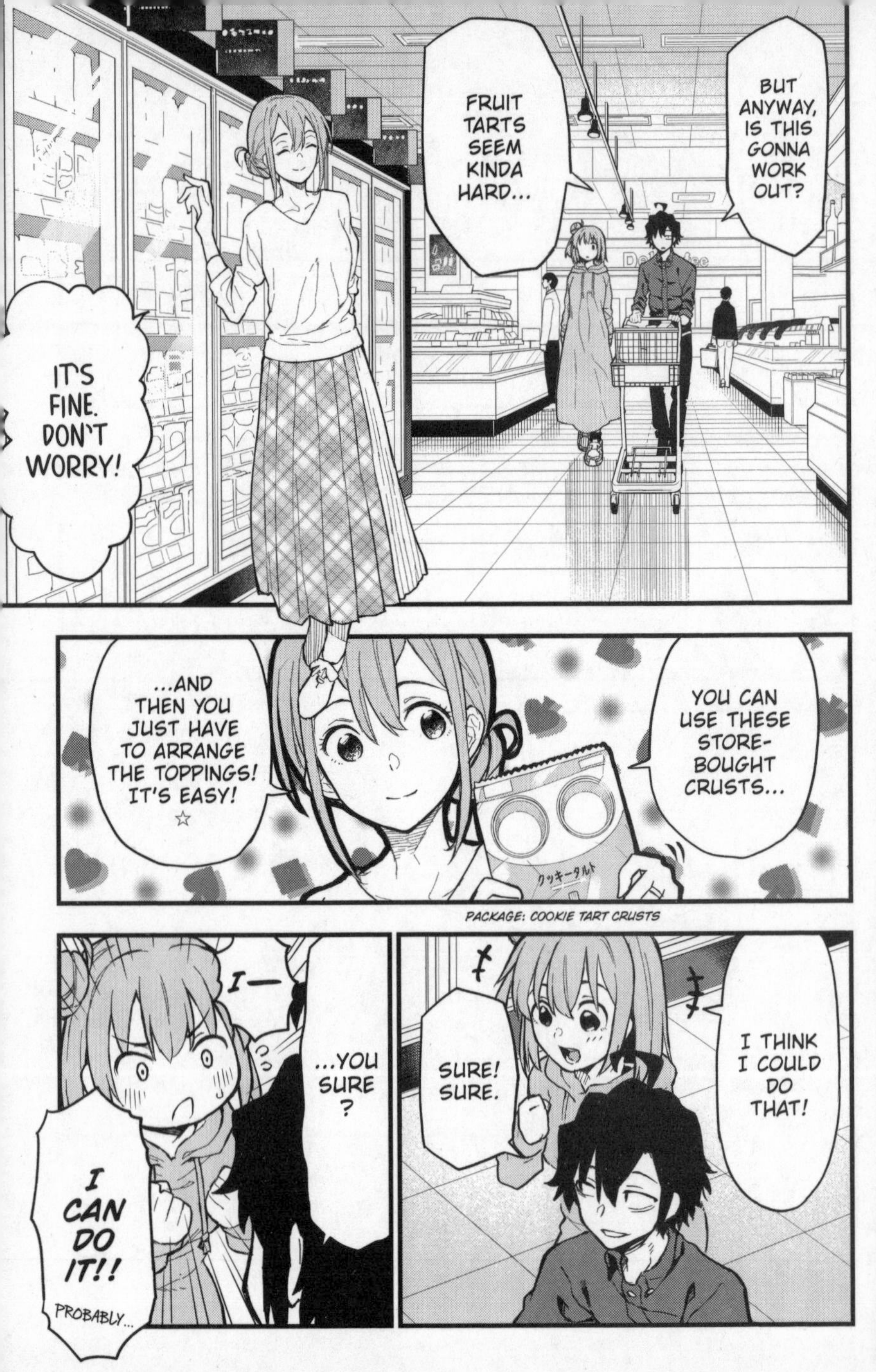
BUT ANYWAY, IS THIS GONNA WORK OUT?
FRUIT TARTS SEEM KINDA HARD...
IT'S FINE. DON'T WORRY!
YOU CAN USE THESE STORE-BOUGHT CRUSTS...
...AND THEN YOU JUST HAVE TO ARRANGE THE TOPPINGS! IT'S EASY! ☆
クッキータルト
PACKAGE: COOKIE TART CRUSTS
I THINK I COULD DO THAT!
SURE! SURE.
...YOU SURE?
I—
I CAN DO IT!!
PROBABLY...

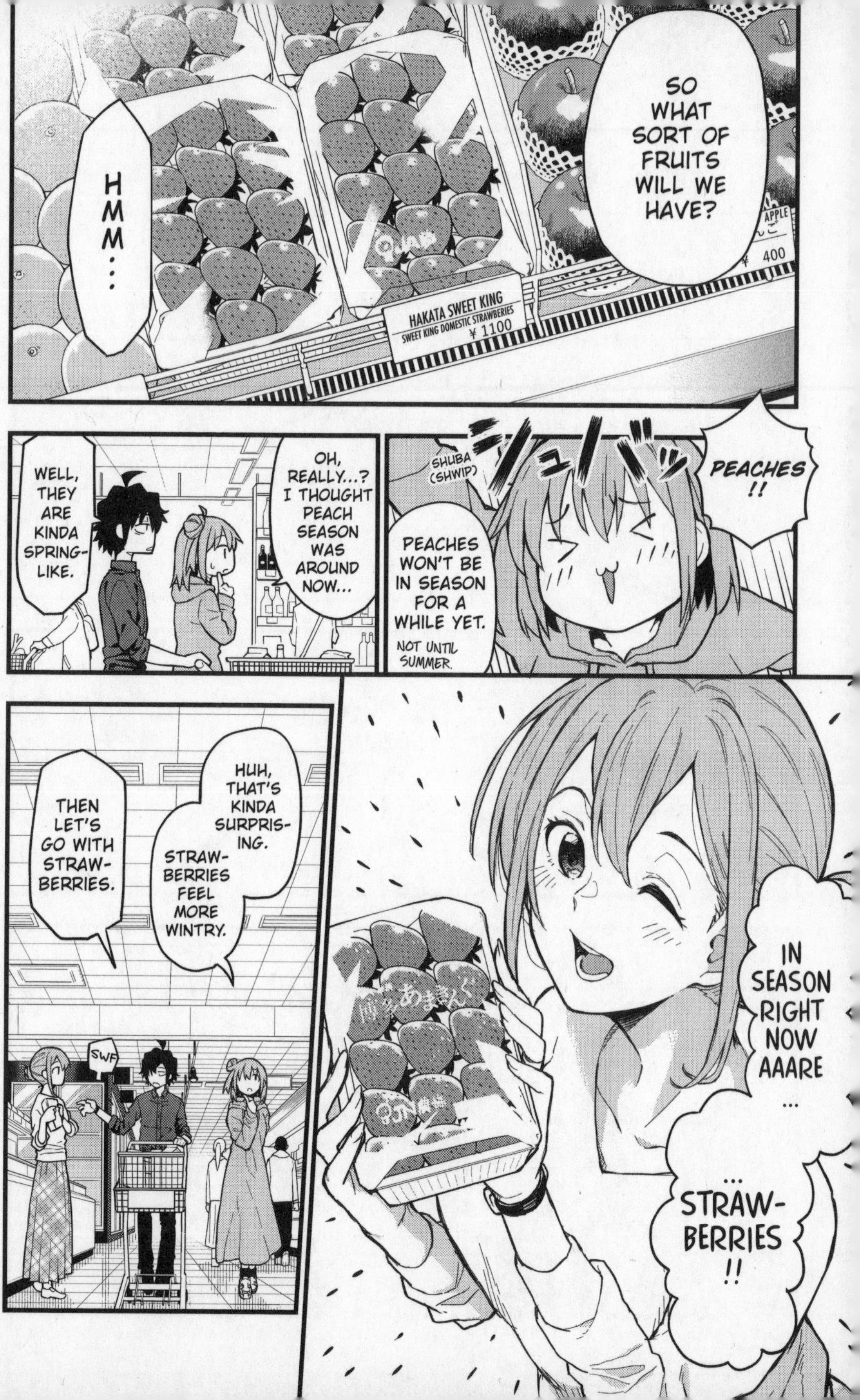
SO WHAT SORT OF FRUITS WILL WE HAVE?
HMM...
APPLE
¥ 400
HAKATA SWEET KING
SWEET KING DOMESTIC STRAWBERRIES
¥ 1100
PEACHES!!
SHUBA (SHWIP)
PEACHES WON'T BE IN SEASON FOR A WHILE YET.
NOT UNTIL SUMMER.
OH, REALLY...? I THOUGHT PEACH SEASON WAS AROUND NOW...
WELL, THEY ARE KINDA SPRING-LIKE.
IN SEASON RIGHT NOW AAARE...
...STRAW-BERRIES!!
HUH, THAT'S KINDA SURPRIS-ING.
STRAW-BERRIES FEEL MORE WINTRY.
THEN LET'S GO WITH STRAW-BERRIES.
SWF

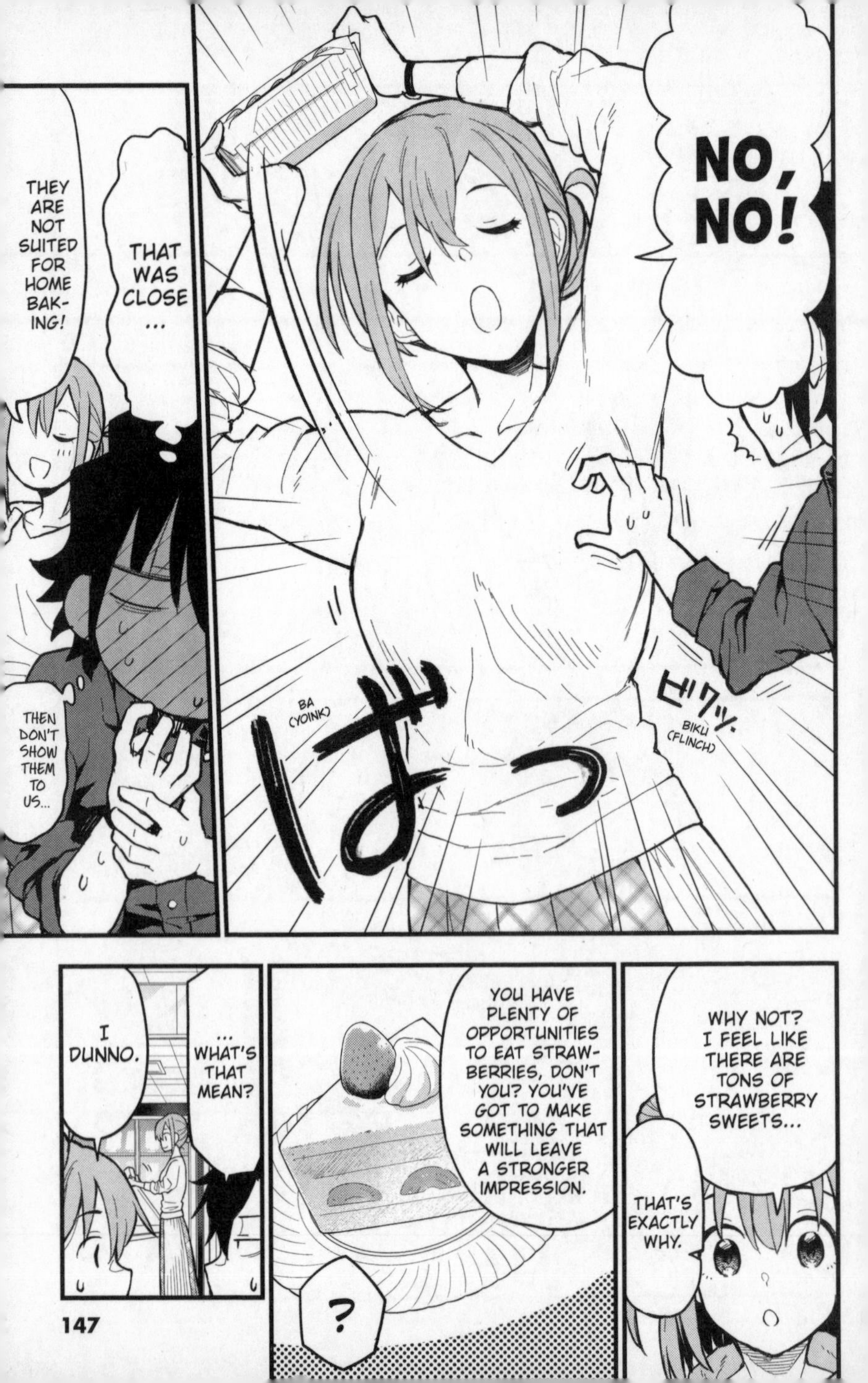
NO, NO!
ビクッ
BIKU (FLINCH)
ばっ
BA (YOINK)
THAT WAS CLOSE ...
THEY ARE NOT SUITED FOR HOME BAK-ING!
THEN DON'T SHOW THEM TO US...
WHY NOT? I FEEL LIKE THERE ARE TONS OF STRAWBERRY SWEETS...
THAT'S EXACTLY WHY.
YOU HAVE PLENTY OF OPPORTUNITIES TO EAT STRAW-BERRIES, DON'T YOU? YOU'VE GOT TO MAKE SOMETHING THAT WILL LEAVE A STRONGER IMPRESSION.
?
... WHAT'S THAT MEAN?
I DUNNO.

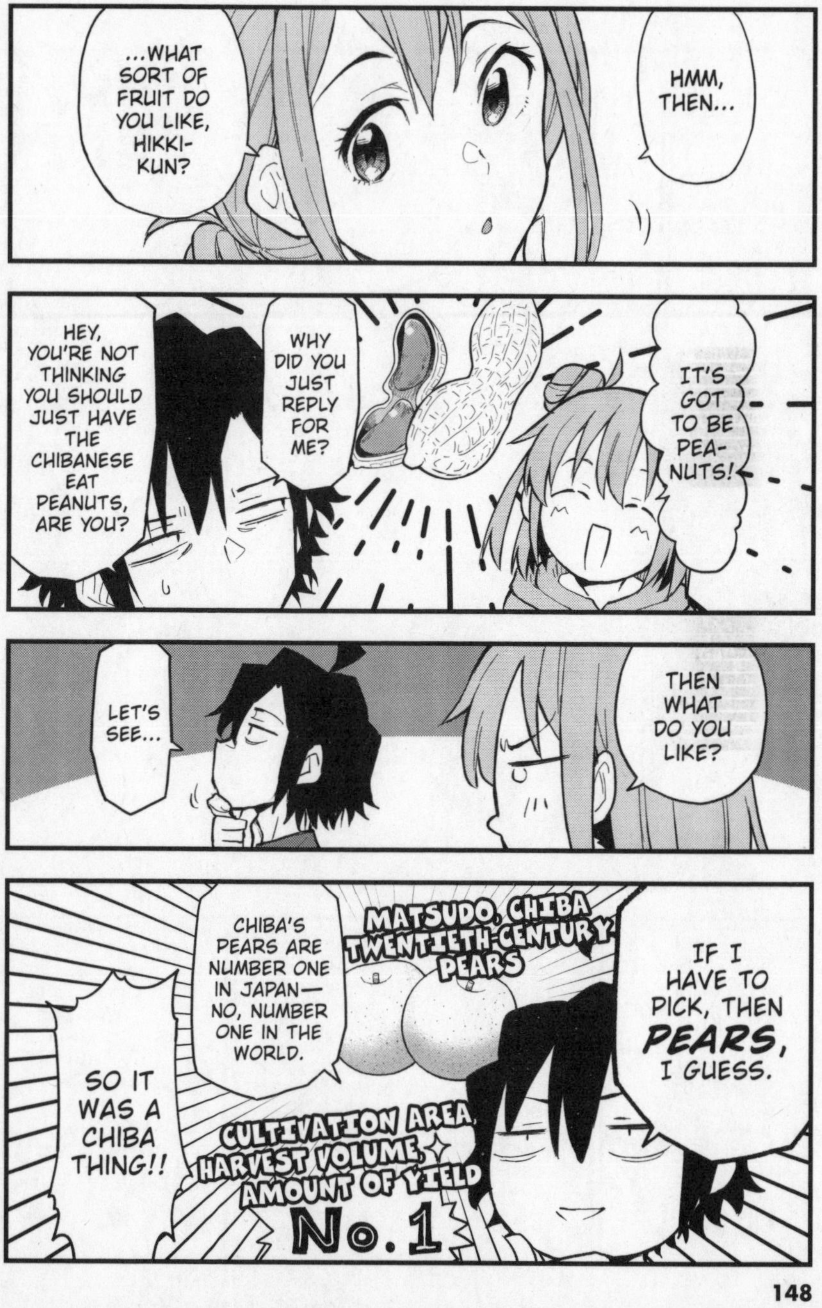
HMM, THEN...
...WHAT SORT OF FRUIT DO YOU LIKE, HIKKI-KUN?
IT'S GOT TO BE PEANUTS!
WHY DID YOU JUST REPLY FOR ME?
HEY, YOU'RE NOT THINKING YOU SHOULD JUST HAVE THE CHIBANESE EAT PEANUTS, ARE YOU?
THEN WHAT DO YOU LIKE?
LET'S SEE...
IF I HAVE TO PICK, THEN PEARS, I GUESS.
MATSUDO, CHIBA TWENTIETH-CENTURY PEARS
CHIBA'S PEARS ARE NUMBER ONE IN JAPAN—NO, NUMBER ONE IN THE WORLD.
CULTIVATION AREA, HARVEST VOLUME, AMOUNT OF YIELD No. 1
SO IT WAS A CHIBA THING!!

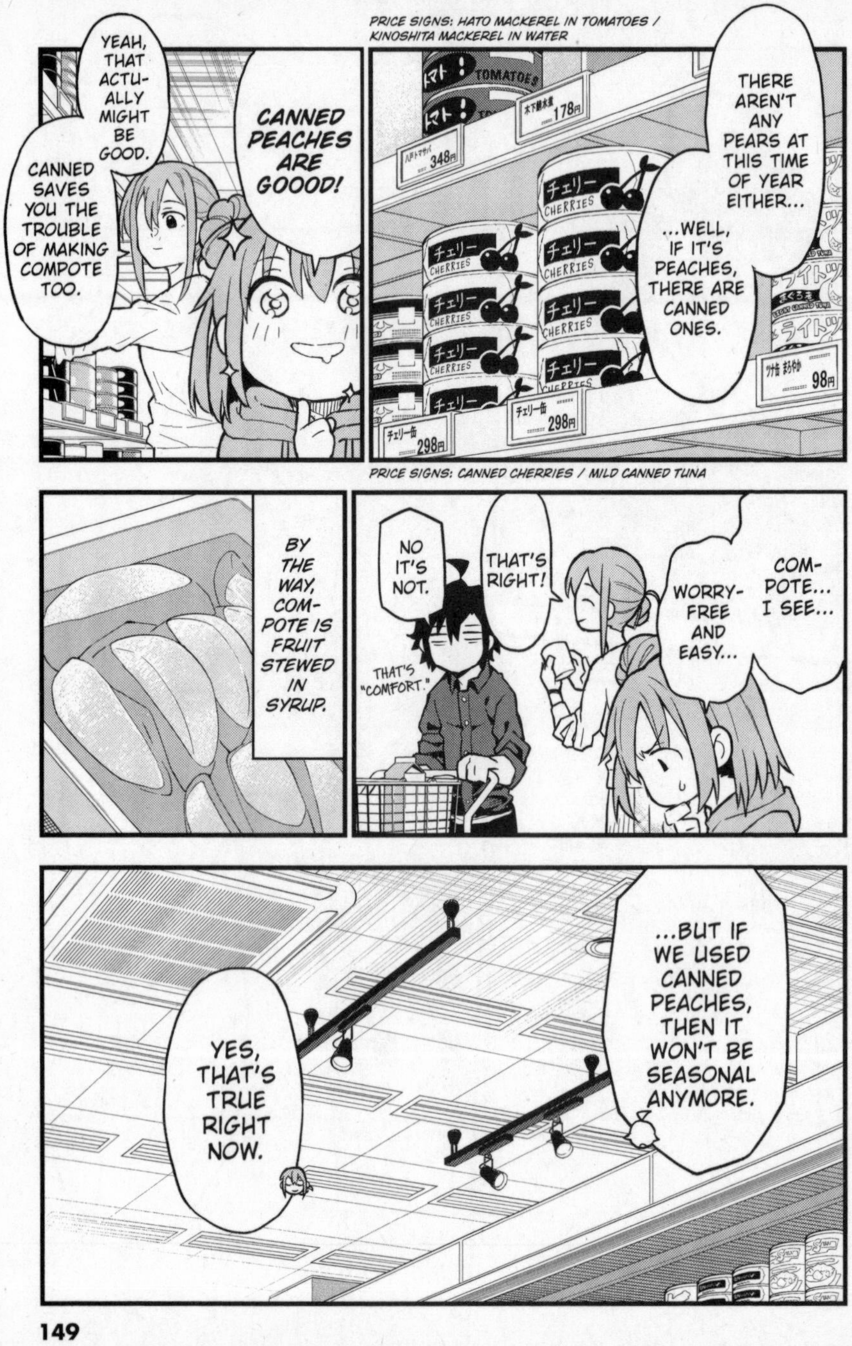
PRICE SIGNS: HATO MACKEREL IN TOMATOES / KINOSHITA MACKEREL IN WATER
THERE AREN'T ANY PEARS AT THIS TIME OF YEAR EITHER...
...WELL, IF IT'S PEACHES, THERE ARE CANNED ONES.
PRICE SIGNS: CANNED CHERRIES / MILD CANNED TUNA
CANNED PEACHES ARE GOOOD!
YEAH, THAT ACTUALLY MIGHT BE GOOD.
CANNED SAVES YOU THE TROUBLE OF MAKING COMPOTE TOO.
COMPOTE... I SEE...
WORRY-FREE AND EASY...
THAT'S RIGHT!
NO IT'S NOT.
THAT'S "COMFORT."
BY THE WAY, COMPOTE IS FRUIT STEWED IN SYRUP.
...BUT IF WE USED CANNED PEACHES, THEN IT WON'T BE SEASONAL ANYMORE.
YES, THAT'S TRUE RIGHT NOW.

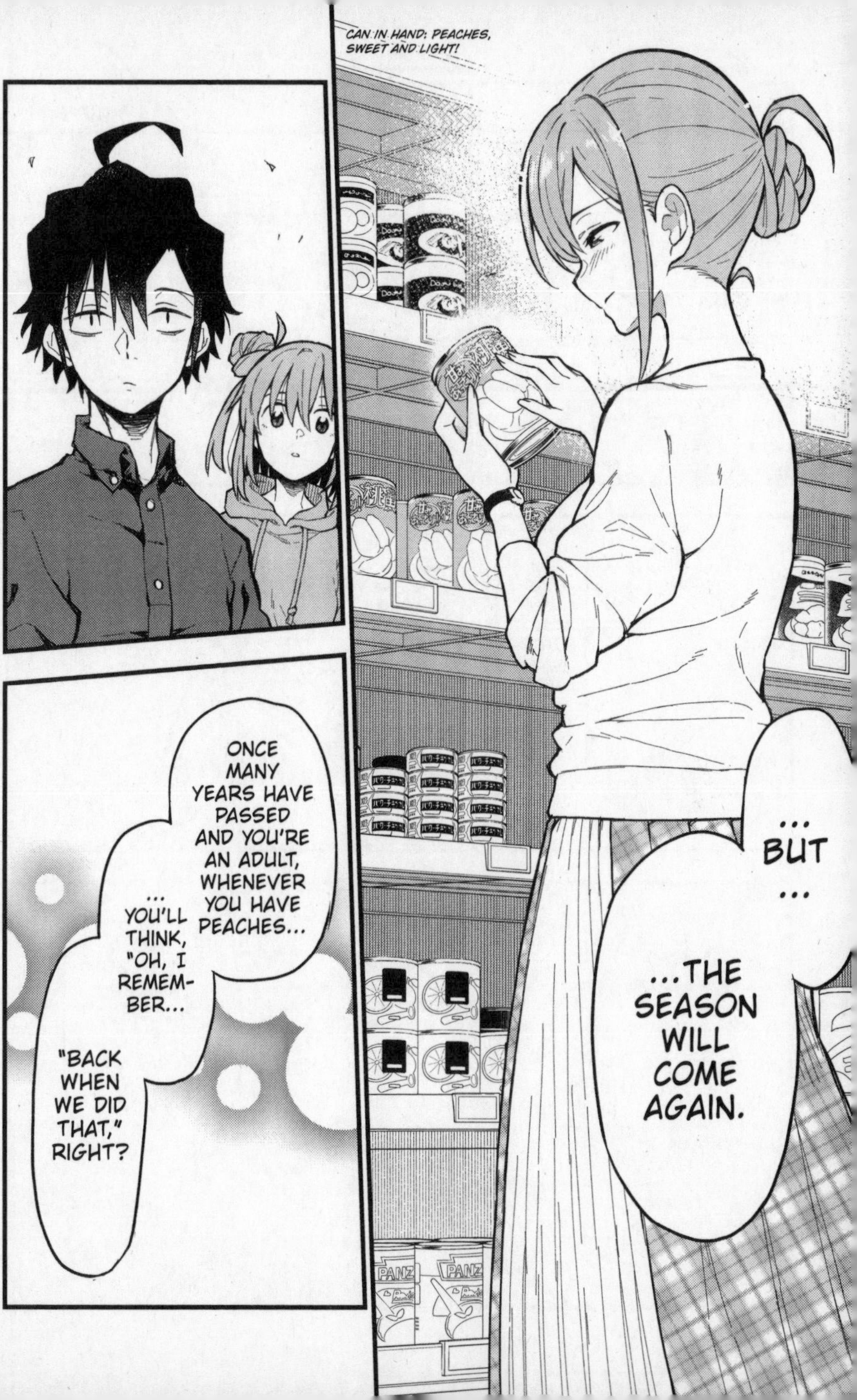
CAN IN HAND: PEACHES, SWEET AND LIGHT!
... BUT ...
...THE SEASON WILL COME AGAIN.
ONCE MANY YEARS HAVE PASSED AND YOU'RE AN ADULT, WHENEVER YOU HAVE PEACHES...
... YOU'LL THINK, "OH, I REMEMBER...
"BACK WHEN WE DID THAT," RIGHT?

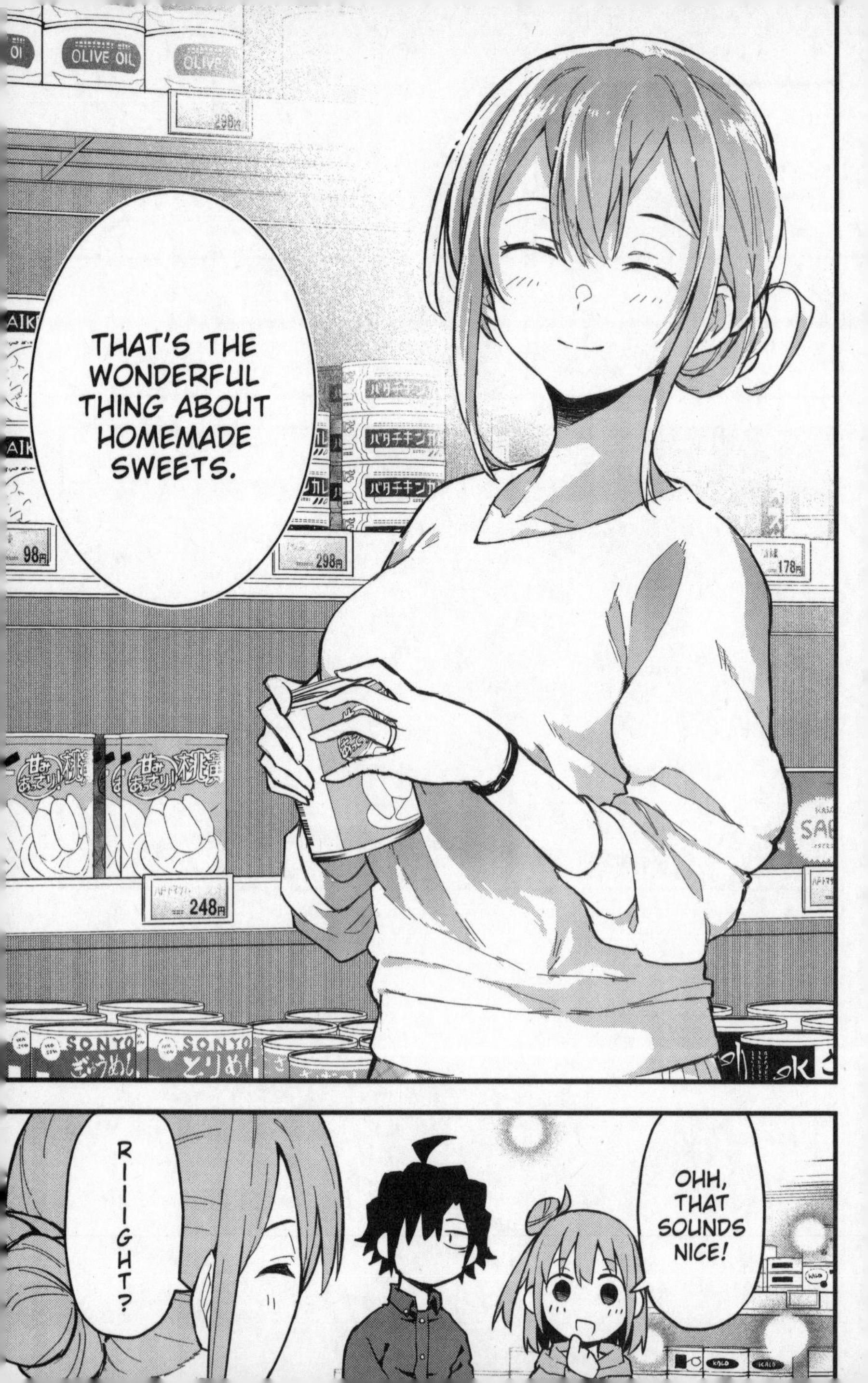
THAT'S THE WONDERFUL THING ABOUT HOMEMADE SWEETS.
OHH, THAT SOUNDS NICE!
RIIIGHT?

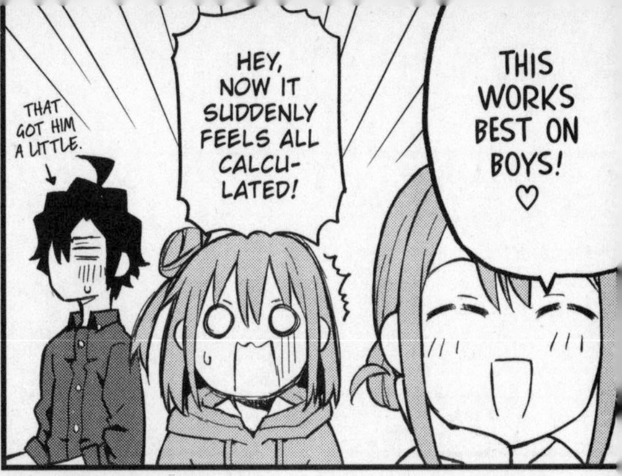
THIS WORKS BEST ON BOYS! ♡
HEY, NOW IT SUDDENLY FEELS ALL CALCULATED!
THAT GOT HIM A LITTLE.
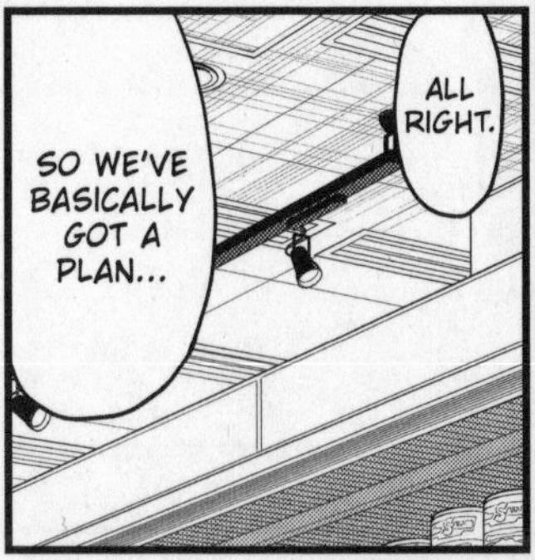
ALL RIGHT.
SO WE'VE BASICALLY GOT A PLAN...
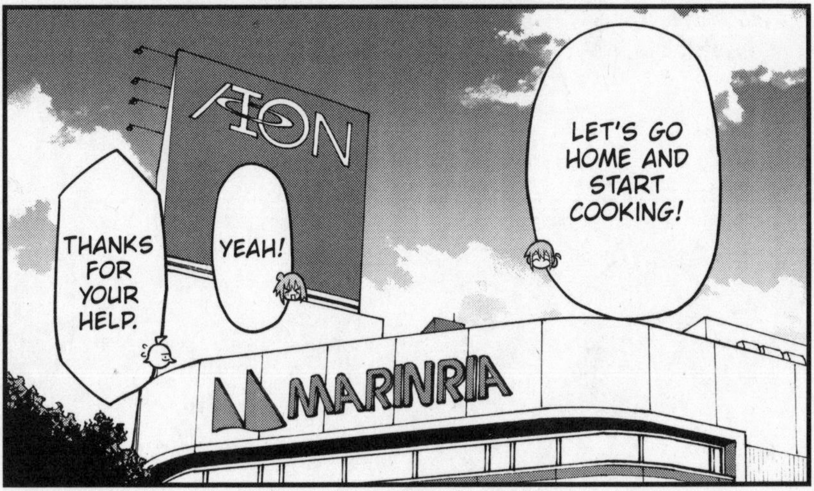
LET'S GO HOME AND START COOKING!
YEAH!
THANKS FOR YOUR HELP.
MARINRIA
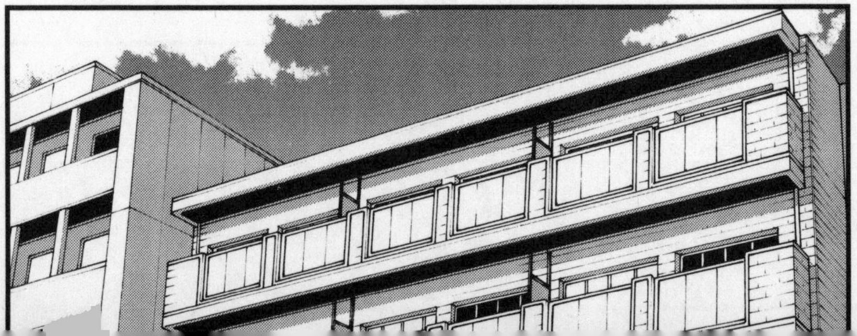

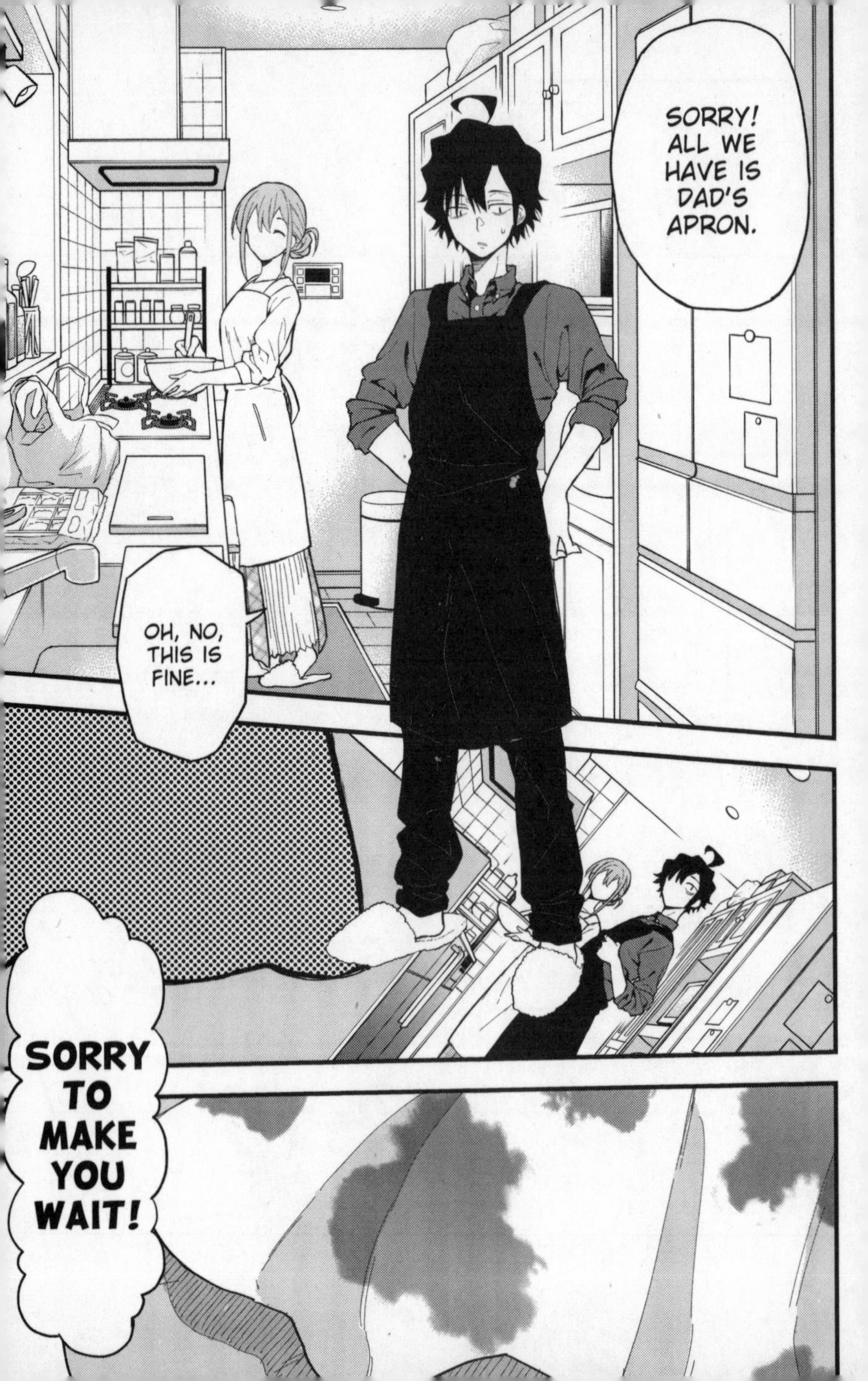
SORRY! ALL WE HAVE IS DAD'S APRON.
OH, NO, THIS IS FINE...
SORRY TO MAKE YOU WAIT!

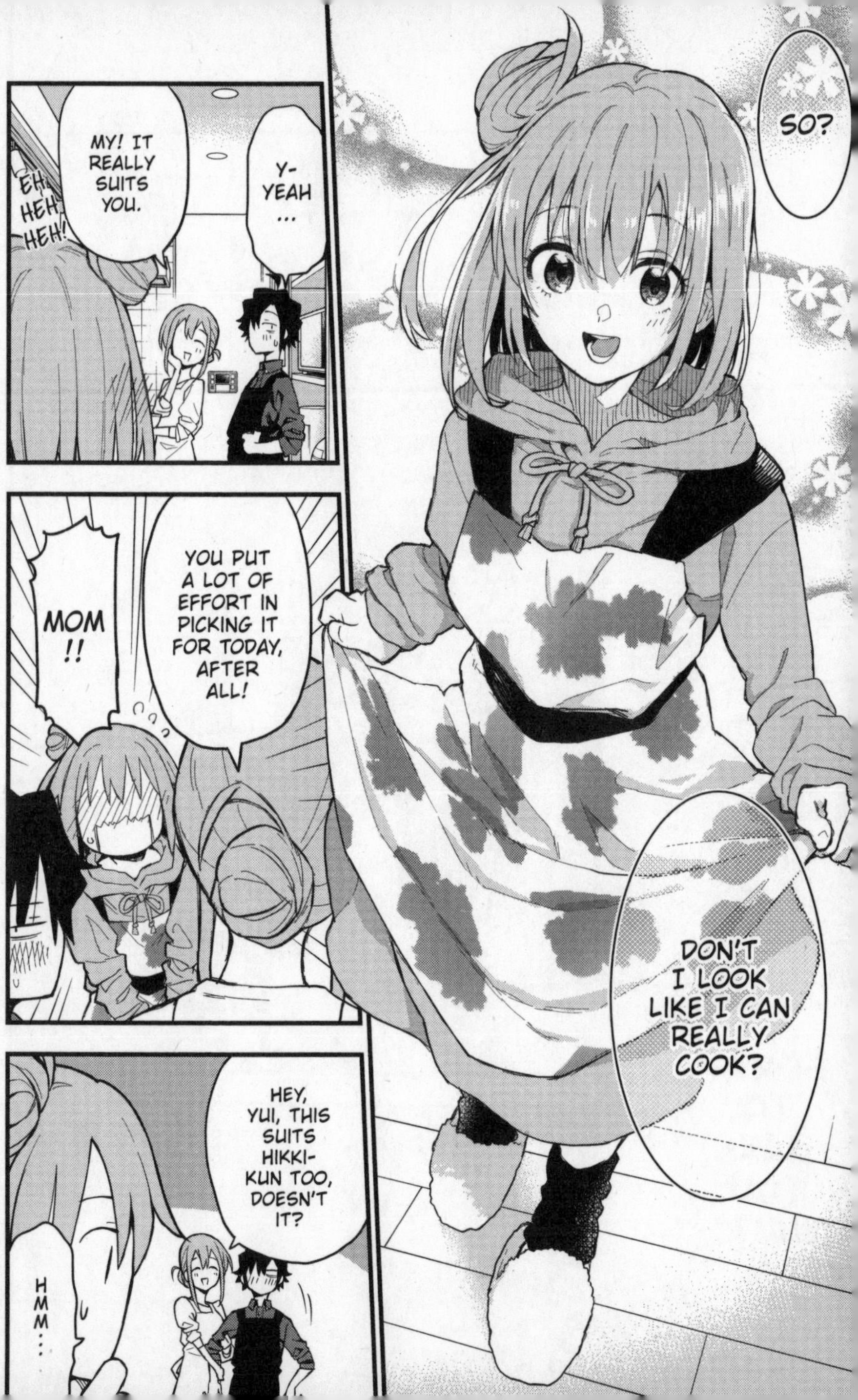
SO?
DON'T I LOOK LIKE I CAN REALLY COOK?
Y-YEAH...
MY! IT REALLY SUITS YOU.
EH HEH HEH!
YOU PUT A LOT OF EFFORT IN PICKING IT FOR TODAY, AFTER ALL!
MOM!!
HEY, YUI, THIS SUITS HIKKI-KUN TOO, DOESN'T IT?
HMM...

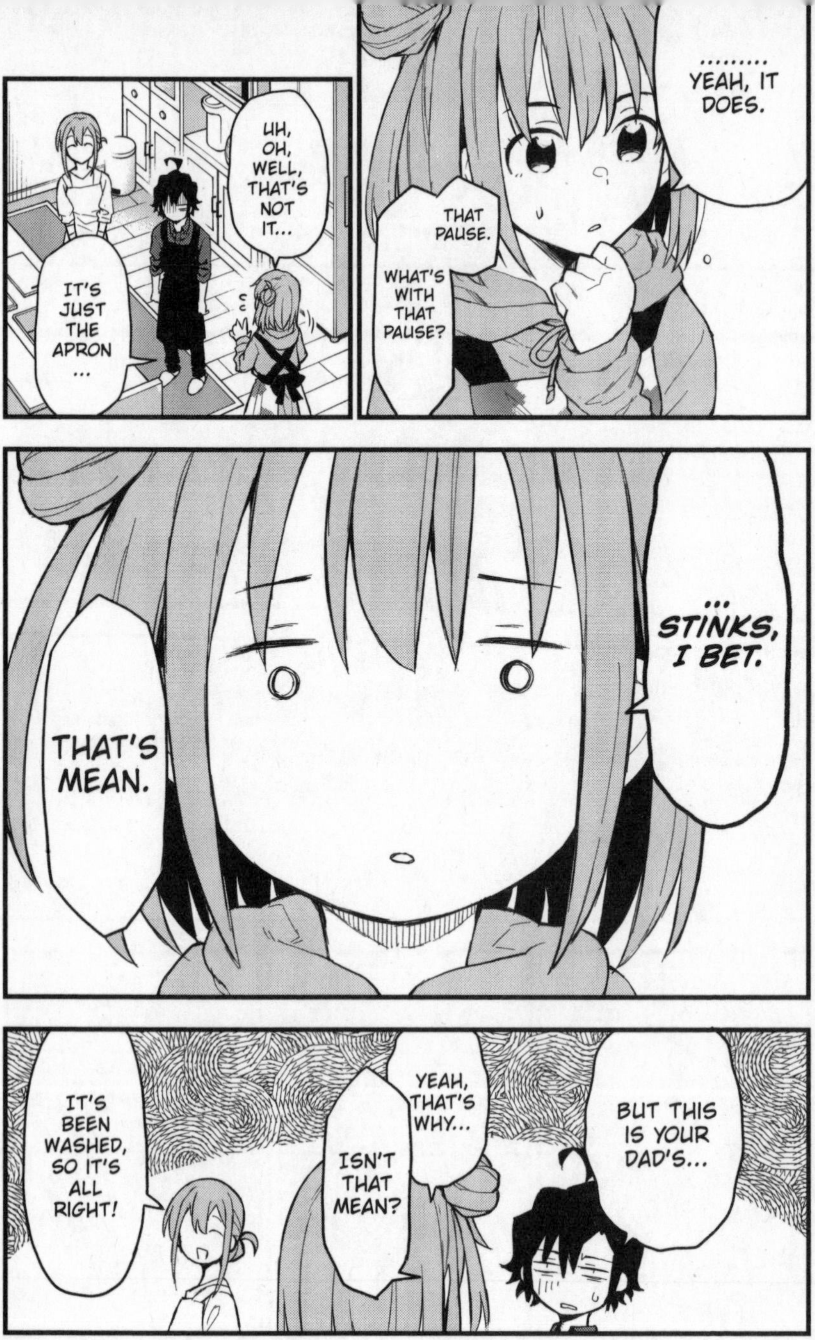
.... YEAH, IT DOES.
THAT PAUSE.
WHAT'S WITH THAT PAUSE?
UH, OH, WELL, THAT'S NOT IT...
IT'S JUST THE APRON ...
... STINKS, I BET.
THAT'S MEAN.
BUT THIS IS YOUR DAD'S...
YEAH, THAT'S WHY...
ISN'T THAT MEAN?
IT'S BEEN WASHED, SO IT'S ALL RIGHT!

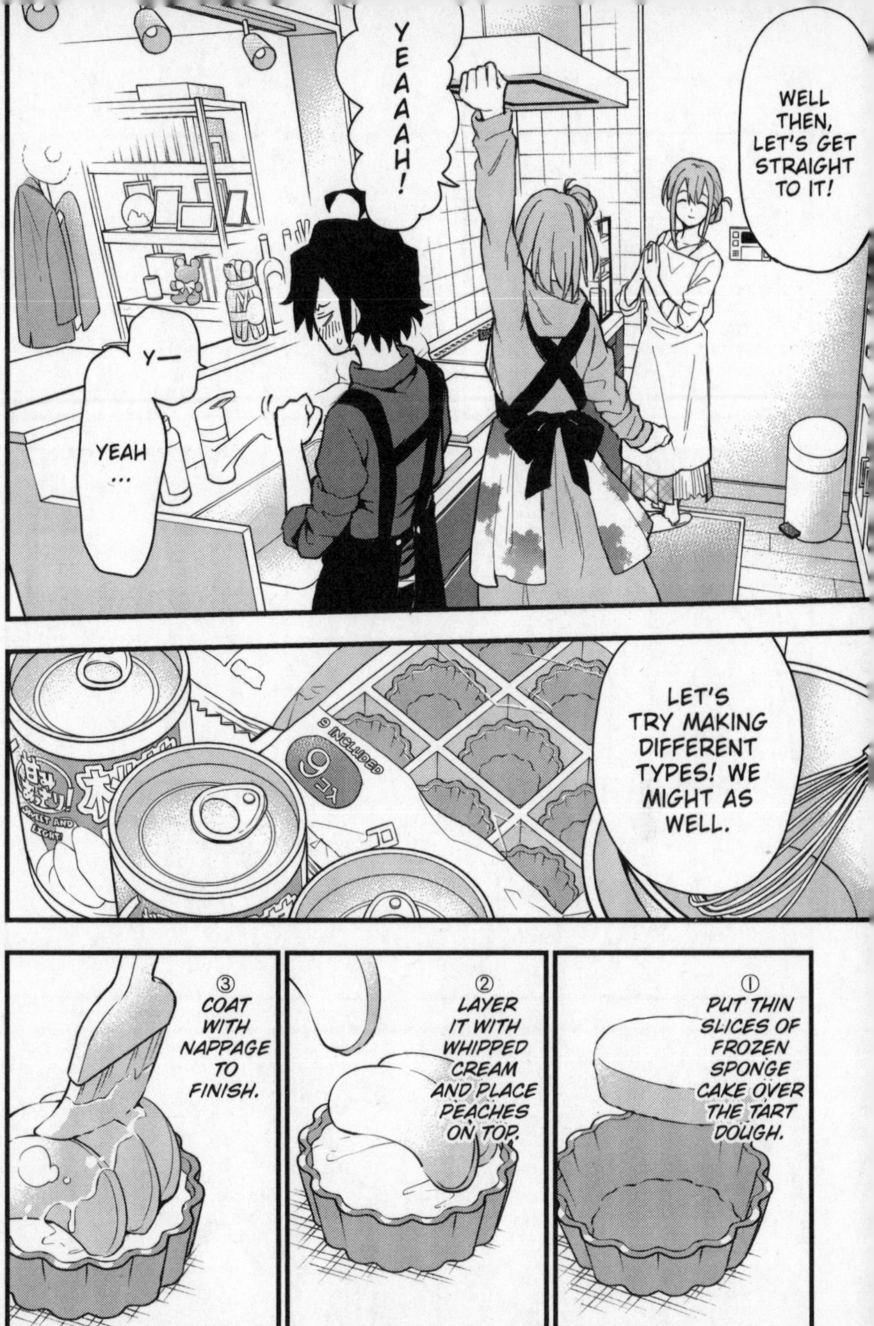
WELL THEN, LET'S GET STRAIGHT TO IT!
YEAAAAH!
Y—
YEAH...
LET'S TRY MAKING DIFFERENT TYPES! WE MIGHT AS WELL.
9 INCLUDED
SWEET AND LIGHT!
① PUT THIN SLICES OF FROZEN SPONGE CAKE OVER THE TART DOUGH.
② LAYER IT WITH WHIPPED CREAM AND PLACE PEACHES ON TOP.
③ COAT WITH NAPPAGE TO FINISH.

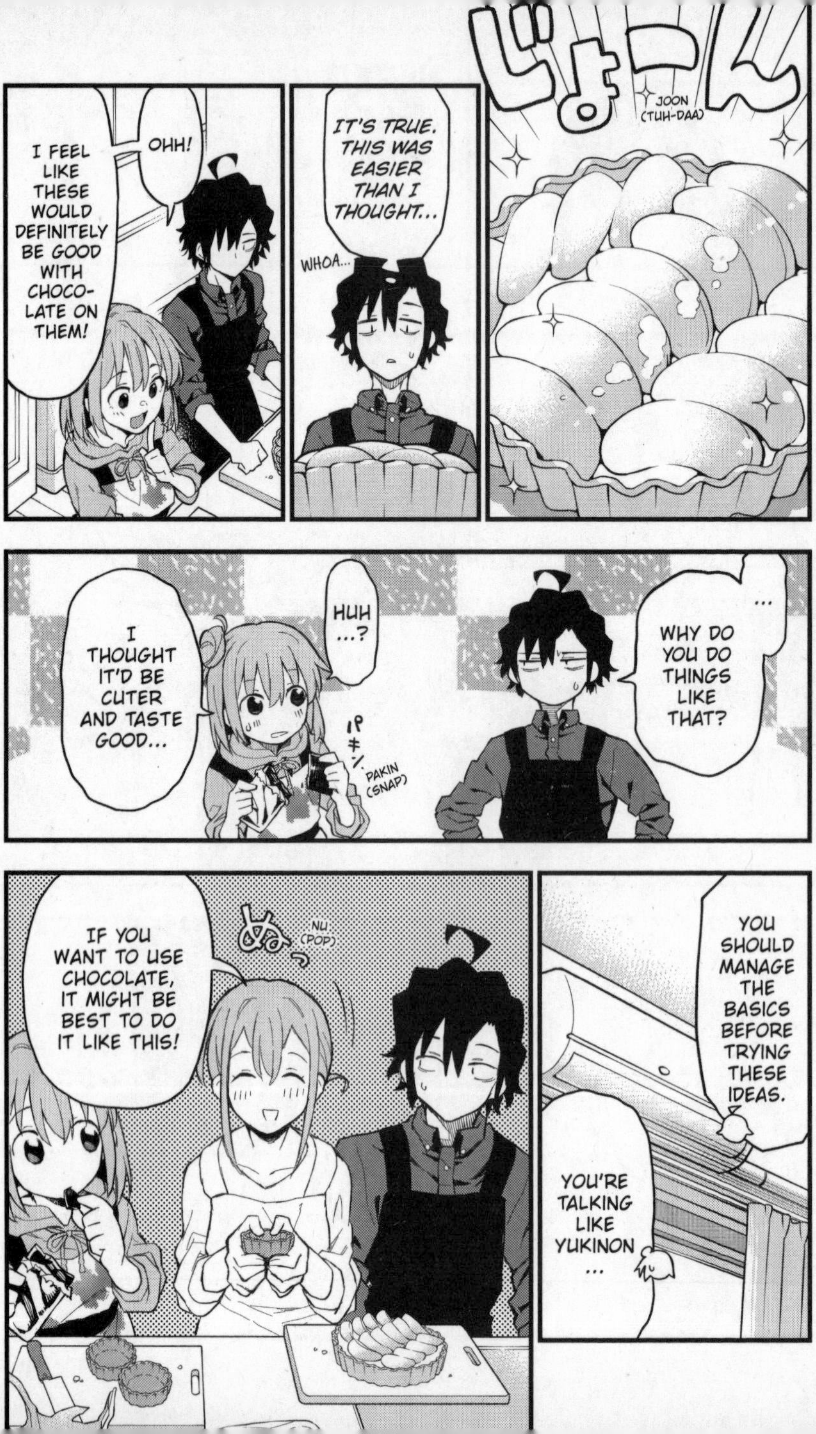
じょーん
JOON (TUH-DAA)
IT'S TRUE. THIS WAS EASIER THAN I THOUGHT...
WHOA...
OHH!
I FEEL LIKE THESE WOULD DEFINITELY BE GOOD WITH CHOCO-LATE ON THEM!
...
WHY DO YOU DO THINGS LIKE THAT?
HUH ...?
パキッ
PAKIN (SNAP)
I THOUGHT IT'D BE CUTER AND TASTE GOOD...
YOU SHOULD MANAGE THE BASICS BEFORE TRYING THESE IDEAS.
YOU'RE TALKING LIKE YUKINON ...
ぬ
NU (POP)
IF YOU WANT TO USE CHOCOLATE, IT MIGHT BE BEST TO DO IT LIKE THIS!

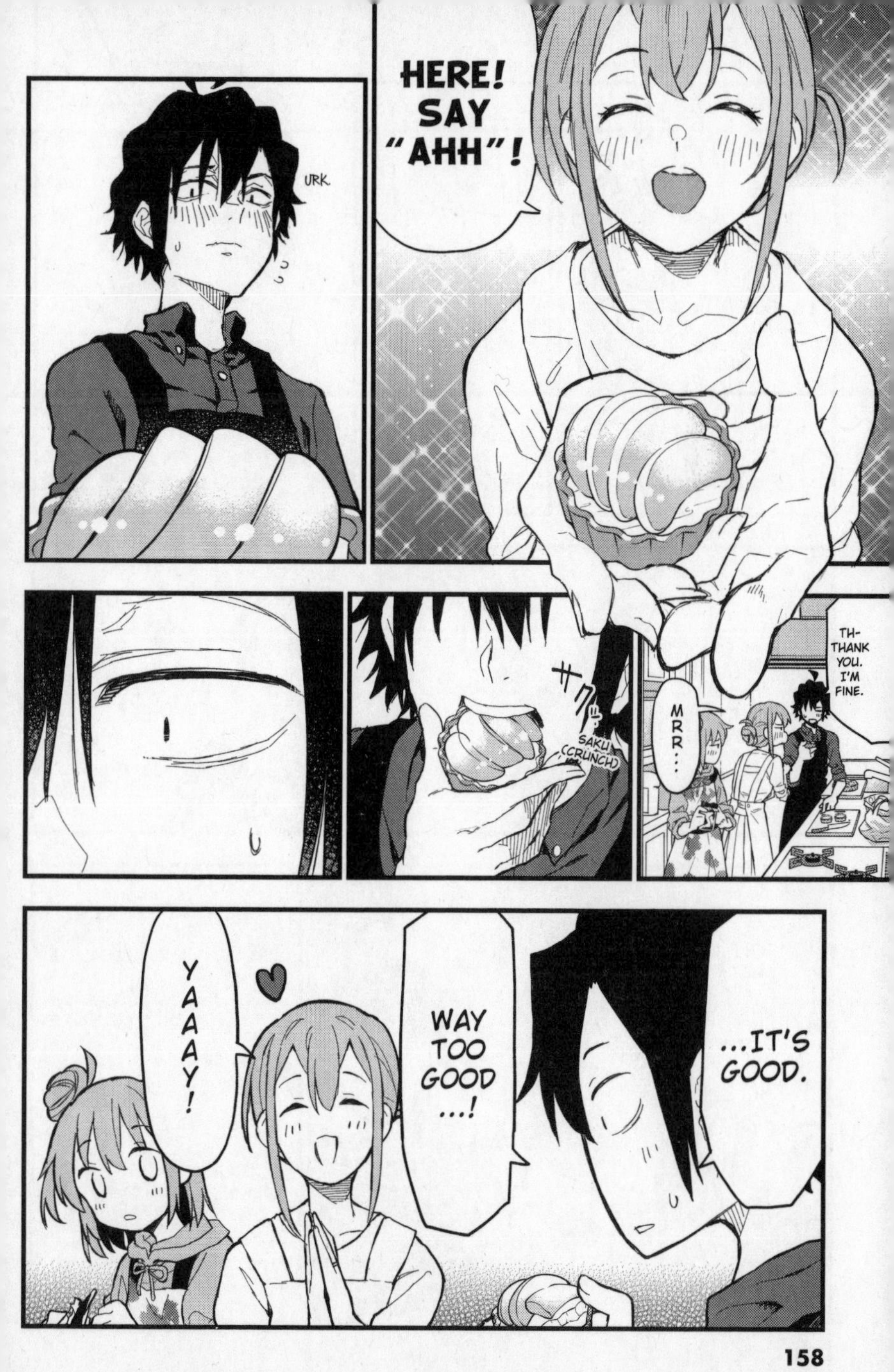
HERE! SAY "AHH"!
URK.
TH- THANK YOU. I'M FINE.
MRR...
サク
SAKU (CRUNCH)
...IT'S GOOD.
WAY TOO GOOD ...!
YAAAY!

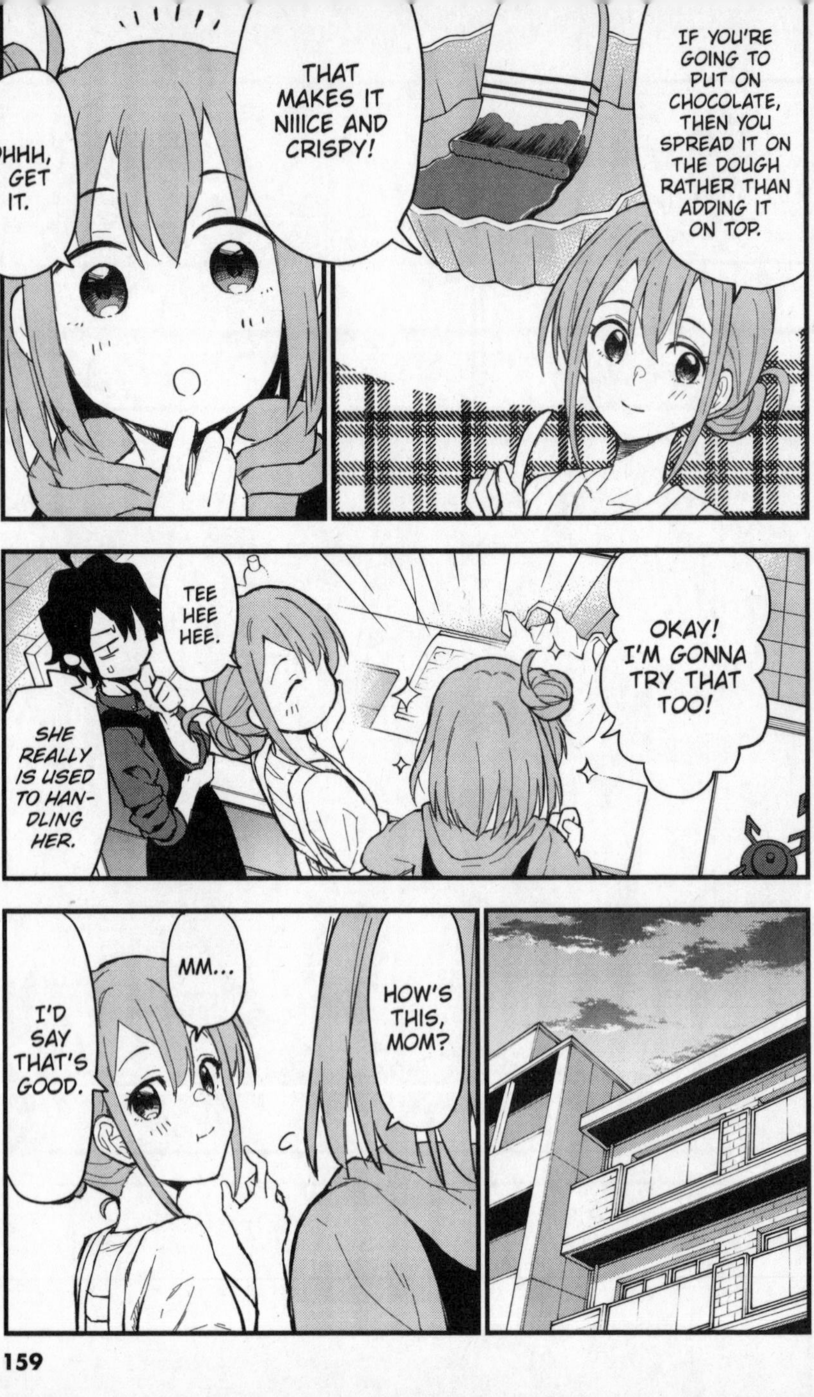
IF YOU'RE GOING TO PUT ON CHOCOLATE, THEN YOU SPREAD IT ON THE DOUGH RATHER THAN ADDING IT ON TOP.
THAT MAKES IT NIIICE AND CRISPY!
OHHH, I GET IT.
OKAY! I'M GONNA TRY THAT TOO!
TEE HEE HEE.
SHE REALLY IS USED TO HAN-DLING HER.
HOW'S THIS, MOM?
MM...
I'D SAY THAT'S GOOD.

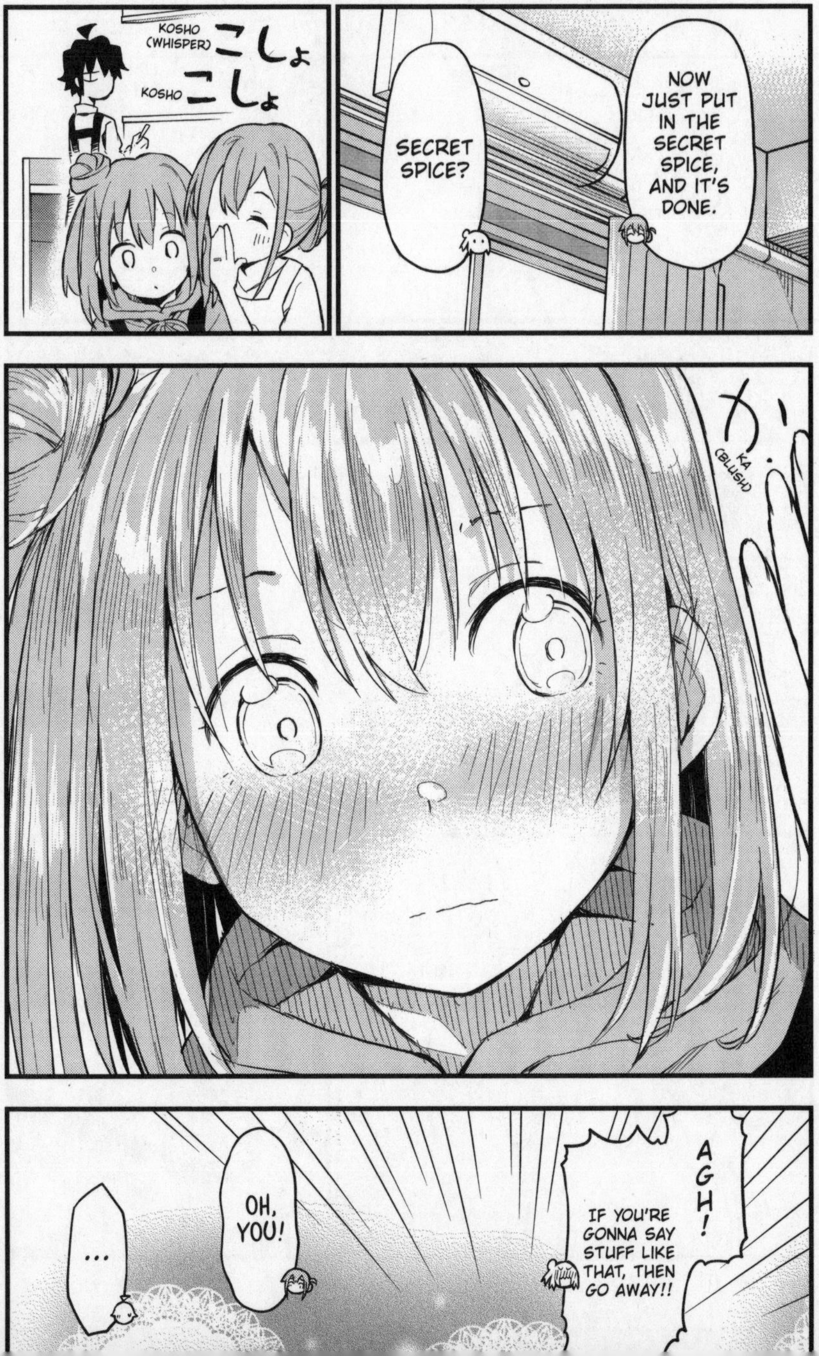
NOW JUST PUT IN THE SECRET SPICE, AND IT'S DONE.
SECRET SPICE?
KOSHO (WHISPER) こしょ
KOSHO こしょ
か KA (BLUSH)
AGH!
IF YOU'RE GONNA SAY STUFF LIKE THAT, THEN GO AWAY!!
OH, YOU!
...

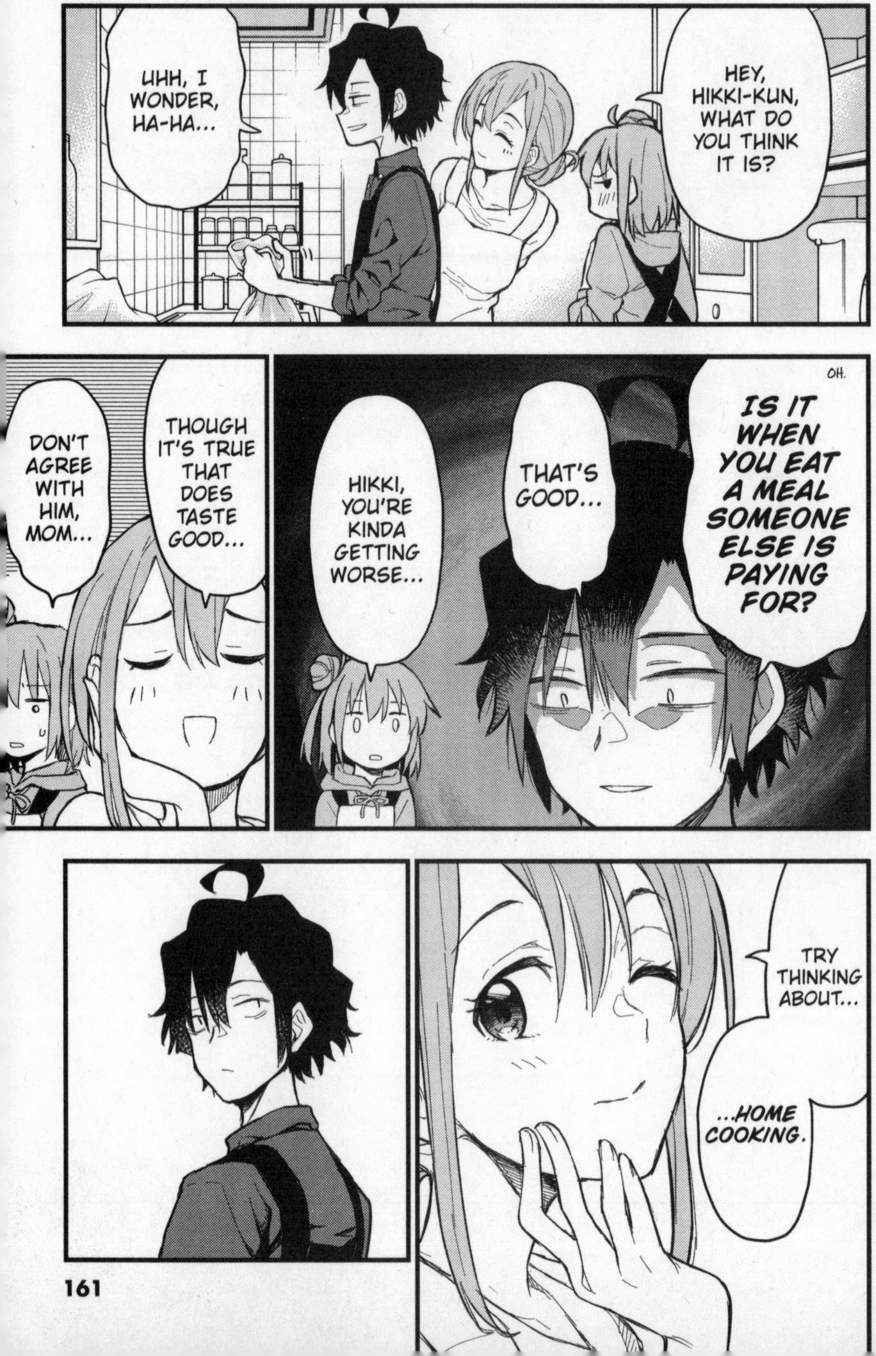
HEY, HIKKI-KUN, WHAT DO YOU THINK IT IS?
UHH, I WONDER, HA-HA...
OH.
IS IT WHEN YOU EAT A MEAL SOMEONE ELSE IS PAYING FOR?
THAT'S GOOD...
HIKKI, YOU'RE KINDA GETTING WORSE...
THOUGH IT'S TRUE THAT DOES TASTE GOOD...
DON'T AGREE WITH HIM, MOM...
TRY THINKING ABOUT...
...HOME COOKING.

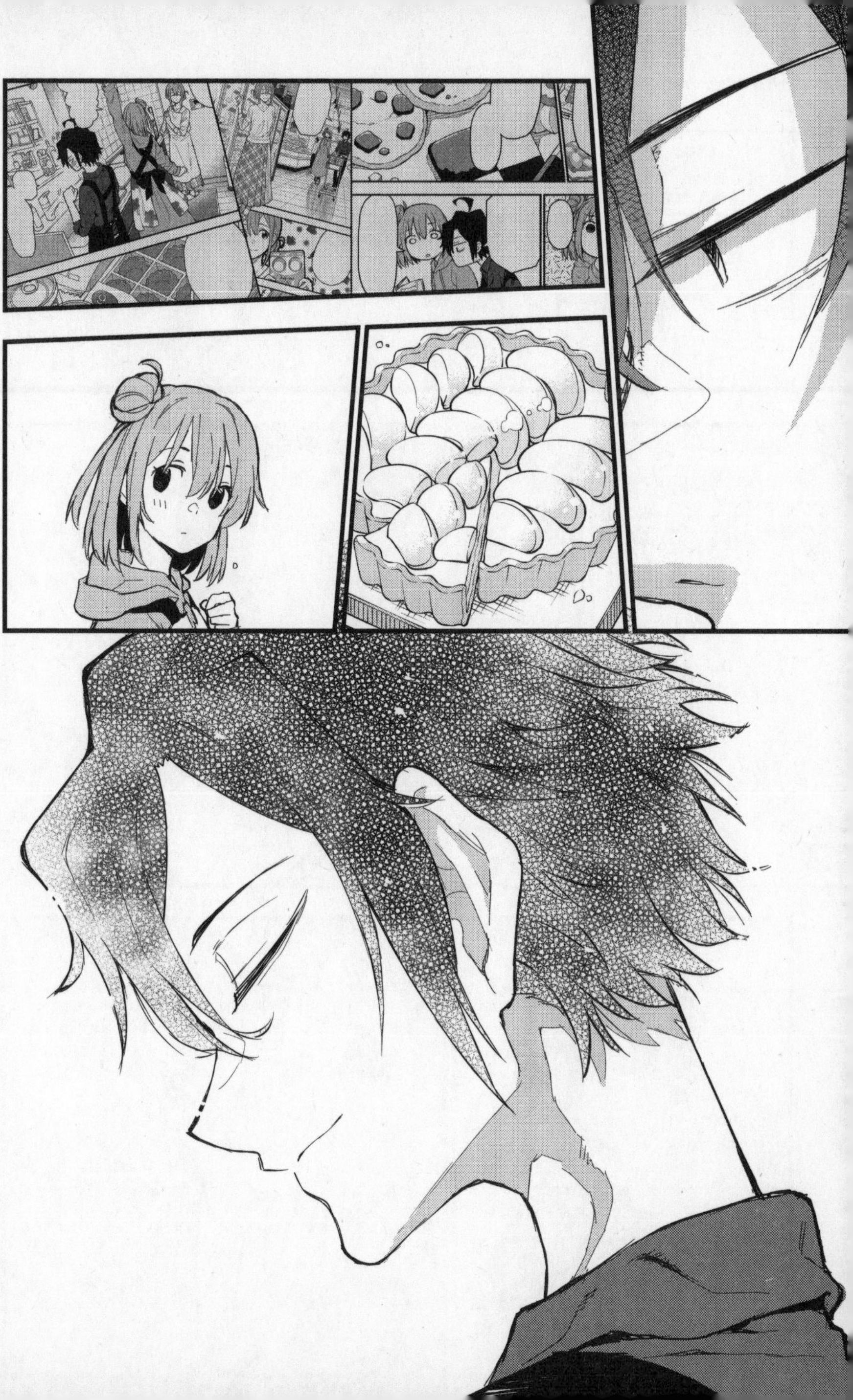

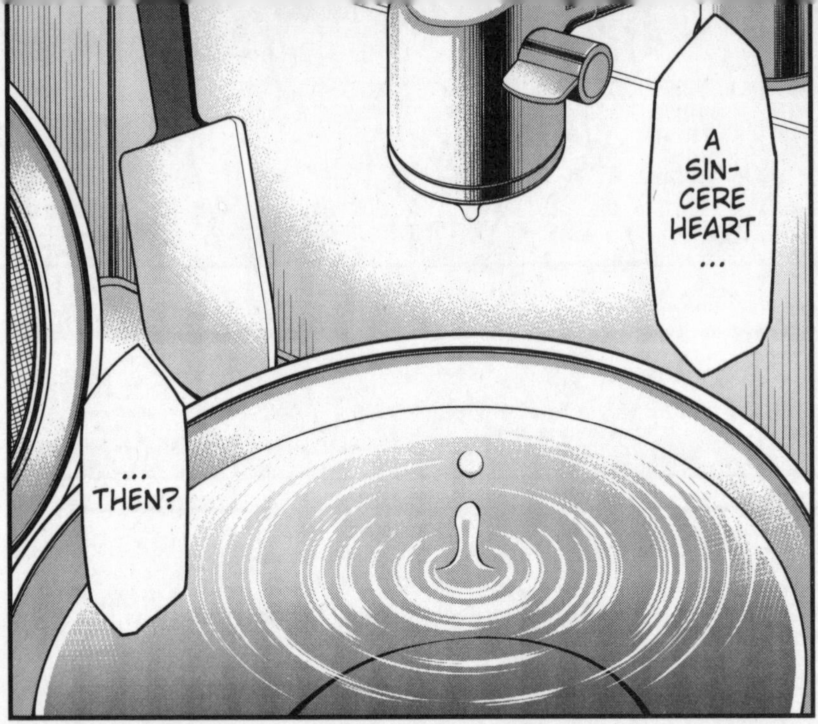
A SIN-CERE HEART ...
... THEN?

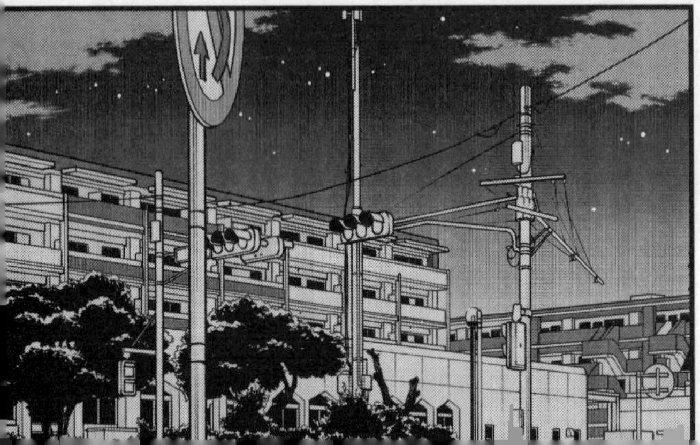

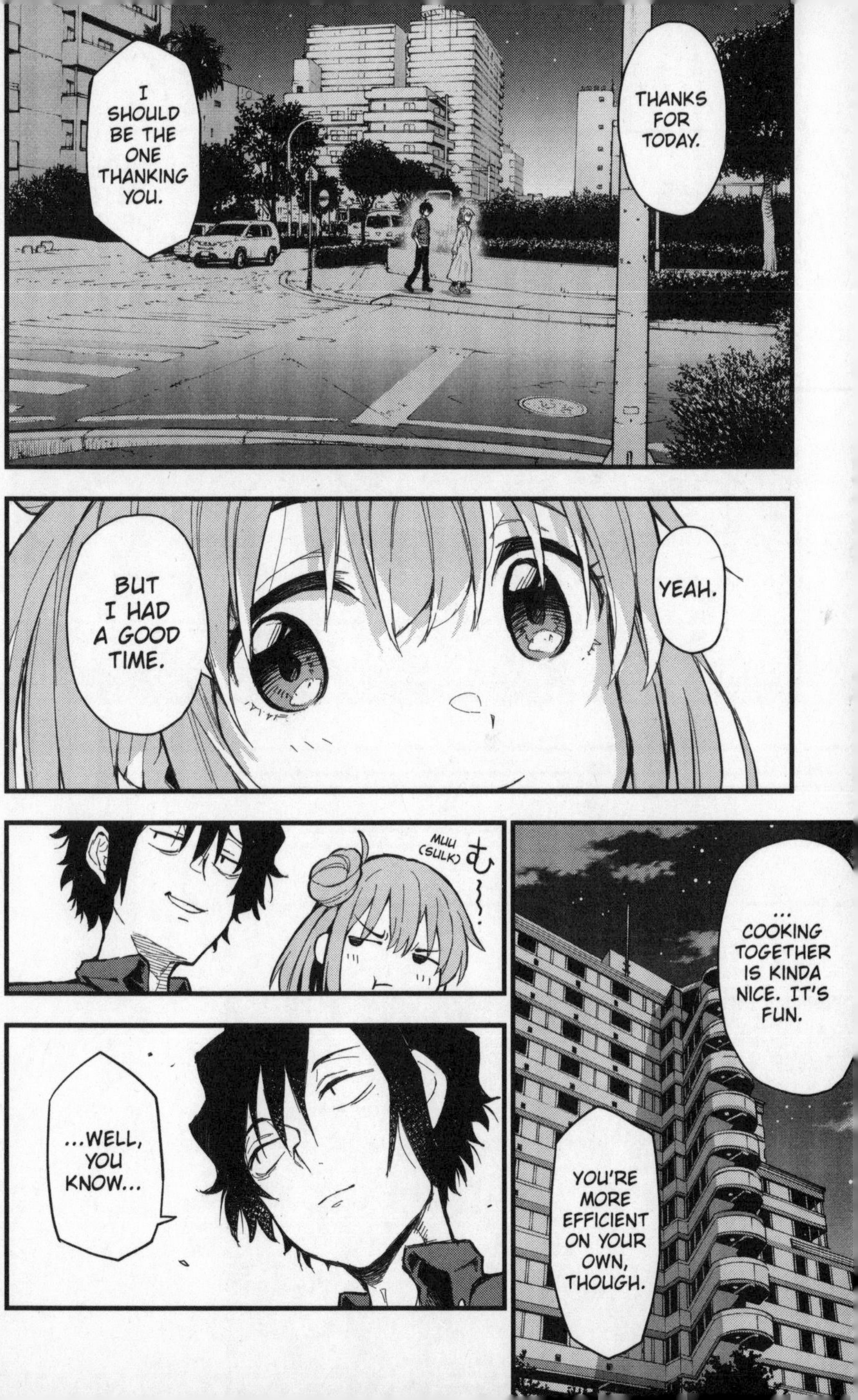
THANKS FOR TODAY.
I SHOULD BE THE ONE THANKING YOU.
YEAH.
BUT I HAD A GOOD TIME.
...COOKING TOGETHER IS KINDA NICE. IT'S FUN.
YOU'RE MORE EFFICIENT ON YOUR OWN, THOUGH.
MUU (SULK)
...WELL, YOU KNOW...

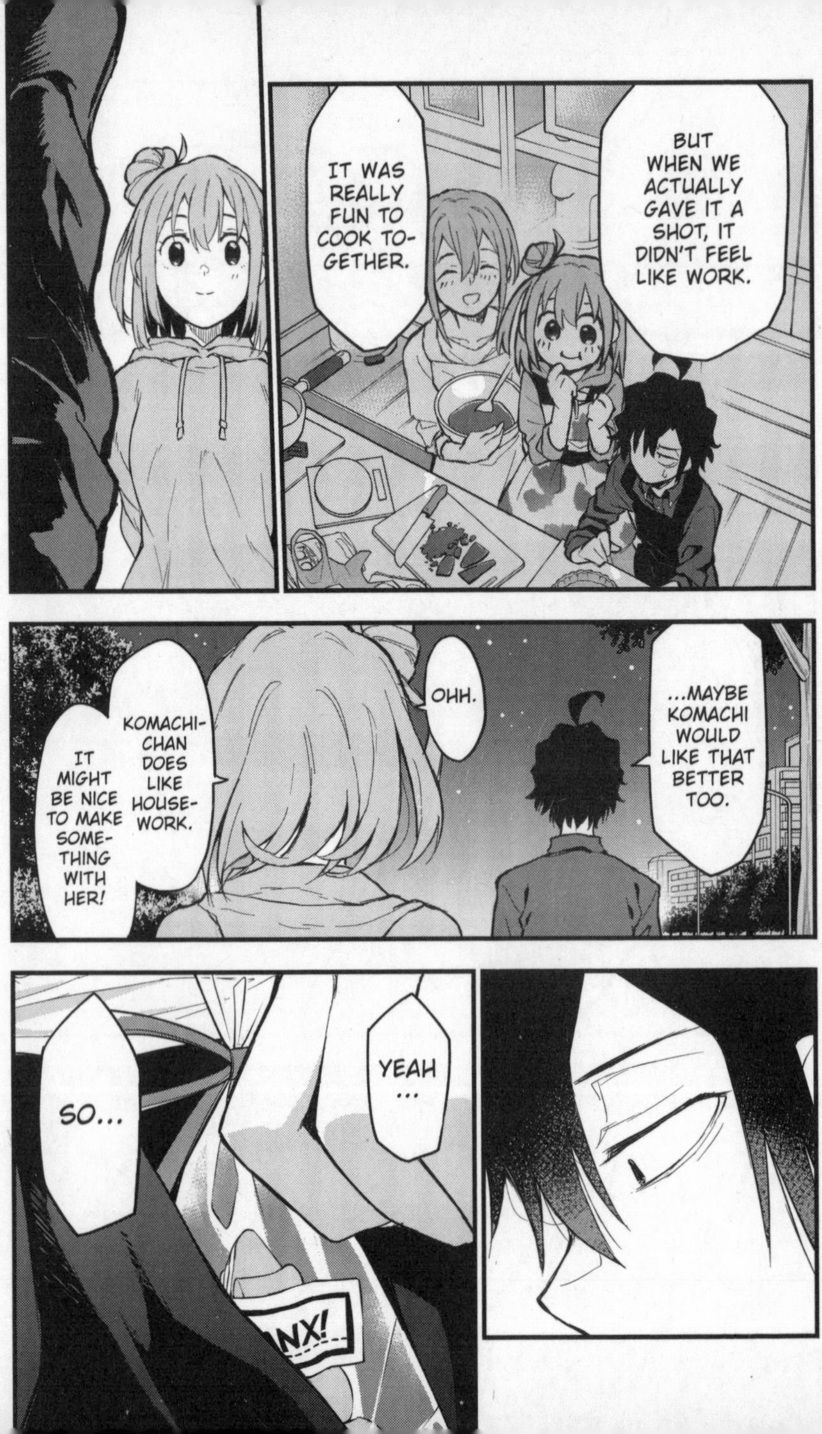
BUT WHEN WE ACTUALLY GAVE IT A SHOT, IT DIDN'T FEEL LIKE WORK.
IT WAS REALLY FUN TO COOK TO-GETHER.
...MAYBE KOMACHI WOULD LIKE THAT BETTER TOO.
OHH.
KOMACHI-CHAN DOES LIKE HOUSE-WORK.
IT MIGHT BE NICE TO MAKE SOME-THING WITH HER!
YEAH ...
SO...
NX!

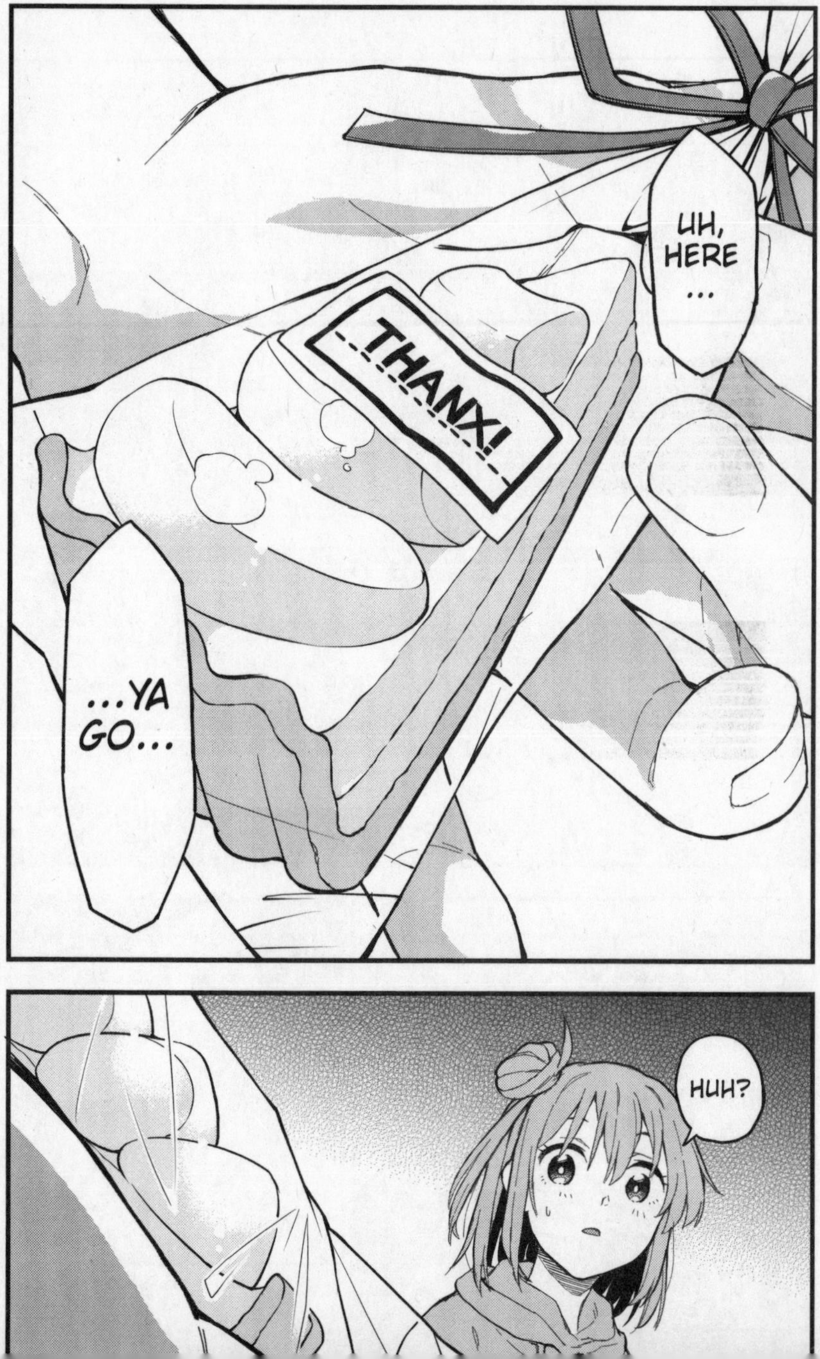
UH, HERE...
THANX!
...YA GO...
HUH?

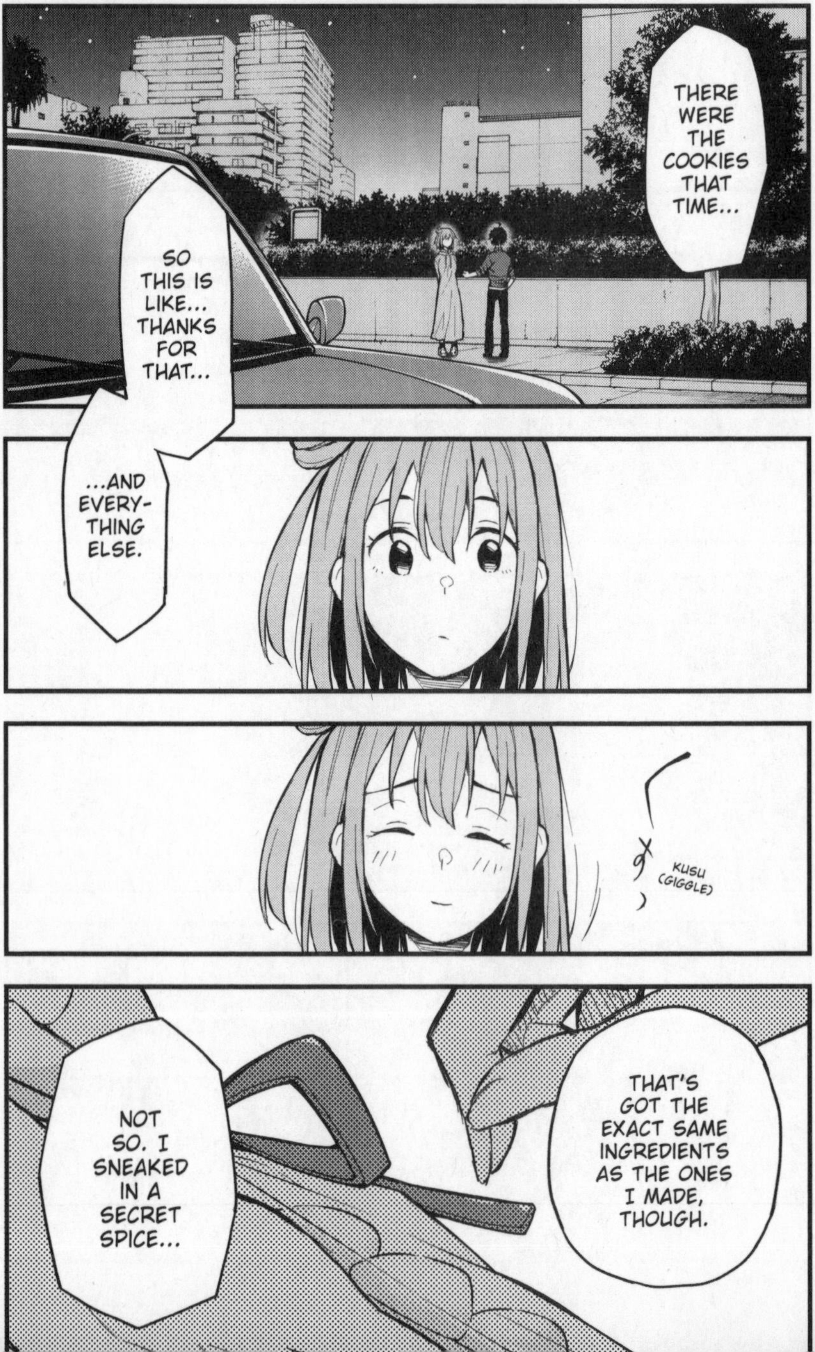
THERE WERE THE COOKIES THAT TIME...
SO THIS IS LIKE... THANKS FOR THAT...
...AND EVERY-THING ELSE.
KUSU (GIGGLE)
THAT'S GOT THE EXACT SAME INGREDIENTS AS THE ONES I MADE, THOUGH.
NOT SO. I SNEAKED IN A SECRET SPICE...

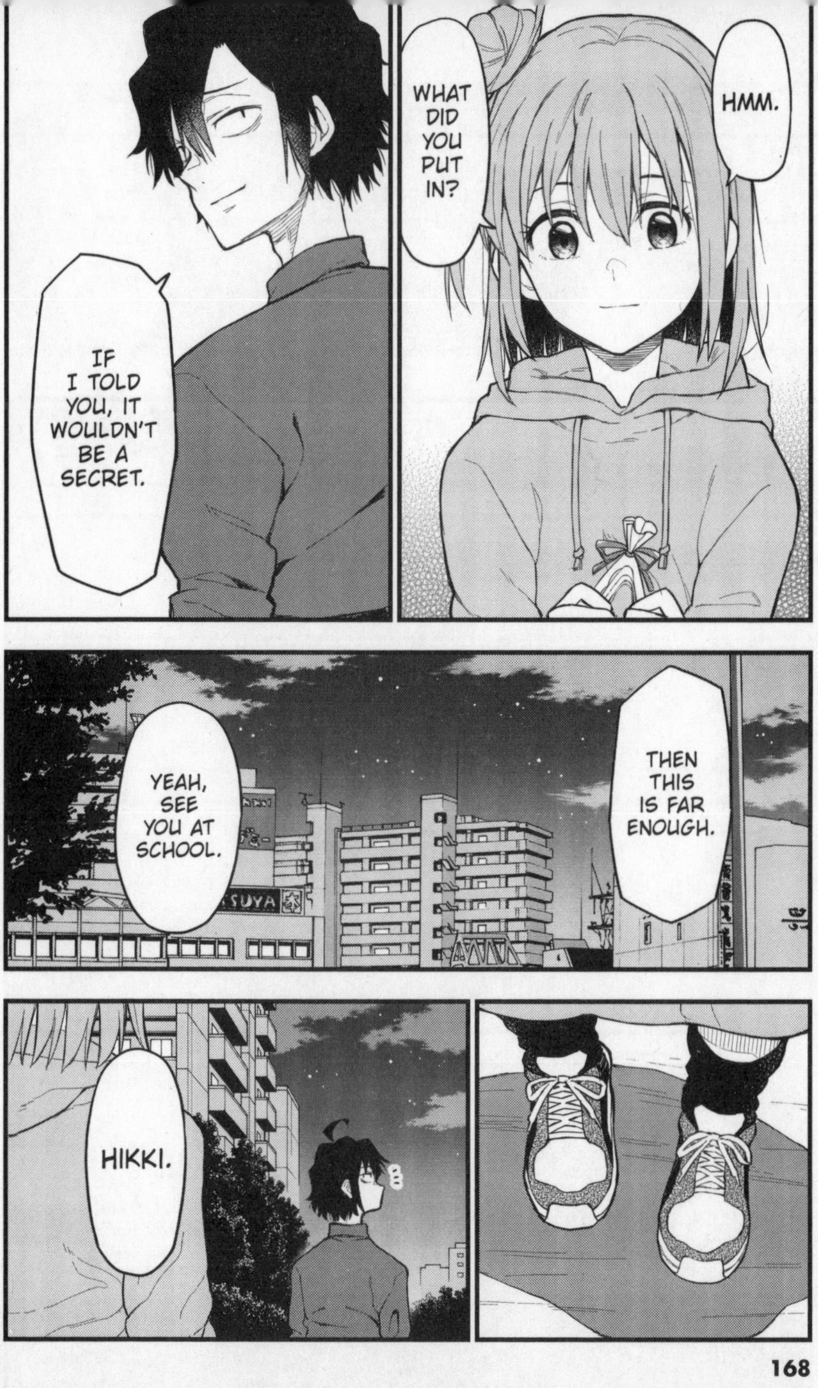
HMM.
WHAT DID YOU PUT IN?
IF I TOLD YOU, IT WOULDN'T BE A SECRET.
THEN THIS IS FAR ENOUGH.
YEAH, SEE YOU AT SCHOOL.
HIKKI.

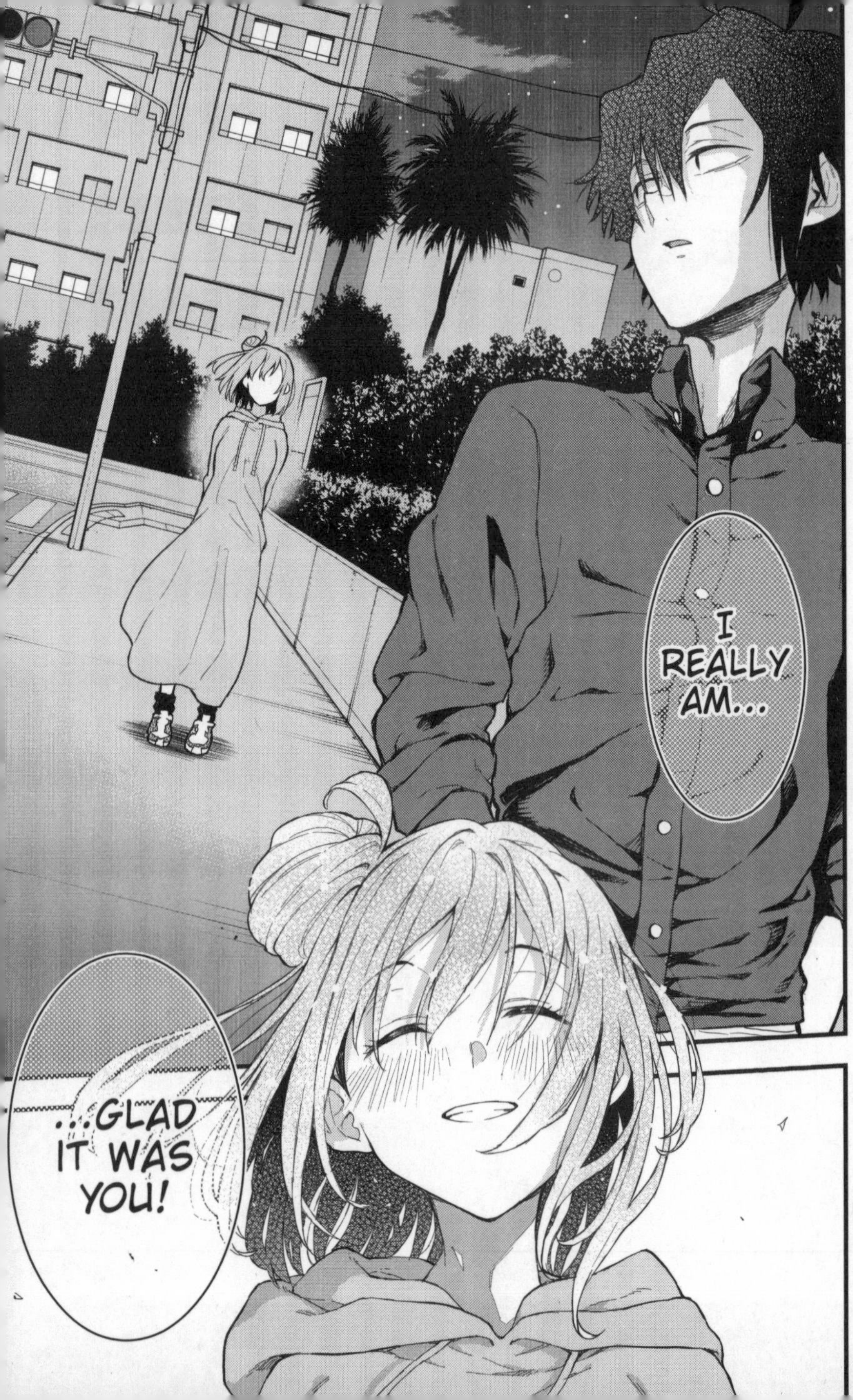
I REALLY AM...
...GLAD IT WAS YOU!

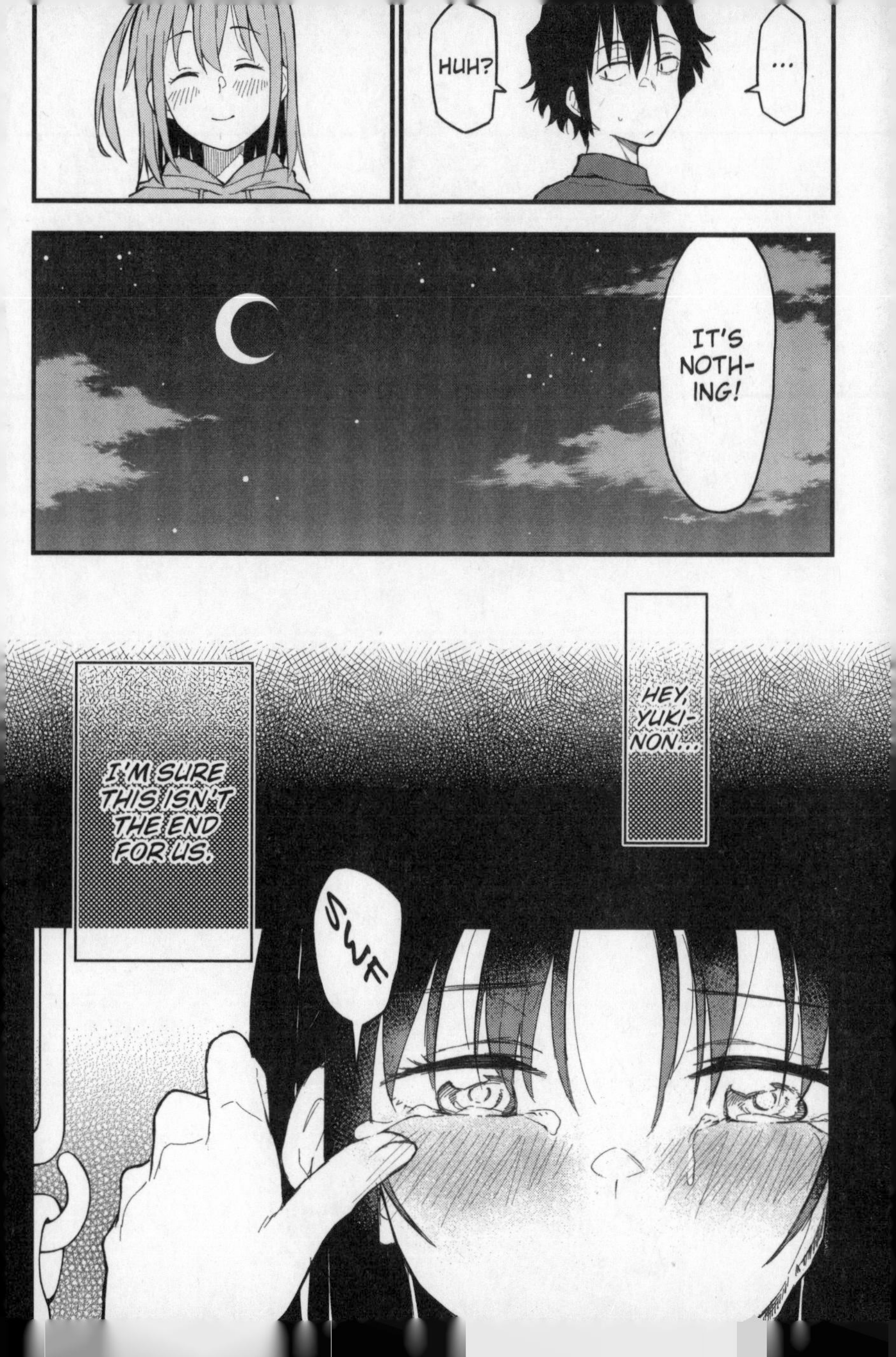
...
HUH?
IT'S NOTHING!
HEY, YUKINON...
I'M SURE THIS ISN'T THE END FOR US.
SWF

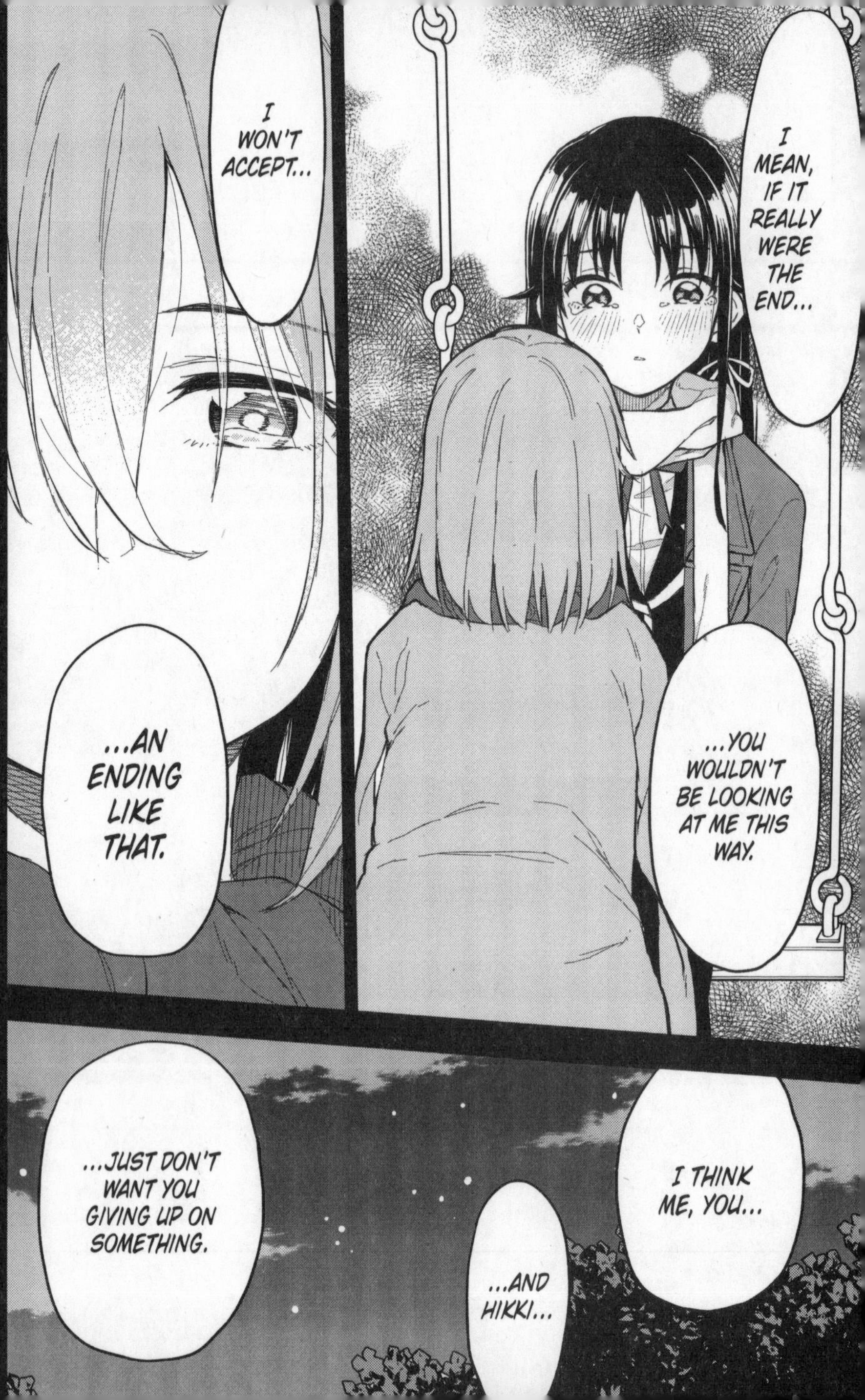
I MEAN, IF IT REALLY WERE THE END...
...YOU WOULDN'T BE LOOKING AT ME THIS WAY.
I WON'T ACCEPT...
...AN ENDING LIKE THAT.
I THINK ME, YOU...
...AND HIKKI...
...JUST DON'T WANT YOU GIVING UP ON SOMETHING.

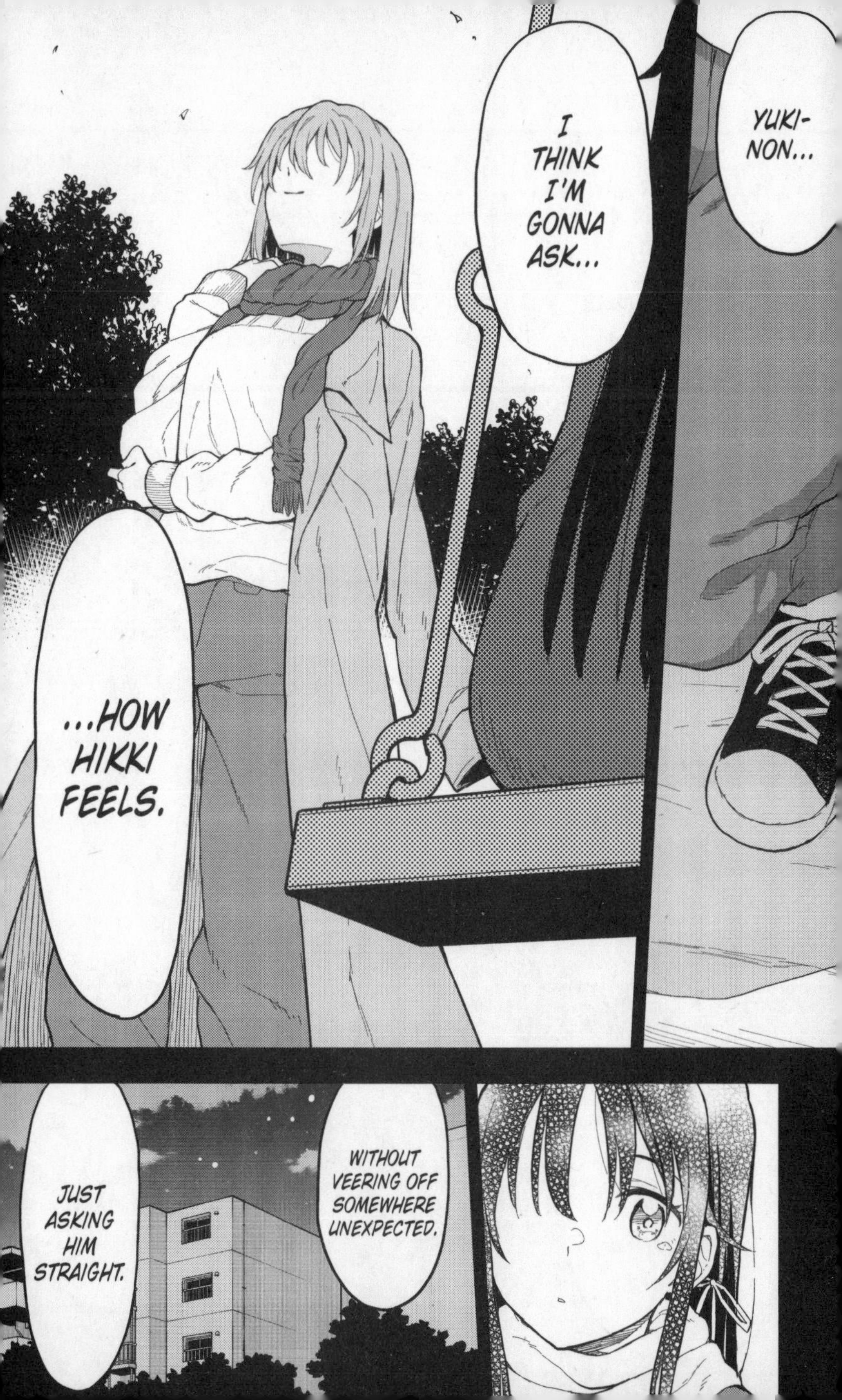
YUKI-NON...
I THINK I'M GONNA ASK...
...HOW HIKKI FEELS.
WITHOUT VEERING OFF SOMEWHERE UNEXPECTED.
JUST ASKING HIM STRAIGHT.

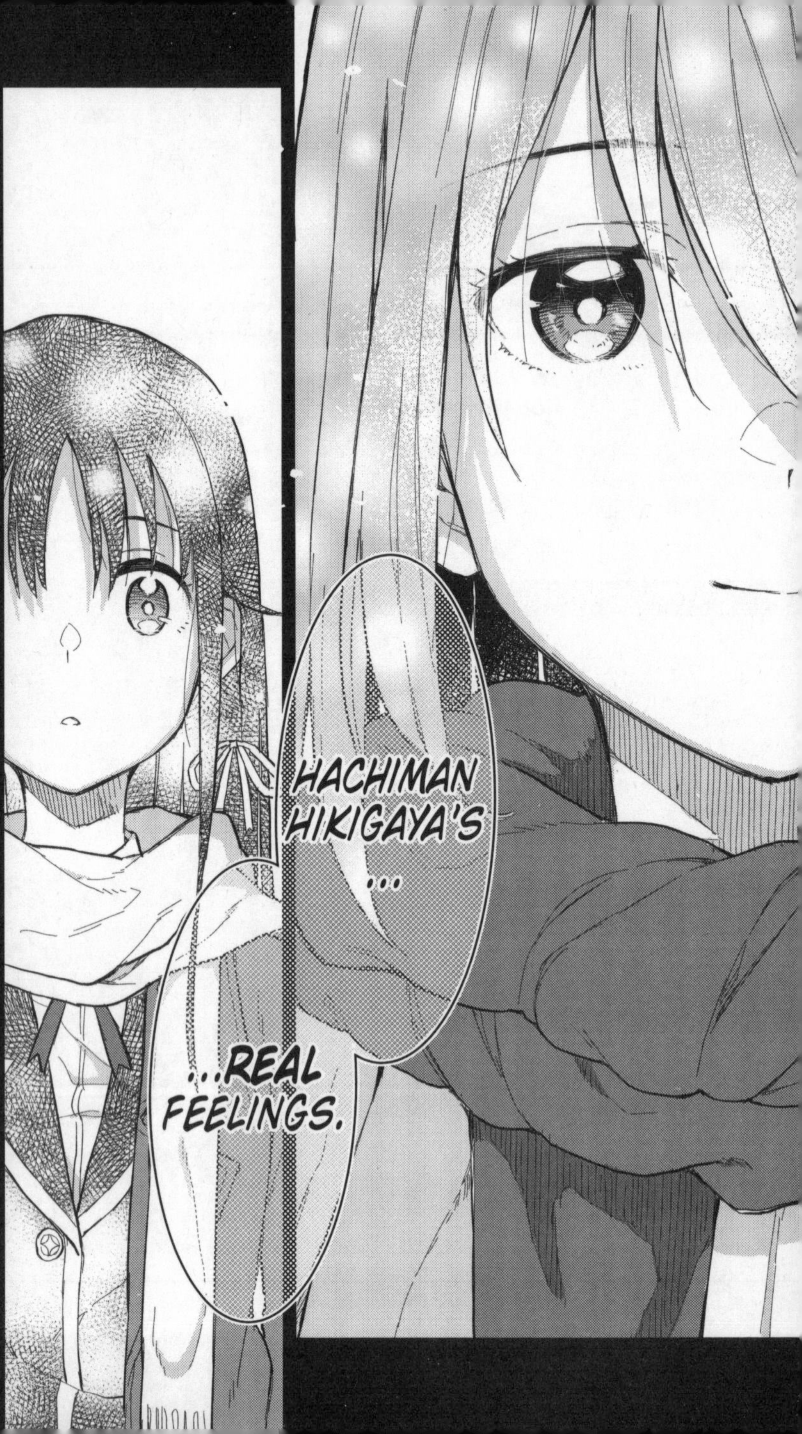
HACHIMAN HIKIGAYA'S ...
...REAL FEELINGS.

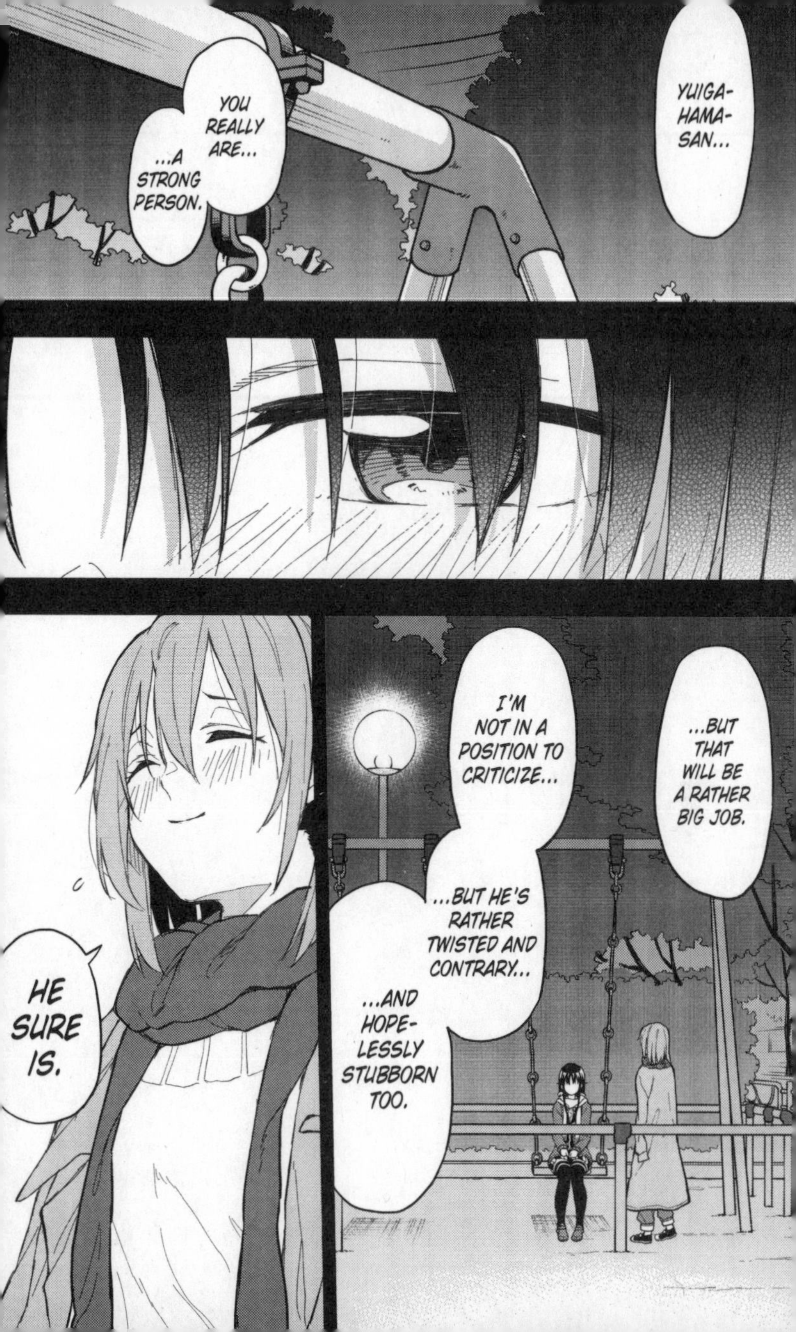
YUIGA-HAMA-SAN...
YOU REALLY ARE... ...A STRONG PERSON.
...BUT THAT WILL BE A RATHER BIG JOB.
I'M NOT IN A POSITION TO CRITICIZE...
...BUT HE'S RATHER TWISTED AND CONTRARY...
...AND HOPE-LESSLY STUBBORN TOO.
HE SURE IS.

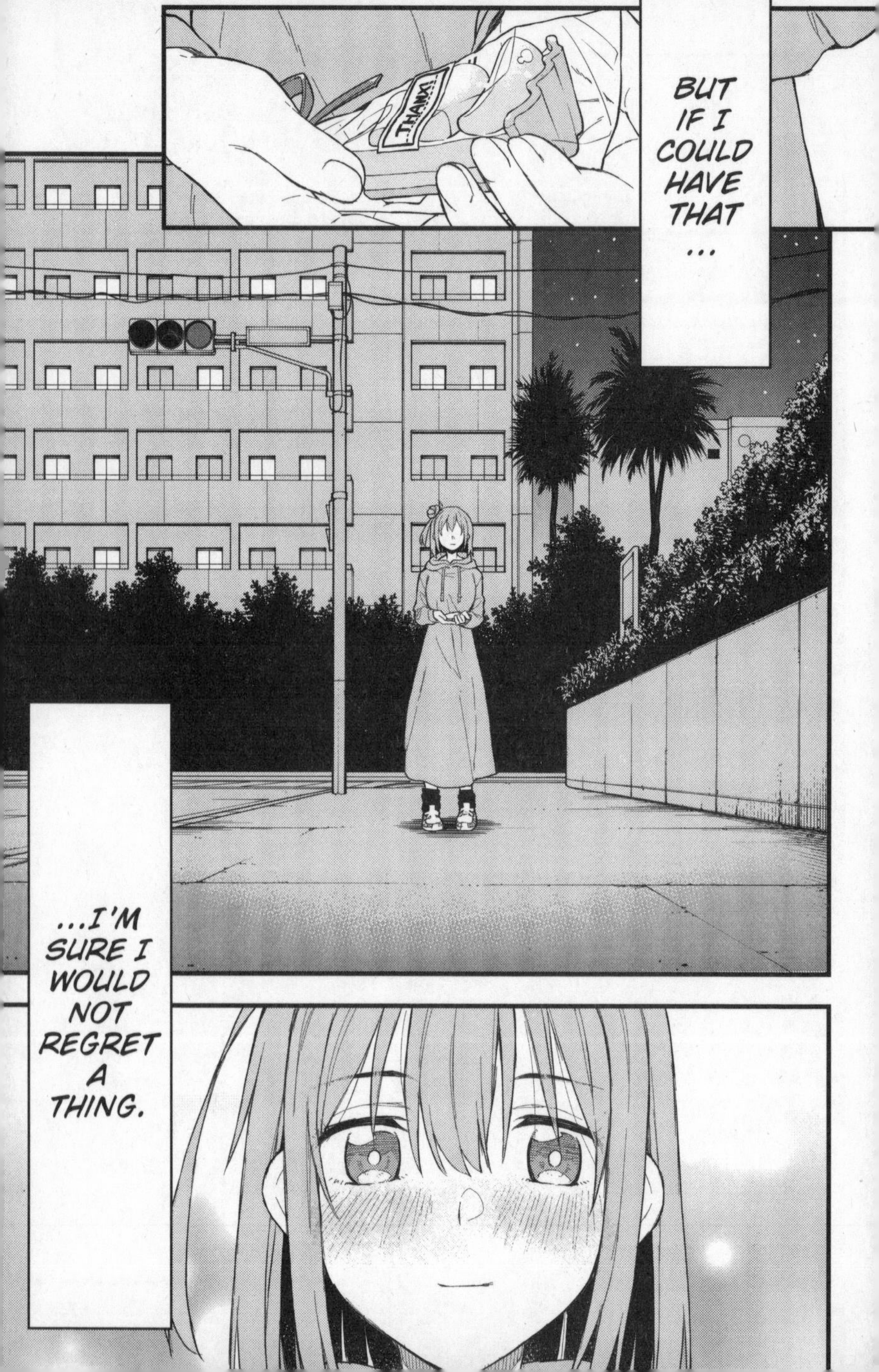
BUT IF I COULD HAVE THAT...
THANX!
...I'M SURE I WOULD NOT REGRET A THING.

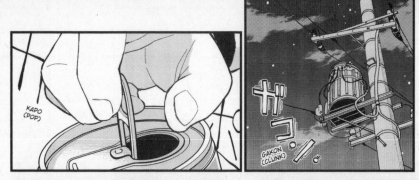

KAPO
(POP)

GAKON
(CLUNK)

MY
WISH
...

HÜH
...?

176

TRANSLATION NOTES

Page 71
"The Nighthawk Star" is a children's short story by Kenji Miyazawa about a bird teased by other birds for being ugly, hated by a real hawk for not living up to the "hawk" name, and even rejected by the stars, but it ends up a brightly shining star itself in the night sky.

Page 108
Royal Milk Tea is a style of tea popular in Japan that has more milk and sugar than other milk teas.

Page 115
M-2 Syndrome, or *chuunibyou* in Japanese, refers to the kind of cringey behavior one expects from a second-year middle school student and what someone that age would expect to sound cool and mysterious.

Page 144
Aion Marinria is a parody of an actual shopping mall in Chiba called Aeon Marinpia.

Page 146
Sweet King is a reference to a Japanese cultivar of strawberry called Amaou (literally "sweet king"). The Japanese version of the manga called its version of the strawberries "Amaking."

Page 156
Nappage is a French term for a fruit glaze.

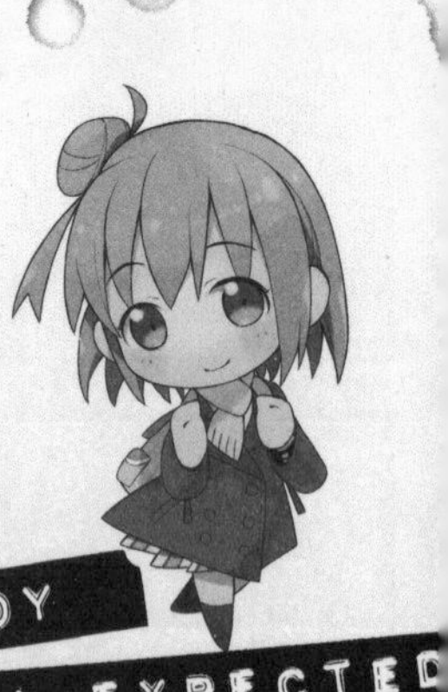

MY YOUTH ROMANTIC COMEDY IS WRONG, AS I EXPECTED

...To Be Continued.

CHAPTER 105.5 … KOMACHI'S BIG BROTHER IS A BIG BROTHER, AS EXPECTED.

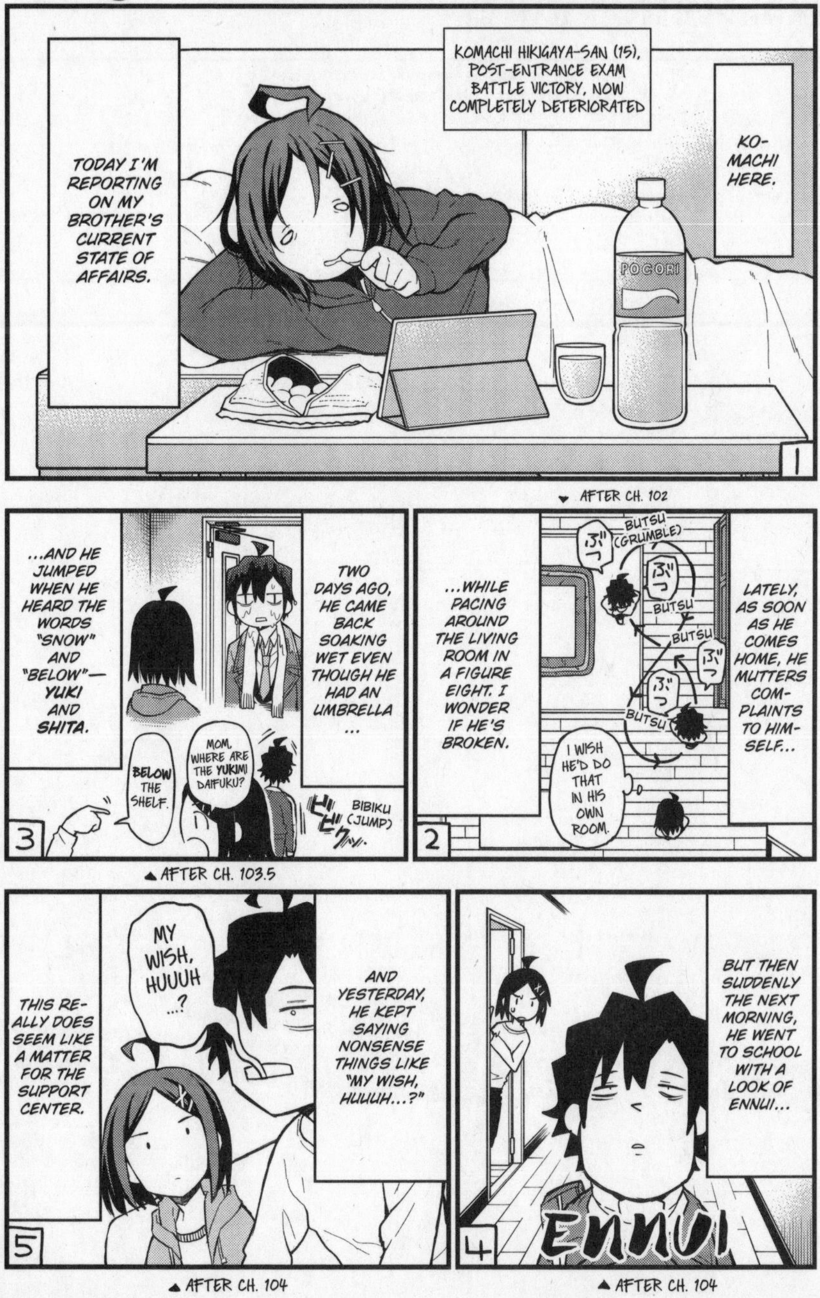
KO-MACHI HERE.
KOMACHI HIKIGAYA-SAN (15), POST-ENTRANCE EXAM BATTLE VICTORY, NOW COMPLETELY DETERIORATED
TODAY I'M REPORTING ON MY BROTHER'S CURRENT STATE OF AFFAIRS.
POCORI
1
AFTER CH. 102
LATELY, AS SOON AS HE COMES HOME, HE MUTTERS COM-PLAINTS TO HIM-SELF...
BUTSU (GRUMBLE)
ぶつ
ぶつ
BUTSU
BUTSU
ぶつ
ぶつ
BUTSU
...WHILE PACING AROUND THE LIVING ROOM IN A FIGURE EIGHT. I WONDER IF HE'S BROKEN.
I WISH HE'D DO THAT IN HIS OWN ROOM.
2
TWO DAYS AGO, HE CAME BACK SOAKING WET EVEN THOUGH HE HAD AN UMBRELLA ...
...AND HE JUMPED WHEN HE HEARD THE WORDS "SNOW" AND "BELOW"— YUKI AND SHITA.
MOM, WHERE ARE THE YUKIMI DAIFUKU?
BELOW THE SHELF.
BIBIKU (JUMP)
3
AFTER CH. 103.5
BUT THEN SUDDENLY THE NEXT MORNING, HE WENT TO SCHOOL WITH A LOOK OF ENNUI...
ENNUI
4
AND YESTERDAY, HE KEPT SAYING NONSENSE THINGS LIKE "MY WISH, HUUUH...?"
MY WISH, HUUUH ...?
THIS RE-ALLY DOES SEEM LIKE A MATTER FOR THE SUPPORT CENTER.
5
AFTER CH. 104
AFTER CH. 104

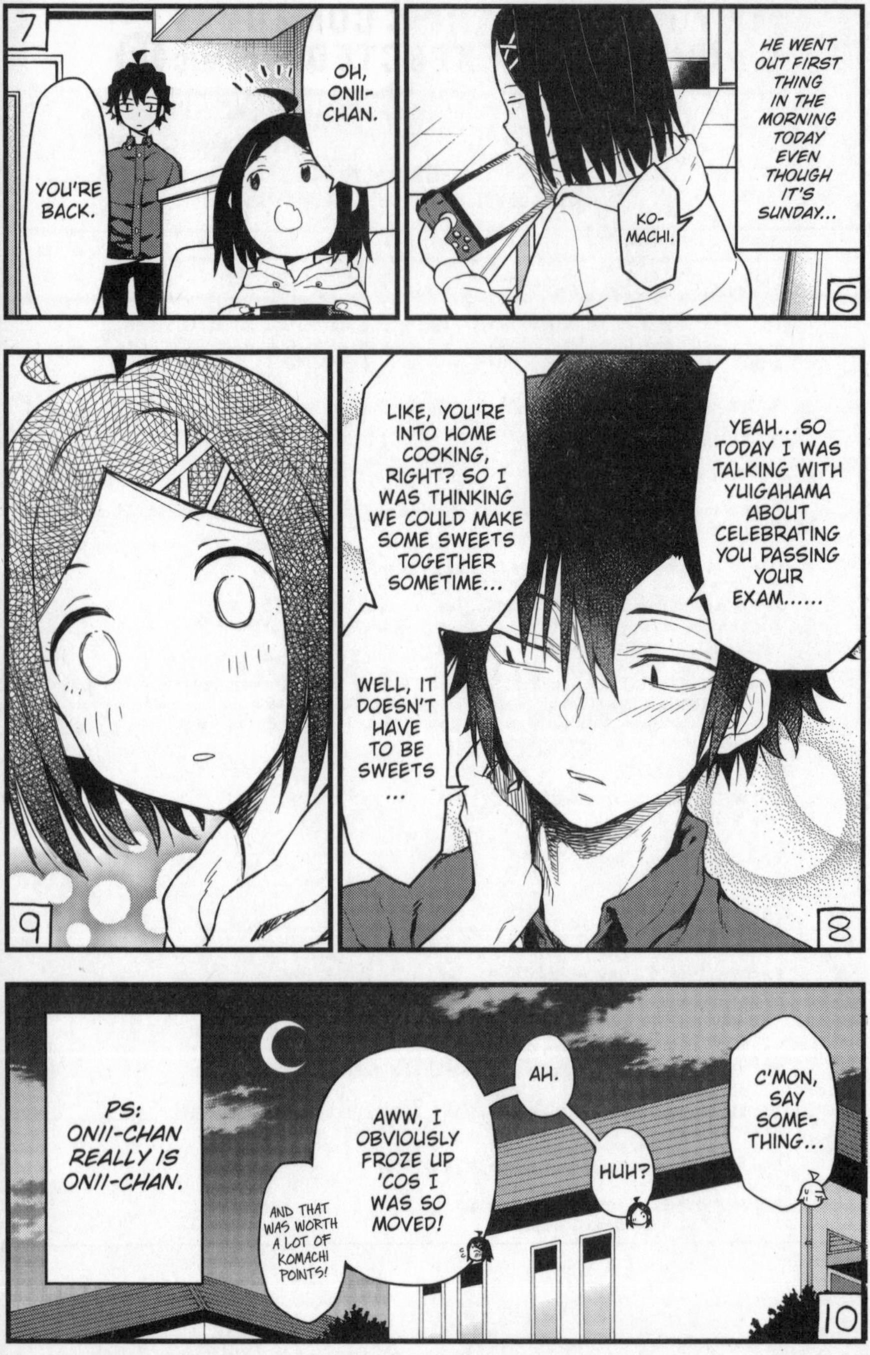
HE WENT OUT FIRST THING IN THE MORNING TODAY EVEN THOUGH IT'S SUNDAY...
KO-MACHI.
OH, ONII-CHAN.
YOU'RE BACK.
YEAH...SO TODAY I WAS TALKING WITH YUIGAHAMA ABOUT CELEBRATING YOU PASSING YOUR EXAM......
LIKE, YOU'RE INTO HOME COOKING, RIGHT? SO I WAS THINKING WE COULD MAKE SOME SWEETS TOGETHER SOMETIME...
WELL, IT DOESN'T HAVE TO BE SWEETS ...
C'MON, SAY SOME-THING...
AH.
HUH?
AWW, I OBVIOUSLY FROZE UP 'COS I WAS SO MOVED!
AND THAT WAS WORTH A LOT OF KOMACHI POINTS!
PS: ONII-CHAN REALLY IS ONII-CHAN.

MY YOUTH ROMANTIC COMEDY IS WRONG, AS I EXPECTED

Original Story: Wataru Watari
Art: Naomichi Io
Character Design: Ponkan⑧
ORIGINAL COVER DESIGN/Hiroyuki KAWASOME (Graphio)

Translation: Jennifer Ward

Lettering: Carolina Hernández

This book is a work of fiction. Names, characters, places, and incidents are the product of the author's imagination or are used fictitiously. Any resemblance to actual events, locales, or persons, living or dead, is coincidental.

YAHARI ORE NO SEISHUN LOVE COME WA MACHIGATTEIRU.
@COMIC Vol. 19 by Wataru WATARI, Naomichi IO, PONKAN⑧
© 2013 Wataru WATARI, Naomichi IO, PONKAN⑧
All rights reserved.
Original Japanese edition published by SHOGAKUKAN.
English translation rights arranged with SHOGAKUKAN through Tuttle-Mori Agency, Inc., Tokyo.

English translation © 2023 by Yen Press, LLC

Yen Press
150 West 30th Street, 19th Floor
New York, NY 10001

Visit us at yenpress.com
facebook.com/yenpress
twitter.com/yenpress
yenpress.tumblr.com
instagram.com/yenpress

First Yen Press Edition: April 2023
Edited by Yen Press Editorial: Carl Li
Designed by Yen Press Design: Lilliana Checo, Wendy Chan

Yen Press is an imprint of Yen Press, LLC.
The Yen Press name and logo are trademarks of Yen Press, LLC.

The publisher is not responsible for websites (or their content) that are not owned by the publisher.

Library of Congress Control Number: 2016931004

ISBNs: 978-1-9753-6034-4 (paperback)
       978-1-9753-6035-1 (ebook)

10 9 8 7 6 5 4 3 2 1

WOR

Printed in the United States of America